About the Author

THE OF

Adrian Lincoln was born in Lincoln, United Kingdom. He was raised in county Lincolnshire and a village in Nottinghamshire. It was in these early days that odd events were to shape his later view of the world. Several houses moves later, he spent his teenage years near Manchester and now lives in North Wales. A tough childhood led to a lifetime of working in industrial production. A hard decision and fate allowed travel to become a big part of his life – as is looking closer at strange events with an open mind, whilst reserving judgment – his politics being shaped by his experiences.

to Sandra "SARAH"

for all your help

Dedication

I would like to dedicate this book to my long-suffering partner, Sarah, without whose detailed memory to pick, much of the travelogue element of this book would be bare bones indeed.

Adrian Lincoln

Life and Times of an Average Oddball

Austin Macauley Publishers™
London * Cambridge * New York * Sharjah

All of the events in this memoir are true to the best of author's memory. The views expressed in this memoir are solely those of the author.

A CIP catalogue record for this title is available from the British Library.

ISBN 9781528981682 (Paperback)
ISBN 9781528981699 (ePub e-book)

www.austinmacauley.com

First Published (2021)
Austin Macauley Publishers Ltd
25 Canada Square
Canary Wharf
London
E14 5LQ

Preface

My real name is not important, I am one of the millions of "Little People", as some of the less savoury of the "Great and Good" would have us known.

I am a relatively private person, not a highly sociable man, I do not do well in large group situations, I prefer the company of one or two. So, some of the time, my confidence is not high, due to my shortcomings. Like many, I will try to mask this by being overly verbose in stressful situations. I shall call myself Adrian Lincoln for this autobiography.

One of the main reasons for anonymity is that some of my early recollections are contentious to say the least, and I do not want to lay close relatives by association to possible ridicule. Though I remain open minded, this contentious subject runs in a compulsive thread throughout my life.

Personally connected people mentioned in this book will have their names shortened, changed or abbreviated. The events and places are real, though the nature of some of my earliest recollections is very much open to conjecture. Some of my workplace locations are deliberately vague, close relatives and friends and other people – past and present will know who they are if they come across themselves in this book.

My life's narrative includes recollections of early life, health, locations, hobbies and interests, a sprinkling of humour where I find it. Life events – both working and home, travelogues, compulsive interest events. Developing political leanings and commentary, lastly, an Addendum of a selection of relevant events I have acquired knowledge of, mostly from leading investigative authors over the years, some events making brief appearances in mainstream media, a few of these mentioned earlier, leading to my tentative, logic-based conclusions of my most compulsive of interests – putting me firmly in the "Oddball bracket".

Chapter 1

As I was born in the late 1950s, it is the early 60s before I recall much. As I mentioned in the Preface, my memory has always been poor, one of my stock phrases is "I was born with dementia", as when my life partner "Sarah" fills in the details of some of our past life – I will only remember brief highlights. Some of the memories are there when prompted – unprompted accessing is the problem, and always has been, even in childhood.

So, the fact that one of my earliest recollections is also one of the most contentious, it is only in later life I realised why it has stuck in my head – as I started to join the dots.

At the ages of three to four, I experienced what might be described as recurring "screen memory" waking dreams that went as follows.

I would get out of my bed in our terraced house in Lincoln, in what seemed to me to be a bluish twilight and go to the window. I would look out across our backyard to the backyard of the house opposite, there I would see, floating, wobbling up and down in slow motion as if in something thicker than air – three basic kites of the day, short top triangle, larger lower triangle, with the two wooden supports that formed a cross, complete with trailing ribbons, only these three kites all had a pair of large solid black teardrop turned sideways, shaped as eyes in the top section of each kite. There was nothing beyond this *that I recall* to this "dream", except that I had this so many times at that age that it has stayed crystal clear in my head for life.

There is another set of recurring "dream" that may be related to this early experience, these occurred a little later – after we had moved to a village on the Lincolnshire/Nottinghamshire border. Throughout my childhood, I had all the usual type of dreams, including recurring ones and some nightmares, literally – monsters under the bed type and later – being chased, but nothing like the above mentioned, or the one I will recount shortly, these were different in that there was no progression.

I will get to that latter, first a bit of family background and hazy memories of my early pre-school days. As I recall, my mother worked in her mother's fish shop, but soon went into nurse training. I have no recollection of my true grandfather. My father became a Quantity Surveyor for most of his life; he must have been in the early stages of that career in those days, working on the building of power stations, which explains why we moved house every so often. I was told we moved to Swansea for a six-month period during the first two years of my life. But for most of my pre-school years, we lived as described above, in a terraced house in the Lincoln area.

I do remember that at the bottom of our street, there was a main road and across that road was a steep embankment with a railway atop this, as sometimes we used to go to the bottom of our street to wave to someone, possibly my grandmother, who must have set off from a nearby station. Sadly, I cannot remember for certain, though it must have been a regular occurrence for me to remember it.

I have no one to ask, as both my parents are deceased and my brother "Ian" was not yet born, my sister "Jane" a year younger than I. I have vague memories of my mum's brothers working on motorbikes outside our house.

Apart from standing on a chair, playing with plastic salt-filled submarines, that would rise and fall in a sink of water, I have little else to recall from that era of strange "dreams".

I have been told that while my mum was pregnant with my sister, she had a bad time of it, and I went to live with my paternal grandmother for some time. There are rumours that my paternal grandmother worked as a servant before and during the WW2 period in the home of some local nobility in either the Worcester, or Grantham area and so maybe my true grandfather was of noble blood! Good story…

I may have stayed there for periods of weeks, as I have memories of baths in a large kitchen sink there, along with my sister, one year younger.

My paternal grandmother, who was married to a man (later than my father's dad), lived in a terraced house with a back extension, the upper room of which was my bedroom, this had an internal window above the door to the landing. We used to feed chickens and collect the eggs from a run that ran along the wall on one side of the back garden. My gran originally came from the Worcester area, how she ended up in Lincolnshire I can only speculate – that she met my true paternal "granddad", who was maybe in the armed forces, and she then moved to where he lived from Worcester to Lincolnshire. Her sister lived in Worcester unmarried all of her life. That is all I know of my father's family.

Chapter 2

At age four to five, we moved to the above-mentioned village on the Lincs/Notts border, where we lived in a bungalow, this had a Rayburn fire heating system, so my dad must have been doing OK by then.

I remember my dad growing runner beans and other vegetables there, and we had a goldfish pond in the front garden. I remember one Christmas, it could have been the bad one of 1962-63, going outside in snow up to my waist, dressed up in my new cowboy outfit complete with twin cap six guns. As mentioned, I started my first infant/primary school there. The school building was older than most of the village, it could be reached by walking along a lane at the bottom of our back garden that emerged on a main road not far from the school. I remember two friends from those days, (names altered), one was David Hadley, the other – Nigel Whitmore, whose hay barn we used to make a den in.

I must have struggled at school with writing from the start, as they forced me somehow to change from left to right-handed. To this day, I do some things better (though not writing) with my left hand than my right, and in sports from football to badminton, I led with my left foot, I played snooker left-handed, though I was never ambidextrous. So, mixed up from the start!

I do not know if this has anything to do with my poor memory and concentration, (left and right brain coordination) or had more to do with some of my night-time problems of my early primary years.

I mentioned earlier that the "Kite dreams" I had a year or two younger had a follow on set of recurring dream/events, I don't know what to call them, which I now believe might explain some strange behaviour of mine concurrent at that time, both happening aged from five to about eight. At night, I would wake up with a feeling of unease, after a while (it happened so often) I knew what to expect next – although my eyes must have been shut – there would be a dull orange glow, with vague shadow movement in front of my eyelids.

This would be accompanied with a very strong tense feeling, that I can only now compare with being treated in a dentist chair!

There was no more to these events than that, *that I recall* though it happened often enough for me to remember thinking after the glow went dark, something along the lines of, "At last, I can go to sleep now" – with a feeling of relief.

Many who read this may conclude that it would have been his parents switching the light on – the glow seen through unopened eyes. No, this was something very different. The orange light was much duller than any electric light, more like fire embers.

The strange behaviour I mentioned concurrent with these episodes, I now think could have been a response to the above. After being put to bed, quite often I would throw my head from side to side "singing myself to sleep". I used to tell my parents, I made noises, something akin to TV theme tunes, like early Z Cars for example. This went on for a couple of years as far as I can recall.

Compulsive interest/speculation – joining the dots with hindsight, it was my way of trying to block out, or prevent those "Orange Glow" events.

Any psychologists reading this will no doubt have a field day, and I rather hope someone will be able to explain the above night-time recurring events. Others will know where I am going with the above descriptions. I remain to this day open-minded and do not have enough proof – one way or the other as to what occurred. I hope there is a mundane explanation, as the alternative is not one I would like to know too much about, though I sometimes wonder if these two sets of "dreams" are responsible for my later compulsive interest in the UFO phenomenon. There, I've said it. As I am not a believer in something I cannot prove, I remain open-minded.

This is why my autobiography has names changed and some locations vague as I do not want relatives tarnished with the inevitable ridicule the above will attract, even though I make no claims as to what actually went on.

I have since gained enough knowledge from authors such as **David M. Jacobs** and the late **Bud Hopkins**, as to what some of the more outlandish explanations might be, though I rather hope not. I have since learnt a US/UK cabal had the microchips and gravity amplification craft, even then, and the motives to use aliens as scapegoats for possible abductions, for chipping for control and, or study purposes.

I recall little of this first infant/primary school activities such as basket weaving, and going on nature walks, Easter egg hunting, making paper chains for Christmas, very little of schoolwork, though I must have struggled with writing as it was while I was at this school that I was made to switch from left to right-handed writing.

I do remember one school trip of note – some type of large whale was supposed to have swum up the River Trent. We were taken to a bridge at Gainsborough to try and spot it – we never did, of course.

My sister "Jane", a year younger, and I were sent to Sunday school. In those days, mid-sixties, we were allowed outdoors for longer periods to play with friends at younger ages than generally happens now. I spent most of these times with one or both of the two lads, David and Nigel, mentioned above.

While at primary age, my mum, Liz, stayed at home or may have worked part time, my dad, I remember having one of those black cars with a small runner board and orange indicter that flicked out sideways, this changed to a two-tone green car with rounded lines at some point whilst we still lived in this village, so his surveying must have started to pay quite well.

Home life had its ups and downs, I recall many rows between parents, my mum often defending us, children, from my dad's strict ways, table manners and food eating, being typical bones of contention. My dad took a belt to my backside from time to time, I probably deserved punishment, as I started to bully my younger brother, though this could have been a case of chicken and egg…

I do not remember well my status at school, but it was fairly low – a trend that was to continue throughout my schooling. I grew up a thin but tall boy which made me a target for bullies, and I think fear at home of my dad kept my confidence level low.

I seem to remember from time to time being taken with my younger brother "Ian" to a darkened room with other young kids, in our underpants. There was a bright, broad column of light set in the middle of this room, I think the heat from this was supposed to help our asthma which by then had made itself evident. Anyone recall this "treatment" in the sixties?

Chapter 3

There was one other strange recurring dream of note, (all others being typical nightmares – monsters under the bed type and other standard growing-up dreams) odd to me was a dream of looking down from high in the clouds – sometimes from between cloud layers – at the ground, seeing it as it looks now from an aircraft at holding pattern height, a few thousand feet up. What was odd is this recurring dream happened long before I ever flew in an aircraft.

In 1967, we upped sticks and moved to Manchester, my dad's work on a new power station taking us there.

This meant my last three and a half years of primary was spent as six months at one school, then we moved to Stockport, where I finished my primary education.

This Stockport School was another old building, attached to a church, I remember desks with inkwells and a bell, hand rung in the corridor for breaks. The head teacher was a good one, he laid great emphasis on everyone learning to swim, may have been just good sense, or may have had a back-story, never knew, or cannot remember.

It was at one of those swimming lessons I remember first paying attention to one girl as she swam a perfect underwater breaststroke pool width. I was to develop my first crush which followed on to the end of the secondary school we both moved on to, though I never got close. I was far too parallelised into inaction by bullies and aware of her seeing my torment by them, to try any contact.

Not sure exactly when, but sometime after we moved to Manchester, my step-grandfather died, his name was Albert, I cannot recall his face or anything of him. My paternal grandmother Francis eventually remarried to Fred, whom I remember more of.

Fairly often, five or six times a year, we would travel through Derbyshire to one or both of my grandparents, in Lincolnshire. My mum's mum lived in a bungalow, being on her own, her husband dying in the late 1950s. The two oldest of my mum's three older brothers lived in that area for some time to come, although the oldest, Bill, was in the Army, I first remember as a Warrant Officer – he left as a Major. His kids hated him, I saw later, for being a tyrant, his wife leaving him. The youngest, John, moved to live in Stockport soon after we moved, he was a stonemason, though he broadened his building skills in time. I, my brother and sister fell out with him after first Bill, then my dad died, both times this brother taking possessions he was not entitled to.

Peter, the middle brother was in sales of some sort, he must have done quite well, as when we went to stay it was in good houses in the suburbs of Birmingham. He was married to Jenny, they divorced years later with the children living with Jenny.

My father was an only child, his father unknown, to me at least, the only family I knew was his mother's sister, Emily, who worked in one of the pottery factories near Worcester, possibly Royal Dalton.

Fred, my paternal gran's second husband, was a much more amiable character, who developed my interest in chess, first taught to me by my dad. Fred would show me the importance of trying to dominate the centre of the board early in the game. By then I also used to cut up bits of paper and draw military ranks on them, or cowboys and Indians, I would put them on the floor, all mixed together, shut my eyes and turn them over at random. Depending on if they were face up, would decide who survived. Part of the title of this, my story, includes the word Oddball for more than one reason!

Strategy was to dominate my interest in games from then on, games of chance held no interest for me.

Chapter 4

My parents used to take us to either Scotland or Devon/Cornwell in my late, primary and early secondary years. In earlier days, from Lincolnshire, it would be a caravan at Mablethorpe, Skegness, Cleethorpes or Grimsby. Scant memories of Grimsby included seeing a "life-sized" Dalek in an arcade, and sadly a dead or nearly dead dolphin or porpoise on the beach, with blood from slashes along its side, so possibly alive at that time.

Cornwall/Devon memories consist of one stay on a farm, with the attendant smells! There was a stay at a caravan park – where I fell in love with a small dog staying next door, that I did not want to part with, and the usual rock pool fishing with a mussel on a string, with a net underneath for crabs.

Scotland holidays seemed to us, kids, as far too long in the car, Dad losing his temper with Mum's navigation at times and a lot of rain.

There was one event one time when we stayed in a cottage near a place called Dalmally near Loch Awe. Us three kids were out on our own, in the forest (must have been near to the cottage) when we came across some soldiers on exercise, they were bivouacking, there were three or four of them that I saw, they pointed to far ridges and said the "enemy" were over there. I was shown what I think was a Stirling submachine gun, which was the highlight of that memory.

In my last two years of primary, I only remember one close friend there, he was called Wayne, he was a very good swimmer, went on to swim at county level. I seemed to gel with friends that were the opposite to me – outgoing and quite popular.

One odd event took place when the headmaster took a few of us kids, in his VW Tourer (probably those showing an interest in books) to the home of the Bronte sisters. I do not remember much of the trip, apart from on the way back, on a sharp bend was a deep lay-by, with steep rocks behind. In this lay-by was a circular powder blue object on three legs – with a ladder up to a door. It had round windows spaced around the circular building? It was **not** a UFO, it did not look like it could fly, it was the late 1960s – weird stuff about. This house was stood in the lay-by, I was amazed. The odd thing was that no one else in the VW seemed to notice it! We had gone around the next bend a few seconds later so I never mentioned it, some Hippy with a lot of money, wanting to make a statement? Stuck in my head! Since then, I found out a few of these were made from a Scandinavian design, this must have been one in transit.

I had started to read books by then – Biggles Books were the first I recall, it did me no good when it came to the eleven-plus exam. I failed it. I think my parents may have expected it, I don't remember their reaction, probably quite disappointment. I was a bed wetter till quite late in my primary years. I think a nervous or anxious disposition or stress was the reason, the cause, fear of underperforming for my dad, or just my genetic make-up, or even the strange events mentioned earlier, I do not know.

My brother and sister both passed and went on to their respective grammar and high schools.

Unless you can be just thick by nature, I believe my memory and concentration were both compromised early in my life and left me as a quite nervous worrier, for most of my life, or like a boomerang – I could just be a throwback!

Secondary school turned out to be mostly, though not all, a private hell for me. It would influence a major choice I made later in life.

Due to my being quiet and introspective, but tall and thin, I soon attracted my peer bullies, not so much in the first tear, (as it was then) before the streaming was sorted out, but from then on, when I was settled three-quarters down in the sets, I had a tough time.

We lived by then in a large four-bedroom semi-detached house, in a decent area of Stockport, a 15-minute walk from school. My mum had gone back to nursing and was a Staff nurse. My dad was still in Quantity Surveying, which by then he hated.

Chapter 5

I learnt to compartmentalise my life at secondary school. It was nearly the end of my school years before one of my teachers told my parents of my being bullied. I remember them being upset and asking why I had never told them. It was mostly low level, and I thought I could cope. Low level but constant and distracting. I worried about the consequence at school of telling my parents – being thought a cry baby, or the retaliation if people were singled out as a result of my telling.

Wayne from primary went with me to secondary and was a continuing friend in the first year or two, before I ended up in a lower class. Lynda, (also from primary) whom I had a crush on, also to my pleasant surprise turned up at this school, though in the first year was in a different class, only later to join me in a lower set – much good it did me…

Most of the bullying I experienced was away from teachers' view, break times, corridors between lessons, dinnertime, though later I used to cycle home in the hour-long dinner break for some peace. I was never badly beaten up, just lots of menace, threats (which I took to heart), neck holds and arm twists. I was never able to concentrate in lessons until we were able to choose optional subjects after a couple of years.

History and Geography were by far my favourite chosen subjects. By this time, 13/ 14-years-old, I had joined the Air Training Corps, or ATC, as it is known. I had a nerdy friend called Paul Massey, who encouraged me to join. I was into History by then and that included WW2, aircraft, I cannot remember much of the "lessons" at the ATC but I remember there was a lot of boot polishing and marching involved, so much so that our "Squadron" won a Regional Drill competition with me in it! A rare success for me.

I went through a short-lived phase of going with other ATC members, armed with binoculars and a book (with all the registration no's of all the civilian aircraft in Britain in it), to Manchester Airport, the idea being to spot the tail number of every plane we saw, find it in the book and underline it – an aviation version of trainspotting. A source of great pride was to have pages full of underlined tail No's. Got to wonder how many were added without being seen by some, I soon lost interest, I was not as keen as some – a sort of semi nerd!

I do remember going on an ATC trip all the way to Heathrow, just for the plane spotting, we also went to the Farnborough Air Show and one other I forget the name of. Part of the lessons I do recall included aircraft recognition from silhouettes. I don't know how many of our squadron went on to join the RAF, but I was not one of them, I never actually went up in a plane whilst in in the ATC, some of the more committed did, I joined the Navy instead - more of that later. I became school friends with a lad, Hong, whose dad owned a Chinese restaurant, he was in the ATC as were a few at school. We both enjoyed table tennis that was often the highlight to look forward to after "lessons" at the squadron hut.

My dad also built a set up that would attach on top of the dining table (so not all bad from dad), we played there often in later school years. Another interest started when Hong came out with the statement "Bruce Lee's dead".

No one in Britain, apart from the Chinese community watching late night cinema, had heard of him. So I got to learn a little about him just in advance of the tidal wave of martial arts films that were to follow soon. I became an avid fan for some time. It was far more interesting to me than western boxing.

Something about the controlled use of the whole body fascinated me. Apart from a little Judo, I was not to try it for myself until in my thirties – more later.

Back at school, our history class was of those where participants chose that option, so more interested, less disruption, and this teacher ruled with a rod of iron – which I liked! As I was able to concentrate on a subject I discovered I liked, unlike some lessons which were ruined by a hardcore of troublemakers who pushed as far as they dare, to slow the lessons down, though in the 70s things were less liberal than now, where those sort of kids know all of their rights and none of their responsibilities, the rot starting with Blair and his wife.

I became interested in the cause and effect of demographic population shifts – from Roman times to the early formation of Britain. The Middle ages, learning the succession of kings by rote, being of less interest to me. The formation of the empire, from Elisabeth 1 onwards, regained my interest, as it mainly involved maritime adventures and operations, logistic preparedness seeming to be the key.

The scale of the logistics and the necessary organisation needed on such a relatively small platform as a ship and the skills to navigate and sail, as well as the fighting, all became of great interest to this teenage lad. The hardships, loss of limbs and the brutality of press gangs, iron discipline were all glossed over in my still young mind, wisdom only comes early to the brilliant, not the likes of me.

More of my historical knowledge came from fiction writers, who kept to the broad sweep of fact and inserted individual characters, both imagined and known – such writers as Conn Iggulden, Bernard Cornwell and many more maritime-oriented authors such as Julian Stockwin, to name one.

Ben Cane, Harry Sidebottom, Robert Fabbri and Simon Scarrow were some I read for Roman history. James Clavell was one of my most influential writers of my late teen years, with *Shogun* being one of my all-time favourite books, though I read and enjoyed most of his far East adventures, such as *Noble House*. I like exotic, as long as the detailed background is included, usually with far more than two protagonists pursuing their own agenda. I suspect that in the lower streams, education was bare bones, unless like me, the subject was a chosen one after age fourteen. I was OK at English language, but then, as now, poor spelling, usually vowels, made me a poor pupil, comprehension not making up for this in a system where Dyslexia was not recognised if not chronic.

The early Middle Ages, the Crusades, and the clashes with Eastern empires, combined with the Mongol incursions West and the pressure thus put-on European populations, this was the history that led to my interest in geography, as you needed this to understand history. I was no good at remembering the succession of royalty, unless key events were tied to a change.

Other subjects such as Physics were lacking in motivation at the time, I wish I had paid more attention at the time, beyond such knowledge as how lift is created in a wing – which was aviation-motivated, motivation is always the key. Until such time as I became aware and interested in hard science fiction and contentious fact, not fantasy (*The Lord of the Rings* being the exception), Physics held no motivation at that time, something I was to regret later, as all things space-related became of importance to me.

Chapter 6

In the last two years of school, I became friends with Kevin, someone who very much enjoyed the outdoors. I used to spend a lot of time at his house; he had three older brothers. Until that time I had little interest in pop music I saw on TV. It was Ian, an older brother, playing Deep Purple, Led Zeppelin, Pink Floyd, Genesis and the like, in the back room that spiked my interest. It was to be a lifelong interest. It was this type of rock music, not some of the less talented (in my opinion) that gained my attention. I would go to concerts of the likes of Fleetwood Mac, Rush, a Canadian trio, folk rockers Jethro Tull. For me the musical content was as important as the vocalist, whose voice had to be strong enough to be on a par with the powerful music, female rockers, such as Stevie Nicks, Belinda Carlisle, the American band, Heart, were all part of my pantheon. Among concerts that stand out were Rainbow and also Rush, both at The Apollo in Manchester, where the opening track for Rush, *Xanadu*, with the two guitarists, waist deep in dry ice flanking the drummer, all silhouetted, the multi-coloured lights playing over the sea of dry ice while the music gradually built, will always be sharp in my mind. This track was replayed on The Old Grey Whistle Test, which was the only rock music on TV in those days. The same venue also hosted Fleetwood Mac just after the *Rumours* album came out, the concert being memorable for its hypnotic tracks such as *Rhiannon*.

The most memorable concert was at Knebworth in 1980, just a week after returning from a Hebrides month (detailed later), where Led Zeppelin performed their last major concert before John Bonham was to die. The sequence of Jimmy Page playing *Dazed and Confused* using a violin bow, standing inside a projected green Lazar pyramid, will also stay with me for life.

With Kevin and his friend Brian, who became my friend (I seemed to like being part of a trio), I started to go fishing – both sea and freshwater.

One of the dafter things I did in this pursuit was putting my hand in an underground wasps nest trying to get the grubs for bait – when we thought we had smoked the wasps out, we had just made them angry! My hand swelled up to twice its size with bites.

One of the highlights of a journey in the dark back of a van to one sea fishing trip (at age fourteen or fifteen) was Brian's successful attempt to light up a fart, it cheered up a long trip to Whitby.

One rainy weekend day, Kevin and I, at about age 13, took a train to Disley near Lyme Park, for a bird-watching day, we entered the park from a side entrance, after much tramping around we had seen nothing more interesting than a Jay.

We ended up at the main house, (later used for filming *Pride and Prejudice*), we sat around the back facing the pond, under the shelter of the house, as it was still raining. Our attention was drawn to a duck that seemed to only have one leg (we had no idea then they stood on one leg routinely). I had my BOAC flight bag (from ATC days) with me for sandwiches. We took pity on the poor duck – Kev caught it – and we zipped it up in my BOAC bag, intending to take it back to Kevin's house, which had a big back garden.

Which we did, only with the bag making funny noises and strange movements on the train, drawing some attention from other passengers, and the train not stopping at our stop, we ended up going all the way to Manchester Piccadilly. The animated bag drawing more stares there, while waiting for a train back to our local stop!

I don't remember what happened at Kevin's house, but I recall that the duck was taken away by the RSPCA while we were at school on what was likely Monday. My bag was a write off…

I took a Thursday and Friday eve and Saturday job in a local Finefare supermarket, where, much to my pleasant surprise, I saw my school crush, Lynda, working at the checkout. I had no idea she worked there, it was pure chance, though I think she believed otherwise.

I think she warmed to me a little there, saying "I should be more like I was there – at school". She was always aware of my interest, but my low social status at school prevented her from acknowledging it. Apart from a few pleasantries, I was too nervous, still putting here on a pedestal, and never got to ask her out, the closest was one evening after work I started walking home with her, saying this way was as quick as the other way for me (which of course it was not). It was the longest conversation I ever had with her (about ten minutes) before her dad drew up alongside, less than halfway to her house and whisked her off home. She was out of my league, but if we had the whole walk home, I think I would have had the courage to ask her out. I was a very late developer.

I took my CSEs, getting middle to low grades all except Modern History, where I got a grade 1, equal to a mid O-level. It was all about interest and being relaxed enough in the classroom to concentrate.

I left school, knowing I would never see Linda again.

By chance, a few years later, I bumped into my now-retired History teacher, I reminded him of my grade 1, and he remembered it. He said my essay about the state of the country – Union domination and the Cold War, and how nuclear fusion power (still waiting) was going to be the future, was good enough for my spelling to be overlooked.

By this time, my reading had turned to Eric von Daniken's Chariot of the Gods, (only partially discredited), J Allen Hynek and other contemporary UFO authors. I was starting to build my knowledge of the subject, though I knew enough to keep it mainly to myself.

I set about joining the Royal Navy, though it was to be some months before my intake at HMS Raleigh, at Torpoint, Cornwall.

Meanwhile, I got a job in the stockroom upstairs at a British Home Stores in Stockport.

One of the girl supervisors turned out to be the older sister of my years' long crush, Linda, and still I was too wary of looking the fool, and asking after Linda, I think part of me did not want to know if she had a boyfriend. Faint heart and all that. I worked bringing stock down to floor level with a guy called Frank, who was amiable enough. There were girls aplenty, but I must have been still too shy, as I never asked any out.

The time came to leave BHS to join the Navy, I was not long seventeen.

I do remember overhearing, from upstairs, at some point before I left home for the first time, my dad saying to my mum, 'Maybe they (the Navy) can make something of him.' I was clearly a long-standing disappointment to him. I was acutely aware, since failing the eleven-plus of that, especially with my brother and sister both passing.

Chapter 7

I remember the very long train journey to Torpoint, near Plymouth. One strange memory remains of that trip. I must have been talking to someone about the subject of UFOs, and a person, not the one I was talking to, spoke up from the opposite side of the gangway and told me, 'There is a village on the west coast of Wales with an RAF base next to it, and at night people from the village above have seen the ground open up on the sea shore, where a wide tunnel, could be seen going under the sea.' Why would this base have an undersea extension – a far out but possible reason coming later…

HMS Raleigh in Torpoint, Cornwall was, when I joined back in 1976 (and still is), the Navy's basic training base for ratings (not officers or engineers), it is where you are drilled, given basic Maths and English lessons, along with basic sea-related training, and in those days, until quite recently, given a NAMET test, which is mainly Maths and English oriented, the result of this test allowed the Navy to decide what specialisation training, once basic training is completed, is open to you. I was told that I could either be a Radar operator, or a navel airman, that is working in the Fleet Air Arm (we still had one in those days), only now recovering, with one of the two new carriers nearly ready.

I arrived just after new accommodation blocks were built, complete with laundry facilities. We were head-shaved, issued with No 1's (best) kit, and No 8's, our working kit.

Memories are somewhat hazy now, but the No1's, ceremonial, and leaving the Base kit, had to be ironed with special creases in the trousers, along with all other kit, as well as boot polishing of course, that I had experienced in the ATC, ironing, not so much.

Living in communal rooms of about twenty lads proved not so good for me, who was never good in a crowd. It was like being back at school. I found life hard, getting up around 5.30 am, at age seventeen, was bad enough, gym training, being still stick thin, must have improved my stamina.

I do remember having silver nitrate treatment for ingrowing toenails. At some point, we were asked if any of us wanted to volunteer for diver training, we were told we would get a pay supplement, as qualified divers. I went for it, I will never forget the Mud Run, it had a reputation as being tough – it was, very.

No more than about 100 yds long, it was on a very muddy part of the beach (hence the name), we were kitted out in a diving dry suit, very hot out of water, with a diving weight belt added. All you had to do was "run" to the pole and back again, simple…

Most of us made it to the pole – barely walking after the first few yards in what turned out to be sucking mud about a foot deep. With the weight belt added, most of us crawled on hands and knees most of the way back. A few people had to be pulled out of the mud, I made it unassisted – just. We lay on our backs totally exhausted; all of us ignoring the petty officer's shouts to get up, so tired were we.

The only actual diving I did then was round in a circle in a seawater-filled tank with other people's flippers almost in my face most of the time.

There was a lot of ox liver and cabbage in our food canteen, I remember that much and little else of the food there. At some point, we had to sign the Official Secrets Act, as are all military personnel.

We did some live firing with old Lee–Enfield .303 rifles, cannot recall how well I did, though I got my Marksman's Badge in the ATC, getting five .22 bullets grouped within the circle of an old halfpenny at 25 yds, at Stockport Armoury.

There was also the gas chamber, this was to let us experience what it could be like if we were sent to control a riot somewhere.

We were put in a room with gas masks on, then CS gas was released, we were told to remove our masks, kept in the room for twenty or thirty seconds – we were then let outdoors, where we coughed and spluttered, eyes streaming, some being sick.

I have forgotten the details, nothing horrific happened to me, but the environment must have been enough of a torment for me, that when we were given leave, told of a possible job by a mate, with no early get ups or other controls. I wanted to leave the Navy. My dad was not happy, though I think not too surprised.

I went back to Torpoint, told my class petty officer, who tried to persuade me to stay, telling me the worst was over, but I had made my mind up, being still under eighteen, you could go PVR – Premature Voluntary Release – which is what I did. I completed my basic training, did the "passing out parade", after which one last attempt was made to persuade me to stay in, but I was having none of it – I was out. I think I was put in the Navy reserve for some years.

I should have known better than to put myself back in a communal situation, but at that age, you only think of the exciting times to come – not the nitty-gritty, I am not quite a loner, but as said, I am happier in my own company or small groups.

In retrospect, I often wonder had I stayed in for what probably would have been nine years, which was the standard period at that time – whether, if I had taken up Radar training, would I have ended up in a radar room on HMS Sheffield, or Coventry, in the Falklands War. Strange how fate works…

The Radar Room was how and where the Exocet Missile homes in on a ship – the French being very diligent in making sure the Argentinians were well supplied…

Chapter 8

I was home, I needed to find a job. I cannot recall if Burrell Colours (now gone) was the first interview I had, but I got the job. I do remember my parents being pleased that my job as a plant technician was a staff position, on a monthly salary.

Everything on this Organic Pigment production plant was either very acidic or very alkaline. Dressed in overalls, Wellington boots and long rubber gloves, my main work was to "strike" batches of red, orange, though mostly yellow pigment dyes.

My plant supervisor was a John Parry, who was of the old school, but a good teacher, as I soon learnt how to follow the batch Formula Book, the plant worked like this...

The warehouse was next to the road at the bottom of the hill of the site (now mainly an Aldi supermarket), sent the raw materials around the side up the hill on a forklift truck, which were then thrown down wooden chutes, where one of the hourly paid men would stack these bags (some 50 kg) onto the top level stillages next to the initial mix vessels.

Much of the process stages relied on gravity. The hourly paid men would then mix the required raw materials with water, some were steam heated up – including caustic soda. Everything hinged on the right pH, the acid/alkali level. Most yellow Azo pigments, for example, were "coupled" that is mixed together in a base of water with either acetic, or hydrochloric acid, down to a pH of between 3.5 to 4.3-ish, the art was to add the first 5% of so of the aniline-based "second component" to the base – rotating in what could be a house-sized vessel – then start adding the diazo, benzene-based dye to the mix.

The aniline would react with the incoming Azo pigment, the trick was to keep enough, but not too much aniline surplus in the mix – for the Azo to react with – too much Azo and you would end up with a dirty "off-shade" batch, to keep the pH up, you could add some sodium bicarbonate, but you had to be wary of adding too much as the batch could end up frothing up so much it could start spilling over the top of the mixing vessel. This striking of the batch was the plant technician's and supervisor's job as this was the skilled, critical part of the job, sometimes, if there was too much for us, other people from the labs could be brought in to strike some batches, (this was to be the thin edge of the wedge later) as there were nine plants, and you could be striking two or even three batches at once.

It was all about keeping the flow rates just right. I was sometimes stretched to my limit, but I enjoyed the satisfaction of producing a good batch or two simultaneously. I would sometimes spend afternoons in the lab testing yesterday's batches against an ideal standard batch of that shade of yellow. I used to spend my dinner hour (it was an hour in that job), eating my food, playing chess with one or two lab techs, Ted K, and a John H, who I was mates with from the main development labs at the other end of the site. I started to learn to play the electric guitar from him, but he was indifferent about playing by then, and I gave up in the end.

Chapter 9

Even in those late teen years I was aware of politics, as far as Britain fitted in, as I was and still am quite patriotic. I was not party blind, I knew they were, as now, faction riven.

We had not long since joined what was then the EEC, having been refused twice in the sixties by De Gaulle, who very slyly, after the first refusal, said, if we could persuade the Americans to give France nuclear weapons, they might think again about our joining.

We got the French what they wanted, and asked again to join, only to be blocked again by De Gaulle, this was all kept quite when we were finally admitted, (I don't think he ever forgave us for sinking the French fleet holed up at Oran, North Africa after France surrendered to the Germans. When their fleet refused to join us, we could not let them be captured by Germany. I was too young to vote on joining in the early 70s, but I would have voted against as I could see, we were to be fleeced even then. And we were, from the start.

We had to give over sovereignty of our fishing grounds, which cost many British jobs. We also had to subsidise (and still do) French, and many other farmers to gain admittance, De Gaulle must have been laughing his socks off! Along with many others.

My knowledge of politics in all its complexity was to grow with age and experience and observation beyond the headlines, where most politicians do not want you to look.

I had kept up my friendship with Kevin and Brian, there was also John, a joiner, who worked with Kevin, a bricklayer, and a guy called Wayne (not the one from early school), who was a smooth-talking office worker – in freight forwarding. His sister was John's girlfriend for a couple of years. At that age, Kevin, Brian, another joiner (and more expert Angler) than Kevin and I used to go to a snooker club in Stockport, from which there were two events of note.

The first I am a little reluctant to recall here, but I will, as I have never laughed (along with everyone else except the players) as much again as we did that night. Picture this scene if you will – if you have ever watched snooker on TV, it was as quiet and tense as that, as the place was shut to the public, the manager and assistant manager were playing a game for money…

We three teenage lads, being well in with them, were locked in with them, sitting dutifully quite watching while they played their game. Pete, the assistant manager, had the upper hand in this game and was just lining up to pot the black for a win…

Now there was small bar at this club, and I had developed a taste for Guinness stout by this time, you may now see where I am going with this, but two things made it exceptional. As I said Pete was just "cueing up" for what should have been the winning shot, you could have heard a pin drop. I started a fart that went on forever, at least three times as long as I have ever done since – to be crude. There was a disbelieving pause for a second or two, as Pete tried to hold his concentration, then threw his cue on the table in disgust, by then, us three lads burst out laughing for so long, after the tension of the game and the unintentional perfect timing, that we were all in tears with laughter by the time we had finished – the game was abandoned!

The second event was not so much what happened at the club – but what it led to…

There was a one-armed bandit slot machine at this club, and Kevin, who used to play on this more than I or Brian, noticed it had started paying out all the time – the manager also spotted this, so the manager shut the machine off – until closing time. We were then allowed to play this faulty machine until we had emptied it. The manager must have taken a share, but our share for the three of us amounted to nearly 140 Pounds Stirling. Late 70s, that was a good amount, we decided to keep it until Saturday night then go to the in pub at the time and get really drunk, which we did. Not only did we sink a lot of beer, but because of all the money we had, we downed double chasers as well, which in my case was Pernod for some reason, maybe the others were on it, but not something I normally drank.

Don't know how I got home, but when I did, what happened next, I thought was a dream when I finally woke up the next morning, it was not. I don't know how it started, but when I got in that night, I must have started smashing things, I threatened my dad with Bruce Lee stuff I said I could do to him if I wanted to, all so totally out of character, I vaguely remember it as a dream, but as stated, it was not. Suppressed anger at my dad, let loose with being so drunk most likely.

I was told that if I ever came home in that state again, I would be out. I never did.

I think I gave him quite a scare. To this day, I have never drunk another Pernod.

In my bedroom I had been allowed to have an aquarium, which I looked after fairly well. Then one day I came home to find the thermostat had malfunctioned, and the heater had stayed on and cooked all but one very hardy angelfish, which had a brown burn on the front half of its body, this fish lived for quite a long time afterwards.

Chapter 10

Going back to the year of leaving school, Kevin, with his older brothers, had gone up to the Outer Hebrides for about three weeks. His oldest brother, David, was an engineer who had previously gone out to work on a power station out there.

The next year, my first at the colour works, I took all my holiday entitlement in one go to go with them, along with Brian. That first year up there, John and Wayne (who never went) were not on the scene yet.

It was the closest I have been to going on an expedition. Having already been there, Kevin said there are no worms for fishing bait, as the soil was peat, and too acid, so as the time neared, we had to dig up large quantities of said worms and store them in gallon ice-cream tubs.

That first year (of five!) was to be the one that I remember the most of, though I may mix up some events from later years, it was so long ago.

In later years, we went up in long wheelbase Land Rovers, a Dutch, Auto Union 2-Stroke Jeep, properly equipped expeditions then. But that first year all they had was a 1-litre Simca hatchback. There were four of us that year, Kevin and his older brother, Ian, who was a telephone engineer, myself and Brian. As we were taking camping gear, Sea and Course fishing kit, shotguns (I had got a licence by then), lots of 12 bore cartridges, food, mostly tinned, spam, corned beef, Fray Bentos Steak and Kidney pies, tinned veg, that sort of thing, it meant that only two could go in the car and ferry, and two by rail and ferry.

Of course, Kevin and his brother, Ian, went in (to be fair) their car, taking it across to The Isle of Skye, at the Kyle of Lochalsh, which at the time had a chain link ferry (now replaced with a bridge).

They then drove to Uig in the north, (as have I in subsequent years), to catch a ferry to Lochmaddy on North Uist, then a drive down across a causeway to Benbecula which had the nearest shop to our campsite on the Machair in the west of South Uist.

They were to set up the tent, as we were to spend the first two weeks of our month that year in our tent, then two weeks staying with an elderly couple nearby, called Morag and Euan McMillan, at their croft.

Meanwhile, Brian and I had to catch a train from Stockport to Crewe first, (Crewe was the only connection to Glasgow at the right time), for the train to Oban, where we got on a Caledonian MacBrayne ferry that was supposed to take five hours to reach Lochboisdale near the southern end of South Uist.

Kevin and Ian were meant to pick us up from there at around 6.30 or 7 pm, I can't remember the exact time, anyway, it did not happen until much later...

The stretch of water between the west of Scotland and the Outer Hebrides is called "The Minch" and had a bad reputation, Brian and I found out why.

The crossing to South Uist that was meant to take five hours took nine hours; the sea became so rough and mountainous, that the two-thousand-ton ferry could not chance turning back to Oban, as to turn side on to the massive waves could have risked us capsizing. So the ship ploughed through the waves, with the whole front of the vessel disappearing underwater at times, with great shudders, then reappearing, white water spilling of the deck, no one able to stand up much for many hours, before finally getting through the worst of the storm (the worst sea trip I have experienced).

We docked at Lochboisdale sometime between eleven and midnight, wondering if we would see the red Simca with Kevin and Ian in it (no mobile phones then) – it was there! We were very relieved to see.

By then, even at midnight up there, it was still half-light, so being taken by Kevin and Ian to our lonely tent in what to us was the middle of nowhere in this eerie half-light was a very surreal and exciting experience, I remember well to this day.

Then there was the corncrake, croaking away like mad all night! We could not see it, but I have to confess we eventually took potshots in the general direction of its croak with our shotguns in the middle of the night! We had no near neighbours, which was just as well, but the sound must have carried a fair distance.

The croak stopped for a while but would then restart, so we must not have hit it fortunately, though we did not think so at the time!

The next day I can only recall due to the fact that we had to perform the following ritual every year we went up there. Although it was my first year, Kevin and his older brothers had been going for a couple of years, since David, his oldest (very opinionated) brother had worked (as an engineer) out there. He had worked all over the world, sometimes where they actually had servants, he was a smug, very self-assured person.

By then, he had stopped going up there, but between them, they had built up quite a few crofter contacts, and within a day or two of arriving up there, if we did not call at every one of them (there must have been half a dozen!) to be fed soda bread scones and tea usually with whisky in, the very efficient bush telegraph had someone mention to us – if we missed calling in somewhere!.

Needless to say, by the end of the day, and sometimes two days, we were so stuffed and half drunk! We did not need to cook any of our own food.

Chapter 11

The location of our camp was somewhere close to what is called on the map in Galic – "Rudha Ardvule" – we called it "The Point" as it was a promontory sticking out from the miles long white beaches which are a feature on the west coast of South Uist.

The nearest settlement was a few miles to the north, called Stonybridge, only a few stone houses and the ruined small seventeenth century Ormiclete Castle, the area closest to us was called Bornais, pronounced "Bornish" which is a scattered hamlet, not now recognisable as such. There was a small shop further north at Howmore, on what was then the single track (north/south) "main road" that had periodic passing places.

There was a larger shop just over the causeway on Benbecula at Creagorry, and on the west coast the small Township of Ballavanich, which had a small airfield nearby, must have had a shop, though I have no memory of it. The only time I recall going there was to a Ceilidh, a Scottish folk dancing gathering/party, where a then unknown band outside of Scotland's West coast were to perform – they were called Runrig and went on to become famous briefly, years later on *Top of the Pops*.

There is a township called Dalibourgh, in English, some miles to the south, though I only remember it for its proximity to a pub/hotel called The Borrowdale, which is still open today and has been extended – it is where we were to spend many a night getting drunk over the next five years. The above then, and the occasional trip to the Polochar Inn, right on the southern tip of South Uist were the extent of "civilisation" to be found on these month - long trips.

The following are the main pastimes we got up to, though I cannot now say which year or years of the late 70s or early 80s with certainty, as these events took place so long ago.

One of our main pastimes was to go rabbit shooting on the many miles long, but only quarter mile wide Machair, a stretch of grassy, sand dune bordering open land next to the beach on which Croft lands grew a few crops along the inland border. There were hundreds of rabbits living on the Machair, plus polecats and birds of prey living off this population.

So did we – to an extent, we were encouraged to shoot the rabbits by the Crofters whose crops suffered from rabbit raids, we would spread out, look for ears sticking up from the grassy tussocks, always upwind of us so they did not get our scent, though the sandpipers would often give us away.

We found many different ways to cook what we shot, but first was the nasty bit. Skinning was hard but doable, gutting however, especially if there was no wind in which to hold the carcass downwind, was a terrible job, I managed not to be sick from the smell, but just barely.

We did have one solution to this, the adage "If you can't solve a problem – move it" applies here. When, between us, we had a few rabbits to "clean", we took them across to Loch Eyenort on the eastern side of the island, which is much more rugged than the West coast. This was a sea loch, and on its southern shore, a rough track led to the skeletal remains of an old pier.

So after skinning, we would cautiously edge our way along the thick beams of the pier, and when out over the water, gut the rabbits, letting the contents fall into the loch.

One year, not sure if it was the first, we had been told by the locals, that migrating mackerel sometimes entered this loch at that time of year, so we took our sea-fishing gear with us on a gutting trip and, with mackerel feathers attached, cast them in straight after the rabbit innards were dropped in.

Luck may have played a part, but Loch Eyenort is big, and maybe the smell transmitted over a large enough area, that it attracted a big shoal, as on one day the three of us who fished, (Ian does not fish) caught around fifty mackerel, far more than we could eat. One of the Crofter families, we or rather Kevin's older brother knew at least, took our excess fish and salted them in a barrel for winter eating. Shop food out there is very basic, so the locals would supplement their diet, they would shoot Cormorant, for example, very greasy, but one of the few wildfowl, apart from a few ducks, up there, though I got the impression they had to be hard up to eat it.

In return for the mackerel, we were treated to a meal at their house. By the late 70s, most, though not all, Crofters had a new house, built next to their small old stone Crofters Cottage, the family who took our mackerel had a new pebble dash bungalow. Peter W and his wife had about eight children, not that unusual among the staunch Catholic population of South Uist, where the pubs do not open on Sundays, at least then. Kevin and another of his brothers, Steven, who was not with us that year, were both to claim two of the older girls of this family as "holiday girlfriends" in later years, though this led to trouble for Kevin that I never learnt fully about as it was after I had married, and he had gone up there to work. I think he had to go back to Stockport in a hurry and lay low.

Chapter 12

We also had one other source of local protein, Rainbow Trout. There are a lot of small "tarns" on the flat western side of the island, and I am not sure who came up with this idea, but it worked a treat…

If you recall, I mentioned that prior to us going up there, we collected large amounts of earthworms, stored in moss and soil, in ice-cream tubs. Now one of the problems of angling in these small tarns was that they were on mostly flat land, and quite shallow, so if you were not fly fishermen, which we were not, it was too shallow and weedy to float, fish.

So we put quite large worms on our hooks, and nothing else, cast them out, where they did *not* sink, as they would have, had we not first injected air into the worms using a syringe that Ian's girlfriend (who happened to be a nurse) had supplied him with.

So the worms stayed on the surface, easily visible and irresistible to the trout. As we caught many using this method, though they were usually less than a pound in weight, it provided a valuable addition to our fare. There were only a few tarns we could get away with fishing, and there was one snag.

While having a fair few trout in them, many of these small tarns were also full of eels, which we were not desperate enough to want to eat, they would often get to the worms before the trout did. We resorted to putting night lines out with many hooks attached, cannot recall if we used our precious, finite worm supply as bait, but we usually pulled quite a few out the next day. Eels are hard to kill, being out of water is no problem for them, they can slither large distances from pond to pond without difficulty. We had to stand on them near the head and cut the head off. The rest of the body would writhe for some time afterwards.

Memory is a bit hazy on this, but I think we used eel as bait when we had it, when we used to go out with a lobster pot fisherman, who let us trawl our lines while he went out and then back from his pots. We could not fish while he was near his pots for risk of entanglement, but we caught a few pollock, a bony fish, but sweeter than cod.

Once, while I was out on my own, rabbit hunting, I came across a large whale vertebrae, about two feet across, which I duly carried back to camp and all the way home, where it rested on top of my wardrobe for some years, I don't recall what happened to it.

Another time whilst on my own, on the Machair, I crept up to the top of tussocky dune, peered over the top looking for rabbits and spotted a large polecat – so intent on hunting, as like me it was, that it never saw me take my Parker PARKA coat off, creep up to it and dive on it catching it with my coat! I do not know what I thought I was going to do with it, maybe just take it back to show the others. I never got the chance, within a few seconds, it had bitten through the coat into my wrist and then escaped. It was almost white, and twice as big as any ferret I have seen, so it must have been a polecat. I have since learnt they had been introduced to control the rabbit population.

We used to stew, fry, grill and skewer rabbit, sometimes taking it up to "The Point" to cook over an open fire. But there were two other things we had to do before we got that far. First was to look at the liver, to make sure there were no white areas on it. If there were, it (the rabbit) was "mixed", that is to say it had Myxomatosis and was unfit to eat.

We would know if there was a rabbit with an advanced case, as when the others saw, or smelt us and ran down their burrows, these poor animals, sometimes with swollen eye sockets, and blind, would be left above ground, oblivious to the danger, smell lost, along with sight. We would shoot these, to put them out of their misery. It was the ones with no outward sign, in the early stages, that we had to check the liver for.

In the five years I went up there, only one year, my second or third, was there a widespread outbreak of the disease, that year rabbit was off the menu.

On some of the Machair, cattle roamed, owned by a collective of local crofters, we never shot near them, but still young as I was, I was up for a laugh, so not entirely sensible all the time. Kevin and Brian were walking a short distance ahead of me, I had my old Russian Baikal single barrel shotgun with me, they were just walking past a fairly fresh cow pat, about six feet away, I shot it, it went up like a landmine! I don't think they got much on them, I know I was and sworn at.. I DIDN'T AND WAS SWORN AT

A year later year, we collected, scraped and salted the pelts of some rabbits, I remember having a mottled ginger and black one, we tied these to the roof rack of a Land Rover we were in that year – to dry out the pelts on the long journey back home. I think the idea was to make a hat or gloves from them. I don't recall any. We must have looked like something out of the Beverly Hillbillies going along the motorway. We spent a lot of time drinking up there, as lads of that age do.

The Borrowdale Hotel, near Daliburgh Township, was our favourite watering hole, darts, pool, the usual. One time Steven, who did not drink and had dropped us off there, agreed to pick us up later. Closing time he was still not there, so we, I think four of us, all somewhat drunk, started walking north, along the "Main Road", single lane with passing places, in what was the half-light at that time of summer, in the middle of the night.

We had taken some carry-out cans of beer with us, and after walking some distance with no sign of Steven, we sat down in the middle of the road in a circle and started drinking the carry-out cans!

There was not a lot of traffic on this road, but if someone had come along I am not sure we would have been quick enough in our state to get out of the way – as I think we were sat in a bit of a dip! Steven did turn up before we got back to what was by that year a builder's caravan, basic but big enough for us all. It turned out entertaining, one of the local girls there was the reason he did not turn up to pick us up, which was fair enough.

Chapter 13

One last footnote from our first year there – Euan McMillan, the crofter we stayed with for our second two weeks of my first year up there, who looked to be in his late seventies, took us out to his peat diggings, we thought the least we could do was to help him while we were there! We tried to dig peat, we made little impression, Ewan was as tough as old boots and he put us youngsters all to shame. There was a knack to using the long, narrow-bladed peat spades.

We found out that when some of the crofters were out in the cold working their crofts, doing everything from veg, to sheep, and including collecting "Tangles" which turned out to be collecting large amounts of seaweed from the shoreline, to be processed at a plant I never saw and sent to Japan in those days, they, the men at least, carried a whisky flask, and the trick was to stay a little drunk only, all day – to keep out (or ignore) the cold while they worked.

Kevin and one-year Steven, as mentioned, both had dalliances with local girls, one of which sent me a letter, to my great shock, at home, after my last visit, saying she wanted to see me and could I go back up there! I suspected in my panicked mind that someone had put her up to it, (such still was my low self-esteem), as she must have obtained my address from one of the other lads. I did not respond, never spoke of it, and it was not brought up by anyone, so I will never know.

Other events of note, I cannot recall what year, close to 1980, but anyway, Kevin and Ian had someone up there make a two-man fibreglass open canoe, to fish from, which we did a fair bit of. We also had a one-man kayak, we decided that particular year to paddle from "The Point" all the way down the West coast to the southern tip of South Uist to Polochar, about ten miles away.

Kevin and John were in the open canoe, and guess who in the kayak, we stayed close to the shore, in my case, a little too close, as a small wave turned me over, and there was too little water under me to right myself. So I struggled to get my head out of the sand, I eventually managed to turn on my side and surfaced, coughing and spluttering until I had got rid of seawater I had inhaled in my panic. We resumed our trip, me staying a little further out after that episode.

Stephen met us at Polochar beach, in the long wheelbase Land-rover they had by then, both boats fitting on the roof-rack. You could see Eriskay from there, the southernmost of the Outer Hebrides, less than half a mile away. We spent some time in the Polochar Inn, me trying out Glenlivet as a beer chaser.

With it staying half-light all night in the summer, we decided, having obtained an old fishing net from somewhere, to weigh the bottom down and walk/swim the length of one of the small lochs that peppered the island. We were not sure if anyone owned this pond, so not sure if we were poaching or not. The fact that we decided to go to the pub first and wait for it to get as dark as it would get – suggests it was poaching. Kevin, John and I, all half drunk, walked and swam a little. It was mostly about four to five feet deep, pushing the net, which had floats along the top in front of us. The pond, too small to call a loch, was no more than twenty feet wide and about seventy feet long.

We felt nothing in the net until we were near the end, and then one fairly large trout managed to jump free near Kevin, so we ended up with nothing for our efforts.

Apart from the last year when Julie and I got together, too close to the time we were going up there to back out, there were no other events of note up there that I retain with my poor level of recall.

Chapter 14

Going back to work was a shock after a month up there, but reality hit hard, going home from work, where, despite having a shower at the end of the working day, my pillow was still yellow from the colour absorbed in my pores, as the pigment, once made, was sent through a press, neutralised with water, then pressurised into a cake or slurry, dropped into tubs and shovelled onto trays, (very hard work) only tried it one year, following the last batch downstream before Christmas, fed onto trolleys, which were dried in ovens into a powder – which hung in the air, as the trays were tipped into drums for blending with other batches, to end up with the right shade.

Heaven knows how much I breathed in over the years. In another building, blues were made, in a shift process. I did not work in there (thankfully) as the process was very different to the orange, yellows and reds I used to make. The air in the blue plant was literally blue, if you looked from one end to the other, workers wore paper masks, but not all the time…

I was allowed to do a two-year day release, City and Guilds course in Process Plant Operation, at North Trafford College, learning mainly in a plant lab, which had a few small pumps, and pipes to practice with. I learnt about liquids, and gasses under pressure and heat, learnt about different pumps, some basic maths, physics and chemistry. Some of it quite relevant to my current job and future employment. I do recall the dinner break was about an hour and half long, so playing table tennis or a drink in the student union bar was enjoyed, but I did get a credit pass on my practical exam and passed the theory test.

By the end of the two-year course, the company was starting to come under pressure from competition, and as part of the all-round belt tightening, I was not allowed to start a more advanced C and G day release course.

Away from work, one of the more unusual later fishing trips out with Kevin and John and Kev's brother Steve, I think, was a trip to Arnside, a village on the Cumbrian Coast where the River Kent reaches the top end of Morcombe Bay.

Nice though this quite seaside village is, it held an unusual secret, in that small flatfish could be caught without the use of net or line, or any sort of bait…

There is a railway viaduct that crosses the large expanse of beach at Arnside, and on the inland side of the viaduct (at that time, 1990s, maybe still) was a large tidal pool, around 100 yds across, and about waist deep in most parts at that time, being sandy bottomed, it may have shifted by now, but then, by chance, we were greeted by the site of a guy in shorts, seemingly walking around, bending down now and again, only to stand up and throw a small flatfish (dab) ashore!

We had taken our sea fishing gear with us, but after a conversation with the guy picking fish out of the water, it being a hot sunny summer's day, we stripped to boxer shorts and waded in…

What was happening was that the flatfish came in with the tide and were trapped in this large tidal pool, so if you walked around, every so often your foot would trap a "dab" on the sandy bottom, if you were expecting this, instead of jerking your foot away from the sudden movement of a flatfish trying to get away, you simply bent down and firmly grabbed the fish, waded to the shore and threw it to one of the lads with a bag, then repeat. As I recall, we went home with half a dozen each, my mum cooked some I took home. Don't know if this is still possible, or if it is done anywhere else.

Chapter 15

The trips out to pubs got less frequent. John had been paired up with Wayne's sister "Julie" for a year or two. She, like Wayne, was a little more sophisticated than John but must have liked his rugged charm. It had petered out a while before I got going with "Julie".

Soon after, Wayne and Kevin and Anne, it turned out, tried to pair me and Julie up, she had listened earnestly to my description of a boat design I had come up with – something along the lines of a clipper but with small wind turbines spaced along the masts, in place of sails, feeding batteries in the hold, which powered an electric engine, the drawings of which I had sent off to Swan Hunter, expecting great things in my youthful naivety. I, still being naïve about girls, did not pick up on her avid attention to my earnest description, as anything more than normal interest, although I wanted to get closer. I was conscious of John, and everyone else watching my every move (as I imagined it), and so even on a night out to a Rock Disco, I never did more than buy her a drink. They gave up on me, John and Julie got back together for a short while. Then John announced he was going to work in Australia. My memory is a little hazy (I did mention that) about when he went, but go he did, I never saw him again.

Sometime around the age of twenty-one, or even two, after a party at our house, I finally started going out with a girl, a friend of my sisters from schooldays. I will call here "Anne" here, she was usually quite in a crowd but could get passionate in private – as I was to find out. My sister warned me against her but would not be specific as to why, though I think years later I could guess, though I have never had this confirmed.

As mentioned earlier, the year we started seeing each other was the last year of my going to the Hebrides. It must have been close to when we were going as I had told Anne I could not back out at this late stage, she did not object. I phoned when I could, before mobiles, this was not very often up there, usually from the Borrowdale.

Things progressed over months to a physical relationship – mainly in cars, as you do at that age! I could not get enough, after being such a late starter.

We went on the traditional dirty weekend to Blackpool, which, looking back, I have to say it was!

Eventually, a date was set to get married, but sometime about two months before that event, something happened that I did not take enough note of at the time, but I now think made all the difference to how things turned out.

We went back to “Anne’s” house while her parents were out, I should mention that her parents were quite old and must have had Anne and her sister in their late thirties or forties, (not as common as it is now). We went to her house as I was saying, not planned, her parents not being in, so being young and in lust, I persuaded Anne to have sex in her room, she was strangely reluctant, though not normally so, we did it anyway, but afterwards, she was crying, she would not tell me why.

Something about her farther (who was an unpleasant man), I could not put my finger on what it was about him, at the time, but I do remember what he said about us getting married, though he did not seem to care much, he said “it won’t last” with glee it seemed, on more than one occasion. You might come to the same conclusion as I, about the one visit to her bedroom, and her abrupt change in attitude to our sexual relationship that followed from then on.

When I used to visit her house, we would all sit there and it would be quite a stilted atmosphere, they were a quite poor, but old fashioned, to the point of her parents calling each other dad and mother instead of their names in front of us, like they used to do in the 40s and 50s, and only now seen in the sitcoms of the day (early 80s).

After that event in her room, things on the physical side cooled, it still happened, never at her house again and not that often. I told myself it would get better after we were married.

Before we were married, another very sad event was to happen first.

Chapter 16

My father by this time was in a state of depression, becoming withdrawn, me being an intellectual disappointment to him meant we were not close anyway, so I confess to not really taking a lot of notice at the time.

We were to find out later, after a suicide attempt, that he was seeing a woman at work, though we kids were told at that time, that it was his work he hated, and the reason for his depression, but after a second suicide attempt, we found out that he had been turned down, by his work mistress, when he wanted to leave us and live with her. My mum was obviously very distressed by this but stood by him to the point where he must have seen some sort of therapist, who must have told him to find a hobby of some sort to become absorbed with.

This materialised as philately, or stamp collecting, which he went into to the point of becoming a trader at Stamp Fairs at weekends. We, my four-year junior brother and one-year junior sister, were uncertain how to react to this situation. I think we believed things had reached some sort of resolution.

We were mistaken. I came home from work one day when my mum was on a late nursing shift, and I was first home. Dad was not in, the garage door was a little up from the ground, it was an up and over.

When I pulled up the door, I saw a pipe leading from the car exhaust into a window, I could see my dad in the front seat, I knew he was dead. His head leaned right back, mouth wide open. There is a stillness that is very different from someone who is dead rather than unconscious. I tried to get the car open, locked, could not break the window, I think because I knew I was too late.

The police got him out, though I must have been taken somewhere else, as I did not see it happen. We were told he had got himself drunk on whisky before he shut himself in.

Apart from my mum, it was my sister "Jane" who was the most visibly affected by my dad's suicide.

I think she was able to reach him more than us two boys, and so could see more of what he (and Mum) was going through, as girls do, than us lads. I am not sure how I processed this, there were a lot of mixed feelings, and I think I tried to shut them out as much as possible. It was left to my sister to make sure we supported our mum as much as we could. I sometimes wondered if my finally getting with a girlfriend was one less problem my dad somehow had felt was his fault, it had taken me so long. So, in my mind it was partly my fault, I had contributed to his depression.

Our marriage was in a register office, not being religious. The usual evening do was had in an upstairs room in a big pub in Stockport.

We had saved enough for a deposit on a small ground floor flat in Denton, a small town about three miles from the edge of Stockport, I did not know that area well, but it was easy enough to get a bus to work for both of us, though I soon got a car, a second-hand Mark 1 Escort Estate. I still went out with my old friends and was suddenly very popular, as for a while I was the only one with transport. Anne, my new wife, would come out with us at first, but this way of life was to change – as it does.

I was to discover that the event in "Anne's" old bedroom was to have a profound effect on our marriage, though I am not sure if things would have turned out any different in the long term. What little physical contact between that event and our getting married stopped soon after we were married.

We found we had little mutual interests to share, and constant niggling soon became the norm. Contact with my former crowd became much reduced and frowned upon by Anne.

It is surprising how over time you can adjust to what with hindsight was a strange relationship, I think I did not want to admit for a long time that this was yet another failure. For her part, I think that her parents' relationship, and possible events in their house in her early life, may have coloured her view as to what married life was meant to be.

We told each other in the early days we would leave children out of the picture for a few years – until the mortgage was less of a burden. So she stayed on the pill, although there was almost no need.

I think within a couple of years we both knew there were going to be no children.

Chapter 17

My interest in UFOs had continued into my twenties. One of the few times, my dad had seemed a little impressed with me was when a few years earlier, when he and my mum had gone over to Canada, (they were not all bad times between them), to stay with some fairly distant relatives, they came back, and dad said with my mum prompting him a little (I suspect) that rumours that dead aliens were being kept at Wright Patterson Air Force Base in the US, were rife. I am sure that before then he was apt to write off my interest in the subject, as more evidence of my low level of intelligence.

The only time I can recall the subject having any impact on "Anne", was on one mid-winter evening, when we had been to a pub, called The Fox, which was out in the countryside near a place called Hayfield in Derbyshire. It was a pub I used to go with my friends, often playing pool, anyway, we were on our way back, driving along a single-lane road back down to the main road, when we saw – across the valley, an orange ball of light about half the size of the moon, moving in slow rising arcs, bellow the summit of the hill.

I stopped the car and started flashing my headlights at it, this alarmed Anne, who told me to stop it. The light continued along and then around the back of the hill, out of our sight. This event quite scared Anne, as she had up till then, very little interest in the subject, or anything else I showed an interest in.

I do not think this was an alien craft. There is a lot of pico/electric activity from the quartz in the rock, in that area, generated from micro tremors, which could have resulted in us seeing released "ball lightning" though the movement seemed quite steady and prolonged. One later theory I heard was that people were known to illegally hang glide at night, and that they used flares, strapped to their ankles to light up their landing area. The movement was slow enough, but seemed too large and to long lived to be the above.

I think it gave Anne pause for thought on the subject.

I kept reading all I could on the subject, at the time most was of American origin, though not all. The sheer number of sightings by pilots, and other events, built up as evidence that if even one out of the thousands of sightings, some of them radar confirmed, was genuine, then we had to rethink the history and the "news" we are being fed, as not the whole uncensored truth.

Around a year or so after I was married, major changes (for me at least) happened at work. The company I worked for was struggling in a crowded market, and redundancies occurred, I escaped the first two rounds, but as the company was put into administration, I was made redundant. My immediate boss,

John P, told me to keep in touch, as there was a chance the works could be taken over.

I got a job in a supermarket, hoping I might get back to the dye works, after about a month or so, I was asked to work a night shift – unloading a large truck with one other person. In twelve hours, we put the entire contents of this truck on the top storage shelf of the supermarket floor.

We had one ten-minute break that 12-hour night, we were very tired by eight the next morning when the manager came in, and said to us, 'Not very tidy is it.' I then did something I have never done since. I told the manager what he could do with his job. It was a bit of a gamble, but my old boss had told me to come and see him about a week on from then.

I went to see John P hoping to restart my job. I was in for a shock, I was offered a job, on the hourly paid work, preparing the vessels and boiling and pumping the finished batches I used to blend or "Strike".

With a takeover and the reduced staff numbers, one of the production chemists – who used to strike the occasional batch (I had called on him myself of the plant) for when I was left in charge of the plant for two weeks of John P's holidays) – was now given what used to be my job, as well as his lab work.

As I knew the processes, I was offered the only job available. I don't think they thought I would take it, but I did.

It was hard for a while, working with people I had technically been in charge of at times, some of them twice my age, but seeing the work, and actually doing it, put me at the bottom of the pile in terms of having to learn the other more physical side of the processes.

Peter Mc was the chargehand of the half dozen men who prepared the Azo dyes, and Anilide bases for mixing or "coupling" into pigment.

Pete was as hard as nails and an old sea salt, and by that, I mean he used to be on submarines stationed at Valletta in Malta – one of the toughest war theatres to live through.

I don't think these men thought I would stick it out, but I was still young, kept my head down and managed to learn that side of the job. I must have physically toughened up, to handle some of the heavy raw material bags, also shovelling tons of ice, from the seven ice-producing plants needed to keep the Di Azo from becoming warm and producing dirty "off-shade" pigment.

This ice went into many oil drum sized steel containers, which I learnt to roll two at a time when empty. There were also endless 50 kg carboys of acetic, or hydrochloric acid to move, lift and tip into the main mixing vessels to add to the water to make the pH a 4-ish base.

Chapter 18

I was gradually accepted, I knew I had to give everything I had to show willing, to accept my new station, no longer in a staff job, though watching John R, the Plant Chemist, in particular, perform what used to be my job, was hard at times. Others from the labs come to do my old work from time to time, it was a bitter pill to swallow.

What was called "the old side" of the production plant, which was situated on a hill and made use of gravity in a downhill progression of the process, was very old, it used to be some sort of mill, and there was an old brick boiler chimney that divided the old side from the purpose-built newer side. The base vessels were made of wood – you used to have to leave a trickle of water running in them in summer to stop cracks – and leaks occurring, and the agitators (stirrers) were basically tree trunks with cross beams for blades, the whole lot powered using belt drives, used in the old mills. The smaller red and orange colours were made on this side, some of these had boiled resin added, the process being quite different from the yellows on the "new" side.

One scary event took place, on this side – where right at the end, an extension housed a yellow Z plant, three times the size of the other plants, the main vessel was the size of a three-story house.

One day, there was a thunderstorm, myself and Dr John R, the Plant Chemist, were at the top of the plant when the glass from the skylights above started to rain down around us, and I saw a blue flash out of the corner of my eye, there was a smell of ozone.

We started to run towards the other end, I did not make a conscious decision to do this, I just found myself propelled by sheer instinct to do this, (not something I have experienced since). The damage was not major, just some panes of glass, but when we went back, there was a blackened area of concrete, about eight or nine feet below a protruding through the low roof, apiece of disused conduit piping, the blue flash I saw must have been lightning that had discharged from the conduit into the concrete, having come down the lightning rod attached to the old chimney, dodged that one!

There are two, or should I say one and half foreign holidays I remember going on with Anne. The half being a trip in an old Viscount propeller plane to the Channel Island of Jersey, not really foreign, though this was the furthest south I had been to date.

We must have hired a car, as I recall driving down high-hedged lanes and seeing long, empty beaches. I think we stayed in a B&B; I remember seeing

Jersey Castle. Not a lot else I recall from there, a bit like the Devon and Cornwall trips we made.

The other foreign trip we took was what then was still Yugoslavia, to a quiet place on the Istrian Peninsula called Porac, near Pula, (of which I have a more recent vexatious memory, to be told later…).

Back in the 80s, Pula Airport was still half military, I recall seeing a line of MiG fighters parked along one side of the tarmac.

In those days, still under Tito's version of communism, more independent of Moscow, that the other "Iron Curtain" countries, there was a fledgling tourist industry along the coast, it was a cheap destination if you did not want the Spanish Costas, Blackpool with sun-type of holiday. We had that much in common.

Pula Airport was not ready for mass tourism, it was a nightmare. Processing through Passport and Customs, you had to carry your suitcase over your head! It was so tightly packed, in what seemed ninety degree heat.

The small town of Porac was pleasant enough, though there was little to do apart from walk the front and eat at the quiet restaurants. Being the first time for us in this humidity, it was quite a surprise how quickly the pavements dried, steam rising, after a brief thunderstorm.

The only excursion I remember us going on from there was by boat, across the northern Adriatic, to Trieste in Italy. A local guide had a clever means of making a little extra cash on these trips. He would go across wearing cheap shoes and come back in expensive Italian ones, presumably with ready customers in Istria, enterprising… Little else I recall of that trip.

Anne and I had learnt to keep to unspoken lines of demarcation after a few years, so we argued less, but behaved (at least it seemed to me) like an old-fashioned, almost Victorian, couple who had been married far longer than we had. I used to go and see my mother on my own by then as it was strained between her and Anne. I think my mother was expecting children, and after two or three years, she probably thought it was Anne refusing to stop work.

From the little I remember of Anne's attitude to children, she would talk of women she knew who had children suffering with arthritis in later years, so I think she was no keener than me on the idea. I by then had come up with reasons for not having children.

I must have picked up the fact that before we were married that "Annc" was in no hurry for kids, though I kept this from my mum, as I had already decided that I did not want to take the chance that any child of mine would be too much like me and have to endure the schooldays I had gone through.

There was something in my mind also, that I would deny an unknown somebody, of my offspring being part of some breeding/experiment/tracking programme. I think I may have tacked this on from my knowledge of supposed alien hybrid abduction stuff that was doing the rounds by then, having never forgotten my early years' "dreams", though I prefer to think there is only a very small probability this is happening. More likely, I had seen other people struggling, working all hours, including night shifts to make ends meet, and knowing I was not going to be a high-earner, life would be a bit easier without kids, though it was the first reason, about my schooldays, that was dominant. I was not blind to any joy, or other benefits children could bring, but the above outweighed this, such was my experience of life thus far.

Chapter 19

Badminton was to be the sport that I would keep playing, though with gaps, usually caused by work changes. In those days, I was in a small club in Mossley, I think the roof of the community centre we played in constrained full shot play, but they did have a coach, and I started to learn correct serving and positional play there, as well as how to hold the racquet, using the thumb to guide shots and enable backhand strength.

I became a reasonable player, though recalling, then as now, scores and serving turns in doubles was and is a bit unreliable, due to my poor concentration, though my playing seemed unaffected.

By this time, I had stopped going to the pub on a regular basis, and I think it was around this time Kevin went to work and live on South Uist, and apart from when he came back under a cloud, that I never did get the story of, though it involved a girl, and after he turned up at our flat, and I went out for a few drinks, this soon fizzled out, though (a bit hazy) I think he had to move again as I think someone was looking for him from the Hebrides…

At about this time, mid to late-80s, my interest in all thing's UFO was at its height, authors such as Stanton. T. Friedman, a retired Nuclear Physicist, who worked on top-secret projects, impressed me with his arguments about "Black budgets". Millions of dollars of US government money spent on Special Access Projects in the aerospace industry and related subjects, such as back engineering of crashed UFOs at such places as S4 on the Area 51 site and the supposed treaty, signed with Grey Aliens, (but maybe others closer to home) in the 1950s offering advanced tech, fed through the likes of Lockheed's "Skunkworks", away from senatorial oversight, whose former director, Ben Rich, near his death, admitted the US had space tech way ahead of anything seen in public. All this and much more, piqued my interest enough for me to join MUFORA – Manchester UFO Research Association, whose, leading lights included Jenny Randles, a noted author, and occasional TV consultant on the subject at the time. There was also a journalist and folklore researcher, Peter H, who co-authored some books with Jenny. His interest in folklore attempted to shed new interpretations on stories of historical interpretation of events involving, faeries, demons, elves and the like, and whether other explanations could explain such "myths".

Meetings were held in what was then the UMIST buildings in central Manchester. The above-mentioned two people pretty much ran things there, sightings were discussed, and people such as Retired Police Constable Alan Godfrey were interviewed at these meetings. Alan claimed to have experienced alien abduction in November 1980, whilst on night shift, following up reports of cattle disturbances on the hills near Todmorden, Yorkshire. He impressed with his down-to-earth recollection of events, in much the same way as the famous American abductee Travis Walton has stuck to his version of events, passing many lie-detection tests over the years. The above-mentioned cases can be "Googled" by anyone interested. A book written by Alan Godfrey of this event has just been released after all these years, of the events surrounding this encounter, concurrent with writing these memories down.

One event I played a minor part in was a showcase of the subject of UFOs, held at Jodrell Bank Observatory in Cheshire. Jenny Randles gave a lecture on the subject, while I and some others sold books and answered questions raised by the public.

Details of the most famous British case started to emerge in the mid-80s, with Jenny Randles investigating, along with local investigators, and producing a book *Sky Crash* co-authored with the two local investigators. (I have a signed copy). The story has been aired on TV on channels such as H2, and more mainstream channels at the time. This book looks at the event as seen from nearby farmers and other local people, as well as the base witnesses.

The main events centre around RAF Bentwaters, in Rendlesham Forest, Suffolk, near Christmas 1980.

Although nominally a RAF base, Bentwaters at the time, was an American-run operation, principally for housing forward USAF nuclear weapons. On at least two occasions, lights were seen by many witnesses descending into the forest near the base. Testimonies vary as to what exactly happened, but a recording by the Deputy Base Commander of the approach to something strange is much featured on the TV documentaries about this case. Some witnesses say the base commander and other officers was seen to approach and communicate with aliens, though the officer concerned denies being there, and this part is not mentioned on some of the TV channels. As well as the above-mentioned book *Sky Crash*, businesswoman and investigator of Georgina Bruni's book, *You Can't Tell the People*, said to be a quote from an interview with Margaret Thatcher about the incident, gives a good perspective of the lengths of cover-up after the event. The mainstream debunker explanation centres around the then operational Orfordness Lighthouse which was shining *as usual* through the trees and seen *along with the craft*, so not mistaken for it. Everyone in the area, including the base personnel, was familiar with this, so to put this forward as an explanation, though worth a look, comes nowhere near the answer to this multifaceted event an SAS security test of the base has recently been put out as another explanation. The multitude of military and civilian witnesses beg to differ…

BBC personnel, who wanted to make a documentary at the time, were prevented at every turn, and the incident was not mentioned in any newscast. Since the famous 1978 New Zealand footage of a UFO filmed from an aircraft on several occasions and broadcast on our TV newscasts, I fear freedom of showing such information has been taken from mainstream broadcasters, all such events to go through a "filter" before they are allowed to be broadcast. Whether or not that filter is Majestic 12, or a modern successor, a group supposed to have been set up in the 1950s after Roswell, in the US, consisting of senior military and scientists, with far reaching powers to recover any tech, and crash survivors, not of this world, and to silence anyone not part of the programme, who had seen too much, will be elaborated on later…

Chapter 20

Moving on to my take on the politics of the 80s, the crippling power of the Unions in the 70s, whilst improving the lives of many in industrial production, had a devastating effect on Britain as a whole, and with hindsight, a swing of the pendulum too far in the opposite direction was an inevitable consequence. What looked like, and was a much-needed modernisation by the Thatcher Government at that time, looks now to have been a too hasty deconstruction of nationalised infrastructure, and while clean energy is much better for our planet, the destruction of the coal industry, and it is destruction, as mines have been deliberately flooded to prevent future use, even in a scenario we're as now – we have barely enough generating capacity to cover demand and have to rely far too much on vulnerable imported gas from unstable countries, or, from grid connections to Norway, and Continental Europe, where Russia could disrupt supplies and so divert the currently available backup.

Even now solar and wind power can only produce about a quarter of needed power and is fickle according to the weather.

Much delayed investment by successive governments in nuclear power has left us short for many years to come of what may be needed, and the suspiciously slow development of nuclear fusion, which would not generate the same income, and so may be, if not suppressed – not supported as the safe priority it should be. It is easy in hindsight to point out the overreaction of those days, but only now is serious attention being paid to those in big business who jumped in to fill the infrastructure vacuum, with too little regulation and integration, instead of the previous too much. And while fracking in the US has resulted in their much-reduced dependence on Mid-Eastern oil, our venture will be much more cautious of any unsafe production methods.

With the help of the partly unwitting Green lobby helped by overseas powers who would like us reliant, directly or otherwise on their supplies of gas, and do not wish to see our return to self-sufficiency as our offshore stocks run down, we run the risk of being forced into such dependence.

This section was meant to be my views on the state of the country in the late-80s, but the decisions taken then, and also lack of others, are so intertwined with our current situation, that I could not disengage the flow of my views based on current hindsight. We are walking a tightrope on which far too many are unaware, or uninterested until what might be too late.

My brother, four years younger than me, having completed college training as a chef, moved to London to learn from and work at several prestigious establishments.

My sister completed her nursing training at Peterborough, though a change of career was on the way, to bank work, both achieved "professional status" in their respective work lives.

At the colour works, things were going downhill, and in the mid-80s would close for good. There is now no visible trace of where it was sited. Part of the site is now a supermarket and car park; it is as if it had never existed.

Having worked the second half of my eleven years there as an hourly paid process operator, we were put on notice, I was the second person to leave, as our production manager knew the production manager at a nearby enzyme and microbiological process plant, closer to my Denton home. I had an interview and got a job as a day process operator that was to last around another eleven years.

I was to learn Fork Truck driving there, as the work often involved packing of liquid enzymes that the shift operators, who were more highly trained, had produced. We would then have to palletise and move these liquids around the back of the converted mill, down into the cellar level.

I, alone among day operators, probably due to my C and G qualification, had a pasteurisation operation of malt colouring as one of my jobs, which sometimes involved connecting several mobile pumps together in order to move product from the opposite end of the site to where the pasteuriser was, and was one of the more interesting parts of my work.

I did have the chance to move to shift work, where the more advanced enzyme work took place, but I did not want to work nights, and so one of the compensations of not having children was having that choice, unlike one or two who worked on days, but more or less had to move to shifts to earn enough when children came along. Normal progression for those living a normal life, among the shop floor level I now inhabited.

The other interesting work we day-men had, hard at times, was producing a liquid mix of dissolved powdered seaweed, that when processed, was filtered and pumped into dropped off road tankers, used in UK-produced beer and lager to create a head on poured draught beer.

If you have ever been to a beach with a lot of washed-up seaweed, you will quite often see a lot of foam on the shoreline, it is that from the seaweed, that was processed, along with a sterilising agent to maintain and prolong the life of what was an organic product. This very small amount, a few grams of potassium meta-bisulphate, was added to a batch that would fill a road tanker, is the main ingredient responsible for hangovers in UK beer.

I don't know if this is still the case, but at that time, German Lager was not allowed to add this ingredient, so may have been responsible for the generally regarded better quality of their beer products. After I was told about this, I often wondered, whilst adding this, just how many hangovers I was responsible for!

The less interesting aspect of our day process work was the blending of powder mixes, of materials, packed of into 25 kg bags on one tonne pallets, to be sent to many UK breweries, to soften, or otherwise change the water used in their beers and lagers.

Hauling these ingredients to the second floor to add to a U-shaped blending vessel with a spinning ribbon mixer was hard work, along with packing the blended mix.

Holding the bags on the runoff, stood on a set of scales underneath and manually shutting this off, until later mixers had an auto-setting, would result in back aching work. The noise from the mixer, which probably contributed, along with the even noisier previous colour plant, and the next job (to be detailed later) led to the slight Tinnitus I experience now.

Some of the rock concerts and headphone volumes of my teen years might also have added to this!

I made one or two friends here, as we often worked in pairs. Ray was the guy I got on best with, he had the ability to create arguments from nothing, just for the sake of it, whatever my opinion was on a given subject, he would champion the opposite and wouldn't budge, this used to keep us occupied for hours of work where possible. Ray was one of those later to move onto shifts, as children needed to be fed and clothed.

One event we both worked on (Saturday overtime) was painting our warehouse ceiling, this involved climbing mobile scaffolding with pots of paint and rollers. The first thing that went wrong was me kicking over a pot of light cream paint I backed into it whilst looking up to paint, the tipped over paint poured directly into a roller tray two levels down without spilling a drop!

I cannot repeat the expletive remarks Ray, who saw this from the ground, came out with, a very cleaned-up translation – you very lucky person.

The other potentially more serious happening was when Ray was on the second from the top level, about 15 feet up, he slipped and fell off, and instead of hitting the ground with a potentially bone-breaking thud, he grabbed a bar one-handed on the next level and swung to another lower one before landing on the ground on both feet. I told him he was wasted there, he should be either in a zoo with the other monkeys, or at the Olympics.

Chapter 21

In any workforce, there is always at least one guy you don't want to work with, the loudmouth and or work-shy guy.

I think my supervisor Joe, who used to be our chargehand, but managed to get into the offices, used to enjoy putting us to work together at times, as I must not have been able to hide my dislike of the air of self-importance he seemed to emanate. Though I suppose Joe knew he had to put this guy with someone who liked to get the job finished, as opposed to running down the clock as much as he could get away with. My frustration with this guy's sly and dilatory attitude was the worst aspect of my time there.

In front of this big, old former mill was a well-kept Crown Green, Bowling Green, which we used now and again in the summer. One summer, there was a doubles competition, along with a party in the canteen, which was a separate building situated at one end of the Green. Partners were drawn from a hat, I ended up with a shift man I was not fond of (full of himself). Gordon was his name, and we were to have a problem later, but for that night, we managed to get on well enough, with the help of a lot of liquid refreshment, well enough to win the event.

I was so drunk by the time it came to the presentation; it was all I could do to accept whatever it was we were presented with.

I recall that most of us day workers, used to work a lot of overtime, including weekends, usually Saturdays until 2 pm, and the occasional Sunday morning, I had a mortgage to pay as did most of us, but I do recall at the end of my marriage, (if you could call it that).

That "Anne" said "I was never there anyway", the overtime was often compulsory, you had to do a minimum amount, which is all I usually did, unless we were saving for something, but it did not stop me from feeling a bit guilty, even though we did not get on that well, I still had a sense of something like duty towards her, it took a long time before events forced the end. I did not contentiously know or plan it, but I gradually must have started to look for a way out.

In hindsight, it is surprising just how much and how long both of us adjusted to a bad relationship, mainly by withdrawing behind safe lines, it is probably why it took seven years to end.

I had my eye on a near six-foot tall dark-haired microbiologist, as usual, way out of my league, but we had been on French lessons together (French-owned company) and got on well, but she had a partner, and I was from a lower stratum, so nothing happened. Little did I know that one of her fellow microbiologists had a thing for me.

She went to the work badminton club sessions, and we had a few words from time to time, and when she suffered a bout of Bell's Palsy, distorting her face muscles for a few months, I had asked her if she was being looked after. I still had a sense of loyalty to Anne, even though we were pretty distant for a couple by then, so though I had a vague feeling she might be more receptive. I was blinded the one I really fancied, so when one day in the main office of all places, she stormed up to me saying, something along the lines of 'You say all the right things, but you never do anything about it,' then getting in the lift for the lab, in tears. Joe, my boss, and the others were all stunned, but not as stunned as me, I think Joe said, 'Didn't see that coming,' which was how I felt. If I had known just how close I was to splitting up with Anne, I may have pursued "Dot", instead, I avoided her.

Sometime later, she left to go and work for Kelloggs. Not sure that had much to do with me, more likely career progression. But ego being what it is, and me being used to relative failure by then, I wondered how different my life may have been if I had decided to pursue Dot, who was a good-looker in a bookish way. It felt wrong, as I had no strong feeling for her, I am not quite that calculating, and was not ready to upturn what was a poor apple cart that was my current relationship. It is strange how easy it can be to maintain the status quo, poor though it was, than be ready to turn things upside down.

When it happened, it crept up on me, but I must have been ready by then – more on that a bit later…

Chapter 22

One Christmas works do in the canteen, I cannot recall what year, but it would be late-80s, as Ray had not yet gone on shifts, we were all getting quite merry, as you do at these things, I was not that far gone, as I started to notice that Ray kept disappearing out the back door, at first I must have thought he was going for a pee, but eventually he came to me and said, 'I have got something to show you,' so I followed him out the back door.

Just beyond a narrow pathway is a rockery, and on this, Ray had placed about ten plates of cakes, trifles and other goodies from the extensive spread not yet touched by anyone inside!

He was on about us taking this lot up to my car boot, it looked like Santa's grotto out there!

I could not believe he had got this lot out there without anyone noticing, or just how drunk he must be to attempt this. Somehow, I got word to one of two trusted people inside, and we were able to get everything back inside without being seen by any senior people, not sure how, but the sight of all these plates placed on rocks outside the back door will never be forgotten by me.

I mentioned earlier that Gordon, the guy I won the bowling competition with, and I were to have a bit of trouble, this is how it went – at weekends, when on overtime, there would be no senior staff on site quite often, the shift chargehand, being in charge, if Joe, our boss had gone home early, as was his wont, often a couple of hours earlier than the rest of us.

Now the car park gate was electrically controlled from the shift chargehand's office and was kept shut at night and weekends. When it came to going home for us, we had to ask a shift man to open and close the gate for us. If the chargehand was not about, another would do this. This had been done before, but sometimes if the chargehand was not about, a shift man might shut the gate just before we got out for a laugh, before letting us go. Gordon, along with his mate, took it too far this time.

I was on my own and for some reason last one out, the usual trick was played, it was a 2 pm finish, I wanted to get home, so when the gate shut, after shouting up to the office on the first floor and getting no response, I went up and pressed open, as of course no one was about, but by the time I got back to the car the gate was shut again! I did the same again twice more.

By this time nearly twenty minutes later, I was so wound up, I went up to the gate and forced one side open, breaking the control bar and drove off, this horrified Gordon, all of a sudden he was running out of the building shouting at me, as he was temporary chargehand, he knew he would get the blame.

Monday morning came, I went to work equipped with a Dictaphone micro-recorder in my overalls pocket, as I guessed Gordon would find me before the work's manager started, this he did, and I made sure the conversation implicated him, I told him that I shouted a warning (which I did) that I would break the gate if I was not let out, he had no real answer. I did not go and see Joe or the manager, I just waited. Sure enough I was called to the manager's office, where I explained exactly what happened and just how many times I tried to get out before I had had enough.

I was sent on my way, without reprimand. Gordon was put on another shift, it seems he and his mate got too giddy when together, it was not the first time they had got in trouble together, although I was not aware of this at the time. I don't know if any warnings were issued, but it was a good job I did not have to depend on the recorded confrontation, as it was so muffled as to be useless.

There was a tough guy, Ernie, who ran the warehouse, whom everyone was a little scared of, I was not aware of what he had done to get his reputation, just that he had one.

He came to see me later the same day and asked me if it was me that went to the manager first, I told him no, he left it at that. Later I learnt he had caught Gordon on the stairs, I don't know if it got physical, but Gordon never referred to the subject with me again. Ernie had a code, you didn't go to the management, never the less, although me and him seemed to had an understanding, you were very careful what you said to him, there was a touch of the "godfather" about him. Sometime earlier at someone's do at a pub, I was drunk, and he was very drunk, though not with him as a mate, we had a shared walk home that involved a canal towpath part of the way, I more or less kept him from falling in and got him to his front door. I think that may have stood me in good stead in the above-mentioned incident.

Chapter 23

One of the more interesting episodes of my MUFORA days was when Jenny invited the Todmorden ex-Policeman Alan Godfrey to talk to us as a group.

As mentioned earlier, Alan was on night shift and was directed to go and investigate a cattle disturbance, along the way he was confronted with an object, blocking the road ahead, lit up, and hovering above the road – a classic UFO – complete with spinning lower half. Alan then seems to have lost consciousness, for a short time, and awoke to find himself, still in his car, some 20 or 30 yards down the road, backing up, he recalls seeing a circular dry patch an otherwise wet road as it was raining.

Alan only reported the incident to his superiors, after he realised he could not recall half an hour, and then other police man also reported seeing strange lights heading his way. The whole episode seemed incomplete, so he eventually submitted himself to hypnotic regression, a somewhat disputed method of memory recovery. This seemed to produce a scenario of a classic alien abduction. This was all recounted in a very matter of fact way to us as a group, no unprompted elaboration was attempted it seemed to me by Alan, the story later got out, and he later resigned from the police. This event can be Googled, and I do believe a book, many decades later will soon be published, giving a first-hand account by Alan. One of the others there suggested that Jenny and Peter used the rest of us as sounding boards – to see how we reacted to new information – and to me, it looked as if we as a group were being observed for our reactions, though I found out later when I brought a "past-life recall" case to their attention, it was followed up, as I will share later.

At home, things were about to reach what to me, looking back, was an inevitable conclusion, I am not proud of how it happened, but it had to occur somehow.

A woman called "Sarah" had started to work part-time cleaning the canteen, and sometimes offices, I sometimes passed her on my way to the car park and we exchanged a few words.

One day near Christmas, her car was out of action, and I offered to run her most of the way home, not all the way, as she was married to a very nasty, sly man, whom I was later to find out, used to hurt her, but never when her two kids were about. This man never used to work, instead sending Sarah out to work two or even three part-time jobs. He was suspected of some burglary.

It was a good job I only learnt all this gradually, as I might have over reacted.

Just before I dropped her off, we exchanged a Christmas kiss, which I think we both knew opened up new possibilities. Things progressed from there, I never imagined myself having an affair with a married woman, but it seemed right.

I used to make illicit short visits to the canteen when I knew Sarah was alone.

Ray and I were going to a leaving do at a local pub, I knew Sarah would be there, we tried to avoid being seen, but I think a few people were starting to notice. Sarah had warned her controlling, nasty husband long ago, that when their kids were grown up, she would leave him, and this she did, moving in with her daughter who had not long since left home.

Then I stopped going to badminton and used those evenings to meet Sarah in various out of the way places, the obvious took place that made me look as if I had been to badminton!

Prior to her leaving her husband, he had been (I found out much later) doing things like hanging Sarah over the banister, threatening to drop her, holding a razor blade to her throat, in an attempt to find out who she was seeing and many other nasty things, though most of the time he was careful not to leave visible marks – an all-round nice guy. It came as quite a shock to her daughter to read a letter written for the divorce hearing, which she went to, about the extent of abuse her mum suffered over the years.

I cannot remember if Anne found out, there was no big row, or if I decided on my own to tell her about my affair, but when I did, she left fairly soon, not wanting anything to do with paying the mortgage, she moved in to rented accommodation, not too far from where she used to live. I gave her a few thousand pounds, all but a few hundred that we had saved, she did not want the flat sold, it was as if she knew we should never have got married, her dad's prophesy had come to pass about us not lasting, I will always suspect he had good reason to know why.

After helping her move, I only saw her once or twice over practical things, then never again, I think it was my sister told me some time later that she had met a German man and had gone to live there with him. It was a very quick split, unlike Sarah's, which was very messy, it was a tough neighbour, who had found out about Sarah's ex slashing her car tyres and finding out from her where he could intercept him on foot, and must have, as all he would say was that he had been warned to stay away from her, doing my dirty work for me, as we never met until much later, where – in front of their children – I shoved him away when he tried to reach Sarah, we were both restrained, that was the extent of the contact I had with him. It took a long time to find out just how much Sarah endured from this man over the years. A restraining order was placed on him after she moved in with her daughter, but he was seen close by, he must have followed her home or knew where they both lived, and so she had to hide when he was seen nearby, twice.

Chapter 24

After some time, "Sarah" started to stay odd nights at my flat, and I would spend a night at her shared terrace. A pet cat, kitten of her daughter's cat, travelled back and forth with me, this arrangement turned in to alternate weeks.

Sarah, as well as cleaning at my workplace, had a main job as a cook at a local school, trying to make ends meet, but not many months after we became an item, she stopped cleaning at my work, but not before it became known we were together.

One of my workmates, John, saw us together, but after she had left her *lovely* husband. Eventually, it became common knowledge we were an item. It was about a year before Sarah moved in with me. We are still together, over thirty years later.

My mother's health started to deteriorate, first with diabetes, then angina, I mentioned she had three older brothers, the two oldest died in the 1990s of heart-related problems. Long after my father died. She had a few months seeing a social worker, but this petered out. She had moved to a smaller house by then.

As mentioned, my employers had been taken over by a French company, thus the French lessons mentioned earlier. All they really wanted was the know how to make certain cattle feed growth enzymes, this took them a while, after a year or two of financial restraints were imposed, that cut our overtime eventually to nil. I then started a KleenEasy around to make up the shortfall.

I had kept my interest in martial arts films, and as for some reason, I was not playing badminton at the time, I decided to join a younger neighbour and start at a Chinese "Northern Shaolin" School, based in central Manchester, but from which the Master would go out to different venue's and train smaller groups. I think this school had around twenty Black Belt, grade members, but it was only the master who taught outside of the main school. The younger neighbour with me was fitter than me and remembered the long "form" sequences quicker than me, but we progressed, eventually getting to second Blue Belt over two years of once or twice a week sessions.

I would practice at work when I thought I would be unobserved, but I was seen, in the cellar, by the work's manager, doing roundhouse kicks against a pillar, by others doing pull-ups on pipework, so it become common knowledge. I was never fitter than the two years I did this Chinese Martial Art that included a lot of fast, spinning movement and a little pole fighting training. I think it is very different to the Japanese approach, which to me was a lot more robotic, especially in early training.

Sometime after Sarah moved in, I started home brewing wine, in demijohns, I tried various book recipes, including Elderflower, and Elderberry, which was very strong brew. I used to bring home 25 kg, brewing sugar bags, sometimes less, at a time from work at weekends, this being used for enzyme fermentation there. As this was the most expensive ingredient in a gallon mix, I could make a decanted bottle for about 50p in 90s' money. My best produce were peach, apple and blackberry and apple.

Some of this was taken to a housewarming, about a year into training at one of the local group of Shaolin students.

All I recall is first being sat on the floor with someone else's girlfriend, nothing going on, just sat with a demijohn of peach wine between us, and getting so drunk, that when it was time to go home, I was walking around the walls, hand over hand laughing, saying, 'I can't find the door!' The room was slowly spinning. I must have been a sight, Sarah, who had not been drinking, got me to the car, which was frozen over, it was that cold. Not sure how I stayed on my feet. I think that was the last time I have been really drunk.

Chapter 25

The first time Sarah and I went on holiday together was a cheap coach trip to a static caravan site near Cavalaire in the south of France. Getting there was a bit fraught, with the coach taking us from Watford Gap on to the ferry arriving late, having broken down.

It made it to the ferry terminal too late to catch the scheduled ferry to Calais, and the whole coachload of us, fed up with waiting, eventually persuaded the driver to switch to Boulogne, he was not happy, but Cantabrica, the tour operator, must have agreed. The driver had to drive a bit further, but it was a lot quicker than losing half a day waiting. Many details of our life together will be down to Sarah's memory which is far better than mine, I remember highlights, she fleshes out many events.

We got to the site late-afternoon, the caravans were set under pine trees, by today's standards the caravan was basic, and there were a few of ants, but we enjoyed it. I recall seeing what must have been a hornet flying overhead, thinking at first it was a small bird, it was a good two inches long.

We went on the usual trips, one to St Tropez, eventually finding a nice restaurant, where Sarah had her first strong garlic-flavoured meal, after we had first ogled the giant yachts, all lined up in the harbour, the occupants showing off to us lesser mortals.

Much more interesting was a trip to Monaco, not for the racetrack, or the casino, that would not let us in wearing shorts, but the Jacques Cousteau Aquarium, perched above the sea, built into the cliff face. It housed a large whale skeleton, and there was a darkened tank with some live nautilus, those strange spiral shelled creatures from the deep, unchanged for millions of years.

It was also my first go at scuba diving, there was a local school with two English dive masters, though I found out later that they should not have let me follow up the morning training dive as I did. Having done the basic theory and sit in a circle "buddy" sharing of regulators, followed by a twenty-minute follow my leader around shallow water, I overheard them and other experienced divers talking about an afternoon dive out near a lighthouse island, I asked if I could go with them.

After a discussion along the lines of 'There are enough of us to keep an eye on him' (there were about five of them), they said OK and told me a pick-up location and time.

I must have had time to tell Sarah, as there were no mobile phones then! Don't recall the boat trip out, however, reminded by Sarah, I do recall struggling to get into a wetsuit, as the previous day had got myself sunburned enough to have Sarah plaster my back with yogurt that night, it was that sore!

What I did not know was just how deep we were going; I got the first hint when they told me we would be making decompression stops on the way down and up. My right ear must have a narrow canal, as when I fly, I have to use a plug to stop it hurting when we descend for landing.

After being kitted out with tanks and buoyancy regulator, mask and flippers, we all jumped in and started descending down a rope, after only about twenty feet, my right ear would not equalise, despite all my nose holding and swallowing, all but one of the others carried on down, I was just about to give up when it finally cleared.

I followed the others down to what I found out later was around thirty something meters, enough to be slightly gloomy. I recall looking up and thinking, *Hope nothing goes wrong* – the surface looked a long way up. I need not have worried, I saw two or three strike out on their own around what I think was a steep circular island, there were still about four of us, I saw nothing remarkable until I was beckoned over to look at a torpedo casing, open at one end, (told later it used to be an Italian testing range years ago), so there we were, in a circle around this tube, about six foot long, and I am thinking – not that interesting – when out pops this head with big eyes, and part body of an octopus, it swivelled around on its axis, it was so funny! It was like a cartoon character, I burst out laughing – promptly filling half my mask with water.

If I had not been shown earlier in the day, to clear water from my mask by pressing the top of it whilst breathing out, I would have panicked, but I did this, and it worked.

The others knew this octopus was resident in the tube but the picture of it twisting around to look at us all will never leave my "highlights only" memory. I do remember the decompression stops on the way back up the rope.

I was told years later on other dives, I should never have been allowed down that deep without the full weeklong course, which I never took. Just did about half a dozen more training dives over my holiday lifetime, not wanting to take that much time away from our joint holidays.

Chapter 26

After two years of Shaolin Kung Fu, I decided to stop going, at the Christmas break, I had earlier hurt my foot at one of the monthly competitions. I had then watched one of the more senior students break his leg whilst trying to gain his second Brown Belt. I was not far of getting to the point of going for my first Brown, and it seemed I was not committed enough as I only started this as a means to maintain fitness. Master Ang was a good teacher, and I enjoyed the relative informality in his classes. I decided I would go back to badminton when I could find a club to join.

Living in a small ground floor flat had its downside, mainly when the older couple upstairs had one of their frequent arguments, and they would stomp up and down and shout at each other.

We settled together, Sarah moved work to other schools, making a lifelong friend, Tracy, at Marple Hall School. It was Tracy who told me about a set up called Spice, where you could do all sorts not activities, it was a sort of dating group, but I just went to the badminton group, which turned out to be at my sister's old school. The standard of players varied, depending on who turned up, but it was fitness training, different from the sometimes back aching daily grind of production work.

One of only two (to date) eastern European trips we have ventured on was to Bulgaria, a two-centre affair in the early years after communism departed, the first to the inevitable sunny beach, in the days when we went, the beach front area entertainment consisted of little more than restaurants (now much more lively), so I've heard.

When we were there, the local version of the mafia had a strong grip on the area, it did not matter where you ate, at some point in the evening, a BMW or Merc, would pull up outside, sticking out like a sore thumb from the rest of the much more modest and older cars nearby, the occupants, hard-looking individuals, walking straight through to the back rooms, emerging five or ten minutes later, no doubt having picked up their "protection money", then straight off in their cars.

A trip to the UNESCO world heritage village of Nessebar was the highlight of that week, situated almost on an island, but with a thin strip of land to the mainland, this little village, of churches, a market and little restaurants around the edges, all old and terracotta-roofed buildings, is very picturesque, and I recall walking through an arch to a vine-covered open-air restaurant overlooking the Black Sea, cannot recall for sure, but seafood is probably what we ate there.

Being a little independently minded, we had taken a bus to Varna, which I don't recall much of. What I do remember is that we were followed, we saw this scruffy character get on the same bus as us, and when we got off saw him a little distance back after we had made a few turns.

I made it obvious to him, by looking back at him with long stares, that we were on to him, he hung back, but was on the same bus back, he didn't try anything, I think he knew we were on to him. Was he waiting for us to separate, long enough to grab Sarah's handbag, I never gave him the chance to find out. There was an excursion to a big top type restaurant with an animal-based stage show, which included tigers jumping through hoops of fire.

It is hoped that this no longer takes place, as I have seen a YouTube video entitled *Last Bulgaria Circus Tiger Walks on Grass for First Time*.

Chapter 27

The second part of this holiday was up in the Rodope Mountains, at what in winter, is a ski resort called Pamporovo, we were there in summer though, having a go on the ski lifts, there was only a little snow to be seen on the tops, but lovely panoramic scenery of endless, forested mountains, misty in the mornings.

Now modernised, the hotel then was basic, as was the food, but we had our most interesting meal out in a hunting lodge/tourist restaurant, with wild boar on the menu, and antlers on the walls, we sat in circular bays.

I may have risked my life, as whilst videoing the olde-worlde surroundings, I deliberately left it running while I hung my arm and the camera, over the next bay, filming guns in belts, openly on display, where the local mafia had just arrived and settled themselves, I did not film for long, whilst looking in the other direction…

With us were some English school teacher tourists, and one retired music teacher was very intrigued by some Bulgarian Bagpipes hanging on the wall, so much so, that he made an offer to the owners for them, which was accepted.

When it was time to leave, one of the mafia guys genially offered us all a lift back to our hotel, that we were allowed to decline, saying it was all downhill and not far away, and being a nice evening, we would walk, thanks…

All of us were a little drunk, and the attempts along the forested road in the twilight of the retired school music teacher to play the local bagpipes had us all in tears of laughter, the local wildlife must have thought we were killing something very cruelly.

Our other visit to what was classed as Eastern Europe, was barely that, and so long ago I cannot recall what year, but we went on a coach to Brno, in what is now Slovakia, not long separated from the Czech Republic when we went. The highlights of this trip included a visit to Prague, the Charles Bridge, the red roofs, viewed from the castle, the whole city looked good on a day trip.

Another day trip went across the border to Vienna, the grand palaces, and the underground opulent food hall, and a visit to a chess set shop, where I came away with a Habsburg Empire themed set.

A hunting lodge trip, complete with a wild boar meal, with dark meat, which suggests the boar was not farmed, was enjoyed. An excursion also took us to Pernstejn, a Gothic castle situated in South Moravia, Czech Republic, about 25 miles north of Brno. This castle was 13th century, very well preserved, and almost deserted, there was absolutely no security, you could have walked off with all sorts, they were not yet used to mass tourism, bet things have changed by now. I would not make any more of those low-cost coach trips across Europe these days, we were younger then.

All I recall of Brno, our base, is old-fashioned trams, and lots of small kiosks selling all sorts. That is the extent of our eastern European travels to date.

Chapter 28

Back to the early 2000, and a mysterious set of files, notes and drawings, collectively known as The Blue Planet Project, (search) emerged from a scientist, Jefferson Souza who worked on "Black Projects" in the USA, much disputed, he has supposed to have had access and taken part in ultra-secret research on various alien species, Black Triangle ships and many other aspects regarding the UFO phenomenon. Although quite detailed, there is no supporting evidence of his work, or of his location, as he is supposed to be in hiding from the US government, and no record of his existence can now be found. It is another one of those names of people who claim to have been on the inside of what the US, British and other governments are hiding on the subject, always, you can search online the above name and make up your own mind, all be it without the necessary proof. I file it under "Hard to believe, but given other evidence – maybe".

By now, you will realise that I am trying to make you aware of the sheer volume of information, rather than verifiable facts that are available, and it is this, the volume, that suggests that if even 1% is true, then governments that have gone to great lengths to hide what they know for fear of loss of control, will eventually no longer be able to use ridicule, and more sinister – family threatening – methods to maintain cover up of some grave mistakes they may have made in the early years of contact.

Moving on to more solid ground, Sarah, whilst driving her blue Mini of that time, was hit sideways on by a car that indicated to turn left of the main road, but continued on as Sarah pulled out to turn right.

This resulted in a long-term neck injury known as "whiplash". Considerable abuse of this injury has resulted in distrust of claims for this, but what I have seen of Sarah's suffering over the years, doing everything from ironing to holding a book for a long period, chopping ingredients for cooking and many other activities, including playing badminton, which she found unable to continue, having started to play. She still suffers to this day with bad upper backache for long periods, after most prolonged arm use activities, so although she eventually received some compensation after many visits to appointed doctors, and subsequent physiotherapy, it was not nearly enough for the now nearly three decades she has bravely endured this pain.

Soon after Sarah sustained her neck injury, she started to struggle to read, or at least hold a book she was reading for any length of time without experiencing neck and upper back pain. I thought I could come up with a solution to this, as reading was a favourite pastime of Sarah's.

I started by tying some bamboo together to make a cradle to lay a book on – this worked after a fashion, but one thing led to another, and eventually I came up with, to give it a name, "The Easyread Bookrest", a lightweight pair of cut-out rectangular box shapes, slightly longer than most opened hardback books, with a sill to rest the base of the book on and two attached "fingers" to keep the book on the page being read, all on the front of the two rectangles, without having to hold it open, a hole drilled halfway up one end allowing string with knots tied to be notched into a notch cut into the corresponding back of this laptop-sized easel, so it could be opened at a choice of different angles.

This helped Sarah, and I soon found myself using one myself, and still do to this day.

I thought I was on to something and went to one or two local small manufacturers and had some prototypes made with a view to finding a mass producer.

Despite paying for an invention company to find a manufacturer, I had no takers. I suspect due to the cost of producing a unit, there was too much work to leave a profit on a selling price per bookrest unit.

I have made a useable, basic version and have indeed made a few over the years, but not something that would sell for enough more than it would cost to make, I even sold one when using several to exhibit some photos at a car boot sale – sold no photos, but the bookrest caught the eye of someone enough to want to buy it.

I am not a good enough craftsman to produce something good enough to charge sufficient premium to make a commercially viable version, even though I am still convinced many people, especially older people, would benefit from not having to hold a heavy hardback open.

I even use it for paperbacks, as it allows me to drink or otherwise be hands free apart from page turning. Some things are just not meant to be…

Chapter 29

There was one short-term recompense which I shared in from some of the money Sarah received – this was our first long-distance holiday. I felt a little guilty that Sarah was paying for most of this, but she was keen to see something different from the money gained from her suffering (most of mine having gone to Anne).

Sarah's first choice would have been a Safari trip to Africa. From her extensive reading of Wilbur Smith novels, and her keen interest and knowledge of nature, both flora and fauna that I have become aware of over the years, she would have loved to experience a close up encounter with the African bush.

Unfortunately, the doctor told her that travelling over rough ground in the back of a truck as you would need to, to get out into the wilds of Africa, would be the worst possible type of holiday for her neck injury.

Reluctantly, we looked for a plan B, this in the end turned out to be a trip to Thailand, with a three-day excursion to Hong Kong included. We stayed on Phuket, near Patong, on the west coast, which a few years later was to suffer many dead from the tsunami resulting from the earthquake in Indonesia to the south.

We stayed just outside town at what for us was a posh hotel, with glorious gardens, with butterflies of a size that at first we mistook for small birds. We stayed in a chalet off from the main building, almost on the beach, and close enough to forest, that you could hear the frog chorus at night. (I should point out that many recalled details of our travels are supplied from Sarah's memory, with my very patchy additions). Some of the Thai food is too hot for me, especially if it involved chillies, but I enjoy Chinese food, and much of South-Asian food as long as it is not too hot, Sarah has a higher tolerance for heat in it than me. I like the spices, just not too much heat.

The humidity is not something I got used to, though I don't think having slight asthma made much difference to trying to climb even short hills without an instant all over sheen breaking out, indeed, soon as you left air conditioning, you wanted another shower within five minutes – being a pampered westerner. The beach was great, Sarah finding hermit crabs wandering about.

The sea there was a different matter. There was a sign up – "No Swimming", after inquiring, I was told the undercurrent was too strong to swim safely. For me – I am afraid I took that as a challenge, I was still quite fit in those days, and so with the insistence that I wear a life jacket, out I went, no problem, until I tried to swim back to the beach.

If I had been any less fit than I was, I might not have made it back under my own steam. The current was in the form of an undertow – out to sea – but with the basic English of the guy I asked, he could not tell me that much detail. I had to learn the hard way…

It took me about twenty minutes of swimming with everything I had to make it about thirty yards or so back to the beach, when I finally made it, I was on my hands and knees, retching for about five minutes before I could get up. It was a lesson I would not forget.

We did have some enjoyable excursions, one being an elephant ride through a rubber plantation, the swaying from side to side and the habit of the Asian elephant stopping every so often and raising its trunk to grab a banana from us (pre-purchased at start) before being willing to continue was a memory I had no problem recalling.

Another was an evening trip to a village where a very basic, unclad breeze block arena with wooden benches, was the setting for local Thai Boxing contests.

The first contestants were older children, then the late teens and adults, with the accompanying high-pitched woodwind frenzied "snake charmer and drum combo" which the contestants first performed a ritual dance to, before a three-round contest commenced.

The crowd of a few hundred went mad, betting on the outcome, the atmosphere was electric, I enjoyed watching the skill and athleticism of the contestants, having learnt martial arts myself, I could appreciate the level of fitness displayed before me.

Dinner there that night at "half-time" was different, I had what I called "chicken on a stick" the correct term is spatchcocked, I am told, it was half a small flattened strong garlic chicken skewered with several sticks, I suffered no ill after-effects as Sarah thought I might, so, all in all, it was a good night.

Chapter 30

Patong is a lively little town, for men on their own, there are the girls and ladyboys aplenty, but the bars do cater for couples with simple bar games, and some very rough Thai whisky, as Sarah will attest to.

We paired up with a young couple from our hotel I will call Paul and Linda, from Leeds Sarah thinks.

Paul and I drank bottled beer and Jameson's Whisky chasers, Sarah tried the Thai whisky! Within an hour, she thought she would show the local girls how to pole dance, I managed to catch her when she fell off…

The journey back to the hotel in an open back tuk tuk was eventful, in that every time we went around a bend – Sarah would bring up a bit more of our dinner, literally, out of the open side, so it was good that the tuk tuk was open-sided.

The one and only time we have ever had to be woken up for an excursion in all the years of travelling together was the next morning, it was early, I was rough, but Sarah was really rough, the worst I have ever seen her on two feet, for the whole day. I think if she had time to think when we got up late, rushing around, she would have stayed behind that day, though it turned out to be an interesting one.

Sarah must have looked bad that day, as at our first stop, a pineapple plantation, at the gatehouse where there were a few trinkets for sale, the vendor gave, not sold, Sarah a drink of coffee, no one else was given this.

We were shown the plantation and told of the high risk of being bitten by a yellow snake that infested the plantation. The fresh pineapple we were given to eat was so much better tasting than any I have eaten since. We then moved on to a ramshackle wood-built jetty where we boarded a longtail boat, with the big motor mounted at the back, the propeller on the end of an eight-foot or so steerable pole.

We were on our way to so called "James Bond Island" out among the vertical island "Karsts" of Phang Nga Bay in the Andaman Sea,

But it was the journey out through marshy waterways where we passed a large sea snake on our way out to the bay, the sight of trees growing sideways out of the limestone, then up, covering these Karsts, was something to behold, numerous narrow, hundred foot or more islands, set in a turquoise sea, that was a sight never to be forgotten.

The speed of the long, narrow longtail boat ensured we were wet from the spray on the trip out to the island, where in the film *The Man with the Golden*

Gun, Scaramanga, aka Christopher Lee, had his hideout. The island itself was almost two islands, with a strip of beach between, where tourist trinket stalls waited for the daily influx, of which we were a part.

As I recall we were not there long, Sarah was still under the weather from the night before, to the extent that at our next destination, a "Sea Gypsy" village, which from what I could see, looked quite well off, compared with the coastal village we had set off from.

The restaurant on stilts over the water looked quite new. We, the tourist group, were well fed, with one exception, Sarah sat on the small pier with a bottle of water, unable to face food. I felt quite guilty at buying Sarah Thai whisky, instead of better branded drink, but we don't drink out on a regular basis, even then, and Sarah paid the price for my lack of judgement in letting her drink the rough stuff, which must have had a very high alcohol content. Entering into the "spirit" of choosing local *produce* is not *always* the best option.

On this marathon trip out, we were then taken by coach to a silk production village, where we were "guided" into the shop, where we bought a large colourful wooden-latted fan, with a stilted village house and pond scene, spanning about three foot when open. This ended up on the bedroom wall for a year or two. Sarah tells me I persuaded her to eat a bowl of soup when we finally got back to the hotel that day.

We went on the obligatory Buddhist temple visit, where, with my humidity covered hands and face, I proceeded to attract stares after touching the gold leaf covered reclining Buddha, fingers then speckled with gold dust, which I must have promptly wiped on my face, must have been a sight, Sarah then has seen what was there after the attention I received, alerted me, I looked at my hands, still speckled, before wiping away the evidence and moving on!

Chapter 31

The last excursion on Phuket was a so-called Safari, into the interior of the island, where we entered a village and saw, much to our alarm at first, a pretty little girl of about four or five, lifting (just barley) the head of the biggest Burmese Python I have ever seen, I still have the photo, I think.

We were told this giant of a snake was her pet, and she was in no danger of being eaten as it was fed a chicken a day to keep it docile. This was the cue for contributions of course, it was worth it for the photo, there is another photo of this snake draped across my shoulders, with its massive head on one arm, the rest of its body trailing behind, it must have been fifteen feet long, with a foot width body. I could barely stand up.

Later on, we were taken to see a trained macaque monkey, roped to its owner, run up palm trees, knocking coconuts to the ground which were then pierced for us to drink. Though this is something of dubious interest as all animals were made to work for the amusement of tourists. The macaque was not scarred by its collar and looked healthy enough, so judgement of the locals, trying to earn a living at that time – around twenty-five years ago – must be tempered. It is to be hoped that these days the enlightened tourist avoid such shows, as most would now avoid dolphin shows.

A snake "exhibition" we went to, where various snakes were let out in a small arena to be "charmed", this was evidently not as safe as was claimed, as the "charmer" did not have all ten fingers left! Sarah was left with one "harmless" snake she ended up having to put back in the basket herself as she seemed to have been forgotten about.

We also went to a "catchynut" factory which turned out to be a cashew nut processing operation, the pulp surrounding the nuts is high pH (almost caustic) enough to need gloves to scoop out the nuts using a large needle, it is a quite labour-intensive operation. I had a new appreciation from then on of the work involved (at that time) at least, to produce the savoury snack we consume at home.

Another highlight of this trip was the three-day "excursion" to Hong Kong, which was still in British hands in the late 90s. Though only a village when it was "ceded" to Britain, it was then built into the vast trading centre it is now by various "Noble Houses" as James Clavell describes them, handing it back to China is the least we can do in recompense for the opium trade we forced on the country in Empire days, not that we now had a choice anyway. Let's hope that China's buying up and "investing" in large parts of the UK's infrastructure, from telecoms to nuclear power, is only a commercial operation and not something planned for other purposes, in memory of those days, as no Chinese-based business "tycoon" is acting without the "consent" of the Communist government.

Back to our trip there, when we went it was on a Thai Airways jet. Compared to the Thomas Cook plane we got to Thailand on, this was like travelling first class, much more legroom, complimentary Courvoisier brandy – with a steak dinner fit for a restaurant, we arrived at what was still then Kai Tak Airport in style, with its breath-taking "washing line close up" approach and landing. What it must have been like to live in a flat in the skyscrapers next to the runway is hard to fathom. We were taken to a hotel, it was then called The New Territories, though as it was "acquired" from China in 1898, new no longer, it was just an "extra" land grab, part of the mainland.

Our hotel was situated alongside the Pearl River Estuary, where we were warned not to eat any fish caught there, as it is very polluted from the industrial cities upstream in China, though it did not smell bad, at least while we were there.

We only had a couple of days there, we walked around the public park that doubled as a zoo, I remember some small capuchin monkeys, and a few big cats, flamingos, it was not a large zoo, but it was very lush, specialising in rare species, well shaded with a lot of tropical plants and trees which made for pleasant surroundings.

Crossing to Hong Kong Island from Kowloon side, we did via an underground efficient tube system, rather than the well-known Star Ferries, which were packed out with large queues.

Chapter 32

Apart from buying a video camera, ruined on a later holiday, and admiring the harbour skyline view, I recall little else of the daytime. There was a half hourly shuttle bus we made use of in the evenings from the hotel in Sha Tin, down to Kowloon harbour, where one evening the group of us from Thailand had a harbour tour by boat, followed by being dropped at a floating boardwalk, I think in Aberdeen Harbour, where we were led through what seemed like a maze, before ending up at what was a smart restaurant, I have no idea where but still close to the harbour.

We were sat around a traditional rotating table with French and American tourists, where we had a great mix of Chinese food.

We then went looking for somewhere for a drink, aware that our pick-up point for our hotel shuttle bus was opposite The Peninsula hotel, famous for its Rolls Royce fleet.

Paul and Linda, whom we paired up with on some Thai excursions joined us, we all felt better as a small group in a strange city. We ended up in an Australian bar for the rest of that evening, I vaguely recall that the drinks were quite expensive, but then it probably catered mainly for western tourists, so was to be expected. What happened next is not something I am proud of, but at the time seemed totally necessary.

Having left the bar, we made our way to the shuttle bus pick-up point. By the time Paul and I reached it, we were both desperate for a pee. Seeing no alternative nearby, and being emboldened with being half-drunk, we left Sarah and Linda at the crowded shuttle stop and walked across the road, bold as brass and up the steps into the foyer of The Peninsular Hotel, and asked a man who was sweeping up if there was a toilet we could use, he pointed to some marbled steps that went underground, we quickly headed down before the people at the reception could intercept us.

The steps just kept on going down, must have been three stories, all marbled, when we finally saw a sign that indicated a gents, we almost ran over – only to find it locked! By then we were both bursting to go, there was no one about down there, though brightly lit, we just looked at each other and proceeded to pee under the locked door of the gents, on the marbled floor! Much relieved but apprehensive of meeting anyone, we shot back up the stairs, being half-drunk, with broad grins on our faces as we almost ran out of the foyer doors, with the reception staff staring at us.

By this time, the last shuttle bus had arrived and Sarah and Linda were holding it up for us, we dived on laughing, but looking across the road to see if anyone was coming out of the oldest, poshest hotel in Hong Kong to chase us, no one did, we were relieved that the shuttle set off straight after we boarded. Only then did we tell the perplexed Sarah and Linda what had us laughing, to disapproving glares. I do remember the following day being a little nervous as we got off the shuttle bus at the same place, but no one came out to intercept us from across the road, different shift hopefully…

I can only recall a walk around the famous night market, followed by a much more basic meal than the previous night, on a street corner, sat outside on rickety chairs that evening. As it was the night market, and was our last night in Hong Kong, again with Paul and Linda, we decided to get a taxi back to the hotel, being later than the last shuttle bus.

And so we did, except that we slowly discovered that the very chatty taxi driver, who was a mature student at a local college and was taxi driving to pay his way, didn't have a clue where our hotel was, he hadn't been driving a taxi long, as we found out. Sarah, after a while, told us she was getting desperate (her turn) for the loo.

As the taxi was nowhere near the hotel, we more or less had to force the driver to stop and let Sarah got to a toilet at a shop, thus relieved, she re-boarded, and we eventually found our hotel, after the driver had done much talking on the phone, we paid the pre-agreed price – he did not get a tip. Poor guy must have spent half the night on our journey, best put down to experience all-around.

Chapter 33

The next day it was back to Thailand, all the events mentioned on these holidays all happened, but maybe not in the exact order described, especially these older trips, anyway, one other event awaited me back in Thailand, and that was a diving trip out near the Phi Phi islands.

Sarah tells me she got the hotel shuttle into Patong that day, just for a stroll, and also had a relaxing hotel sauna.

I had two dives that day, the morning dive was memorable for me, as following the others at the back, they did not notice when I veered off to look at what turned out to be a three-foot long (what I thought was a cuttlefish) that was the same sandy colour as the bottom, it let me get to within about twenty feet before turning away, still watching me with its large eye, we zigzagged like this probably, for only a minute, but seemed longer, keeping a short distance away, but not swimming off, before I realised I was well away from the group.

I turned and could see someone in the distance beckoning me to re-join them. I had become mesmerised by the eye of what must have been a squid, as the eye was big and round, unlike the cuttlefish which I now know have eyes with horizontal slits and do not grow as large as the squid I now know I saw. It kept its tentacles out in front, in the manor of a cuttlefish, not behind as a squid does when swimming fast. This one was not moving fast whilst shadowing me.

The dive group climbed aboard the dive boat for a lunch which I am sure was nice, but it was what happened after that gave me a scare. We had moved off to a different location, not sure what we were intended to see, as almost as soon as we entered the water within a minute or so, I started getting a pain in my head, we were only about ten or fifteen feet down, it was not ear pressure, but the pain gradually got worse to the point that I signalled that I would follow near the surface, which I did, the pain reduced to a level that I could just about stand, I recall nothing more of that second dive, until we returned to the boat and I climbed out. The pain was still sharp in my head and did not start to go until I was sick over the side, after which it gradually subsided.

Not sure if it was anything to do with eating then diving, as my stomach felt fine, but it was a good job it was not a deep dive, as this second dive of the day was not pleasant for me. This was a memorable trip for us, as you might guess, we had a jeep safari into the interior of Phuket, stopping to climb up the extended roots of trees up the side of a waterfall, finding secluded beaches at the end of terrible road/tracks, being thrown about like the trip we avoided going on in Africa, I think due to the heat and humidity, Sarah dodged the worst effects her neck might have suffered in a drier climate. A memorable holiday had come to an end.

Chapter 34

In the summer of 1998, Sarah, knowing of my interest in rally driving, for my birthday booked me on a full-day rally driving experience.

We had been to one or two World Rally, UK legs. In those days, Colin McRae was at the top of the rally world, in his blue Subaru. With my still working video camera, I remember getting some great footage of him "drifting" around a gravel bend, with only a tree trunk between us and him hurtling sideways towards us, only gaining traction about ten feet from us, that picture staying in my "highlights only" memory.

The day was a wet one, we, the participants for the day, had the briefing as to how the day would progress, we then took turns in a Mk 2 Escort 2-litre, stripped and kitted for rally, round an oval, timed circuit, about a foot deep in mud, guess who went first, I managed to spin the car in a complete circle on the first bend, but ended up facing the right way, so was able to keep going, but that lost me any chance of getting the best time on our three circuits. Later, after some food, we all took turns around a circuit used by professionals to train, in a 3-litre, duel control, Sierra Cosworth, pretty much among the bee's knees at that time. The professional driver pushed me to my limit in the use of last-minute hand-break turns, another memory still there in my limited "instant access" recall array.

By this time we were starting to look for somewhere else to live, we were getting fed up both of the very small flat and the noise from above. One good and one not-so good memory were to occur before the eventual move came.

Sarah's birthday in the next year, 1999, was a challenge for me, having been given a special rally driving day as described above, I had to come up with something of equal interest for her.

It came in the form of a short holiday to Padstow, Cornwall, where Rick Stein's restaurant, among his other outlets, is located, even then the town had been re-Christened "Padstein", he owned so much of the place, I believe he owns even more of it now.

We stayed in a little village called Rock, a short distance away. When the time came for the meal in Rick Stein's restaurant, we were quite disappointed not to find him – towel on shoulder, waiting on us.

He was probably off filming one of his food Odysseys somewhere. The restaurant was nice, bright and lively, as was the price of our meal, but Sarah was happy, and that's what counted.

One other event occurred while we were there. I am not a great football fan, but nominally followed the fortunes of Manchester United, and as any fan of any other team will tell you, most of MU's fans do not live in Manchester. After our experience in a pub in Rock, I will attest to that often-bitter sentiment.

Manchester United under the management of Alex Ferguson reached the pinnacle of UK football achievement, not since equalled to date, while we watched it unfold in a pub I forget the name of there, as Ole Gunner Solskjaer (now Manager), forever went down in football history as the extra-time "super sub" who scored the winner against Bayern Munich in the dying seconds – giving United an as yet unequalled triple win of League, FA Cup and European Cup winners in the same year.

In that pub, it was if England had won the World Cup, the place went mad, as if we were in city centre Manchester, not quaint Cornwall. Sarah was more of a fan than I was, having gone to watch them from her teenage years, so it was a good trip all-around. Then life returned to earth with a bump only a few weeks later.

Chapter 35

As I mentioned earlier, my mum had been in poor health for some time, suffering from angina, she had a triple arterial by-pass in the 1980s, and now in the late-90s, with diabetes also, she went into Manchester Royal infirmary for the last time, ironically, the same hospital where years earlier she had risen to the office of Acting Matron in the nursing structure.

After a couple of visits, I received a call telling me she had been moved to another ward and advice to turn up there soon. As soon as I saw the state of the other people in this ward, tucked away in the deep recesses of the hospital, I knew my mum would not be coming out this time. As I made her comfortable as she could get with the pillows, she told me she had renal failure and asked if I knew what that meant, I did not want to take it in but I nodded, we then talked on other subjects.

That was the last time I spoke to her. She had previously made a living will, saying "Do Not Resuscitate" not wanting to prolong her suffering. Within a few days, I got the call.

I do not think my mum was happy that I had taken up with Sarah, who is both a little older than me, and had had a hysterectomy, though I did not tell my mum this for some time, I was not going to break her heart by telling her I had no intention of having children, as in Sarah's and my early years, my mum kept hinting at "when children come along" as mothers do. When she realised that was not going to happen, she was cool then to Sarah. I had a choice – tell her that I was not about to risk another childhood like mine, or tell a half-truth that Sarah could not have any more children, which is what I must have done, though I don't remember the moment.

Sarah, in our early years together, had offered to try and get her hysterectomy reversed, though this is only rarely done, and has little chance of working. As I have detailed earlier, this was my way out of an option I did not want.

So my mum was gone, she had led a life of sacrifice, and with my dad, only a limited happiness. She had told me it took everything she had to make it in nursing, she was not effortlessly clever like my dad, it was sheer hard work and dedication to make it as far as she did and bring up a family. She could be domineering at times, like I am told her mother was, but she was a morally strong person who achieved much, she must have been a good organiser with a cool head to reach the professional level she had.

It is a strange feeling when you lose both parents, even in you thirties, like there is no longer any anchor, or link to the family past, as we (brother, sister and

I) had lost links to relatives in the east of England and had a permanent split off from my mother's one remaining brother, that will not be expanded on here, though I will say it was a unanimous decision of my siblings and mine, in regard to opportunistic activity on the death of his older brother, and his sister (our mum) at the time of my father's demise, as mentioned earlier.

We had a trip to Puerto Pollensa, a quiet town on Majorca, at some stage whilst living in the Denton flat. A pleasant holiday with a fine tree lined beach, the only thing of note we did, (apart from a half-day dive, for me, with nothing I recall from that) is that we both went up in turn on a tandem open Microlight, with a guy who advertised himself as an Ex-Spanish champion. It is quite a feeling to be sat in mid-air with nothing whatsoever around you, and when we went above the sharp ridge line of the mountains on the eastern end of Majorca, the wind hit us so hard we were blown backwards, the front of the Microlight tilted up to the point where I thought I might fall out backwards, but then we stabilised, and I enjoyed the rest of that flight.

I don't remember Sarah was taken up above the ridge line. I don't think the pilot was expecting the strength of wind that hit us, and if Sarah had experienced what I had up there, she would have recalled it when I asked her. Nice beach, with a good bar, otherwise a nice but unremarkable holiday.

We did, however, have one more memorable trip while we still lived in Denton, this was a two-week trip to the West Coast of America.

Chapter 36

We thought we would do a fly-drive trip, but when we looked into the routes available, they all started no further north than San Francisco and headed south or inland from there, not what we wanted. We wanted to see the north-western coast and forests, so we ended up putting our own trip together.

As when visiting most countries, you have to have at least the first night's accommodation booked, so having decided to start our trip in Seattle, and end in San Francisco, we used a travel agency to book a hire car, one night in Seattle and three nights in San Francisco, all other nights we either looked in hotel registries for adverts where we were headed next and phoned ahead a booking, or got used to stopping at the motel strips that are a feature of the outskirts of small town America, as there was still no internet in the 90s – how did we all manage? Younger readers would ask? We just did.

We had to get there first, the plane from Manchester was delayed, so when we landed in Chicago to catch our connecting flight to Seattle, we had to run down what seemed like mile-long corridors to make it to the departure gate – just in time, the staff were surprised to see us and told us we were the only passengers to make it onto the connecting flight. (I would have no chance of repeating that feat now).

We picked up our hire car, a Chevrolet Cavalier, from Alamo. (This trip was the only trip Sarah kept a diary of, so a few extra details recalled here.) The first date was Sept 2nd, just not sure what year, but around the millennium. We eventually found our hotel, visible from the highway but not reachable, on the one-way system, until we figured out the long-winded way to it.

We decided to start our holiday in style, so as we were not far from the Space Needle, we had our first meal that evening at the top of it. Nearby there is a stadium, and we noticed it was filling up as we approached the Needle. At the top, in the slowly revolving restaurant, we could see there was a concert happening in the stadium, we were told later it was REM, who are native to Seattle, a group Sarah quite liked. It would have been cheaper to go see them, had we known, than the price of the meal up there! But it was a good view – over Puget Sound, and in the opposite direction, snow-covered Mount Rainier, the tallest Mountain/Volcano in the cascades.

We took a boat to Blake Island to a very-commercialised Tillicum Indian reservation, then went to the extensive fish market. Before setting off for Enumclaw, where I had booked our first motel on our route south through Washington State, Enumclaw looking about the right distance to end our first day's drive. This was our first taste of "a one horse town", not too far from Seattle, just a pizza meal there that night, but we were on our way. Our objective the next day was the famous Mount St Helens. We must have got up fairly early and we stopped along the way as the views of the cascades, especially Mt Rainier was quite spectacular at more than fourteen thousand feet, it looked like Mt Fuji in Japan. We reached the turn off for Mt St Helens mid-morning, and drove up to the observation area.

There was no one else there, it was quite eerie, silence, but looking out over a view that still, over fifteen or more years later than the eruption, still looked as if an air-burst atomic bomb had hit the area, stripped trees in every direction, only slightly interspersed with small new growth pines. The only comparable sight I am aware of from documentaries is the area around the Tunguska event in 1908, in a remote region of Russia, this is a possible air-burst exploding comet or asteroid, as there is no impact crater. There are other theories for the cause of this massive explosion, which stripped or flattened trees over a wide area, like at Mt St Helens, but on an even bigger scale, but not speculated on here…

Spirit Lake below was still full of stripped trees.

I am afraid we ignored the sign saying do not take any pumice, as it was deserted, we fed some bluebirds and chipmunks with some crackers we had with us, then it was back on the road heading for the Columbia River on the Washington/Oregon border.

Chapter 37

Our next stop was a small town called Morton, I had tried to book ahead, but it was Labour Day in America, and all those that could – headed for the hills that weekend.

We kept going, we had a map, and the scenery, forest and snow-capped mountains, including Mt Rainier, you could see for miles, was fantastic. I am never happier than travelling in new country, we must have worked out that Morton was reachable that afternoon, to find somewhere to stay, which we did, just, second to last room in a motel.

There was a place called The Wheel Cafe we had noted, for an evening meal, but when we stepped out into "Town" we could hear music, but could not see the source, I could tell it was live music, we had to go through an arch to the large back yard of the Morton Hotel, where a band called The Blues Junkies were in full swing.

The tables were transplanted tree stumps, there was bottled beer and Bourbon, and burgers, the food we had to buy ourselves, but as soon as some locals heard our English accents, they would not let us buy our own drinks! Now that's what I call hospitality, not too many of us English must have passed through Morton, as I think we were quizzed on where we came from and what brought us to their neck of the woods, so we had to work a little bit for our beer.

Next morning, we set off after finding a local cafe for breakfast, after which we headed for the Columbia River, but on the way as Sarah recalls, there was a downside, we saw so much roadkill, raccoons, chipmunks, porcupines, even deer, which if you saw the number of large 4X4s up there is not so surprising.

From a *Rough Guide* book, I had phoned ahead to the historical St Martins Hotel, in Carson, a Spa town on the Washington side of the Columbia River, on the Oregon border, I had managed to get the last Log Cabin available. We made good time and stopping at the Bonneville Dam, where you could see salmon leaping up a man-made run, there is also an underground aquarium there, with large fish such as sturgeon. When we reached Carson, it looked like the cabin we had was the last available for a good reason, no bath or shower, or carpet, just old cracked lino, it had been there since the 19th century, and it looked like it – very rustic, leaking bathroom, heat from a through stove pipe, different, here, "historic" meant our room! We had booked a Sulphur Wrap followed by a massage, the local hot springs providing the Sulphur Mud Wrap, my massage afterwards left me feeling like I had gone ten rounds with a Turkish masseur.

The next day we crossed the Columbia River gorge and then went on a two-hour stern-paddle steamer trip, before heading off into Oregon at Hood River, the river town also close to Mt Hood, the tallest peak in the area. We had two choices, we could head towards the coast and eventually Portland, or down the highway splitting the middle of Oregon, as we planned to go through the giant redwoods near the coast of northern California later, we elected the inland route, making good time, I think on Highway 26, heading for Madras, for a good curry? This road split the Oregon we saw into two very different terrains, the high desert to the east, forested mountains to the west, the desert to the east given to the local Native Americans – given the best land as usual…

We turned off to Warm Springs Reservation, stopped at the only building, a casino, had a coffee, then back to the highway, not too impressed with what the Natives were given to live on.

At Madras (no curry eaten), we decided to head for Sisters, named after the three sister mountains close by. I had an idea that we might do a little horse riding.

Chapter 38

The Sisters Motor Lodge we stayed at could not have been more of a contrast to that Spa Cabin, in Carson Hot Springs, the rooms were themed, ours was decked out in Indian rugs, pipes and the like, and was very comfortable, first coffee facilities in the room since we had arrived. We stayed two nights there, as Jim and Tracy the then owners had found us somewhere we could go horse riding the next day.

The town of Sisters is just as you imagine a tourist version of a gentrified Cowboy town, lots of leather and other goods, including Stetson hats, which we duly bought, so as to look the part if we were getting on horses next day. Don't remember that evening's meal, but Sarah said the portions were so big she had what was called they called a child's portion, but what we would call a normal portion. Sorry to include toilet humour, this once only, but I dread to think of their version of a Close Encounter of the Turd Kind – cow pats or us! They say everything's big in America…

We had a good (normal-sized) cooked breakfast at the Motor Lodge and then headed for the Black Butte Ranch where greenhorns were catered for. We were given horses and our guide took us up a fairly steep hill into the forest, where we were able to go at a trot, something that to us, non-equestrian ranked people, was quite a thrill. We followed some trails, seeing some deer before heading back. Sarah fell off as she caught her foot in a stirrup climbing down, not hurt, apart from her pride, as it was on soft ground.

We spent the next day at the nearby Mackenzie Lava Beds, (not so good to sleep on), a local guide explaining the local geology, afterwards climbing a National Trail to a place in the forest called Proxy Falls, Sarah seeing a small snake on the way up. That two days gave us the intended good break from driving.

Next day, we drove on south towards Bend, on the way we stopped at The High Desert Museum, which was more like a mini-zoo, with otters and porcupines, then stopped for coffee at the Mohawk Restaurant, which had on display all manner of animal skins, some stuffed, ornaments, bottles and the like. Around lunchtime, we arrived at Diamond Junction and checked in at the Whispering Pines Motel, before driving up to nearby Crater Lake, a volcanic caldera, created over 7000 years ago when the cone collapsed in on itself, eventually leaving a deep, blue lake, with the beginnings of a new cone rising up in the middle of the lake.

We climbed the 500ft down for a boat ride around the caldera, but it was the climb up the steep steps afterwards in the searing heat that we struggled with, I made sure not to eat before this, as I would not have made it back up. The view from the top was spectacular, the Cascade Mountains snow-capped into the distance. After food and drink, we headed back down to the motel which was some distance away, I actually recall commenting that the view into the deep distance downhill along the dead straight, but undulating, road is like you see in the classic US "Road Movies", I also recall saying you just could not see that far ahead anywhere in the UK, for me to recall that, it must have been some vista.

Heading south west the next day, after a long drive, we stopped near Grants Pass for caffeine, then a Ranger Station near Crescent City, which was our first stop in California, for information on the nearby Redwoods National Park, before reaching the Marigold Cottages, I phoned ahead motel for that night at around 1 pm.

After a sandwich and coffee nearby, we entered the National Park, with its giant redwood trees, we saw a herd of Elk there, before stopping at the "Big Tree" 61ft in circumference and many centuries old.

Our first sight of the Pacific proper, rather than Puget Sound at Seattle, was reached at Gold Bluff beach, where we saw more Elk at the tree line, just a little further down the coast we turned off the road at Fern Canyon, as we just wanted another beach stop.

By pure accident, it turned out to be where they filmed one of the opening scenes of *Jurassic Park, The Lost World*, just inland from the beach, with the massive fallen tree. We had driven close to three hundred miles that day, down from the Oregon Mountains to the North California Coast.

On the coast road the next morning, now in Humboldt County, it was very misty, we could barely see the surf, when we stopped for a break, there were a few bushes in flower nearby, and we saw what we first thought were large insects, but on closer inspection turned out to be tiny iridescent blue humming birds, sipping nectar from the flowers, turning our fresh air and circulation break into something special.

Chapter 39

Reaching Arcata, we turned east, inland, heading for Willow Creek – reputed bigfoot country! We stopped in town for coffee, before heading up into the mountains hoping for a sighting, if there is anything up there, we had no chance of seeing it, as first there were endless roadworks, and then a forest fire, quite close to the road, the smoke acrid, even with the windows shut. Bigfoot could relax and take his whole deerskin Moccasins off but should be more careful with his pipe tobacco…

The firefighters had their work cut out from what we could see, chopping a firebreak to try and stop it crossing the road. Eventually, we got through and passed through Redding, on our way to Lassen Volcanic Park. Mt Shasta was visible further north, I wanted to go up there, but Lassen was much closer, on the way up, it rained, Sarah said the raindrops were the biggest she had ever seen. Having zigzagged to 8,500ft, we parked. There was a couple there from Cheshire, doing a similar holiday to us, but only in northern California. Mt Lassen Peak was still another 2000ft up, not for us, instead we walked the mile and half to Bumpass Hell, and yes that was its real, quite apt name.

It smells like it sounds! The boiling mud and water vents, full of sulphur, smelling of bad eggs, way more than anything even I could produce, even with the assistance of craft beer IPA!

We ended up that night at Red Bluff, about 30 miles south of Redding, in the Sports Motel, big room, comfortable and way cheaper than the first place we tried at Mineral, near Mt Lassen. The Green Wok, just down the road, was our Chinese meal out that night.

Our next destination, we had spotted in our travel book, was to be Clearlake, at a resort called Blue Fish Cove, which turned out to be in Glendale. But first we had to get there. I was getting fed up with Highway 101, so we thought we could cut through countryside and end up on the coast.

Soon lost as there were no signs (no satnav then), we ended up in scrubland, that led straight to one of those prisons in the middle of nowhere you see in the movies, complete with watchtowers, manned be archetypical sun-glassed guards with rifles. We turned around very quickly and found our way back to the 101 after that.

The Blue Fish Cove was a nice "Place in the Sun", we had our own comfortable cabin. Sarah decided to sunbath and read. I went swimming in the huge lake and then hired a Jet Ski, which was a first and great fun. Late afternoon, we walked around town, thinking to spot a likely place for dinner later, we were told The Lamplighter was good, so went back there later. We ate outdoors there, marvelling that we could actually see the Milky Way, not something you are far enough away from lights to see at home.

An American, we were talking to, pointed to what turned out to be a Black Widow spider, weaving a web, thankfully on the other side of the plastic window wind screening. Early start the next day, so thought to have breakfast on the road.

Clearlake was a turn off south east from the 101, so to head back towards the coast, we had to pass through an area called the Coastal Ranges, the roads snaked around the mountains and it seemed we had to reach the bottom, before climbing steeply back up.

Boonville was the name of the town at the bottom, nestled between steep mountains, it was a bit like the land that time forgot, it even had its own language, sort of.

We had breakfast at The Horn of Zees, which in "Boonting" just means cup of coffee.

I wondered if we would be still in the same decade as we climbed up the other side, it was up hill and down dale, with more racoon and skunk (Good name for a pub) roadkill. After we re-joined Highway 101 on the coast, the scenery was great, but I had to keep my eye on the winding road that much I didn't take much in. Only one more nights stop from being in range of San Francisco, we started to look for overnight accommodation.

The prices at Bodega Bay, where they had filmed Hitchcock's *The Birds*, were, in Sarah's words, astronomical, so we kept going, until we spotted a motel at Novato, which we stopped at. After dumping our cases, went for a walk and fresh air in the nearby China Camp State Park, where we bumped into a couple from Cheadle, Stockport, the woman's sister working at Hyde Sixth form College – small world. Back at the motel, I managed to give our once white hire car a hosing down, as we would be handing it back to Alamo the next day.

Having stretched our legs, headed back to the motel, then ate in a nearby, an otherwise deserted, Bavarian restaurant, can't win 'em all.

As we were not too far from the Golden Gate Bridge and our pre-booked three nights in Sam Plank's disco city, we were not up so early the next morning, as after turning on the local TV station, the 101 was backed up nearly to Novato, being the rush hour, so we got up slowly and went to the next-door Burger King for breakfast. The rush-hour traffic eased, so we set off – getting across the GG Bridge at a steady 55mph, kept that way I suspect, by the overhead Police Chopper.

Chapter 40

Armed with a map of San Francisco, Sarah successfully guided us through the one-way system to our hotel, as it was only 11.30 am, we could not check in yet, but were allowed to drop off our bags at reception, before heading off to find the Alamo car drop off, after that, deciding to find Fisherman's Wharf, though we had to walk, as we didn't know the buses yet.

On the way, we heard shots, and thought we had stumbled into a shoot-out, which turned out to be filming for a scene in *Nash Bridges*, that's America for you.

Found our way down to Fisherman's Wharf, had a coffee in a converted warehouse called The Cannery, as used to be. Then headed for the famous Pier 39, where the sea lions stank, fighting noisily for a place on the float, just off the pier. The nearby Undersea World was OK for an hour, we then booked a trip around the Bay and Alcatraz Island for the next day, did a little shopping, then found a bus to McAllister, where our hotel was, checked in, unpacked and showered, rested, ready for the evening.

A restaurant called Lou's was where we found our first evening meal in SF, it was also a Blues Club upstairs, so after having a good Cajun meal, we went upstairs for drinks and to listen to the live band singing and playing the blues. Bit of a sleepless night at the hotel, right across the road from the Police Station, with cars leaving – sirens blearing, on and off, all night.

Next morning we had breakfast at Ems Place just up the road, before getting on the boat for our trip around San Francisco Bay, which was a little cold and misty at that time of day.

Alcatraz itself was not of much interest to us, so we did not book a tour, just went around the island on the boat under the Golden Gate Bridge before landing back at the pier.

Another look at the sea lions, before buying a Seafood Chowder from a boardwalk seaside stall, the Chowder served in a large scooped out bread roll, followed by a ride on the cable cars on the famous hill, then back to the hotel. China Town in San Francisco is one of the largest in the world. We booked an evening walking tour, with the guide telling the history of the Chinese immigrants, railway and mine workers mainly, we ate a good meal there, before an overlong city tour back to our hotel.

After some more (jeans) shopping the next day, we caught a mini-bus to Golden Gate Park, where we spent most of the day. After walking around the lake, the Japanese tea garden was our was our midday tea and cookies venue, followed by a long walk to the Natural History Museum, this had a large aquarium section, and in one large tank, a Pacific Giant Octopus swam over to where I had put my hand on the glass, and attached its suckered tentacles there over an area of about three feet for some time.

The great Earthquake of 1906 was also featured in this museum, with a moving floor plate you can stand on, that is supposed to simulate the ground movement of the quake that devastated the city that year, they are still waiting for the next big one, and all the talk is of whose *fault* it will be, though San Andreas is most likely!

The Hard Rock Cafe was the setting for our last meal out, where you were given wrist bands that let you wander around, looking at guitars and gold disks mounted on the walls, before vibrating and flashing to tell you your meal was ready, can't recall what we ate, only that that portions were of the usual American size – humongous – another close encounter imminent - Der de dur du der… that was that, flew back next day, quite a memorable trip, the recall much enhanced from Sarah's diary.

Chapter 41

With the additional funds added from the one third split of the sale of our mum's house, and the sale of our flat, early the following year, Sarah and I were able to find a small three-bedroom house in Hyde, a town a little closer to where we both worked. It was near the bottom of a dead-ended road, so no through traffic and not far so from the same canal that passed my current workplace.

We were to spend ten years there. There always seemed to be a catch when we moved house, the catch at this one was the back garden, nice and big, which after the little, often waterlogged one at the back of our flat, was a complete contrast, we had wanted a larger garden, just not one that slopped upwards at what seemed a thirty degree angle, while it might not have been quite that much, from the top you could see over our roof!

At one time this garden may have been terraced, as there were a couple of sharpish slopes, one half way down and another near the bottom, below which there was a flat section, held in place with a brick wall, then a small concrete area at ground level, a set of steps, leading up to the bottom flat level of garden. On this bottom flat section, the previous owner had deposited a large pile of large cobbles he had acquired from somewhere.

I knew I would have my work cut out here. We probably got it a little cheaper as the back looked a daunting prospect to me, who had no experience of building or major garden work, and must have looked the same to other prospective buyers. Fortunately, we had a good set of neighbours, John and Alison, (who had an interesting secret I will come to later), who were our downhill (about four feet) semi-detached next-door neighbours, and John was into all things DIY, which was handy…

First of all, after we had settled in, we had the front garden, (weeded soil and a bit of grass), gravelled over, with a few paving stones with some large pots, that were my mum's, plonked on top. We must have kept some money back from our new mortgage for some fitted wardrobes, but then there was no avoiding the back garden.

Like I said, a good set of neighbours, who it turned out, were in the habit of helping each other out when it came to major work on our joint, hilly back gardens. One weekend, three of our hill-bottom neighbours came around and helped us move the great pile of bread loaf sized cobbles, from the flat section of grass, down onto the concrete space adjacent to the walled bottom grass.

Must have been quite a lot, as there was enough to build two terraced walls, with deep enough footings to make a decent lower garden. With advice about having drainage channels included from John next door, who had done similar but with bricks, we hired some local landscapers to start the two terrace walls using the cobbles, which they did, we then decided to let them carry on, using access through the garage to the back, while we went on a short holiday to Cornwall.

Neither of us recalls much of that holiday, must have been pleasant enough, and came back with an oil painting from St Ives.

Sarah reminded me there was a good reason to remember the exact date we came back from that holiday. That date was September 11th, 2001, we knew nothing of the events of that day on the long drive back from Cornwall as we had CDs rather than the radio on in the car.

It was the wall builders, working in the back who told us to put the telly on as something major was unfolding in the US, according to their radio.

We watched the events of that day unfold hour by hour. It was in the years afterwards that some odd facts surfaced, such as the way the third, smaller building collapsed in on itself, according to some "experts" as if charges were placed in the building, and a close up of one of the planes just before it hit one of the towers, showing an unusual shape under the fuselage.

I am no expert on these things, but as with the Japanese "surprise" attack on Pearl Harbour, where warnings were "ignored", I would not put it past the certain sections of the American military establishment to be willing to sacrifice some of their own people to further their aims, just as at Pearl Harbour where all their aircraft carriers, the vessels that carried the day in the Pacific, just happened to be safety out at sea during the attack. Seasoned radar operators on the island were replaced for the day by rookies, who reported the incoming aircraft, but were ignored. In 2001, the military needed a reason to go in heavy in Afghanistan, and one appeared. Sometimes it is convenient for the left hand to not know what the right hand is doing. Tragic as both events were, they proved useful in political/military terms.

I and those with far more expertise in investigative skills could be entirely wrong on both counts, but the US governments record of using its own, often Native American, "citizens", and those of places like the Marshall Islands, as guinea pigs in mind-altering drugs, or as long-term test subjects for nuclear fallout does not inspire trust in the official stories, as with their clandestine development of technologies way in advance of those in the public domain, not just those with military applications, but in the withholding of power generation tech that is so cheap, they would derive no tax and oil revenue income, from the general public, drastically reducing their ability to control our daily lives. Again Google "The Tesla papers" and ask what happened to his notes on wireless absorption and transmission of power – after his death in 1943, why were they confiscated by the government. In the same vein, "search" out the interesting inventor Thomas Townsend Brown, whose anti - gravity research in the 20th century was also suppressed, likely also in the interests of "Big Oil".

Chapter 42

I return now to my own little life, though I will continue as I have to divert from my life to my times and interests, as I see them, and as events and available knowledge at the time warrant.

The fact was that the wall being built from the large cobblestones was looking distinctly wonky, as it had a fair slope, nowhere near level from one end to the other, they said we asked for "rustic" but from the little progress they had made in a week, and the state of it, we decided to pay them off at where they were up to, as I suspected they (youngish lads) had as little expertise at cobble laying as I had, either that or they needed a new bubble in their spirit level!

Fortunately, John from next door was in his element and showed me how to mix the mortar correctly, to include drainage holes, to relieve the pressure on the two walls after rain (water came through these often, so proved to be needed), and I was able to select progressively larger cobbles to correct the downslope on the next layer up and went on to finish both walls, with a paved walkway between them for a washing line. I used the few remaining cobblestones sometime later to build a rectangular area for fruit berry bushes, three quarters up the garden. I also built a half-moon wildlife pond halfway down into one sharp slope.

That just left the flat-walled area at the back of the house. There was a small gap (1ft) between the wall and the house, with a drain at the bottom. We found some professional builders to put a small conservatory, accessed by new French doors in the back-dining area.

This left about eight feet from the front of the conservatory to the lower terraced wall.

John, next door had built a brick, U-shaped, small but deep fish pond opposite his kitchen, while I was not keen on the design, it got me thinking, as I had always liked keeping tropical fish, indeed we had a tank by then in the living room. Before long I had built, with help from a pump and filter specialist, a six foot by four foot, by three-foot-deep pond, surrounded by flagstones, with a Greek style urn at one end where the circulatory pump returned the water after filtration and UV cleaning, complete with green lighting set in the bottom, it looked great from the conservatory lit up in the evening.

I have never since done so much exterior work, but it felt good to have done as much as I could there. My biggest regret, when we eventually moved on, was leaving the Koi and other fish for the next owner.

Before we had moved to Hyde, Sarah had changed from working in school kitchens, to working at Stockport town hall, then back to schools, where by then, she worked her way up to manager at a comprehensive.

At the enzyme factory where I worked, things took an unexpected turn for me, fortunately as it turned out, though I didn't think so at the time. In the roughly fourteen years I worked there, I had worked with many different products, including sampling one liquid enzyme years earlier, that had fermented and gone off, I could tell from the smell! I soon after developed the worst case of diarrhoea I have ever had; I was off work for about three weeks and lost a fair bit of weight I really didn't have to spare in those days. I could not prove this was the cause, but the management never questioned my assertion of the cause of my illness.

Back to late 2000, I started, with others, having to suit up and weigh off small batches of a new powdered enzyme, but I turned out to be highly allergic to this product, my nose and sinuses instantly blocking up the moment the slightest amount in the air reached me, despite having come into contact with many other enzymes over the years, with no ill effects. The site manager was taking no chances, other people, notably in the labs, had succumbed to various ailments though never proven to be work caused to my knowledge. It was determined that the company insurance would not cover me for this, so they decided to look to other sites run by the company for alternative employment to offer me.

They had a site thirty odd miles away in Widnes, processing phosphates, where they were short of a forklift truck driver. The distance put me off initially, but when told I would start on four thousand pounds pre-annum more than I was then earning, I accepted, as the overtime ban the French owners had imposed here (Stockport) was still in force.

My acceptance of this transfer proved to be fortuitous as I mentioned, as within a year and half, the French owners, having stripped the Stockport site of the biotech knowledge they had acquired the site for, shut it down, with the loss of all jobs.

Chapter 43

Returning to my seemingly compulsive interest in the UFO and breakaway human higher tech civilisation that may be secretly existing alongside the rest of us.

Just a little before my work transfer to Widnes, a guy called Gary Mckinnon, made headlines, and his story followed up on mainstream media from time to time as he successfully fought of extradition to the USA, with the help of a certain Theresa May, then Home Secretary. (What did she learn, if she did not already know?)

Gary's crime as far as the Americans were concerned, is about as serious as it gets, as he successfully hacked into both NASA and the Pentagon, using a fairly primitive computer, but great skill, to uncover glimpses of a secret space programme, way in advance of anything seen publicly, apart from by accident, which are probably the triangular TR3Bs or newer replacement, of which Gary uncovered transcripts saying there were about 43 of these, at that time, and 9 of the larger "mothership" type vessels in our "Solar Warden" fleet.

There were also transcripts mentioning ship-to-ship transfers of "Non-Terrestrial Officers", the context meaning not aliens, but human crew – operating off world. If true, and the Americans were (and still are) furious that his extradition was cancelled, due to Gary's Asperger's Syndrome condition that could have left him vulnerable to suicide if forced onto a plane to face charges in the USA.

Gary was looking for information on Gravity Amplifier Propulsion Systems, and Zero Point Energy, both rumoured to have been either acquired, or developed, but not released into the public domain, whereas Gary succinctly put it, 'Pensioners are struggling to pay their heating bills – while this free energy tech is being withheld.'

Those of you who do not remember this saga playing out on the "News", can (as with all other stories on this general subject) simply Google/search it out, it's all there in the public domain, which is why I feel reasonably safe trying to remind people that we are NOT being told everything, for fear of the resulting lack of government control, if even a small portion of the true current and past real world state is confirmed, especially if US/Antarctic German collusion is confirmed from 1954 onwards, after the "1952 superiority demonstration" over Washington. (Search 1952 Washington Flap).

I would like to know why we need a "Solar Warden" fleet. Perhaps I should refer you back to the "Blue Planet Project", again, Google it, this is not David Attenborough's *The Blue Planet*, very admirable though that is.

For those of you still with me, I refer you back to the Oddball bit in the title.

I am not claiming any of this subject to be gospel truth, as I would need proof, just an awful lot of circumstantial evidence available to anyone with reason to look, usually people like me who don't quite accept the "norm" of visible society, where some things, especially historically, don't quite add up.

Back to my life, and my transfer to the Widnes Phosphate Processing Site of the then owned French company that closed the Stockport Enzyme site little more than a year after I was transferred.

Just a reminder first that I am keeping company and personal names false, or non-existent on the off chance that this gets published, and I do not wish people close, or associated with me mixed up with the more controversial subjects I bring up (as above).

I realise that there is more than enough information for a determined investigator to unearth my identity. I see no reason for the casual reader to need to know this.

The job I was given at the start of my time working in Widnes was very different to my last two major employments, at the dye manufacturers and the enzyme and beer water treatment site in Stockport.

In my last position at Stockport, part of my job was moving whatever batch I had produced or packed to its appropriate place of storage – by forklift Truck, the use of which had to be retested every three years, so I was used to driving electric fork trucks. The team I was assigned to at Widnes was the warehouse operation, at least for the first five or so years, before the site was sold on. Then it became more varied. For now, I was one of seven men, on a varied day shift that meant that five of us were working at any one time, six days a week for four weeks, then a week of 11 am – 7 pm, to deal with late deliverers, alongside with one other who was working one late day a week, so a different person each day. At the end of this five-week rota, you got sixteen days off, complicated, but it worked, and I got used to it.

Chapter 44

The fork trucks here were bigger, diesel-powered trucks, with enclosed plastic zip-sided cabs, we had our own red diesel filling station. There were three main production operations on this large site, and two old warehouses, where we were based. Our work was divided into two main operations, the first being stock transfer, this involved moving 1000kg or 1250kg pallets of either large "tote" bags, cling film wrapped onto the pallet, or, from other places, 25kg bags stacked and turntable wrapped, both of these would be stacked in rows of about twenty, by the production operators, for us to transfer into lanes in one of our two warehouses, stacked two or three high, depending on stability and, or, product, in lanes twenty deep, so you could have lanes with up to sixty pallets in them.

There were ramps up to an upper level with ten deep lanes in them, and we did eventually have racking four high in part of one upper level. These warehouses were where we would park the fork trucks we had been using all day, but there was no claim on any truck, so in winter for instance, the trucks with working heaters were the most sought after.

People (including me) would resort to reversing into lanes with two stacked pallets to hide it from casual view last thing, in a bid to find it still there in the morning, it was that sort of place. There was a still strong GMB union at this site, as a result working practices long abandoned elsewhere, with strict demarcation on who does what were still prevalent here. We, the warehousemen, had our own brew cabin, as did all the different production operations.

There is what I can best describe as a parade square where there is enough room for up to about ten curtain-sided trucks to park, well-spaced, either delivering raw materials or picking up finished product. It was rare for that many at once to be there, but it did happen, sometimes building up later in the afternoon if they had come from ports down south. So just as it got really busy, three of the five men in would be going home, the other two on "late's" having a mad two hours to clear the backlog before the 7 pm finish.

Both of the old warehouses had what were called loading docks for twenty- and forty-foot container wagons. An electric ramp would lift up beyond the height of the open-door containers whose driver would then back up to the ramps, the raised extension then released to form a bridge to the container, which we would drive into to either load or unload.

Not as easy as it sounds, as sometimes, if unloading, the container would be packed to the roof, double stacked, the upper pallets not always level, but at all angles, the trick was not to pierce the bag below whilst trying to level the top pallet to lift off in a very restricted roof space. The containers often had travelled from all over the world, so apart from the indifferent loading of those who knew it was not them who would have the job of untangling at the other end, there was also shifting at sea, so not always the fault of the loaders.

If the warehouse ramps were in use, there was also a mobile ramp on the "parade square", which we often used for the most modern production plant that was situated on the far side of the square, about two hundred yards away from the warehouses, and the main plants beyond. This fully computerised plant had its own large canopy where the production men there would leave orders out in rows of about ten pallets, picked from a six high-racked warehouse of their own. It was for us to go over and check periodically to see if there were pallets for us to transfer to our warehouses, or to alert these guys to pick orders for trucks that had arrived for these orders. Some were actually put out ready for us in advance…

They usually only stored high turnover stock in their warehouse, but it fell to us to load what they put out, using the nearby mobile ramp if it was a container to load, which it usually was. The mobile ramp had side sockets for FLT forks to lift the front of the ramp up whilst the driver backed up to it, when forks were withdrawn, hydraulics ensured a slow drop onto the back of the container.

Chapter 45

Out of the other six guys there was only one, Joe who was always looking to criticise anything he could, you may have met the type, usually only talks if he has something to moan about, and as I was the newcomer, I was a target. I found out later that he thought he had someone lined up to take the job I was given, so that didn't help. The rest of the guys were all OK, they, like me, all had their foibles, but that's what makes us individuals not robots.

Once they saw I was willing to do my share I was gradually accepted. When working a late week every five, you would find yourself with a different partner every day for the last two hours, working his one day a week eleven-seven day, as it was not always busy on those last two hours, you could spend half of it in the brew cabin, after running some pallets from the plants for the first hour, and if there were no or few wagons in to load/unload.

So apart from Joe, who would go off and spend time with his cronies if I was on "lates", I got to know the other five lads, Dave the tough, gruff old hand gradually took a shine to me, as long as I knew my place, once that became known, more of the men around the plants seemed more willing to talk to the outsider I was.

The main GMB union guy was called Steve, and he was bright and sharp, a bit of a bully if he needed to be, the management had to take heed of him, unlike at most workplaces that by then (early 2000s) where unions, if they existed at all, had very little power, as most medium-sized businesses had learnt the trick of hiring from other EU countries up to a third, or even half their workforce, so as to make sure there was no union cohesion, as the owners always had the unspoken threat of bringing in more EU labour, if there was any threat of strikes. It is from there you can see where the Leave EU Vote gained many of its number from, where imported workers were happy to take wages that had not gone up for years for the native incumbents, while energy and other costs have shot up.

Back to Widnes, and with Steve and the GMB union, the next five years saw our wages climb to a rate that I would never see again after the ten years I spent there.

It could not last forever, some of our phosphate raw materials came from Kazakhstan, and the suppliers were finding buyers who would pay more than our company – or so we were told – so we started having production cutbacks, and eventually rumours that we were to be sold turned into reality.

The new owners were a bit mysterious, there main plant was Dutch, with an East German plant, and also one in Argentina, and like most takeovers, it signalled changes for us.

First there were a few redundancies, all achieved voluntarily, less than ten percent of the workforce. It was not surprising they got the volunteers, as the pay outs for some of the men, who had been there for twenty years or more amounted to up to sixty thousand pounds, for senior grade-1 operators.

None of us warehousemen left then, however our work was about to get more varied. There was a small blending plant that one or two men used to produce blended batches in, this used to be done by men from the new plant, across the square.

All production men worked a three shift system, we were the only people to work days, and now, one or two of the five in at any one time would have to blend batches in this plant, it was mucky work, as the materials readily turned into something akin to porridge when cleaning out the mixer between batches, so the production men were quite happy to hand over some of this work to us.

The management killed two birds with one stone, as the supposedly (*Times* reading) staunch union guy, Steve K, was offered the job of being our manager, which he promptly accepted. Our union rep, Roy replacing Steve K as site GMB rep. Roy never used one word when he could use ten, but he didn't have Steve's clout, and the management knew it.

Previous to this, Steve K used to run a semi-automated robot packaging plant as part of his job, one of only about three people with the training to run this plant, it would not run all the time, only when certain products were made, usually for week long campaigns. For some reason I was not told, maybe due to my previous production experience, I, alone of the warehousemen, was chosen to learn this operation, presumably as Steve K was now our manager. I was his replacement on that operation, and it was him who trained me there.

Starting this plant from cold was quite technically challenging, compared to anything I had done at the dye, or enzyme works, first you had to hoist a new roll of bags onto a complicated machine that supplied the belt with bags, switch it on to heat up while going over to the main plant about a hundred yards away to check the valves to the pipes ready to blow the powder over to the hoppers in my plant, were open as the computer said they were, as they had a tendency to stick. The hoppers were supposed to measure it out into 25 kg portions, these also were known to stick from time to time, also setting up a laser/photo cell guided printer to spray the bags with date and batch info as it went past on the belt.

The blowing over and the hopper filling was all on the schematics of the computer, and I controlled the valves from there, though the plant's age was starting to show by this stage, as sometimes I had crocodiles to contend with! These crocodiles were bags that had merged into one five-foot long bag that should have been two smaller bags, a hopper having stuck open for an extra cycle, as mentioned above, the bag chopper/heat sealer not cutting until filling ceased.

Chapter 46

Someone earlier had seen this on the belt and called them crocodiles, and I could see what they meant, moving along the belt, five-foot long bags, to where they were picked up, by a large robot arm that I had previously chosen a program to stack to a certain weight in a set pattern, either five, or seven to a layer, either 1250, or a 1000kg. After this was done, if all was working well, the pallet (which was fed from a stack I loaded earlier) would turn at right angles and proceed to an automated turntable, where it would be wrapped top to bottom with cling film, after which it would be shunted to the end of the line, waiting for me to lift it off with a fork truck and stack it outside for my workmates to run to the warehouse.

What I have described was the ideal world. There was three phase safety interlocks to make sure that one finished pallet would not run into another if it were held up, sensors everywhere, the more complicated something is, the more there is to go wrong. Sod's law usually ruled here…

I don't know if it was loose product from a nearby plant in the air, but the plant was far too sensitive, and was forever stopping, the phase interlocks going out of sync for one reason or another, so I spent many a time with my back leaning against a ton or more pallet on the runners, pushing it to the wrapper, or off the wrapper, so the pallets were spaced far enough apart to resume operation. So much for automation. One way or another, I got so I could complete these campaign runs with little or no help from Steve K, and when I was working on this, I was exempt from the batch production, and general fork truck work, which drew some muted resentment from moaning Joe, as I called him, but there was not a lot he could say, as long as I was busy.

In the winter, crossing the old Runcorn Bridge (there is a new one now), heading for the M56 and my long drive home, you could sometimes see thousands of starlings, flocking together in the twilight sky, getting ready to roost on the bridge. I am sure more than one accident was caused on that bridge, forcing me to go the other way to the M62 to get home, by drivers watching the swirling clouds of starlings.

On one of these journeys home on a bit of quiet road near Daresbury, there is a section where two lanes merge into one, with such a long journey home I tended to drive fast where I could, on this stretch, I accelerated hard to pass a truck tractor unit, who was also travelling fast, I just got past him as he speeded up before the road merged into one lane each side. Next thing I knew, the lane opposite deserted, the truck tractor unit shot past me, slammed his brakes on, at the same time slinging his back end in my direction, doing his best to throw me of the road.

I jammed my own brakes on, coming to a halt just short of him, sat there for a couple of seconds, then shot off past him, looking in my rear-view mirror, the road being straight for some distance, I could see that he never moved whilst in my sight. I can only guess at his state of mind at that time, but that is the only attempt on my life I am aware of. Anyone looks determined on the road since then, I give way to.

Around this period (in my forties), I started to suffer from gout, cannot recall exactly when, but sitting for long periods (hours) on fork trucks, either running finished product to warehouses, or loading and unloading wagon's, containers and curtain-sided trucks, does not do a lot of good for the circulation.

Only about one week in six or seven was spent by me on the robot packing plant, or later in the blending plant, but by then it had taken hold, I am told being tall does not help, as when gout strikes, it is usually at night, when the place farthest from the heart, your toe joints allow (at the time of slowest circulation) any excess uric acid build up to precipitate out in the form of crystals from your bloodstream, especially if not enough liquid has been taken in.

I learnt all this the hard way, from doctors and herbalists, it seems logical if you think about it, that if you drink enough liquid, any solids would have a smaller chance of crystallising out, but there are certain foods – shellfish, some cheeses and beer, especially bitter and stout, that are high in purines, which are the causes of uric acid excess. My brother "Ian" also suffers from this very painful condition, we are now both on tablets for life that prevent gout, but I spent many years taking strong anti-inflammatory painkillers that made gout bearable, but not to the point of clearing it quickly.

You could spot a sufferer by the characteristic limp, my manager before Steve K could be seen occasionally with it. In my later years at Widnes, I got gout in my left elbow, possibly due to the constant fast turning of the knob situated on a fork truck steering wheel, which is turned faster and more often than in a car, using your left hand, whilst the right operates the lift, tilt and side shift controls. It looked quite funny, a sticking out red mound on my elbow joint, if it were not so painful, fortunately, that only happened once, though I also got it in my knees from time to time.

I do recall one or two long and painful drives home from Widnes, where every gear change was almost agony, (I do not like words to be over used, like the modern trend to over use the word "need" when "want" is what is really meant). So not quite agony, but I would be shouting out if I needed to use the clutch pedal, so very painful. I would reserve the word agony for people suffering from serious war wounds, or similar, in need of morphine, that's agony, something I have been lucky enough to avoid thus far.

Chapter 47

I did say in the preface that this is part travelogue, and so in the early 2000s, we, "Sarah" and I, embarked on our only visit to date to the African continent, and then only the north-eastern tip – Egypt, on a Nile cruise, from Luxor to the Aswan Dam and back, so nowhere near the pyramids. There is a lot more to Egypt than pyramid selling, and much of this we saw.

Karnak, to me is most impressive, built at Thebes, now Luxor, the temple complex is so large it creates its own cooling microclimate, which we experienced for ourselves, standing among columns so massive, (there are many) that the guide told us fifty people could stand on top of just one, and some of the individual cut stones placed atop and across these weigh in excess of a hundred tonnes, like to have seen the cranes used…

Anyone interested in Egypt can read for themselves far more than I could relate here, but there are one or two controversial characters that I want to touch on, before moving on to our personnel experiences there. I am not sure if we were at the temple in Edfu, or at Karnak, but I drew attention to myself when one of the Ministry of Antiquities guides asked our group of tourists how we thought the hieroglyphs were first translated, as I knew the answer to this, I piped up "The Rosetta Stone", Google if interested, but then he mentioned a very interesting guy from 2700 BC called Imhotep, he was mentioned as an early physician, again I spoke up asking where he got all his knowledge from, as he also was known to be an engineer, astronomer and mathematician, like an ancient version of Michelangelo, who also had many other inventive talents beyond art, drawing helicopters and submarines – way ahead of his time.

When I mentioned this, and that all his knowledge seemed to be too much at once, I was asked, 'Who are you?'

'Just an interested tourist,' I replied, which I was. I also know that the Ministry of Antiquities are very orthodox about how the history of Egypt is described, they do not like any departure from their establishment history to be contested.

The Sphinx, situated near the main Pyramids in Cairo, is one edifice I regret not seeing, mainly due to the controversy surrounding its date of construction, and what may still be hidden underneath, which the Ministry of Antiquities is keeping a tight lid on.

There are two modern scientific-minded authors that have challenged the orthodox dating of the Sphinx, based on the fact (as shown on TV documentaries) that water erosion can be seen around the base of the Sphinx, and as the Nile has not been near the Sphinx or Pyramids in recorded history, this erosion must have been caused around the time of the Great Flood, the latest estimates of which occurred well before the Great Pyramid was supposedly built. The two authors I mentioned above, I think have uncovered much non-conformist info on this, and other ancient civilisations, they are Graham Hancock, and Robert Bauval, Google as always.

By far the most interesting of the Pharaohs to me is Akhenaten, and his wife, Nefertiti, as there were several major departures from the norm, in terms of religion, depiction of form and status of women, compared to any other of the Pharaohs.

First, after becoming Pharaoh, he abolished the multi-god pantheon and replaced it with just the one God – Ra or Aten, the sun god – why is a mystery, but there is something very strange in the way he, his wife, Nefertiti, and they're are portrayed, with very large, conical heads, long thin neck, sunken chest, skinny limbs, pot bellies, not at all flattering, unlike all the rest of Egyptian royalty throughout the dynasties. There are hybrid theories, I will not go into here.

His wife, Nefertiti, was given equal status, again unusual, only Hatshepsut, given Regent status for the young Tutmose 111 (who was to become one of the greatest of Egypt's leaders), she also had the status of a pharaoh.

On our riverboat, it was a little like going back in time, with more than a nod towards the 1920s, with a fancy dress party, and the days of Howard Carter.

There was a small jeweller's kiosk, I had a ring made, and Sarah had earrings and matching pendant. The owners of this little kiosk, known to us as "George and Andreas", were grateful enough for our and another couple's custom, that we were taken by them on two unofficial excursions, the first was to an American chain hotel, where we were fed and treated to a belly dancing exhibition (by eastern European girls), and the second, to somewhere in the backstreets (in the middle of the night) of Luxor, at a little crossroads, sat on a street corner, where a little bar served us mint tea, accompanied by hubble-bubble bottles, placed at our feet, (Sarah did not participate) with leads to different flavoured pipes – giving me a ten-second rush on inhalation, the only time I have ever partaken – when in Rome… We eventually were led walking at three-ish in the morning through a maze of narrow backstreets back to the boat.

Chapter 48

The Valley of the Kings were next, full of dead people, hot and dusty, we also stopped at Edfu, a temple of Horus, where afterwards we then boarded a traditional Falucka Nile sail boat, across to a public garden situated on an island, where quite a few white Ibis could be seen.

One of the most impressive excursions was to the Temple of Abu Simbel, unfortunately missed by Sarah, who on that day had a bad case of the runs and could not leave the boat, so I was told to take many photos(which I did) and took the half-hour flight to just north of the Sudan border, next to Lake Nasser and the High Aswan Dam, where brick by numbered brick, the temple was relocated from what was to become the bed of Lake Nasser, to an area next to the lake.

The temple, dedicated to Ramases 11, with its massive statues set at the entrance, has some of the best-preserved hieroglyphic inscriptions plastered all over the vivid red and yellow painted interior walls, along with various animal-headed deities depicted.

A visit we both made was to the cleverly designed Temple of Hatshepsut, dedicated to the Queen of that name. When you stand at the base of the ramp in front, it looks as though it is a two-story building and was designed to look that way, but when you go to the top of the ramp, the second "story" is set way back from the first – impressive design, especially without the use of a theodolite (presumably!). Some German tourists were killed by terrorists, less than a year earlier while visiting this temple, which would explain the large number of armed guards there…

Being on a boat as a tourist in Egypt is like being in an oasis of calm, as whenever you set foot on land, you are besieged by people trying to sell you anything from a soapstone Scarab beetle (which we bought) to camel rides (which we did not). We did go for a ride, on the other side of the Nile on the edge of the desert.

While everyone else in our party elected to ride camels, we chose horses, though I suspect the horses we ended up on would not have been passed as fit for consumption in France and rejected by Steptoe…

Led out to the edge of the narrow-cultivated area, and into semi desert, where we passed two huge statues, 1500 years old, of the Pharaoh Amenhotep, thought wrongly by the Romans to be the Ethiopian King Memnon and so are still called the Colossi of Memnon.

Apart from a little problem when my horse turned up a dead end and could not turn around and I could not find reverse gear, we had little trouble with the horses.

A basic whitewashed village house was our stop for a drink, where the man of the house wanted to debate British politics with me, which at that time was Thatcher's privatisations, while his wife and daughter served us mint tea and flat bread.

The Esna locks near Edfu was a place where, as we were stuck in one place for a while, enterprising locals in small boats, despite being twenty feet or so below us, would throw up t-shirts and table cloths wrapped in plastic bags, shouting up the price and trusting us to put money in the bags if we bought something, we bought a table cloth that all the colour ran out from, the first time it was washed. Apart from the soapstone Scarab, we have a granite sphinx that is our memento of that trip.

Chapter 49

It is surprising what you can get used to, driving thirty odd miles to and from work to Widnes and back became part of my routine. I got used to avoiding every pothole on the M56, though I still managed to get three points on my licence, when one 6.30 on a Saturday morning, the last bit of duel carriage way leading off the Runcorn Bridge, in brilliant sunlight, rounding a bend, there he was, a policeman with a gun camera at the far end, just him and me, no one else around, got me doing a little over the limit, having just come of the motorway, with the road deserted, he knew just where to wait, he was around the bend, in more ways than one…

There was a railway bridge just before the entrance to the Phosphate works in Widnes, and the road dipped quite a bit under this. Some days the dip would fill with rainwater, drained from the surrounding land, enough so that we had to park down the road, unable to get through, the water being too deep. This also meant that the shift workers sometimes got trapped inside the gates, as there were no engineers or maintenance men working at night to set up a drainage pump, which was done in the daytime if it looked as though the water was rising to high enough levels, about two feet to prevent passage out.

Myself and one or two others, who had long distances to commute, were very wary if there was persistent rain in the day, so that we would leave what we were doing, or wait to a break time, if busy, and take our cars to park at the roadside outside, which was a deserted run up to the site.

One morning I got to work to see a car floating in the twenty foot-ish long pond that had appeared overnight under the bridge. There was no one in the car, can't recall whose it was, but this shift man must have got fed up with waiting to get out and tried to speed his way out. There was a small, locked, walking-only gate the management had the key to, just a little along the embankment, but this guy must have thought he could get through with his car. There is a safety barrier at the side just high enough to climb and walk sideways along under the bridge, which is how we got back if we had moved our cars out before it got too deep, or we arrived in the morning to find it not drivable through, and the management had not unlocked the side gate.

Whilst working at this site, those of us in the warehouse team were given the chance to gain NVQs in Warehousing and Storage, which only two of us took up, mostly it just involved management watching and confirming we did the paperwork involved with loading, receiving goods etc. stock rotation, that sort of thing, as well as using the fork trucks correctly. This minor qualification, added to my online CVs, may have helped in my next work placement.

After the change of ownership, certain managers had let it be known that they were weary of the secretive new owners, and that we might be being used to offset tax, that sort of thing. So I did the NVQ which we were allowed to work on during slack periods, as a possible help in securing future employment, as it complemented my City and Guilds in Process Plant Operation, which had helped me get the robot packing plant work here. There were also rumours that the new bridge being planned, would go across the Mersey so close to us, as to force closure, though to me the takeover that had just happened would not have occurred as the new owners would have assurance this would not happen. Where I work (part time) now in 2018, I have now and then occasion to cross the new bridge, and it does run very close to my former workplace.

Chapter 50

Adding to the thread that may have caused some losses, but hopefully not too many, to the readership of this narrative, as I have always tried only to inform, not persuade people of the veracity or otherwise of this particular subject matter, mainly as I am not an unconditional believer in the origins of some of the information available, only that there is a vast wealth of it, some of it more than just testimony, highly valid as some may be, such as pilots who risk careers for speaking out for no gain, but this is often backed up by radar confirmation, though some recordings has been known to have been confiscated.

It is in this vein that I would like to highlight the existence of a group, or organisation, calling itself "The Disclosure Project" (Google), led by a Dr Steven Greer, well connected to a lot of highly placed military and political "witnesses" to the existence of a vast "black budget" funded, secret parallel space programme, far more advanced than the NASA rockets that are in the public domain, that people like Gary Mckinnon may have gained glimpses of, when hacking into Pentagon and NASA computers.

This Disclosure Projects stated aim is what it says on the tin – to get governments, in particular the US, to reveal what it knows of advanced, partly alien tech, Gravity Amplifier Propulsion and so-called Zero Point Energy, that would free us of much government dependency and control, *good luck with that.* I have not got involved with them. Of periodic returning interest, when I learn something new. But I feel that as I am adding this subject as part of my life and times, and this subject is the reason I am giving relatives and myself other names, so as not to invite casual trolls.

I realise the enormity of what I am asking people who are able to live their lives without any of this subject ever needing to be a credible part of their knowledge base or world view, indeed the more successful and busy life you lead, the less likely you are to see any reason for the world not to be entirely as presented, unless you have experienced a reason to think otherwise.

It is too easy to point at people whose lives are so boring, they just want to believe anything put out there to see, just to relive the boredom. Some of these people muddy the waters with claims, to the point that anything that might be real, is dismissed along with the rubbish, by those who have a lot more to lose if caught looking, much less speaking out. This is very useful to those wishing to keep a lid on any genuine non-conformist info.

I feel obliged to add this pressure group to my list of people worth a look into for those of you still reading this, as they have a large database on the subject, and if only mildly curious and maybe a little amused, the Disclosure Project is worth a look. They came to prominence in the 90s and are still around as I write this. Some of their claims such as "Contact Protocols" stretch credibility, though their high-ranking political and military witness base makes them worth a look, if from a distance.

I have no association with them or any UFO-related group such as MUFON, as I have not enough conviction, only disquiet, that the easily visible world history, which may go back much further than we are allowed to see. The news presented to us daily, does not quite add up to everything even a little digging seems to reveal, without being gullible enough to believe all that is available to read, as hoaxes and disinformation come with the territory, along with "fake news" as with all the genuine misidentification of more mundane objects and weather events.

On a slight but related tangent, there is a place called Puma Punku in Bolivia that is sighted close to the Tiahuanaco temple complex.

But Pumu Punku, (Google), is a site unlike any temple complex, with massive precision cut H blocks, made to interlock but scattered apart by some unknown catastrophic event, some of these blocks are well over a hundred tonnes, but unlike all other megalithic temple sites, this place is almost unadorned by decoration, it looks like something built for an unknown working function, with very sophisticated precision tools, not in veneration of anything, and the locals say the nearby Tiahuanaco complex, that *is* adorned with carvings of "gods" and other art, was built to worship whoever built Pumu Punku.

This place is far more interesting the many temple complexes around the world, as it hints of a world history we are not meant to look too closely at.

Way over the other side of the world, in Turkey, at a place named Gobekl Tepi, a site is in the process of being unearthed, (literally, as it has been deliberately backfilled), by orthodox archaeologists, that has been reliably dated to around 10,000 BC, with some centre stones weighing up to 60 tonnes, and is extensive enough to be called a temple complex, with entire layers buried beneath each level, with stylised human and animal figure's depicted, at a time when there were supposed to be nothing more than stone and bone tools in use.

So our known (orthodox) history is being pushed back further than previously thought, and how the amount of material has been moved, cut and then backfilled, for some reason, is a mystery, it is a temple that looks as though it has been deliberately backfilled soon after all that effort to erect it, as the earth used to surround the stones is, according to archaeologists, contemporary with the stones buried, to preserve it or hide it for the future people to find.

Places like this and Pumu Punku, which was never a temple, are what make me and many others, far more qualified to judge, wonder just how much we really know, or are allowed to know, of our origins. And if our ancient past is not as we are meant to believe it was, then is it such a stretch to consider our present is not quite all as it seems.

Chapter 51

Back to the living of my life, and as you may have gathered by now, my decision not to have children and risk any repeat of my childhood for a mini me (not always a choice for some) has enabled the compensation (I tell myself) of me and Sarah having the variety and frequency of travel far more than someone of my station would normally expect to, not being confined to expensive rip-off school holiday times only, (apart from when Sarah was working on school meals) or child friendly only venues and so.

France is a country we have visited a few times, I have already described the static caravan holiday in Cavalaire on the South Coast in our early days together, so, unable to separate our subsequent trips there, only to say that apart from a recent trip that included Sarah's daughter and her son, mentioned later, our other three trips were all car crossings, in the late 90s or early 2000s, neither of us can pin the exact years, so I will try with Sarah's help, as always to recall some of the highlights.

Starting with the earlier of these three trips, we had pre-booked a series of one or two-day stops through a travel company, our destination being the Dordogne region in the south west.

But as we had a drive from near Manchester, to Dover and a ferry crossing, our first overnight stop was in Clecy in the Calvados, region of Normandy. I would like to have seen Caen, with its stunning Abbaye Aux Hommes, but we had to find our pre-booked accommodation for that night in Clecy. Interested in history as I am, I know that town, which we bypassed, was held by the Germans for some time after the D-Day landings, where the British and Canadians had, with an ever-cautious Montgomery, a hard fight to take, the Americans landing further west, where resistance was not as hard, after the landing fights, but able to have a moan about our progress, as I understand it.

A pleasant Auberge, in a square, and a Calvados brandy-soaked apple desert with our meal is all either of us recall of Clecy.

Having no written record of this trip I can only say that we decided, looking at our French map, that we thought that we could follow the D and N roads all the way down to our destination, and that picking in advance the towns and villages we wanted to go through, or close to, was the way to navigate in France, without using their Toll Motorway, and so it proved, as long as you stuck to one golden rule of navigating the French roads, as road numbers are not advertised on the signs, you looked at the "*toute* direction", or through routes signs, as they give a list of the towns on that route, so if your pre-picked your next town, and was on that signpost list, that was the way to go, the actual road no appeared a little down the road you had selected in a little six-inch square sign.

We successfully followed the gloriously straight Roman and then Napoleonic paved over roads, around Tours and Poitiers, on the E5, then the N10 all the way down to Angouleme, passing mile after mile of sunflower fields, on their almost empty summer roads, as this was a year Sarah was working at a school. I had a Daewoo Nexia at that time, which had the blessing of air conditioning, as it was scorching hot, even at sixty odd mph, which you could do for large stretches of the straight roads, where you could see little towns and villages rising like islands in the distance in a sea of sunflowers.

Often these small towns were almost medieval in their antiquity, built on rocky ramparts, or just full of impressive old buildings, we stopped in a Tabac for a Croque Monsieur, a handy French staple of the Tabac snack, no idea now which town, but it kept us going. Angouleme, on the Charente River, was our overnight stop, just north of the Dordogne region, the hotel was of the old, faded elegance variety, a river walk, and evening meal ended that day’s travel. We then stayed near a town called Les Eyzies, in a charming Auberge, in a ground floor room leading out into a well-planted garden with swimming pool, which as it was still scorching weather, we could not wait to use.

Sarah, thought it quite funny that I had Linguee, which turned out to be fried chicken gizzard, which tastes better than it sounds.

The town of Sarlet is as pretty as advertised with its narrow medieval streets and restored Chateax.

A trip on the Dordogne River, with its limestone cliffs and the caves with stone age art, was due a revamp… the Lascaux Cave, the first to be discovered, is closed to tourists, except Banksy, but we were shown a lesser-known cave with images of aurochs and other animals highlighted.

The return route took us to the Loire Valley, Saumer, on the Loire, was our next stop, with its large château, with the characteristic conical towers, so prevalent in France, set on a hill back from the river almost directly behind our river front hotel, and lit up at night, it looked good, it was once an army barracks and then used as a prison by Napoleon, it is now an art museum.

I managed to find a man with a boat who gave us a tour, showing us the large rodents, Coypu, not native but introduced, that were eroding the riverbank with large, deep-tunnelled burrows.

Chapter 52

As we cannot recall much of interest on our return journey I will recount our other places of interest on subsequent trips, the nearest of which was La Rochelle, with its twin round towers, harbour, large aquarium, and electric-assisted bikes for hire, and lively, nice waterfront.

On the Ile de Re, further north, we decided to hire some bikes for some exercise and fresh air, it was flat country, and good weather – at the start, what happened next has put Sarah off bike riding for life.

When we had ridden about half an hour, when the heavens opened, with a deluge we have only seen equalled in the far east, it did not let up, we were drenched, could barely see in front of us it was that heavy, Sarah said she was crying, but no one could see it. Never persuaded her to ride a bike since.

Further north, the town of Saint Nazaire was of interest to me for its still intact German U Boat pens, great concrete structures, one of which had, when we were there, a 1950's French submarine, accessible for tourists, to give an idea of the narrow confines of the submarines of that period.

We visited there whilst staying in a quaint thatched cottage called La Chaumarie in the French equivalent of the English Fens, called La Briere, a national park area, situated just inland of south east Brittany. The whole network of canals there is overrun with Coypu, we went to a lake where whole families could be seen swimming – of Coypu, that is. Charming as they are, they, as in the Loire, are eroding the banks with their large burrows. They are known in France as Ragondin and are treated as pests, though introduced for their fur at some point, from South America.

Within a day's return driving of our little thatched cottage to the east, we visited the Cote Savauge at the south-eastern edge of Brittany, which is situated I think on the Quiberon Peninsular. it must have been good weather, and the sea reasonably warm, as on the causeway leading on to the peninsular, we saw people picking what turned out to be oysters from the seaweed covered rocks on the beach – we joined in, don't know what we used as a container, but we brought an awful lot of them back to our thatched cottage in La Briere.

Over the next two or three days, we boiled them open, having no oyster knives or anything close, we had them on top of pizza, in omelette, fried, until we could eat no more that week, all sat in front of great log fires, that we built and fed from the large supply stacked against the outside wall – very cosy.

Not far from Quiberon is Carnac, we went to have a look at where literally thousands of megalithic standing stones look as if they are marching down in long lines into the sea, as though when these were placed, sea level must have been lower than now. It must have taken a staggering amount of effort to erect so many of these stones, for some reason. We cannot begin to guess at the motivation for this, history again keeps its secrets here, at least from the public domain.

A few miles north east of Carnac is Auray, a pretty town situated at the top end of the Gulf of Morbihan, we had Moules-Frites at lunchtime and decided it was so pretty there, we would come back for our evening meal on the waterfront, in the Saint Goustan quarter, where the Auray River runs into the gulf. Having a smart phone now with maps is very useful, as without which the exact locations would have had no chance of being recalled accurately.

The meal in a very picturesque harbour area is memorable – as some of it was still alive, on the massive, iced seafood platter salad presented to us. My memory may be playing tricks with me as the Escargot in my mind were crawling across the iceberg lettuce, and the part where the snails shrank back into their shells to avoid the winkling hooks we were given to get them out, is not my imagination, they were that fresh! They must have tasted OK, as we did eat them.

On our way back from this holiday, we stopped first at Mont Saint Michel, the Breton, big brother to our own St Michel Mount in Cornwall. As the Cornish and Breton people share a history, I can only assume that our, much smaller version must be a later imitation, Eiffel and Blackpool towers being an apt comparison in my eyes! If they built three Eiffel, it would not be a trifle…

The first thing that caught my eye at Mont Saint Michel was the glint of the golden spire that I seem to recall as having a crescent glinting in the sun on top, though now there is a saints statue up there now. Looking at a phone image now, it was his arms raised that I thought looked like a golden crescent…

When we went, you could park on the sandbar, on the tidal causeway, just short of the Mount, which we did as the tide was out. These days, I understand you have to park on the mainland.

It being a hot day, we never made it to the church at the top, built in 708AD at the request of St Michel who appeared to the Bishop of nearby Avranches, (so he says), mmm, convenient, instead we looked at the endless souvenir shops on the very busy circular walk route up. What Samurai swords, which I recall seeing for sale there, had to do with the Mount, I will never know. A drink up there will have been imbibed, though I don't remember it.

Later, on our way up to the Cherbourg ferry, we had time to visit Arromanches, one of the landing beaches on D Day, and also the nearby Bayeux Tapestry, which we saw mounted in a glass U-shaped case, listening to some translated "Norman Wisdom" (sorry) as we walked around it, we saw it turned out to have been an arrowing experience for Harold and his army being too hasty to battle – groan now. We have visited the south of France more recently and have another trip planned, these will be mentioned later.

Chapter 53

A combination of factors came about that made us decide to downsize from our three-bedroom house in Hyde, the main reason being fairly sure redundancy was imminently to be announced for my job in Widnes, then things like the need for a new heating system, still working, but iffy, keeping the grass in the steep back garden cut in the days before I successfully got on Allpurinol, for the rest of my life, freeing me from periodic gout attacks, making lawn mowing less daunting.

The search was on for a smaller house, which with the sale of our current house, would clear the mortgage and hopefully leave us with money left over.

We settled on a two up, two down terrace near Houghton Dale, which divided the Houghton Green end of Denton from Hyde, we told ourselves that being close to the dale for walks would make up for the lack of a proper back garden, instead having a small backyard, overlooking some allotments, one of which we, or rather Sarah, were to acquire the use of, Sarah, having in the past grown veg, in a previous life…

The biggest regret leaving the Gee Cross, Hyde house, was having to leave my Koi and other fish to the new owners, but the son of the buyer, seemed interested, and after showing him the pump and filter system and feeding regime and telling him that the next-door neighbour, John, would help if he had any problems, he never got back to us, so hopefully they are OK.

Transferring an aquarium with live fish from one house to another successfully is quite an operation, as anyone reading this who has done it will testify. I may have had to leave my pond behind, but not my tropical fish, this meant transferring a large quantity of tank water into other containers, though not all could be saved, as the three-foot tank held about thirty-five gallons, but you needed a reasonable amount of tank water to put back in so the fish would not be too shocked and stressed by too much tap water being added at once.

We were fortunate in that Elisabeth, the woman we were buying the terraced house from and whom had already moved out, was happy for me to transfer the tank the day before the official move date, (the estate agent being kept in the dark to avoid any problems) with about six inches of water and all the fish in it, into a small corridor to a downstairs loo at the back of the house, (that we were subsequently to extend into a small conservatory the width of the kitchen). The saved tank water slowly added back and topped up in stages with about 1/3 tap water, which the heater brought back up to twenty-five degrees. I lost no fish, thanks to our vendor, with whom we had already established a good relationship, buying a bookcase we still have with us now as well as one or two other things that were not wanted for her move.

If you have ever downsized, you will know that the weeks leading up to moving is consumed with making hard decisions about what is coming with you into a smaller space, and what is to be given away or taken to the tip.

As the house we were moving from had an attached garage and a loft, and the terrace had neither, there was lots, from an old VHS recorder/player and tapes, to the old Van Gough original in the attic, if only!

Not knowing at the time that a conservatory would be possible in the new place, we left the wicker chairs for the new owners, along with a dining table and chairs we would not have room for in a terrace.

Having a garage with all sorts of oddments and leftovers from garden improvements, and with there being a workbench, complete with mounted vice, I had a lot of clearing out to do from there, as, if there was space, I did not throw anything out if I could think of any conceivable reason to keep something I was no longer using – was my general rule until this move, when old rolls of carpet and everything else under the sun seemed to be going to the tip, surprising what you can fit in the back of a Fiat Panda 4 x 4 I had bought (after not being able to get up the hill to the main road the one year we had bad snow, having to park at the back of a petrol station at the top for near three weeks).

The terraced house we had moved to was in the middle of a row, that at the bottom end, had the road run downhill into the Tame Valley that separated Denton from Hyde and was a nice walk around on a sunny Sunday morning.

We had fitted wardrobes put in our bedroom, and then the corridor running down the right side of the backyard leading to a downstairs loo, extended out to the left, to make a small conservatory, just big enough for two chairs and a small coffee table.

This all happened within a few months of moving in. We should have waited a bit, as it gradually became clear, that a few near neighbours were not the most amiable, one next-door occupant seemingly alcoholic, licking his wounds from a split, getting occasional visits from an ex, with kids in tow. Another guy next one down was full of himself, doing a lot of bossing about of his partner, that we could hear in his backyard, with the inevitable noisy dog left out to bark.

The lady on the other side was OK, but it was clear she was living hand to mouth, which made me feel a little guilty, spending money on the conservatory and bedroom, going on expensive holidays, whilst she was struggling along. It dawned on us that we would never be comfortable there long term…

Chapter 54

Not quite sure when we did this, sometime late 90s, but in summary (won't have been winter), we did our version of Billy Connolly's televised *World Tour of Scotland*, by that, I mean we went up the West Coast, turned east across the top, and down the east side, roughly speaking. As we have made several trips to Scotland, I will do the same as with France and incorporate as many recalled highlights as I can from other visits as I recount this trip.

After crossing into Scotland near the Ayrshire Coast in our aged BMW 316, we turned south west near Annan, onto the river estuary, as we wanted to start our trip with a little barbecue, having bought with us a one time – tin foil kit and a couple of burgers and barms, along with a flask of coffee. It was a nice sunny day, and a bit of fresh air, after the M6, was just what we needed.

Passing Loch Lomond, with a quick coffee stop at Luss, to admire the island filled southern end of the loch, before continuing up the A82 as far as Tarbet, where a turn left took us to Arrochar, at the top of Loch long, where we found our first B&B this trip, for the night.

I managed to hire a little motor boat the next day, with my little telescopic rod and a few spinners, we were advised to head for the confluence with Loch Goil, where a mix of currents stirred up food for the fish, sound advice I heard, as while Sarah kept the boat moving, I caught a couple of mackerel at this confluence, we gave the fish to the boat owner, who looked a little surprised we had caught anything.

I had found a phone number of a guy on Mull who did whale watching trips, but when he answered, he was on his boat – in Norway (hopefully not whaling…), so that was out. We found someone who did wildlife safari's on Mull, so headed for Oban (for the ferry) a nice-looking town with its Mcaig's Tower, a Victorian folly/nod to Rome's Colosseum, built on Battery Hill to light up the town… Staying nearby, we walked to the harbour, where we, and others booked with the same outfit, were met with a mini-bus, that boarded the ferry with us for our Wildlife Safari, which a little to our surprise, lived up to its billing.

After landing, the first thing I recall on our trip across to the west of the Mull was the funniest dog I have ever seen, as it was very cleverly made of Wellington boots, inserted together, must have been on a wire frame, strange animals here at the side of the road. Taken to a remote location on the West Coast, where we were treated to the sight of a mother sea otter and two young on the seaweeded rocks, within good binocular range, the mother periodically diving for food for her young.

After this rare treat, we were given a packed lunch each, before heading off to our second location – opposite cliffs, where a pair of white-tailed sea eagles had a nest atop the cliff. These eagles were extinct in Britain, but have been reintroduced from Norway, in selected remote areas of Scotland.

Again we were lucky, seeing these massive, deep-winged birds, larger than golden eagles, soaring on the thermals near the cliffs, I think then there were only about six pairs reintroduced in the whole country, though now there are about ten pair on Mull alone. Somewhere further up the coast, we were shown a pair of golden eagles, further away from us than the Fish Eagles but close enough to see where the name comes from.

Our trip went around the top of the island, where we had a coffee in the colourful main town of Tobermory, before catching our ferry, past the magnificent Duat Castle, just out from Craignure, on our way back to Oban. The Mull visit was later than our "World Tour of Scotland", but I am recounting as best I can recall highlights from south to north, so, digressing to our actual "world tour", Callander, on the A84s was one of our overnight stops. A short walk down from the road is the River Teith, where Sarah was bitten by a horsefly while we stretched our legs, having been bitten myself years earlier, on South Uist, I know it is painful. There was, and may still be a Chinese restaurant next to the river there, Sarah tells me we ate upstairs, overlooking it.

Heading north and west, the next day, past Crainlarich, which in earlier times was a stopover on the way to the Hebrides recounted earlier, we turned up the A82 on our way to the Isle of Sky, past Tyndrum, and up through Glen Coe, which in September, when we passed through, was breath-taking in the morning mist, as those who have been there will know is a wide, long valley, with gradually rising hills, a half mile or so away on each side of the road.

Having decided that there would be no problem finding B&Bs on the hoof, it made us inclined to find somewhere by mid-afternoon, we could then explore the locale, knowing we had a bed for the night.

As our next intention was to explore as much of the Isle of Sky as possible in one day, I intended to find our overnight stay in the vicinity of the ferry crossing (as it was then) at the Kyle of Lochalsh, but first, having been this way before, I wanted to show Sarah the stunningly sighted Eilean Donan Castle, set on a spit of land at the neck of Loch Alsh. Used in many brochures, it is one of the most picturesque sights in Scotland. The castle itself is not that large or impressive, it is all about the location, set as it is – jutting out on a spit of land into the loch.

Chapter 55

Just north of the ferry terminal, are one or two small villages, though I confess to not knowing which one we stayed at, but I know it was only a short drive back down to the ferry the next morning.

As mentioned, we must have found our B&B early enough in the afternoon, as was our wont, that we drove up to Plockton, the setting for the TV series *Hamish Macbeth*, with Robert Carlyle, for which the village is renamed Lochdubh, it also featured in *The Wicker Man*, and *The Inspector Alleyn Mysteries* series. Set on the shores of Loch Carron, you could see why it attracted the attention of TV producers, the epitome of a pretty Scottish coastal village.

SKYE The Isle of Sky is a large island, so the idea was to stay overnight as close to the ferry as possible, so as to spend a full day exploring, returning to the same B&B that evening. When we crossed, it was still the chain link ferry, the toll bridge was not yet built, we got there fairly early, crossed in about half an hour, and headed west.

I knew that Ian Anderson, front man of Jethro Tull, in for me, one of the best groups of the Prog/folk rock genre, with their totally unique, musically rich sound), had bought an estate on sky, SKYE I knew not where, only that he had a salmon farming business there.

Had Google been available back in the 90s when we were there, I might have headed south to Strathaird, his estate on the peninsular of that name, if not to knock on his door for a cup of tea, then at least to find Dun Ringill, the iron age fort that is the title of a short but very atmospheric acoustic guitar track, sung by the above-mentioned genius.

So as I said, we headed west around the forested Cuillin Hills to our first stop of the day, which was the Talisker Distillery, though not to buy any of that very smoky tasting whisky, as I knew it to be, as Sarah's dad used to like the stuff, but just as a place of interest. It was only a short turn off from the main coastal road that led up to Dunvegan Castle, the seat of the Macleod Clan since the 13th century, being the longest continuously inhabited castle in Scotland, set on the shore of its own named Loch, the castle has pretty gardens, and Dunvegen village close by.

Tea and scones was taken there, but we soon moved on as Sarah and I wanted to reach as far north as Uig, where I (apart from the first trip) used to get the ferry to the Outer Hebrides with Kevin and Co. Uig is a small village, but with the benefit of a sheltered deep bay, where the Caledonian MacBrayne Ferry can dock against the large pier, where a basic restaurant is situated, being early afternoon

I think we had fish and chips there. Then it was back down the same road, as going right around the top of Sky would have made us late for the ferry back.

Portree was our last stop on Sky, tea or coffee imbibed in the "capital" of the island, a pretty coastal village not as large as Tobermory on Mull, but similar, different coloured houses creating a pleasant picturesque sight set on its own sea Loch of the same name.

Sarah tells me we had to wait a while to cross back to the mainland, as the sea was too rough, so we likely had a cuppa in Kyleakin, but we did get across that evening and back to our B&B. From there the next day we headed up along the A 890, as there was no coast road, turning west to Gairloch as we wanted to stay as far west as the roads would allow whilst heading north.

Sarah recalls seeing a lot of jellyfish there, I remember the beach, but nothing else. Ullapool was our destination that evening, it was raining and windy when we arrived, the sea having white caps on the waves. Quite a contrast to 2017, when I took Sarah across to Stornoway from there, it was nice and sunny on that visit, to be elaborated on later. I seem to recall seeing and being told that quite a few Russian deep-sea trawlers used Ullapool on their way around to and from arctic ports. We stayed in a bungalow B&B that trip.

After looking at the map that night, we decided that faithfully following the map north along the West Coast would cost us too much travelling time, so the next morning, after heading north, we cut out the far northwest corner, when we reached Ledmore Junction, took the right turn across country, following the River Oykel east on the A837, taking the north western turn at Rosehall to Lairg, where we turned north through the tundra like landscape typical of the far north eventually reaching the north coast in Caithness at the Kyle of Tongue, so cutting the far north west out of our route. By this time, our old BMW318 had developed a blowhole in the exhaust manifold, not serious – yet, but fortune was to smile on us in the most unexpected of places. Following the A836 east along the north coast we reached Scrabster, just short of Thurso.

At the tourist information there, we found what turned out to be a very special B&B, also booking a ferry/coach-day excursion to the Orkney Island Mainland, for the day after tomorrow.

Chapter 56

That done, after food and drink, we pressed on, past our turn off to our B&B as it was not much further to John O'Groats, which turned out to have a hotel, car park with a signpost for Land's End – 874 miles, or New York – 3100 miles, and a pointer to the Orkney and Shetland Isles. There is a village full of tourist shops nearby, but having reached the iconic northern tip of mainland Britain, after a hot drink, we retraced our steps back as far as the turning for our B&B, which turned out to be no more than a quarter mile from the Castle of Mey! Hidden from the main road by trees, the castle is facing the sea a little elevated from sea level, and walkable from our accommodation, our high spec B&B, the same distance in from the coast. The owners were a nice, retired couple from the English midlands.

I will not forget the huge rosewood-dining (in our case breakfast) table, complete with silverware and China everywhere, there was also a silver lining to our stay there, as I alluded to earlier. The man of the house had a workshop equipped with a lifting car ramp, from where he fixed our blowing exhaust manifold.

While he was doing that, we went for a walk down the lane towards the coast, the further you went down to the coast – the more you could see the Castle, where it turned out, the Queen Mother was in residence, who we could see stood with her entourage just in front of the castle, smaller than the suits, but standing out in a pale blue coat and hat, she was there to witness what we found out later was a substitute fireworks display launched from a Coastguard vessel, in place of the then still in service Royal Yacht Britannia, that used to fire a signal rocket when reaching the castle with the Queen aboard, to which the castle would reply with a rocket of its own.

This substitute display was put on for the QM, who was always at her northern retreat at this time of year, due to Britannia, along with the Queen and Duke, being in Canada this year when the above-mentioned tradition normally took place.

There was a turn off lane that led towards the royal castle, so we started along it – to see how far we would get. Not very far, two plain clothed guards at a guess, soon set off from the Royal party, towards us, so we about turned, back towards our B&B, we were not to be part of the Royal tradition it seemed.

A meal at the Castle Arms Hotel on the main coast road was that evening's night out.

Next morning, our trip over to Orkney booked for that day, after breakfasting in the poshest of breakfast/dining room, followed by a binocular viewing of a resident feral Cat family, complete with kittens, living in the shelter of the stonewall at the bottom of the garden, we set of back to Scrabster for our excursion across to Orkney.

Skara brae, is a Neolithic settlement on the west coast of Mainland, the main island of Orkney, not far north of Stromness where we disembarked, and was our first stop, still in the process of excavation when we visited, it is situated just up from a beach, dug into the ground, you could see the bed alcoves dug into the walls, and the stone hearth cooking area, it must have been a tough place to live, still is.

That day was a sunny one, and we had time for a stroll on the beach before moving on to our next stop – the Ring of Brodgar, the Neolithic stone circle that we had seen Billy Connolly dance around naked on his *World Tour of Scotland*. We kept our clothes on…

It is a large circle of standing stones, no Capstones like Stonehenge, the stones set too far apart for that, but impressive enough to make you wonder at the motivation of its builders. A stop off in Kirkwall, the capital, where a walk down the high street provided food and drink, along with souvenirs for those wishing them. If we bought any, they are long gone now. Returning to the mainland, from mainland (Orkney) that afternoon, we headed back for our last night at the Castle of Mey's next-door neighbours, the breakfast room next morning being our royal treat.

From then on it all went south, our route that is, with our royal next-door neighbours very kindly having wielded the offending manifold blowhole shut, our next stop having passed through Wick, which caught our interest was what is now called North Lands creative Glass, near Lybster, about ten miles south of Wick, just short of the A9. After watching glass ornaments being blown, Sarah bought a perfume spray bottle and tray there, which she still uses.

Continuing down the A9, our next stop, was where I inquired about work, as one of the Sixteen Men of Tain (now 24) at the Glenmorangie Distillery, located on the south side of the Dornoch Firth. There were no vacancies, but as it is my tipple of choice, I had to try…

The distillation process is not labour intensive, the stills there being the tallest in Scotland, fed from the nearby Tarlogie Springs, but the maturing of the original 10-year, 12, 18, and 25-year-old Malts is what takes the looking after. The casks are grown in their own forest, located handily nearby – in the Ozark Mountains of Missouri, where Jack Daniel's bourbon is matured in them first for the Original 10 years range for four years, sherry and wine being used for the special blends, which for me loses the unique taste I treasure.

I ration myself to make a one-litre bottle last about two months, Sarah only occasionally partaking. Not being cheap, it is bought when it is on offer. Given the many years of maturation, the warehouse space needed for product turn-around is vast, the air quality in these single-story warehouses is also thought to affect the finished product – works for me!

Chapter 57

From Tain, it was down the A9, across Cromarty Firth and the Black Isle, then the Moray Firth to Inverness. At this point I now digress to an earlier visit, where we boarded a hire boat at Inverness, at the top end of the Caledonian Canal and the Great Glen, as it is known.

Loch Ness, Loch Oich, and Loch Lochy were all linked together, to form a continuous passage from northeast to southwest, down the geological split known as the above-mentioned Great Glen. Designed by Tomas Telford, (busy guy) and completed in 1822, as a safer alternate route to Cape Wrath and the Pentland Firth for the wooden ships of the day, it also provided much needed employment in a Scotland barely recovering from the clearances. Google for more detailed history, as I now continue with ours.

Having been on the Norfolk Broads in the past, skipped in this narrative, the Caledonian Canal and the Broads have just one important thing in common – next to no locks, (Fort Augustus only) these two being the only major constructed waterways without such in the UK. With just two of us to manually open and close countless loch gates, that is not our idea of relaxation, and so the Great Glen, with its one manned set at Fort August, was our remaining boat trip of choice in the UK. If I am still writing this by May 2018, a planned trip on the Canal Du Midi in France, again with only manned Lochs, (remember I said that…) will be recounted later.

For now, Loch Ness beckoned, 23 miles long, holding more water than the whole of England and Wales combined, and the nearest I have come to piloting a boat at sea, at around a mile wide in places.

When the wind gets up there, you are ploughing through serious waves at times for a boat of less than 30ft. For a loch this long there are very few stopping places, including the River Ness, where you start, it is about ten miles to where everyone must stop on their first night, that being Drumnadrochit.

After the first couple of miles, when you realise that not every line of distant waves is the back of the Monster, you start to appreciate the somewhat bleak scenery, the east side being the starker of the sides.

As on all these boat holidays, you are given a detailed map of you route, so we knew to look out for the somewhat ruined Urquhart Castle just past the inlet on the west side, Drumnadrochit set in the lee of the inlet. There, a "Nessie" exhibition centre, with a grey painted Concrete Nessie is set in a little pond. Alleged sightings are recounted, along with the known hoaxes.

I err on the sceptic side of this, as Adrian Shine, the long-time Nessie hunter has given up, after mounting large-scale Sonar surveys over the years, though I do recall seeing an interesting picture of what was supposed to be a Plesiosaur fin on one of the documentaries on the subject, the general consensus is that there are not enough fish in the loch to support a creature that size, should it have survived this long, the same legends also abound in such places as Lake Champlain on the US Canadian border. We ate at the Drumnadrochit Hotel that night, the only place in town.

Next morning, after a wander around the ruins of Urquhart Castle across the inlet, a place of disputed clan ownership, dismantled at one point to deny the Jacobite's its use, it was never to be rebuilt.

Casting off, Fore and Aft, we set of down the loch, into a rough bit of weather, after a few miles, against advice not to, if it was rough – we headed for foyers, on the other side of the loch, where Sarah nearly went in as she tried to climb onto the rickety old pier there. She slipped, and I could not leave the wheel to help her as I had to keep the boat lined up with the pier.

Sarah managed to recover and gain the pier, but not before first trapping her leg between the cruiser and the pier. She had seriously bruised her leg it emerged, turning her thigh black and blue for a while, with hindsight we should have kept going for Fort Augustus, heeding the warning not to try for Foyers if rough, I take the blame for this. We did manage to eat at Foyers Cafe, Sarah's leg not stiffening to a painful limp until the next day.

At some stage on Loch Ness, I tried some spinning with the telescopic rod I had with me, letting most of the line on my reel out at times, Sandra keeping the boat heading slowly south, but with the water being very peaty, the visibility of my spinner, would be very limited, to what is a sparse fish population, so I was not too surprised to get no bites.

That evening Fort Augustus at the southern end of the loch was our overnight stop, the monster having kept out of sight…

We had fish and chips there. I recall it being a nice sunny evening, as the midges made an appearance while we sat eating our food, admiring the view, we had a drink at a local inn later, naturally.

After breakfast the next morning, the locks through to Laggan Avenue were to be navigated, Sarah having to pull the boat to a mooring spot on the first of the five, 180ft locks, the mooring line being let up or down, depending on the lock being filled or drained, to keep us stable while the lock filled or drained (as on the way back).

Laggan Avenue at the other end of the locks, is the canal that joins Loch Ness to Loch Oich.

The thing I remember most about Laggan Avenue is the flowering yellow Gorse along the banks, masses of it along its four miles or so, where trees did not line the banks, then through the lock gate to Loch Oich. Compared to Ness, or even Loch Lochy, Loch Oich is a small narrow loch, about the same length as Laggan Avenue.

Chapter 58

At Invergarry, halfway down the loch, is the ruined castle of the same name, we stopped there to have a wander around and stretch our legs, before continuing through the lock gate at the bottom, through to loch Lochy. This loch being about 10 miles long, less than half the size of loch Ness, but still impressive, from here you can see Ben Nevis amongst the other peaks off to the south, to the west of Fort William, our ultimate destination.

Before that, about two thirds down the loch on its east side is the Great Glen Water Park at Kinlochlochy, near Spean Bridge, where Scandinavian-style wooden lodges are available for hire, set back from the loch. Moored here for the night, the only thing we recall from there is ending up at a traditional Scottish Ceilidh, encouraged to join in one or two reels after we had a drink or two.

The last day of heading south west took us to the lower end of Loch Lochy, which runs to the river of the same name, from which the lower section of the Caledonian Canal (The Great Glen Way) draws its water. We passed Gairlochy the village just in from the start of this lower section.

This last section is about six miles long before you reach the top of Neptune's Staircase, and our turnaround point. Eight locks down the Staircase to Loch Linnhe and the sea, for those vessels heading that way, and we did have one or two larger boats pass us on our way down the Great Glen capable of that. For us, mooring up at Lochaber at the top end of the staircase was a chance for a shower at the canal side public shower block the next morning.

First, as the run from Kinlochlochy down the last three or so miles to the Great Glen Way and Neptune's Staircase was no more than ten miles in total, we must have arrived there around lunchtime. Walking alongside the locks took us down to the Caol end of Fort William, where after a wander around we had lunch, not sure where (so long ago). I, being still able to climb a hill, after eating in those days…

That evening, crossing the top gate of the staircase, we walked alongside a park to a nice inn we no longer recall the name of, but it was recommended to us by someone at Fort Augustus. After a most welcome shower at the above-mentioned public block in the morning, we started our journey back to Inverness, sixty miles to the northeast and three days away.

Nothing of interest comes to mind of the return journey, so we will have stopped at the same places, there not being other choices, so to sum up, apart from Sarah's leg injury whilst mooring at Foyers, it was a good holiday. After this digression back in time to our Caledonian Canal trip, now back to our version of BC's *World Tour of Scotland*, I will resume what we recall of our journey down the east of the country.

From Inverness, we turned east onto the A96, heading through Nairn, intending to travel as far east as we had time for, which only took us as far as Forres before deciding to turn south on the A490 through Grantown-on-Spey, where we crossed that famous river, where many famous brands of malt whisky draw their water from.

Not using the A9 that we had travelled up on our way to Inverness for our boating holiday, from where you pass Aviemore, and can also see the Dalwhinnie Distillery in the distance, that's whisky to me at least, having a dry, almost liquorice like after-taste to it, not something I would buy in preference to Glenmorangie, we must have tried it on our travels one evening up there and liked it enough to buy a bottle – much later at home as I recall.

As I was saying, on this trip, heading now south, we were determined to travel as much as we could through the east, so not the A9, we continued south east on the A839 into the Cairngorms, past Tomintoul, the highest village in Scotland, set in the stunning landscapes of the Glenlivet Estate.

Chapter 59

Somewhere up near there in the Cairngorms, we found a cattle farm for our next B&B, set high on a bare hillside, just the basics, the farmer having a herd of Aberdeen Angus, not surprising as we were not too far west of Aberdeen. The east coast there was just too far away with the time we had left, of the week we booked off work. Having found our overnight stop, we followed the farmers recommendation for a pub meal, which was some distance away through the nearby forest, Sarah recalls having Langoustines, saying it was a nice pub, my memory does not run to that much detail so far back, unless something stood out from that time.

I do recall that for some reason, we got a bit lost on the forest roads, with no other traffic about, and it being very dark so far from any village or town, we must have missed a turning, but found our way back to the farm eventually, though Sarah got a little scared after a while of lost bearings. Poor though my recall is, I would have remembered a rescue party…

Not certain but looking at the map now, it could well have been the Balmoral Forest or close to it, as we ended up on the A93, stopping at Braemar Castle for a break the next day, after passing Balmoral, where we would have called in for tea, had the owners not been in Canada at the time…

Braemar Castle was built for the Earl of Mar, it was burnt in the first Jacobite uprising, later occupied by government troops after Culloden, it is now the only community operated castle in Scotland. Heading now south past the Spittal of Glenshee, and its Ski Centre, on down through Blairgowrie, then Perth.

Only having time for one more overnight stop we stuck to the M90 down from Perth, sorry about this narrative being scant on detail, but unlike West Coast USA, we have no written record of these north of the border trips, so only highlights and routes are recalled. Passing Dunfermline and crossing the Firth of Forth, through Edinburgh, the Granite City, we were looking for somewhere to stop for a break, having made good time on the motorway. In the centre, in sight of the castle, we tried in vain to find somewhere to park, so kept going until back on the coast just east of Musselburgh at a little place called Fisherrow, where we ate a late lunch.

Staying on the coast, North Berwick was our last stop, a small seaside town, where we found a B&B in sight of its beach. After having a walk around, late afternoon, a last meal out was Thai, so Sarah recalls, hot and spicy being more her thing than mine, I would have eaten something more Chinese, no doubt on their menu.

Next day was heading home time, and after a short run down the A1, we turned south west via Selkirk and across country along the A708 down to Moffat and the A74, and the M6, stopping twice for food and drink, a long run, but home (Hyde) that night.

At various times in Scotland, we had visited places like Callander, Blair Athol and Pitlochry on the A9, also stopping somewhere near Aviemore to look at a protected Osprey nest, this road having been travelled a few times by us, but I have tried to generally stick to our Billy Connolly's world tour route, digressing to the Great Glen boat trip when passing Inverness, so as to try for some sort of continuity.

For us little people, work, especially when as in the 2000s, when I spent all of it at one place, having described most of what I can recall of work there, makes it looks like I spent most of it on holiday – if only. Having no kids had some benefits, travelling was one. Work for us Drones is Groundhog Day on steroids, with only limited written interest, once outlined.

As previously mentioned, my health started to deteriorate whilst at the Widnes phosphate site, sitting three quarters of the time on fork trucks is not good for your health, especially your circulation, as increasingly severe bouts of gout were to testify for me.

Indometacin was then the strong anti-inflammatory/painkiller, keeping me going when it struck, able to limp along and make the thirty odd miles commute to work, only once or twice getting bad enough to struggle with the clutch, my left foot being worst affected, though my left elbow, no doubt due to the fast rotation needed for fork truck steering, also suffered now and again, as did my knee to a lesser extent.

It was many more years before I managed the transition to Allopurinol, as it actually gives you gout before it gets into you system, I tried it once and gave up going back to Indometacin for pain relief before making the transition, as I have now, being free for a few years, apart from hints of it if I try eating shellfish.

Chapter 60

After watching a *Place in the Sun* on *Chanel 4* in the early 90s, and as both of us liked Greece, having been to Zakinthos (Zante) and Corfu, having money in the bank, we thought it a good idea to buy a holiday home there…

It is a good idea, but only if you can spend enough time there to justify it, but thinking it a good investment, we went ahead anyway, buying from an English developer at the western end of Crete in 2004, where there is a sizeable British expat population surrounding the former capital, and pretty Venetian developed town of Charnia, with its picturesque harbour area, the town itself being far older than the Venetian Era, and since occupied by the Turks until 1898, with Britain actually meddling to maintain this to so late a date, as it feared Russia might try for a base there, as the Cretans did not want to be part of Greece for many years, Britain, only allowing Crete its freedom when it became part of Greece, this being a very potted history of the island, Search online for much more if interested…

Half an hour's drive east from Chania Airport is the very pretty village of Almirida, with its perfect shallow beach cove and small harbour. A short drive-up steep winding road passed Plaka, where houses first took my interest, then up passed Kokkino Chorio, where the film *Zorba the Greek*, with Antony Quinn was made, and where *A Place in the Sun* featured a gay couple, Brian and Andrew, having a house built, and having a giant window put in for the view over the sea (we used the same developer).

You eventually reach a plateau where a small village called Drapanos is situated, about a ten-minute drive from Almirida and the coast. This is where Cretan Traditional Homes (now defunct) had a half-built development, and where we bought a small, one up one down half built corner house on a development where seven of us shared a pool, the corner giving us a private back garden,

The fact that we could only ever spend a maximum of four weeks a year there did not diminish our enthusiasm, as we told ourselves we might retire there eventually, and if not it would be a good investment, remember this was 2003 and holiday house building boom time, all around the surrounding area you could hear the ground pounding rock breakers in the distance like woodpeckers, new house foundations being dug out, these having to be dug deep by law, as frequent small earthquakes were possible there, though in our five years of ownership we never experienced any.

It was from Maleme, to the west of Charnia, (where during WW2 the Germans paratrooped in and from there took the whole island), that we had stayed while we were shown various houses under development - and chose Drapanos. Not sure, but it must have been 2003 when we paid our first third, followed by the second instalment about six months later, getting emailed photos on building progress.

It would be spring 2004 before we took possession, paying about 40,000 Stirling in all, though small, it had an upstairs terrace with views over the pool to the front, and the village to the back, being situated at the side and attached to next doors wall, which having no windows there, made it a nice private outdoor space, accessible from the bedroom, with a covered archway underneath leading to the back garden.

I used to put my sun lounger under there when it was too hot for me in the sun, and leave Sarah to bake, as was her wont…

The back garden was just soil, and seeing what people had done with earlier finished houses, I enlisted the help of Mick, a retired builder and a great guy who lived out there full-time, in laying a plastic membrane, and wheelbarrowing delivered white gravel on top, with holes in the membrane around the wild Cactus and other succulents, along with Oleander bushes that were native to the area.

We paid Dave and Marian, who lived full-time in the house nearest the lane that passed the small complex, to maintain the pool, shared by seven of the fourteen houses on the development (the other seven having their own pool), this couple also watered the garden when needed. A small town called Vamos was the administrative centre for the area few miles inland, and where we paid our water and electric bills once a year.

A basic but homely restaurant that used to be a small school in Kokkino Chorio, that was known simply as Yanni's, the owners name, became our main local watering hole and eating out first choice, again used as a setting for interviews with Brian and Andrew, the developer, and *A Place in the Sun* Presenter, not sure which one, but with a great sunset view over Souda Bay, and a family typical of Crete that welcomed you as if long lost (paying) friends, Yanni is the archetypical outgoing Greek host that made you feel instantly at home quoting from memory what was on that days menu…

We only ever in five years ate indoors there, near a great central fire, that was the only year we went in winter. Getting there in winter was a two-flight affair via Athens, as no one flew direct to Crete, from Manchester after October, until mid-April, in the period we had our little house there. The first trip of the year, usually in May, had me painting over where a persistent winter wind always took some paint off, usually from the terrace wall.

Over the five years we had the place, we managed, from the ground level and up a trellis to the terrace Pergola, to grow a lovely Bougainvillea, that eventually dapple-shaded the whole terrace and looked very pretty and gave the house real character. A grapevine was planted to grow up the back-garden terrace Pergola later - but needing more water (which it probably didn't get) we never got that patio shaded.

Chapter 61

One of our favourite places to visit while out there was Georgioupolis, a pretty, smallish resort about ten or so miles across the other side of the plateaux from Drapanos, situated where the coast changes from a north/south direction to an east/west line heading along to Rethimno, before a southerly dip at Heriklion, the Cretan Capital, a nearly two-hour drive from Drapanos, we know because we switched to flying and driving from there, as Chania became much more expensive to fly to.

Back to Georgioupolis, and what it had going for it, a river for a start, it wasn't navigable inland very far, it was more of a wide inlet, with a few fishing boats working from there. You could hire small motor boats, to take up "Turtle River" as they call it to tourists, so called as when you got to the end of the navigable (about ¼ mile) bit, it ended in a round pool complete with lily pads and – you guessed it – a few long-necked turtles.

Part way down the river, still in town, a few restaurants line the narrow road parallel with the inlet, with wooden-shaded terraces overhanging the river in a very pretty setting, one called the Blue Moon also has a few rooms, and if we ever go back to Crete we will try to stay at, if still open. It is what we both like – small and charming, like the town itself.

Over the last fifteen years or so, I have suffered from an as yet undiagnosed condition that only seems to affect me after I have eaten. This caught me out in Crete.

I have a pain in my chest proportionate to any exercise, especially uphill walking, even a gradual slope will bring this on if I have eaten a meal in the previous three or so hours.

I have had a Stress Echo Cardiogram, and in 2017, a cardiac profusion scan, that amounted to thirty X-rays taken in rotation around my torso, both these tests say I have *not* got Angina, which my mum and two of her brothers died of. My brother, Ian, has recently been diagnosed with the condition, having two stents inserted, so I am still plagued with this mystery condition that will allow me to play badminton or go for long walks in a morning, as long as *I don't* eat until afterwards.

I let myself get caught out in Crete, when, I think it was 2005, we sought out a restaurant recommended in a guidebook, on the harbour front in Chania, it was a hot, humid evening, and I think these conditions, simulated the exercise of walking uphill, as within five minutes of finishing my (very tasty) Prawn

Saganaki, I started to feel the pain in my chest, even though we were walking on the level ground harbour front, forcing my to walk quite slowly back to our car.

I drove back the half-hour journey to our house in Drapanos, with only mild pain whilst driving, then went to lie down, expecting the pain and the tiredness to fade overnight, but whether due to the stress of the pain and, or, the heat and humidity, that night I suffered the worst asthma attack I can remember, even using Ventolin, as well as my preventative spray could not clear my breathing for much of that night. It got to the stage that we were considering Sarah having to take me to the hospital near Charnia if I had not improved by morning, which I eventually did, recovering completely, though this took until the early hours before I could sleep.

The next day was spent resting on a sun lounger, as I was very tired after this combination attack, which I have not let happen to myself since, though I have to go through life planning any significant activity before a meal, only eating small amounts of food at work, only having a main meal in the evening. I have given up on the doctors.

I will now mention a few of the more interesting places in Crete (which is 150 miles long) that we found during our five years of bi- or tri-annual trips there.

One of the longest, but enjoyable day drives involved us getting up very early for a long drive west along the north coast as far as Maleme, before turning south up into the western White Mountains, passing narrow, cultivated valleys high up in the hills, before reaching Kandanos, where we stopped for a coffee, which was made very slowly for us by a woman, dressed all in traditional black, who could have been a hundred years old.

The Mountain Town of Kandanos was the centre of resistance in Western Crete during the German invasion of WW2. There is a monument there to the fallen of the town, many of whom were killed in retaliation for the activities of the resistance.

Driving up through the mountains in our hire car is a pleasant change from driving along the two-lane north coast road that serves as the main east to west artery on Crete, where it is the practice of many natives to drive very close behind before overtaking. You soon learn to leave a large gap between yourself and the car in front to minimise the time a car is up your backside before it overtakes, the police drive the same way along this road, so not surprising Greece at that time had the second worst car crash record in Europe.

Chapter 62

Continuing down to the south coast, which is very rugged and has no coastal road unlike the north, we eventually reached Pelakanos, with its small harbour, in time for the 11 o'clock ferry to the very special beach of Elafonisi, named after the island of the same name just offshore. It is just about possible to drive to it down very long rough tracks, but most people get the ferry that comes back at four in the afternoon to pick you up.

The reason this beach is so special, is that it is two tone and looks just like raspberry ripple ice cream, the reason for this is that pink sand is blown across from Libya in large enough quantities and is of different enough particle size, that the native yellow sand and the pink sand, form into separate congregations to create the raspberry ripple effect over the low lying peninsular near the island. There is, or was when we were there, nothing there but a small beach shack selling bottled drinks – essential as there are no trees, no shade of any kind, and surreal as it is, we were glad to see the returning ferry at four.

Another very nice remote beach, again well away from the resorts, was told of to us by an expat called Elisabeth who worked in Almirida, our closest beach village, she also used to work with Andrew, of *A Place in the Sun* fame, in the same restaurant. Always on the lookout for somewhere new, this beach was at the base of the north western most peninsular on Crete called Khania, the beach itself was called Phalasarna, about ten miles west of the town of Kissamos, there were orange groves at this end of the island, which otherwise as a whole is fairly arid.

There is a very small village near this beach where we had a meal in the shade of a grapevine-covered pergola, so prevalent in the more rustic parts of Greece, and a major part of its charm. After a long wander along this pristine beach, which we returned to another year, it not being quite so remote as Elafonisi.

Getting up around 4 in the morning one day enabled us to manage a day-trip to Santorini, seventy miles to the north of Crete. This involved getting picked up by minibus in the nearby town of Kalyves, being taken to Rethimno, where you boarded ship for the trip. Breakfasting on the ship after our 6 o'clock sail, we relaxed until about two miles out from Thira, or Santorini as it is better known, when the ship was suddenly surrounded by dolphins, it seemed like hundreds of them were leaping out of the sea, not sure what species, but they had a fair bit of white on them, as well as darker shades, so maybe Striped Dolphins.

As we were in sight, but not yet close to Santorini, the ship had not yet slowed down, and though the dolphins were fast, they could only keep up with the ship for a minute or so, but it was to be our only major sighting to date, though we were taken to see an Orca pod some years later of the coast of Vancouver Island – to be mentioned later. As this route was a regular crossing, you wonder if so many dolphins being in the area at just the right time – it was a routine they were used to, riding the bow wave, though there were far too many for that, some were a good hundred yards from the boat on both sides, all happening too quick for photos, but it is imprinted in my usually poor memory for life.

Arriving at the port, you are struck by the sheer cliffs that almost surround the re-growing Thira Volcano in the centre of the sea less than a mile offshore. This volcano a few thousand years ago is probably responsible for the destruction of the Minoan civilisation, after the massive eruption created a Tsunami large enough to destroy the main Minoan city of Knossos on Crete, though not a complete wipe out of inland settlements, the Minoans never recovered their status as a major power, the island being invaded by opportunists soon afterwards…

As the trip was a package, you are then taken around the island on a coach, much of the lower slopes on the outer side of the island is given over to farming, but it is the view from the top of the Caldera, with the multi-coloured layers of the cliffs, and the villages perched with whitewashed houses and churches topped with blue domes that everyone is there for. Oia is the cliff top village where the majority of the iconic picture postcards are set.

I for one did not mind paying silly money for a coffee and snack, simply to sit and stare at the breath-taking view before me, with houses built almost on top of each other. Unless you wanted a donkey ride down, you made your way past the trinket shops to a funicular ride down to Ormos Athinos and the ferry back.

No dolphins to see us off, they must have been on the morning shift that week, but we were back on Crete by about 8.30 that evening.

Chapter 63

Evenings on the terrace, watching the sunset, and just before complete darkness, watching for the three of four bats out on the wing for moths, was a nice way to end the day, usually with our Greek version of the Spanish hot chocolate drink – La bomba – made with brandy, but our version being made with Metaxa, the closest Greek equivalent, and my favourite Greek drink, as I do not like Ozo and Raki only in small doses with food, the Raki quite often being produced *very* locally if you were eating out of town, if you know what I mean…

As the financial meltdown of 2008 arrived, we decided somewhat reluctantly that as we had seen a lot of western Crete and had only a few weeks each year available to go there. That and there also being rumours of redundancies at work, that we had better sell up before the price dropped too much, and so after five years that we enjoyed trips there, we eventually sold to a British retired builder, for a similar price that we paid for it, he planned to spend half the year there and extend the house into the back garden – with Greek planning laws. I hope he was not in a hurry, but of course I said nothing, wishing him good luck. One day we will have to go back, stay at the Blue Moon Inn at Georgoupolis and go take a look at our old house and nearby haunts.

Whilst on our last trip there as we completed the sale, I got a text from a job site I had uploaded my CV to, when back at work the rumours had firmed up to specific numbers that amounted to two thirds of everyone there on notice of redundancy. Asking me to attend an interview with an agency that controlled sole supply for non-company staff at a large pharmaceutical company about ten miles from where I lived, much closer than my current commute to Widnes.

Redundancy volunteers were asked for, and after having an interview, and being told I had a job, albeit about six weeks away, I asked for my redundancy settlement figures, which were quite good for the years I had spent there. I accepted, having found out from the manager of the warehouse at the pharmaceutical company where I would be working, that agency staff usually got taken on after a couple of years if seen as good workers, I was prepared to take that chance, as the pay was better than most other positions I had looked at that did not involve night shifts.

The number of people to remain at the Widnes Phosphate site was such that only one part of the site would run at a time, then production would move to another section, all employees having to work shifts, including nights, so me being one of the later starters there, it was unlikely I would have kept my job, even if I was prepared to work nights, which I was not, so all in all I knew it was time to move on, especially as my next job was secured and before the compulsory redundancy date.

When something appears to be going too well to plan, I usually find a way to mess up somewhere along the way, and of course, I found a way to keep up this tradition with this transition…

On the day of my leaving Widnes for the last time, after saying goodbye to my workmates, I was in good spirits, to the extent that on my walk from our brew cabin to the changing rooms at the security weighbridge, in a show of bravado, still in sight of our brew cabin, I did the jumping click of heels of someone in high spirits, and of course I landed badly, going over on my left ankle so badly I thought I had broken it.

Got up quickly grinning at our cabin, not wanting them to know how bad it was, but as I hobbled away, I could tell I had done serious damage. How I drove home the thirty-five or so miles, with my ankle swelling all the time I will never know, all I had in my mind was that this being a Friday, I had only the weekend to be fit for my induction day on Monday for my new job.

My ankle and half my lower leg swelled up like a balloon overnight, a combination of strong anti-inflammatory tablets, and comfrey Sarah boiled, helped get the swelling down by Monday, but I still went to my new workplace with a slight limp I could not hide, just barely getting my foot, with no socks on, into my safety boots. Fortunately this being an induction day, myself and a batch of about a dozen new starters, not all warehouse staff, spent more than half the day sat down being given info about the company, receiving security passes, passwords to our new online accounts, being shown how to access all needed sections, including online payslips etc.

Chapter 64

Halfway into the day, we were shown to a welcome cold buffet in the lobby area of the main offices, which also served as a local canteen area, this led to more drama for me. It was not enough for me to be nursing a half-crippled foot, I then, after eating sandwiches, picked up and took a bite from a mince pie, straight away I knew this contained ground up Brazil nut, which is the only thing I am allergic to, being fine with all other nuts.

Normally if there is any of this nut about, individual particles in the air will sting the back of my throat, and I know to steer clear, but due to the nut being in the mincemeat gel, I had no warning, Sarah checking ingredients on any mince pies bought for home. Soon as I felt the feeling in my throat, I got rid into a napkin what was in my mouth, but it was too late, not enough to cause serious anaphylactic shock, I nevertheless had taken in enough to feel like my throat had a wire brush in it.

All I could do was drink as much water as I could get my hands on, and endure about two hours of the soreness slowly subsiding, my throat not quite closing, so there I was, hobbling about, my throat burning, trying to pretend nothing was wrong on my first day, you could not make it up, but there I was, living the dream… I made it to day two and into the warehouse and packaging areas.

There are two main jobs in the warehouse that supply the drug packaging operation, order picking from the six levels high racking, using location tech on board the Reach Trucks, about five or six people would be doing this, leaving the picked orders on pallets in a transfer area. The second job, and the one I started on, was picking up the palletised orders using a sideways driven, three-wheel delivery trucks that lifted the pallets a few inches from the ground, for transfer to the packaging areas, set on three floors, accessed by driving the small delivery trucks into industrial width lifts.

The drivers of these trucks, of which usually there are two but can be three or one, all have to carry a phone, which is the bane of this operators life, as although drugs and the appropriate packaging materials are requested through a computerised-ordering system, all the supervisors of the packing plants have the phone no of the delivery drivers, and if orders are slow to arrive, (in their view) the delivery driver is the first point of contact, and so the guy who has to explain that the order has not been picked yet, then on return to the warehouse tell the pickers that so and so is chasing such and such an order, and then receive flack back for being the messenger putting the pickers under pressure.

The drug packing machines are up to about fifty feet long, and there are very strict driving, drop off and pick-up areas for packed product. It was a bit like a high-pressure milk round, where you got to know who was a pain to deal with, and who understood you were doing your best to get what was asked for as soon as possible.

It sometimes got to the point that when someone was being unreasonable, you had to resort to playing one line supervisor against the other, by saying something along the lines of, 'Shall I leave such and such's order while I fetch yours?' They usually balked at that, knowing we would tell the delayed order receiver who had claimed priority. The normal operating procedure would just have you pick up picked order pallets from two lanes in the warehouse at random, unless you had received specific requests from a line for a ready order.

In theory this job, once you had learnt the locations of pick-ups and drop-offs, and got to know the related people, was fairly simple, in practice, due to the packing lines having set targets of production to meet, the supervisors, depending on their capacity to absorb pressure, passed on some of this pressure to the only point of contact they saw on a regular basis involved in getting what they needed, that person being yours truly, or his team mate.

When once asked how I saw my job there, I used an analogy, citing the guy you used to see spinning plates on the top of canes, constantly having to move between them to keep them spinning and not falling off, this was quite well received. When you are doing this job, you look at the order pickers in the warehouse with envy, as they are far removed from the front line of contact with the ever-ravenous packing lines, us being the buffer.

The grass is always greener on the other side, and so after about ten months, having had my Reach Truck refresher, I was transferred to order picking, a month or so after requesting this…

Chapter 65

As in any job, there are pressures that are not apparent to those not doing it, one being product not in the location it's meant to be, so the order has to be reset, and as you are expected to get through a reasonable number of orders, these orders are for an exact number of drugs, together with enough of the associated packaging for this number, the packaging materials are usually rounded up in excess of what is needed, so there are always "returns" to log and store, as the packing lines are not allowed to retain any excess for future use, apart from a few items that are on large rolls, and are used by all the lines on that floor, these being delivered independent of any drug order.

Newly arrived product has to be put in allocated spaces, pallets with very little product consolidated with others of the same, all this to be recorded on the computer stock control system. If anything was not exactly as it appeared on the stock control system, there is a long rigmarole of procedure to go through to put things right, there is no simple adjustment to be made on the very rigid SAP system, though to be fair, you could be putting an order together worth up to a quarter of a million pounds.

There would be quite an investigation if some drugs were not accounted for, and rightly so.

As far as I know, there was never any theft that I was aware of in our area of operations, losses were usually down to someone not inputting the correct numbers when something was being moved or used, the difference then had to be traced back to its real location – loads of fun.

Work stable again for now, wanderlust, something we were both susceptible to, started to raise its head again, Sarah being quite into wildlife in general, had been watching a programme about Orangutangs and the deforestation of their habitat, and the idea of going somewhere a little different from the usual holiday haunts also grew on me, and before long I had found a hotel near the town of Kota Kinabalu in Sabah, one of the two Malaysian states of northern Borneo. This was duly booked. Fast forward to…

The hotel we had found was the Rasa Ria, a resort in itself, with its own private beach, set on north coast on the shore of the Sulu sea, and having a small wildlife reserve attached, which opened into jungle, where on one evening, I waited a long time to catch a glimpse of a rare Civet cat, a very shy animal, lured by bait left by the park rangers, for the benefit of such as myself, a tourist wanting to see rare animals. It had a head that looked more like a polecat than your normal cat, but I saw my Civet, after waiting on my own late in the evening in the hide set there just for this.

There were excursions that set off in the middle of the night that allowed the younger and not so young but fit people to climb the Mt Kinabalu Volcano, to get to the caldera for sunrise, but at approx. 13,500ft, in my state of health, with asthma, among other things. We decided instead on a trip that explored the rich flora of the foothills of this mountain. One of the highlights of this walk was to see a "Stinking corpse Lily", so-called due to the smell of rotting flesh it gives off to attract insects for food, this gigantic flower can grow up to four s high, and the one we saw must have been not far off that, its yellow and purple quite striking, the smell very sickly…

Another interesting day-trip was to Poring Hot Springs, a place developed from natural springs by, of all people, the Japanese occupying forces during WW2, one of their very few beneficial legacies from that era. Set now in the Kinabalu National Park, a series of open-air tubs channel the springs, opening a rickety tap diverts some of the sulphurous hot water into your own personal tub, very relaxing and supposedly good for your health – as many smelly things seem to be.

Nearby, in the same national park, was a rope bridge jungle canopy walk, not to be missed, except we did, as the place was shut for maintenance work, someone must have fallen through it… In the small nature reserve behind the hotel, some very young, orphaned Orangutangs are hand reared, encouraged to wander a little way into the jungle but always returning to be fed at regular times, this of course being a great draw to us tourists.

While this was good to see, what had really drawn us to Borneo, was a trip across to the east coast, the location of Sepilok, the renowned Orangutang rehabilitation centre, and then also for us, a three-hour trip up the Kinabatangan River to stay at Uncle Tan's Wildlife Camp for three nights. This was not a hotel excursion, I had booked this separately, this being the main reason we were there, we would lose three nights from our hotel stay, so we made sure the hotel reception knew we would be absent those nights.

Chapter 66

On our day-trip previously mentioned, walking the paths of the jungled lower slopes of Mt Kinabalu, we stopped at a local village for refreshments, ours being a coconut, with the top chopped off, with a straw for the very refreshing milk, it was there I bought a Parang, an 18-inch blade Malay machete, in the hope that I would be allowed to take it on the flight across to the east coast city of Sandakan.

We had a choice of a nine-hour bumpy bus ride to Sandakan from Kota Kinabalu, or a half-hour internal flight, which turned out to be as quick at the airport as getting on a bus, as for the Parang, at the check in I just handed it over, they wrapped it, put my name on it, for storage in the aircraft hold, I picked it up at Sandakan with no fuss, imagine that in England now…

No one batted an eyelid when I took the 18-inch-bladed Parang out of my bag at the check in, can you imagine doing that at an English airport? I would have been on the floor with my hands zip tied behind my back, and half a dozen guns trained on me within about thirty seconds, then made the national news… None of that drama there.

At Sandakan Airport, the taxis were in designated different colours, set prices to zoned destinations, to stop rip offs, good idea.

Uncle Tan's transit stopover bunkhouse was known to the taxi drivers, who must have a steady stream of tourists heading there, the bunkhouse being in a village around half hour inland along their "highway". Twenty-two, near to the junction to Highway Thirteen, the main Sabah arterial road we would have taken if we had bussed it from Kota Kinabalu, this road eventually crossing the Kinabatangan River, where we would take the boat to the Jungle Camp.

Having dropped our rucksacks at the Transit Bunkhouse in the late afternoon, we had a wander around the village, young children following us, one old guy asking us why we were walking around in the afternoon heat, us explaining we had a long journey to get there and needed to stretch our legs, which he nodded to with a gap-toothed grin.

There was a small bridge over what looked like an agricultural drainage stream, and just a little way down was a two-foot-long baby crocodile sunning itself on the muddy bank, we were defiantly out of town. Back at the very basic bunkhouse, we were given a sticky rice meal with the darker meat you get with wild fed chicken, this and a fruit breakfast was included in the booking we made on the internet at home, staying two nights there, as the next day we had booked through Uncle Tan's to visit Sepilok Nature Resort as it is now known, though at the time we were there, it was known as Sepilok Rehabilitation Centre, accommodation there doubtless much expanded now.

Double bunks in a small dormitory were our overnight beds, an overhead fan giving little relief from the humidity, but we knew what we had signed up for. Early the next morning, about 6 am, I was woken up by a deep rumbling noise, Sarah never stirred, I got up to look out through the window slats, no glass in the way, to see truck after flatbed truck in a convoy on the main road, all loaded with hardwood tree trunks raided from the jungle, all destined for Japan, we were told, at that time, forbidden from chopping their own hardwoods down, instead importing it on the cheap from all-over South-East Asia.

The convoy must have had at least twenty trucks, and we were told this happened every day, it was the reason we went when we did, to try and see Orangutang in the wild, while there was some wild left. The flatter areas these trees were taken from would be replaced with giant palm oil plantations, some of the oil no doubt used to grease certain official palms…

Sepilok was not too far away, so we were there by late morning, Sarah stumbled on the steps up to what I will call the briefing room, knocking my video camera out of my hands, this being a fairly large object in those days, I picked it up, switched it on, came on OK, the viewfinder picture looked fine so I switched it off.

DELETE

We were briefed in in what is probably now called an Education Centre or some such, as to what they aimed to achieve there, which is pretty much what is says on the tin, taking young, but not baby Orangutang, these coming from such places as the Rasa Ria's Sanctuary, that take in orphaned babies. Here, they then gradually got them to spend more and more time out in the jungle, returning to a raised feeding platform that we were all positioned to one side of at a distance, at a set feeding time, to await the returning juveniles.

To facilitate this, two or three thick ropes were attached to the platform, at about ten feet of the ground, snaking of a hundred feet or more into the jungle in different directions, these acting as guiding highways for the Orangutangs, so they could swing along, hanging upside down to the approx. 15ft by 15sq raised food platform, where bunches of bananas and other fruits and vegetables awaited them.

Chapter 67

It was good to see about four of them turn up, one passing over our heads along a rope to the platform. Unlike other primates, I don't remember any squabbling, just calm breaking off of bananas, and eating for about a quarter hour, before disappearing back into the forest, returning less and less frequently we were told, as they got used to finding food in the jungle, rehabilitated.

We would have had our own refreshments at some point. Somewhere on the way back, we stopped at a Sun Bear Rescue Centre, orphaned cubs found after their parents were taken for the Chinese, who extract bile from living Sun bears for superposed medicinal purposes, I don't know if this trade still goes on, but it a sad reflection on us all, as testing of consumer products on animals for us, Westerners, is just as bad as the numerous animals killed for oriental dubious medical benefits, some of which may have real use, but not to the point of species extinction.

After another night in the airless, stifling overnight heat of Uncle Tan's transit dorm, the next morning getting we were picked up by a feeder truck on a long trip, turning south off highway Twenty-two, onto Highway Thirteen, in an increasingly bumpy ride down to a bridge over the Kinabatangan River.

Here, along with around eight or ten, mostly far younger people, we boarded a large long-tail boat for the two to three hours journey along this switch back meandering river, packed with the sights and sounds of the varied wildlife, from brightly coloured hornbills cawing overhead to Howler monkeys in the trees along the banks, small to medium-sized crocs (six feet-ish) on small sandy, mangrove beaches, this is why we were here, I was videoing everything, it might have been a two to three hours trip, but it was over too soon, although it was starting to get dark by the time we arrived at what passed for a landing stage, a little bamboo jetty sticking a few feet into the river, with no sigh of the camp beyond.

One of the young camp workers on the boat, returning after leave from the camp, where they spend a month at a time, led us through a jungle cleared path almost in the dark from overhead vegetation and the evening gloom, about five-minute walk to the camp, emerging into a clearing, not sure what we were expecting – we were told basic, and that's what it was.

Sleeping accommodation was an open air raised platform, about two feet above the baked earth with a corrugated galvanised steel roof, (tin would have rusted in a rain forest in short order), beds were mattresses in rows on the floor, set well in from the roof overhang, with mosquito nets attached to roof support posts and tucked in around the base of the mattresses, though Sarah in particular was to find out just how limited this protection was.

We were gathered together on the raised eating platform, built similar to the dorm, but with benches and tables, with a makeshift bar and cooking area at one end, here we were told of camp procedures, such as a roll call in the evenings, not as daft as it sounds, as especially in the dark, if you were more than ten yards away from the camp, you might never see it, the jungle was that dense there. There was no shower block, just an old oil drum full of water and God knows what else, that you ladled over yourself, you had a permanent sheen within minutes anyway.

After a meal and some bottles of beer, (that was it from the "bar"), we were told to wait quietly, the camp guys, all young, led by a lad called Lan, had thrown the evening meal leftovers a short distance away, on the edge of the clearing, within half an hour very tall but narrow dark-skinned wild pigs, with piglets in tow, turned up to polish off the leftovers, as they did every night.

Later in the night, a pair of Civet cats tided up the bits of food left over on the raised platform, the lads not sweeping up as they knew the "cleaners" would be along later, I never saw them, but on the following night Sarah, who did not come on that nights "Jungle walk" sat in one of the permanently strung hammocks and was there to see the pair of Civets "cleaning up" after us.

That night's jungle walk was an experience, in as far as you did not dare lose sight of the small group of seven or eight, a guide at front and back on the single file "trail" that was all but invisible to the rest of us, we may have been only a few hundred feet from the camp, but in the total darkness, it might as well have been miles if you lost sight of the camp guys.

One of the strangest sights to see there at night are small forest birds, no larger than a robin, that sat without moving on branches no more than five feet off the ground whilst three or for torches were pointed at them, I joked that they were stuffed and tied to the branch – they were so motionless, being dazzled did not scare them. But any vibration of the tree would scare them away, as it was tree snakes, they were wary of being supper for.

While walking in single file, guess who was the lucky one who a got in the way of a column of fire ants on the march, the first I knew of them was a feeling of pins and needles on steroids on my lower legs, I soon got out their way, not that big, but their name was apt… Our guide spotted a large black Tarantula which we all stood around – at a respectful distance, it was the size of an average hand, not something Sarah would not miss seeing.

Chapter 68

Early the next morning, I got up before Sarah, it was only just light, I had been told that a couple of Monitor Lizards hunted the nearby small lake, which was not much more than a large weed-covered pond really, but sure enough, after sitting quietly for a while, two lizard heads started appearing above the surface every so often. I did not see them enter, but they climbed out after a short while, the larger one was about three foot long, the second, presumably its mate, a little shorter, I was told they sometimes came to the camp on the scrounge, though we never saw this.

Sarah said she was not going on that morning's boat trip, not having slept well, but with everyone getting up she changed her mind at the last minute, getting on the second small boat, not the one I was on, we set off to where a troop of Proboscis Monkeys were known to nest overnight, I remember little of this, but Sarah says we saw them, I do recall crocodiles on the riverbank, not big, but I was not going swimming…

Later in the day, after brunch, we went out in two groups, on the lookout for wildlife, and any Orangutang nests set high in the trees, our group saw none, but did see elephant dung reckoned to be from the night before. A place was shown to us where a King Cobra had been seen the week before, it was pot luck what was nearby, we did see a foot-long centipede, on its way to the shoe shop no doubt, must be like the forth bridge, no sooner one end sorted, than the other end needed new…

Being armed with the Parang I had bought along from Kota Kinabalu, came in handy, as we were asked to cut some green shoots of a certain plant for use in that nights Stir fry. Basic jungle-survival info included being shown Liana plants that held drinkable water, if lost for a day of two, this might be the difference between making it out or not, the Parang came in handy as only the guides and I had one.

Just as we were getting close to camp, one of the guides from the other group came to us saying their group had spotted an Orangutang, our guide set off at a fast pace, we were nearly running, getting spread out trying to keep up, making sure we did not lose sight of the person in front soon became our priority, Sarah and I being about twice the age of everyone else there. After a long hot very sweaty chase, the trail had been lost, a roll call was counted after we returned, exhausted from the exertion in the stifling jungle heat, the head count was OK, not sure about the bodies.

That evening, our last in the camp, thunder started to rumble in the distance, and as it got dark, lightning lit up the sky, it turned into one of the most surreal nights of our lives, the thunder and lightning became sustained, it started raining as only the tropics get rain, on the corrugated roof of the dorm, it was deafening, and then the Howler Monkeys joined in, no doubt stirred up by the storm, if you can imagine a mixture of Salvador Dali, and Picasso paintings turned into sound, then you get the picture!

This went on for hours, if we slept it was not for long, we all got up the next morning bleary eyed, ready for our boat trip back to so called civilisation, by this time Sarah had been bitten far more times by mosquitoes than the rest of us, and it was starting to become something needing attention. The boat trip back was delayed a while as the engine would not start, but it was fixed eventually, and before setting off, I gave my Parang to Lan, saying it would now be more use to him than me.

I spent the river journey back filming with my video camera, the crocs, monkeys, and toucans, thinking what a visual feast I had captured for back home. We made it to Sandakan Airport early enough that we were able to get an earlier than scheduled flight back to Kota Kinabalu.

On getting back to the Rasa Ria Hotel, Sarah asked to see the hotel doctor, who was not long in responding, Sarah told me he was amazed at just how much she had been bitten, saying her rare blood type must be the reason. Sarah was given an Australian cream called Soov, a name she has not forgotten, as it worked as the name sounds, and quickly.

Still with a few days left of our holiday we had a quiet evening, and also next day, giving Sarah a chance to start healing from the jungle 633 Squadron mosquitos. That evening, the hotel had as entertainment the Murat Bamboo Dance, check out YouTube for this, local tribesmen hop between increasingly fast tempo bamboo poles that are moved together at foot level, the pièce de résistance being the star guy doing it blindfolded at the fastest tempo. We were of course invited to have a go, which I did, managing not to get caught at a medium speed, the sound being as mesmerising as the sight, which of course I was videoing.

Chapter 69

Out on a trip the next day to the coast, and also a small island not far out, given a packed lunch, we enjoyed the beach, off from which I went snorkelling, whilst Sarah sat reading at a bench under the trees, still recovering from the camp mosquitos. Having flippers on made me quite confident in the sea, and I soon had twenty something feet of water under me, just as I was about to turn back, a turtle, bigger than me, moved off the bottom, from a little behind me. If it had not moved, I would not have seen it, being well camouflaged against the bottom.

It swam up underneath me, still more than ten feet down, heading out to sea, it was slowly rising and I tried to keep up with it, which I did for a little while, but it was leaving me behind, and I realised I could no longer see the sea floor, so, happy with what I had just seen, I turned around for what now was quite a distant shore, with flippers on I made good progress but felt a little nervous, looking behind me every so often, wondering what might lurk in the deep blue just beyond my limit of vision, I got back to where the marker buoys signalled the safe distance out, realising I must have been three times that distance out before turning around. When I got to the beach, Sarah must have seen me come in, as she was close by with a towel and a tea shirt, I followed her to the bench and table set under the trees set just back from the beachfront footpath.

While we had our packed lunch, she told me that one of the park rangers had to chase off some Macaques that were trying to pinch her food, a little later as a ranger was passing us I asked him about the large turtle I had seen, and from my description of large raised segments dividing its shell, he concluded I had seen a Loggerhead, and that they were quite rare in the area, he asked where I had seen it, I told him it was a bit beyond the marker buoys in less than twenty feet of water, not wanting to say just how far out I had gone.

Somewhere in Kota Kinabalu there is a square, like a market square, but with bench tables and chairs, and surrounding this courtyard area are, or were when we were there, restaurants, with the fresh sea food on display that you queue up and order, to be carried over by a waiter to where you had chosen to sit on the bench area, which was a collective eating area for all the surrounding food shops/restaurants.

Most of the food on offer was still alive in tanks, fish, or in my case tiger prawns. You pointed out which one you wanted, and as each one was nearly a foot long, one was all you needed, served with ginger and spring onion with rice, and served on a palm leaf – it was scrumptious. I left the palm leaf! Sarah did not want to condemn a particular tiger prawn to death that was a bit too fresh for her, so asked for an already dead one, they probably caught two in the same net swoop, but she did not see that, so was happier for it. The next day was our last but one out there, we had a dip in the pool, and a walk along the jungle-backed beach, before settling on loungers on the private hotel beach.

Not long settled, two men, one older man walking behind the younger, the elder with his hand on the shoulder of the younger, clearly blind and being guided around the beach. They looked like monks, they were offering reflexology massages, I was a little sceptical, but when the elder was engaged with others, the younger came to us offering his services, I proceeded to ask him if he could diagnose what was a problem for me, using fingers on my feet, using this technique, he said it was possible, and after a short while, he said I had a problem in my left lung, with breathing, not aware my left was the problem, but he had diagnosed my asthma, which I was exhibiting no symptoms of, having used the preventative spray that morning, he proceeded to massage a specific area of my foot for a while, the theory being as I understand it, that there are nerve endings from all over your body that end at your feet.

This fellow, who referred to the elder as his master (they looked Chinese rather than natives of Borneo), offered their services for the next few days, saying they could improve my condition, but I had to let him know we were flying back to England the following day, so I will never know…

That was Borneo, quite a memorable trip, as I had to ask Sarah for few of the details from there.

Chapter 70

Back at work (Pharma Warehouse) an amiable, down-to-earth guy called Martin was our warehouse manager, who was loyal to his subordinates when it came to defending his department against the endless bickering between warehouse and line packing supervisors, usually getting to the bottom of reasons why something was amiss in the supply chain, often discovering that requests for items came in later than stated.

Security was such here that we all had to undergo "Aviation Security Vetting" soon after we started, included soon after was a session which included having a decommissioned automatic pistol being handed around to feel the weight of it, not quite sure why, I don't think they expected us to find one in incoming or outgoing orders, but part of required training, as much of the drugs produced there ended up in air freight.

It was while I was working here that another of my health problem started to manifest itself, in the form of heart palpitations, starting suddenly, usually whilst standing up after being bent down, a rush of blood audible internally, would be followed by an irregular heartbeat, and a resulting loss of strength, also a gradual increasingly strong pain at the back of my neck.

This first started to happen in the middle of playing badminton, and at first going somewhere private and lying flat for two minutes or less, would bring about a resumption of normal heartbeat as suddenly as it had become irregular, this did not happen in the early half of my time at work there, while I was delivering stock on the little side driven supply trucks, but later, whilst order picking in the large warehouse, not usually occupied by more than one or two people at any one time, and so I was able to slip back to the deserted charging room for a quick lie down that restored my normal heartbeat quickly, these events being weeks apart in their occurrence in the first six months of these episodes.

I should have reported this, but being an agency worker, I knew it was very easy for such as I to be removed from my job, and so as the problem was reversible in its first few months of manifestation, I kept silent about it at work and from Sarah at home at first. As time went on, this problem first forced me to give up badminton, as I could not keep leaving games part way through and expecting people to wait for my reappearance two minutes later, at first letting someone waiting to play to take my place until I was back, but as lying down soon stopped being a quick fix, that was the end of that for now at least.

During the last few months of my time at this drugs warehouse, as this problem got worse, I got lucky, if you can call it that, in that on two occasions, when these episodes started to get worse, it was late on Saturday morning overtime, when few people were about, there being few lines working to be supplied and only two or three of us warehouse staff in on an overtime rotation every other week or so. We had separate jobs to do as so were well separated, which was fortunate, in as far as not bringing my employment there to an early end on health grounds.

The first more serious occurrence requiring much longer lying flat to return my heartbeat to normal, the second being something of a nightmare, where having only just made it to the quite truck charging room, I actually passed out, before I got the chance to lie down, only realising this by the fact that my head hitting the floor hard had brought me around, the irregular heartbeat, dizziness, weakness, and increasing back of the neck ache, still there.

Again fortunately, for my job continuation point of view, it was going home time that Saturday midday, the others in work that morning long gone by the time, I slowly got changed and started the normally five-minute walk out of the building along the internal back road to the warehouse car park near the top gate.

It took me about twenty-minute slow walk to make it to my car, another five sat down, before I felt able to drive off, when I did, it was all I could manage to stay conscious every time I had to stop at traffic lights, the pain in my neck getting gradually worse, only the act of shouting at red lights, and of driving itself, keeping myself awake by sheer willpower got me home that day. When I did get there, there are half a dozen steps to climb to get from the road to the footpath along the raised terrace to our little two up two down.

If anyone had seen me trying to climb those few steps, they would have thought me very drunk, as I climbed those steps on my hands and knees, very slowly puling myself to my feet after the five minutes it took me to get to the top, leaning on the wall, to make my way the last few yards to our front door, the street being totally deserted the entire time it took me to get from my car to my house door, about ten minutes in all.

Chapter 71

When inside and sat down, I told Sarah the whole episode, omitting the bit about passing out, knowing she would insist on me going to the doctors, instead, slowly going upstairs to bed to await the return of my heartbeat to normal. Not sure how long it took that afternoon as I was asleep when it finally happened, the sudden change back to normal waking me up, to a flood of relief. This was an ordeal I knew I was lucky to get away with, not least the fact I should not have driven home, but I was too concerned about losing my job, nevertheless I knew I could not expect to get away with another event like that again.

The next time the rush of blood came in my ears, signalling the start of another palpitation episode, I knew the game was up, it being a busy weekday afternoon/evening shift, I got word to the manager, Martin, claiming this was something new, not experienced before, trying to minimise the repercussions, fighting for my job, but taking no chances, an ambulance was sent for, and I was whisked off to the nearest hospital, in Macclesfield.

By the time I got there, my heart had returned to its normal rhythm before the ambulance even got to me, so although I was hooked up to a heart monitor, and kept in overnight, they did not see my heart palpitating, and so I went home with the hospital having no data to diagnose, my GP giving me a 24-hour heart monitor, that again recorded nothing unusual, as indeed I felt fine when those episodes were not occurring. I was allowed back to work, having been given some tablets and told take things easy, easy for the doctor to say, but I still had a living to earn…

By this time rumours were rife that as the company was suffering reduced profits, mainly due to some of the main drugs the company sold now being at the end of their patent period, during which no one else could sell a generically similar product, so enabling a high price for these drugs, having to be now much reduced in price to compete with new generic competition, now allowed, and so pushing down profits, until new patented drugs could be brought to market, all this likely to result in agency staff being purged, as had apparently happened before.

So it proved, in September 2011, we were on a short break in a log cabin in North Wales, when I received a text from the agency, saying that my contract, running out at the end of September, would not be renewed, along with many others, as I found out when I got back to work.

A few people with the agency, less than a quarter, who had been there over four years, were to be taken on by the company, the rest of us, we, to be finished on our three-monthly renewal date, this way, as agency staff made up less than a quarter of the workforce, they would not be hit by a sudden sharp drop in numbers, giving time to adjust down production, they had it all worked out, this being a repeated cycle from what I could gather.

So back I went back on the online job sites, with my CV updated to include the last eighteen months or so at the drugs company.

If there was any time between finishing there and my next job, it can't have been much, as I soon found myself starting, again through an agency, at an Overhead Crane Manufacturers out in Chapel en Le Frith, about the same distance out from Hyde, but southeast into Derbyshire.

This work was very different from drug trafficking and involved a variety of jobs, the only one in common with the last job being a small amount of fork truck work, mainly loading a parked trailer, with a mix of products each afternoon.

This company made a mix of small overhead chain lift cranes, some made by sub-contractors in Italy, that had to be quality checked and photographed, then uploaded onto a database by me, among a few others, then having small kits of fixing screws, bolts and other bits and pieces added, before being packed and sent to customers.

Much larger cranes were also made by this company, these being mounted on overhead I-beam gantry, picking kits for some of these and checking over and photographing key sections of these were gradually added to my work, as was checking over the creation of the daily manifest for what was going out on the trailer, larger cranes going out every so often on large flatbed trucks.

Chapter 72

This job in general was quite interesting as I gained more skills, working with milling tools among other work, such as photographic QC that I had done little of before, this being a much smaller company, you generally find yourself having a larger mix of different work to do, this being agreeable for me.

However, it was not to last, as the palpitation episodes continued to plague me, only occasionally, about once a month, the first couple of times there, I managed to find a hidden storage room to lie down, effecting a cessation of the debilitating irregular heartbeat within a couple of minutes, returning to its normal beat as suddenly as it went iffy. I got away with this for a few months, but it got worse, and disappearing for a few minutes lie down no longer worked quickly.

The end came when, after trying to restore normal heartbeat by lying flat, and it not working, I knew the game was up. Again, I had to confess to my manager what had been happening, and that it was no longer recoverable, with a quick lie flat session, and therefore I would have to finish there. It was a shame, as I was learning some good skills there and could have seen myself integrating well there in the long term, but it was not to be.

I was seen by a heart specialist at Tameside Hospital, given a Stress Echo Cardiogram, which is basically an ultrasound scan, whilst on a treadmill, being wired up to heartbeat sensors, I tried to induce a palpitation episode by deliberately eating some stodgy food a little while before this test. The pain I get in my chest after eating does not seem to relate to the palp episodes, and of course none were induced whilst I was wired up.

I was then again given a 24-hour home monitor in the hope that it would pick up an episode, didn't happen, and I was beginning to think the medical people would start to wonder about the veracity of my claimed episodes.

I was also trying to figure out where to go from here in terms of earning a living, between Sarah's job and my pension I had opted to take, just before the government changed the rules to only being able to start taking private pensions from age fifty-five, instead of fifty, that and my large redundancy payment from the combined Enzyme and Widnes Phosphate job, plus what we had gained from downsizing, meant we were OK for a while, but I could not fritter away our savings forever.

So being tired of being at the whim of agencies, and the uncertainty of any long-term stability, and the fact that there was no point trying to get back into work busy enough to induce palpitating episodes anyway, I decided to buy a small van and do some courier work, in the hope that mainly driving around would not cause much in the way of palp events.

When I had been last checked at hospital, they had told me of a procedure where a surplus nerve bundle in the heart could be burnt out! This excess node causing the regular signal from the brain to regulate the valve at the junction in the bottom the heart to an artery, could arc instead to this excess nerve node some people had in their heart, causing the irregular signal to the valve, it getting conflicting messages to open and close.

Burning this excess node out would then stop the diverting electrical signal, causing the palpitations, and thus ensure this signal came and went only from the brain ceasing the conflict of signals that was happening with increasing frequency. I was told the procedure did not always work, but did in a high percentage of people, given the option for this, I agreed to it, but it would be August 2012 before I could have it done at Wythenshawe Hospital.

While I was getting organised and familiar with how couriers worked, fate intervened in the problem of getting my palp episodes recorded, and I suspect, verified. Whilst at home, something or other set one off, and wanting to get proof to the doctors, Sarah drove me to the local surgery, it being only five-minute drive away. I had made no appointment, so even though I was gradually feeling worse, I was told to sit and wait for the doctor to fit me in…

Which she did about a quarter hour later, when I told her I was in the middle of a palpitating event I was told to lie down, she then proceeded to try various techniques for shocking my heart into returning to normal, all to no avail, an ambulance was then called to the surgery, this taking me to Tameside Hospital, Sarah getting there before me.

I was taken into an A and E booth, where doctors tried the same procedures the GP had tried, again none working, I was wired up to a heart monitor and could see my pulse up and down all over the place, but averaging up near 200 BPM, I was then told of a procedure that was only used when nothing else worked. It would be a heart-stopping event – quite literally. My analogy was that it was like unplugging the power, hoping for a reset, as that is more or less what happened.

I was given an injection that stopped my heart, beating for about three or four seconds, by the end of which it was starting to burn, then my heart started beating, at a normal, regular pace, they had done it. They now had proof, in spades, that this was a real, serious problem I was having, one that had forced me out of work, twice, they may or may not have always believed me, but they had no evidence until this episode, which provided heart-stopping proof…

Chapter 73

The world of courier driving is, or was when I was involved, fairly cut-throat, in that there were three basic ways to get work, there was an online site where jobs were put out for tender, speed of pick-up, and lowest quote got the work, or you could do as I did, and find a local courier company, and turn up in your van and get your name on their distribution board.

The third way, and the method I should have used in hindsight, was to get on half a dozen companies reserve board, these are the people they called when a job came in that none of their primary board drivers could cover, all being busy. But I, being new to the game, turned up at the nearest company to where I lived, they took a look at my little Fiat Nemo, asked if I was on the books of anyone else, I told them they were my first try, and they put me on their books. That was that, they would call me in the morning when they had a pickup for me.

You needed only four essential bits of equipment to make courier work possible, one was a satnav, as about only half your work was repeat customers, and you had to find them all a first time, there were also diversions to get around, and sometimes there were multi-drops to route plan. Then there was the Bluetooth ear piece, for hands free calls, needed for updates on progress, and the next job, then a hand trolley, to save multiple trips with three of four boxes of documents in and out of a building, sometimes many floors up in London, or more often Manchester, usually solicitors offices.

Last was a spider, a collection of stretchy cables with hooks on both ends that you could attach to various points in the back to keep unusual or heavy loads immobile on sharp bends or sudden breaking when someone pulls out in front, or breaks sharply without warning, which happens a fair bit, if you are on the road enough.

As mentioned, many runs were repeat jobs, so after a couple of the same, the satnav was not needed. At first, I preferred the longer runs, as parking was often a problem, and parking on yellow lines became a necessity, I was never booked, commercial traffic being given a little more leeway, as long as you were not actually blocking access.

The problem with long runs, when getting work from only one provider, was that quite often there were no return pick-ups, so being self-employed, all the petrol, and dead time (running without loads), was yours to absorb, and although I had a good accountant, I could not make enough to keep going, often waiting till nearly midday before I got my first call for work. The longest run I did involve driving to a private address in Bristol, then across the country to Central London, then back home. This was possible only by setting off at about three in the morning, getting home mid-evening.

What I should have done from the start, but was not aware that some drivers worked this way, was to not commit to one job provider, even if at the start you are given plenty of work as I was, as unless you are one of the earlier to register with the company guys, when work gets slack, you are given the least priority, the bigger vans getting the lucrative multi-drop work.

Instead, as I learnt months later from another driver, to register on the reserve list of about half a dozen providers, or even more, enough so you are turning down some jobs due to being busy, being careful not to register with so many, that you end up turning down jobs so often, they stop calling you. About a third of jobs were solicitors' documents, picking up was usually from outlying towns, but into busy city centre offices, often late afternoon into rush hour, so getting back home was slow.

Then again you could end up picking up a hired cement mixer, being top heavy, this had to be well strapped in, trying to find an underground drop off on a new multi-story car park with a satnav that is not programmed for this, is a bit of a detective job, trying to narrow down the actual people who need it – loads of fun, satnavs are often only good for private addresses, with commercial, which is 90% of courier work, satnavs only get you in the ballpark, you can take an hour to get within ¼ mile, then half an hour to actually find the drop off.

One of the few advantages of being self-employed was getting time off when you needed it, as a courier you simply told you work provider you would not be available on a given day, or period, this came in handy when at short notice, I was told there was a cancellation slot in June, for my planned August procedure to try to stop the palpitations, I accepted, I had as hoped, not yet had any episodes whilst courier driving, these usually happening when doing sustained physical work usually after a bend down then happening just after standing back up or badminton, so the choice of courier work was a good one from a health point of view for now. Long term, not so healthy I think, too little exercise.

The day came for the procedure, having previously been to Wythenshawe Hospital to establish if my heart looked as though it had the excess node, and therefore the likely culprit for the diverted signal. A local anaesthetic was administered for where the camera and hot tool were inserted in a large vein at the top of my leg, I was conscious, laid flat and watching the whole procedure on a screen above my head, the doctor taking only about ¼ of an hour to guide the camera and burn out tool to the offending node, then activating the burn out, me feeling very little, no pain throughout.

Full marks to this NHS doctor, who delivered a complete cure for my palpitations.

From that day to this, I have never had a palpitating event, so to date a 100% success, I did ask if this problem was related to the pain I feel when trying to walk fast or uphill, or do heavy physical activity only after food, but was told it was a separate problem, and as mentioned earlier I still suffer this, but at least by minimising my food intake at work, I could do enough physical work to take an average industrial job again.

Chapter 74

Which is what I soon decided to do, though maybe I should have tried switching to the multi-provider option first, but I could see the roads getting more crowded, with the immigration flood gates wide open, the roads getting jammed more often, the M6 being the worst example, so I decided having had my successful Ablation, the excess node burnt out, I would try to get back into company employment as soon as possible.

By August I was offered a QC checking job at a company specialising in reselling used CDs, electronic games and quality second-hand clothes, there are not many companies doing this, but I continue with my policy of not naming my work places, just in case there are legal complications in naming any.

This place of work, at the time I worked for them, was in the south of Stockport, though they have since moved the operation I was working on – the clothing resale sector – out to a new site in Macclesfield. I had the option of transferring back to the CD checking operation, which was to me – going cross-eyed looking for scratches and other blemishes, not going to happen…

Working with traded in clothing brands such as Superdry, Asos, Lacoste, Ralph Lauren, Ted Baker, those sort of brands, checking for stains, scuffs, holes, bobbling, anything that would stop them being fit for display, and resale on their website, subject to close customer scrutiny, this was better than CD checking, and when I graduated to checking the photos of clothes, then sending them on to the website operation, the work became more absorbing.

Checking coat-hangered batches on wheeled rails, against declared stock, making sure that what was on a railed batch, matched the number and items actually added to the computer database and reconciling those which did not, which happened enough to keep you on your toes, this, as well as preparing and wrapping passed clothing on rails for weekly transfer to the online sales operation, was work I quite enjoyed, though the pay was not much above minimum wage level.

Having sold the little one up – one down house on Crete, for about the same as we bought it for five years earlier, not such a good investment, but given the worsening state of the Greek economy, and the banking crash in 2008, just glad to get out without a major loss, though in the long term these things tend to settle down, and looking at it now, in 2018, so it has proved.

We took a trip to Western Cyprus, in the autumn of 2014, a couple of months after having secured the employment mentioned above, and deciding we needed a late holiday somewhere warm before winter, this turned out to be a little town called Polis on the west coast, a few miles north of Paphos, where many British Expats have made their home.

Apart from a trip up to a richly decorated monastery in the Troodos Mountains, and a jeep "Safari", driven by a Cypriot guy who played guitar in a rock band and loved the Scorpions, a British band, and who took us to a Phoenician Bridge up in a forest, that had an ice-cream van parked at the bridge, miles from anywhere, there is not a lot else to recount from this trip, a boat trip to Aphrodite's Cave, I am sure one of many such in the Greek world, a trip to some tombs near Phapos, and last but not least, Sarah got treated to a beachside pedicure, where she put her feet in a container with fish in it, that ate her dead skin…

Whilst we were there, we reflected on the fact that every time we went away, the cats had to spend that week in a Cattery, this led to a new plan, that instead of having a second home we had to fly to, only a very few times a year, we would look for somewhere we could go for long weekends, not too far away, that we could take the cats with us to.

Back at home we started looking at static caravan parks, and we soon narrowed our choice of sites down to somewhere we could get to in not much more than an hour – North Wales – but not too far in, just far enough to feel we were on holiday, but far enough that places like Anglesey would be in easy reach of day trips from the site.

Settling on a site about eight miles inland south of Prestatyn, near a village called Caerwys, and only a couple of miles south of the A55, the main artery into North Wales, we could be there in about 1 ¼ hours, not too much of an ordeal for the cats, though they did always not see it that way, sometimes meowing most of the way in their back-seat baskets.

This idea worked out well, the few years we had the 30ft x 12ft static, with views of the Clwydian Hills, we were able to get there for around eight or nine long weekends each year, usually four days, booking Fridays and Mondays off, and going on the Thursday evenings, going about every three weeks from late April to October.

Chapter 75

As we had hoped, within a couple of days of the cats arriving at our caravan, they were allowed out, under supervision at first, hoping they would not disappear, never to be seen again. We need not have worried, they gradually expanded their circle of exploration, and after a couple of trips, they had a window left open, with an outside table on the patio for then to climb in from, so that we could go out for half a day or so, leaving them food and water, usually finding them curled up on the settee when we got back, having gone out for as long as they wanted, a much better outcome than a Cattery stay.

We had bought a book on Flintshire/Denbighshire moderate to easy walks, three to five miles, and we spent the first year or so finding some of these, interspersed with visits to places like Anglesey, and Rhos on Sea, where we would walk the promenade. Another good walk along the seaside is from West Shore, on the opposite side of the Llandudno peninsular, down to Deganwy and back, often watching paragliders or windsurfers then have Brunch at a local cafe, it had to always be this way, a walk followed by food, as whatever ails me would make eating first then trying to exercise a painful, or on the flat, an uncomfortable experience, as previously mentioned.

Now and again, when the weather had promise, we would get up earlier for full-day trips further afield, driving to the base of Mt Snowden for example, and then taking the train up to the top, where we were fortunate enough to find a sunny clear view for miles in every direction, before brunch in the large cafe up there. Another fine day-long trip is the Lynn peninsular, with the long beach of Morfa Nevin on the north coast, ideal for a long beach combing walk on a sunny day, or on the south coast, Pwllheli, with its extensive harbour, followed by a run down to exclusive Abersoch, I say exclusive, as the prices for anything there excludes much hanging around for us commoners, not a place for bargains, pretty as it is.

Living in our terrace in Houghton Green, Denton, was starting to feel claustrophobic, with the less than agreeable neighbours, at least on one side, being the reason we were starting to regret spending money on the property, as we came to the conclusion that we could not settle long term there.

Not wanting to move out of the area, we started looking at property around the Hyde area, and wasting little time found a new, but small two-bed town house on a development in the Newton district of Hyde, the developer buying our terrace a bit below market price, but cutting out the long-drawn process of finding a buyer, and having more than doubled the selling price we bought the Gee Cross house, we decided to take the hit.

There was a communal car park, and a little bit of garden overlooking a steep banking down to a stream that ran into the River Thames, on the other side of which, there was an old industrial pond, not exactly picturesque, but not bad-looking. The house was small, but having got rid of a large amount of excess baggage during the last move, we squeezed in, quickly settling in.

We did it again – spending money on the place within a year of moving in, first having fitted wardrobes put in ours and the tiny second bedroom, and then a little later I saw this idea of something called the Midnight Sun, now a little more mainstream, with Eon offering a version, but at the time being little known.

The idea being that as well as having solar panels installed on your roof, you also had a converter and storage battery, that took a charge from the panels, anything in excess of what you were using in the daytime, which in spring and summer was little, instead of being returned to the national grid, (for which you were paid an allowance, based on your panel wattage, now withdrawn), you then used your stored charge in the evening, a light sensor switching us to stored battery power, based on the time of year.

This all cost thousands of pounds of course, supposedly being recovered in about ten years of saved bills, and for a year or two, we paid next to no electric bills in the summer and very little in spring and autumn, winter, in this country saved us only a nominal amount, maybe 40 pounds in three months.

Chapter 76

Returning again to the travelogue element of this story, as we did when things were stable, we took our first venture into the southern hemisphere, Mauritius being our destination, while the tropical sand and sea was a draw, it was something a little unusual that I spotted on the internet whilst checking out things to do on this island, namely Walking with Lions, that got both our interest.

With Sarah reading Wilbur Smith's African based adventures, and liking wildlife in general, this was something that got her interest as well as mine, as you could apparently go for a walk with young lions, just like it said on the tin. This was the decider that put Mauritius above the Seychelles for activities, as snorkelling would be about it for Sarah there, and I would not leave her alone for long period's scuba diving.

So, having first booked the holiday, I then booked us in via the net for the above-mentioned Walking with Lions. Getting there involved changing planes at Paris, the closest we got to that town with the extra-large Blackpool Tower without the ballroom dancing option, though not strictly needed…

An interesting Island, with a chaotic history, a mixture of British and French Colonialism, mixed in with migration from Africa, India/Sri Lanka, and even a small but growing Chinese presence, building their own new town, this looking like a state sponsored push into an offshore business operation, though it could also be part of their push into the mineral wealth of African countries, where they build roads for the locals, as long as these run close to their mining operations…

Back to our visit there, we stayed near Grand Bay, in the north of the island, cannot recall the name of our resort, but stayed in a duplex apartment on a small nicely planted complex, its restaurant and bar, with its small dancing stage and pool in front, being the centre of things.

It was while sat around this pool that I noticed the hanging nests in the trees, one tree especially full of them, bright yellow Weaver Birds building these. I put my David Bailey hat on, leaning on a large rock near the tree in question, I took enough close up photos of them building their nests, that back home I was able to pick three, depicting the circular-hooped start, middle and resulting finished nest, framed and on the wall of our current second bedroom in linier fashion, as though I had captured the same bird from start to finish, though in fact chosen from many taken, in the hopes of producing just such a result.

Two photos were taken in what is known as the Pamplemousses Botanical Garden on the edge of the capital, Port Louis, one is a zoomed in picture of the giant water lily pool, and the other a close up lotus lily in another pool in the same park, these were subsequently painted very well by Sarah in fine detail, and as a pair with red border, hang in our bedroom, I would not be parted with these, as with a pair of rural scenes she painted from photos I took from our time on Crete, now on our living room wall, our house is livened up with items, photos and pictures, painted from the former, taken on our travels.

The interior of Mauritius has large sugar cane plantations, and a small but craggy mountain range

On the way to being taken to a catamaran excursion, I was struck by the fact that most road sighs are in English, and yet the predominant language spoken there is a French patois, though English is understood in the tourist areas, where your money is spent – funny that.

The above-mentioned Catamaran excursion was a pleasant enough experience, being let off for a bit of snorkelling on a shallow reef, getting a bit too much sun on the deck, and then going ashore on a mangrove surrounded island, where I was able to wander off far enough off the beaten track to photograph in one picture two Fiddler Crabs, one with a red large claw, and one with a blue large claw, beckoning the other over, or at least that was what it looked like, rather than the mate attraction it was.

On the way back we were passed by a mock pirate ship with bright yellow sails, full of mainly black folks singing, bongo drumming and dancing, clearly having a good time, such was the mix on this island.

But as mentioned at the start of this episode, the most memorable part of this trip was the excursion to the Casela Nature Leisure Park, this was set up by a couple fleeing the regime in Zimbabwe, and was a small to medium-sized park, divided into large enclosures with a few monkeys and other animals, but the real attractions were two enclosures, one with juvenile lions and tigers in, that you could enter! You were given a walking style stick that you had to put stood up between you and the freely wandering small – big – cats! If you know what I mean, some of these cats being quite boisterous, chasing each other round the enclosure, there being around a dozen cats in this bit of enclosed parkland. There were a couple of rangers in there just in case of problems, can you imagine being allowed to do this in Britain…

The other smaller enclosure had two cheetahs, you could go in with, though we did not do this, what we did do was what we came here for, went for a walk, with two 18-month-old lions, called Bowser, and a very laid-back Malaka, a white lion, so Sarah tells me, (don't think I recalled details like that with my scrambled brain do you), these two were from a group of about half a dozen lions that went for the same walk in rotation, trained by the owners and rangers to respect the walking stick you had to keep stood up between you and the lions, the route was less than half a mile of woodland, with frequent stops for photos, both yours and their professional set ups, where they would entice the lions up fallen trees with pieces of meat on the end of sticks, out of the photo of course, you standing just in front and slightly below the lions, facing the camera, hoping the young lions were happy with the meat on the stick! The best picture up in the living room, though we had many others of us stroking the young lions and tigers.

There were freely roaming peacocks, and giant tortoises, quite a mix, along with the large cafe, it was a very unique experience, well worth the visit.

Apart from the cockroaches gathering in the eyes of the wooden-roofed bar and the large one I stood on in the bathroom of our duplex in the middle of the night, the wildlife, nature reserve especially, were the highlights of this trip.

Chapter 77

Again just briefly – when you are least expecting it – I would like to draw your attention to a guy called Clifford Stone, formally in the US Army for twenty-two years, who tells of being in a special unit that was used for UFO crash retrievals, if this man is a hoax, (always possible), he has extensive information of procedures used, processing and hiding of Special Access Projects buried so deep that only need to know personnel are allowed contact with the results of these events, either that, or he has a very extensive imagination.

Those with an open mind can search "Disclosure: Sgt Clifford Stone", on YouTube, for an interview with much more information on the subject, likewise with a former Canadian Minister of Defence called Paul Hellyer, who claims UFOs are real and their presence concealed by world leaders – go figure…

Just thought I would throw these guys in to keep up my Oddball credentials.

Returning to my then current employment, at the second-hand CD/games and clothing traders, a new problem loomed, as mentioned earlier, due to lack of space, the clothing operation was going to be moved to a site in Macclesfield, which was not good news, it was one thing commuting there for reasonably good pay at the drug packaging site, it was another going that far for little above minimum wage, so I updated my CV online and started looking.

The alternative to moving with work out to Macclesfield was transferring back to checking CDs and games, for scratches and the like – no, thank you.

My salvation at that time came from Sarah's daughter Sue, who worked at a factory in Stockport building and refurbishing domestic smart gas meters this was mainly assembly work, she told me they were soon to move on to 12-hour working days there, and as I was currently working a 12-hour day, and the money was reasonable at this Stockport factory, I thought them worth enough attention to write a covering letter mentioning I was currently working a 12-hour day and was used to production targets, together with my CV, I sent this to their HR dept on Spec, though they were not currently recruiting directly, they were taking on agency people, that was plan B for me, if they referred me to the agency, I would try through them. I got lucky, after an interview, I was taken on, with five other people as an employee, we were to form the nucleus of a new type of production cell.

I said my goodbye's in the clothing dept and was given a multi-signature leaving card, depicting a guy making good his escape over a wall – very apt. I just hoped it wasn't out of the fire into the frying pan…

The new place was another one of those companies that take on a mix of direct and agency workers, convenient if there is a reduction of output needed, just shed a few agency workers, as they had at the drugs company I worked at a while back.

This new employer, like the CD/clothing recycling company, took on a good third to a half of eastern European people, as many companies do, thus making it hard for any bargaining power for the workforce trying to get a pay-rise, which is exactly the intention. As I touched on earlier, regardless of what the remoaners would have you believe, that it is all selfish (not wiser of course) older people who voted for Brexit, but is as much native workers having to compete (1) with EU directives allowing companies to bring in people from lower wage-earning countries, and (2) when actually getting a job, seeing these people used to keep pay pegged at low levels.

So is it so surprising that people like me, not high achievers, but willing to work hard, given a real vote, (not first past the post, where you can come second in a hundred constituencies, getting millions of votes but no MPs, but a straight national percentage vote,) turned out in high numbers, despite Project Fear telling us we would be hit by an asteroid or worse if we dared vote to leave the Soviet Union, sorry I mean the European Union of course, no, not so surprising is it.

Though the vote was close, I believe many leave minded voters were cowed into believing they had no chance of winning, and so did not turn out, hopefully, they will believe in themselves if anti-democratic plotters succeed in forcing another vote, or succeed in watering down the leaving conditions (as with the fishing industry for example) to the point of not regaining control of our own destiny.

House shortages, strained NHS, overcrowded roads, all can be traced back to Blair, it does not matter what colour skin, you cannot open the flood gates, and then a few years later have the gall to point at the current government, hamstrung by EU Directives (apt word that – Directives, no pretence at democracy there) saying the above problems are all the current government's fault, when millions are let into the country, or any country, in a short space of time, and expect its infrastructure to cope.

Chapter 78

As far as I am concerned, Cameron did one good thing whilst in power, blinded by privilege (not his fault he was born to it), he kept to his word on calling the promised referendum, forced on him by Farage, and his millions of alienated voters, Cameron, not believing for a minute he would actually lose, just not realising how unwilling the EU would be (as many before him) would be to contemplate any reforms that would compromise their federalist agenda, and so the silent majority finally had its say.

It is really very simple in my humble view – the further away the government, the less responsive it is to local needs. Our MPs, will no longer be able to claim everything good is their doing, and the bad stuff is out of their hands – EU regs, no, they will have to drag a civil servant, (misnomer if ever there was one), like public school, the exact opposite in reality) kicking and screaming as it is forced back into accountability, again no longer able to blame the EU for all things bad.

I am not blind to the very few good points of the EU, one I will give them credit for, is standing up to giant US corporations in recent years, in particular the multi-media and computer companies, that use certain countries to shelter their tax liabilities, whilst paying a miniscule amount to the countries where they make most of their profits, whilst also ignoring the misuse by subversive elements, in corrupting young impressionable minds, in this the has EU led the way, our own country now following (or promising) to follow suit. It is a pity those in Brussels are not as progressive in their democratic credentials, where we seem to be showing them how to do it.

Latest rant over, I return to my employment at the Smart Gas Meter factory, set on one of those industrial estates designed for small to medium-sized operations, it was about twenty to thirty minutes' drive from home, depending on the time of day.

Though the 12-hour day was coming, it was a 6 – 2, 2 – 10 operation when I started there, I, with the five other new starters, were to be added to another half dozen experienced operators to commission a new type of production cell, at least new to this site. Instead of a long line with the various stages of assembly strung out along its length, there was being built a U-shaped production cell, the first of at least five such, though the limited floor space was going to be very cramped, and the supply and finished product chains would be somewhat strained, as it would require a "just in time" level of supply to function – fine in theory, the practicalities entailed good communication with the warehouse, which was situated in the second of two buildings the company occupied, so when a component was close to running out, one of us would have to leave his/her station to go tell the distribution reception people that we needed such and such a pallet or crate of whatever.

While the new cell was being finished off, we newbies were inserted into the existing production lines to learn the operation skills we would need, though some would be a bit different on the new cell. After a few weeks, the new cell was ready to try out, individual operations were tried out and tweaked until the whole cell was declared operational.

In theory this new cell was to get priority over the older production lines, as this first of the new cells was more compact than the long lines, and so was supposed to speed up the assembly process, the meter case having been fixed onto and registered on the rollers by the first operator, then sent a much shorter distance to the first circuit board soldiering operation, transducer addition, all the other gubbins added, gluing, the helium gas test stage, more soldiering, more glue, then testing to see if the finished shell worked, before the whole thing was added to a mobile multi-level drying cart for curing and retesting once dry.

The female operators, having smaller hands, and maybe a little more deft, tended to do the soldering work, as this was precision work that had to be done at speed, it was not something I was keen to try, as it gave the operator eye strain and headache having to focus for long periods, my concentration would not have been up to it. The one compensation for doing soldiering was that you got to sit down, these operators swapped to different jobs after two hours, I learnt four station operations, the unit signing on and fixing, gluing, helium testing, and final assembly and test.

All these other stations were stand up, and as anyone who has had to stand in one place for any length of time will tell you, your feet soon start to ache, absorbent mats were provided at these stations, and they made a real difference, when we moved to 12-hour working, they were essential, even so you soon learnt to volunteer for anything that involved walking somewhere, and if that was not happening, everyone went to the toilet when allowed, whether or not you needed to, just for the movement, and break, however short.

Chapter 79

It was a high-pressure environment, there were a lot of eyes on us, being a new operation, and we got used to a lot of visitors, from company bigwigs, to customers like British Gas, who were our biggest clients, our company keen to show of its new quality control and therefore (in theory) its improved consistency of fault free end product.

As time went by we melded into a team, got used to each other's strengths and weaknesses and personal quirks, we were encouraged not to talk much, but we were human, no robots yet, so we managed to produce a few laughs from time to time, anything to relieve the boredom. Anyone walking past got checked out, I remember asking in all innocence how a woman who always put a plastic flower in her hair managed to water it without getting her hair wet – that got a few chuckles, that sort of thing kept us going.

Debbie, our supervisor was a wise lady, firm but fair, only occasionally showing the strain of being responsible for us meeting production targets, with short fits of temper if someone caused delays by missing something out or talking too much and slowing the line down.

For me the helium test machine, where you put two part assembled meters to test for gas integrity became my favourite job of those available to me, and after a half-day training course about gas safety, was given the added job of gas bottle changer, a simple operation, but a welcome change from the usual repetitive actions that almost made robots of us. Having to go fetch nitrogen/helium new bottles from the isolated bottle enclosure outside and return the empties was an excursion away from the cell, though it was not done at leisure, as production was halted whilst the changeover was done.

Again, I might give you the impression that we spent large chunks of our life on holiday, but in reality there was only ever one main trip abroad in a year, apart from two or three to the Crete house for a few years, but for us little people, not part of the professional, or elite classes, the equivalent of the Equestrian classes of old Rome, most of your life is Groundhog Day, only slight variations on a very repetitive theme, and it is only the lack of children on my part that allowed me to take Sarah to far flung places of interest to us both, and to help compensate her for the hard life she endured with her ex.

Admiration for me goes to some of the most important people on the planet, the innovators, some rich, but there by virtue of their own effort, not from old money, or a rich or famous parent, but the people who have got there by finding and exploiting a demand in markets before anyone else sees them, the innovators, who come up with new tech that makes life easier, genuine artists, as well as original entertainers, in books or films that allow the vast majority of us less talented people to forget (temporally) our groundhog days.

I do not begrudge these people their riches, perfect example – Elon Musk, who, having made his fortune one way, now pushes this money and scientific talent into (Space X), to possibly lift our civilisation beyond our increasingly crowded planetary base, that we will need to take the pressure off very soon, as the people Gary Mckinnon and others, have got a glimpse of, show no sign yet of releasing the possibly much more advanced tech free energy, developed or acquired from elsewhere, or from innovators like Nicola Tesla and kept under wraps for commercial (oil) interests (Note the choice of name for Elon's Musk's electric car). It will be interesting if the parts of NASA, not in the public domain allow this non-government space tech to flourish, maybe as a useful diversion?, though if too much is accidentally seen, likewise with Japan, China and India's Luna expeditions, limited top level Disclosure may become necessary to these countries governments, depending on what they see…

Following close behind these mega talented people, are those who get up each morning really looking forward to their days work, what they do each day may not benefit millions, but they are lucky enough to have found work that gives them real satisfaction, building up a small business, or developing a skill to the point that they can chose how they use that skill, as it is in such demand, some able to relegate their income to secondary consideration behind their desire to express their natural or sometimes hard learnt talents.

For people like myself and probably many others, I just hope the above mentioned realise how fortunate they are in having these talents, and brains organised enough to express them, unlike those of us with just enough brain function to pay our way, aware of those unfortunates with not even that much dignity, and so grateful for what function we have, if we have any sense.

Unlike those intelligent but cunning people who have had their lives warped enough at some stage to turn to exploiting and hurting others with smart, opportunistic tricks, as found in many (not all) politicians, these unfortunately prolific people who exploit divisions, sometimes for profit, others, misguided by early misfortune into putting all rich people including the innovators into the same selfish category.

This could be the reason the secret keepers remain such, though their motives could be darker, maybe having made such a catastrophic mistake with a 1950's secret treaty, those of who we trusted, and now having to maintain global secrecy for its own sake, for fear of revealing that massive error of judgement in partnering up with the wrong group. I would prefer to be totally wrong in believing any of the contact scenarios, and turn out to be one of the gullible, then this version being the truth.

I rather hope that the truth of any contact is a more positive one, such as the one Clifford Stone espouses, (though it could be a mix of both good and bad), and that we are being guided away from our wasteful, destructive, short term outlook, if and when that is achieved, we may then be granted open contact with those ahead of us.

Chapter 80

Back to the only world I have proof of, and having once again gained employment that looked as stable as any, we got itchy feet for travel again, this time to Canada, specifically Vancouver, and its namesake large nearby island, the Pacific north west having been experienced by us as far north as Seattle some years ago (related earlier), we were keen to see more of the wild north west.

Vancouver Airport is a statement of Canada's keen awareness of its environment, you are greeted with a waterfall in the concourse, along with a large aquarium, trees planted in this bright and airy building. We boarded the automated Sky Train that took us into Vancouver, with partly elevated views as the name suggests on the way into the city, where it also went underground, getting us close to our hotel, (not now able to recall its name) but somewhere on a main street in the Downtown area, so maybe on Seymour St, within a half-hour walk of the local China town. Which we found disappointing, as its seemed spread out thinly, overpriced and top of the range from what we saw when we went out that first evening, hoping for a Chinatown like San Francisco's, with its plethora of choice of restaurants, there were probably more than we saw, but we ended up in an Indian restaurant that first night…

We had a couple of days in town before we picked up the hire car, we spent one of these buying a tourist bus pass that you could hop on and off all day, getting off at Gastown, the oldest and most elegant part of town, though his name sounds as if it comes from something a little less elegant, its founder John "Gassy Jack" Deighton, (let you guess why the nickname), not so, he talked too much instead. Gastown, grew from Gassy Jack's Tavern, to the smart leafy district, full of galleries, boutiques, and top-class restaurants it is now, along with its unique steam powered public clock.

Back on the open top bus, we headed to Stanley Park, with its Beaver lake, lost lagoon, and miles of wooded walkways, and beaches, but the real treat when we were there was the Vancouver Aquarium's Beluga whales, one of which was a young calf born there and closely attended by its mother, these white whales with their mobile heads were great to see, though the verdict is open as to the rights and wrongs of captivity of these intelligent mammals.

My view being that no more mammals should be captured, but those born, or so long ago taken they could not survive if released should be given the best possible care, with no coercive training, minimum stress being top priority, while they live their lives out. There were Sea otters, and a few penguins there, but it is the Belugas I will not forget. We ate that night at the Vancouver lookout, a somewhat overpriced revolving restaurant on the waterfront, an overindulgence we could have done without, and not to be compared with Seattle's Space Needle.

At some point we caught the ferry across to Granville Island, (not quite an island) and its open-air market, nothing must have impressed, as we came away empty handed. If timings are hazy, we wrote nothing down, not anticipating the need for detailed recall, nothing more of note other than we breakfasted those three mornings in a Chinese all day eat in cafe, fifty yards away on the nearest street corner to our hotel, no frills, good food, and much cheaper than the hotel franchise restaurant. The time came to pick up our hire car from the basement car park of a big hotel near the cruise ship docks.

Other than the car was described as "Compact" a saloon and automatic geared, as most cars over there are, and possibly white so Sarah says, I cannot recall the rental company, but well known, may have been Alamo, or not, as that had also been in Seattle years earlier. This being some years ago my phone then had no satnav, none in the car, so we missed a couple of turns on the map taking us to the ferry terminus at Tsawwassen, at the southern tip of Vancouver, just north of the Washington State US border. But we got there.

The crossing to Vancouver Island was less than two hours, over the Salish Sea, crossing US territorial waters, then close past islands and through the Swanson Channel to the Swartz bay terminal, we then followed our map along the Patricia Bay Highway (17) about twenty miles south into Victoria, the island's capital, and our two night stay there.

The hotel was not hard to find, with an underground garage, though not large, the hotel situated within walking distance of the coast, and after checking in, dumping the cases in our room, headed out for a stroll along the seafront, which was a gently curving bay, the town of Victoria not being that large, the most striking building being its red brick town hall, complete with clock tower, ornate gardens in front.

As mentioned, with my brain having a very poor long-term memory, only able to recall what my brain classifies as important events, with Sarah filling in some details I had forgotten, now having a smartphone, with its browser at your fingertips, is the only reason you are reading the descriptions I had forgotten, but being able to find, using this invaluable tool, the town hall above, and all other descriptions recalled after a few keystrokes, I do not regard this as cheating, as seeing online photos brings out the memories in there, just not readily accessible without prompts.

Chapter 81

If this means I have Alzheimer's, then I was either born with it, or had my brain scrambled at a very early age by whatever happened with the recurring "dreams" the first of which, if I were to describe now, would be like a screen saver – as described in the early pages of this narrative, the second sequence, a few years later, just a dull amber light, but accompanied by a feeling of great tension, and in the year or so to follow, the vocalisation of a familiar tune such as Z Cars, with my head rocking side to side, this happening soon after bed time, I know this is a repeat description, but if that last described episode was not an attempt to block some night time event out, then it was also not normal.

I may just trying to blame something exotic for the fact that we are all different, having different levels of brain efficacy in different areas, but it is strange to me that amongst my life long poor memory recall and concentration, also having normal dreams that are forgotten soon after as per normal – the above-mentioned stand out crystal clear after all this time, different for some reason, my connecting the amber light/tension sessions with the follow on bed time head rocking period only recently, though the blocking out theory is only that, a theory, it has a certain logic to it, as the amber/tension sessions were not pleasant, though not terrifying, at least in my conscious recall. These came *before* my noisy, "blocking" head rocking, so, I repeat, not parent visitations to quieten me down, I also recall those…

As mentioned before, my brother and sister have much better memory recall, both passing the Eleven Plus that I failed. To this day, my concentration is still very easily broken.

Still, if we were all blessed with good brain function, who would do all the boring and repetitive work that needs doing, I having long ago settled for that, as opposed to those with really serious mental and physical problems that prevent even the near normal life I have made, opting out of reproducing being the only abnormal choice, made from the bad experiences my resultant personality brought upon myself, having not good social skills, especially when younger, when anyone a little different was picked on, my dad was the same, my brother had two mildly autistic lads, so who knows if it is all just in my DNA, much easier to put everything down to that, rather than more exotic botched interference, as botched it would be if some of us are literally just Blood Vessels, for some planned evolution, that being the case – my line stops here, though extraction of anything is possible, as we as a species are already dabbling with cellular reproduction. Wheels within wheels…

I have to say I have no recall whatsoever of any strange experiences in adolescent or subsequent years, though from the (possibly crank) books on the subject I have read, I would not be aware anyway, any more than a rare animal does, being tranquillised and checked out by us, trying to make up for the devastation we had caused that species.

All the above having nothing whatsoever to do with our Canadian holiday, apart for the admission of using a smartphone to recall places visited, hazy or lost to my dire recall functions, just reserving the right to go off on a tangent, reaffirming my oddball status from time to time, maybe frustrating those who have by now decided to read only the work and travelogue parts of this book, though I can well imagine some of this as a psychologists dream case study, then for them, the rest is of this is the more juicy, as I am sure they will have an answer for everything, classic X, or perfect example of Y syndrome…

Now, back to the walk along Victoria's Waterfront, and as you see at most tourist areas, the kiosks are set up to take your booking for the trip to somewhere just a bit special, better than where you are now, only in this case, they delivered what it said on the tin.

This, being a boat trip tomorrow, out to the wild coastline where we were promised a good chance of seeing an Orca pod, reasonably, they could not promise a certain sighting, but they said this pod had a hunting territory it was known to frequent, and we would be taken there. Keen to make the most of our one full day in Victoria, we booked it, then carrying on with our stroll around the mostly low-rise pleasant seafront, with lots of boats moored as you would expect, though it was where half a dozen planes were moored, as in sea planes, with twin floats almost as big as the planes themselves, we booked a table in a restaurant overlooking them for that evening.

I was glad (and so I suspect was Sarah) I had already booked the boat trip for the next day, as a sightseeing floatplane trip would have been very tempting, despite it being above my pay grade.

And so we had an upmarket fish and chips meal next to these planes that evening on a raised patio, so it must have been pleasantly warm in the September sunset. I can still visualise that place, so one of the anchor points of my recallable memories there.

Chapter 82

True to their word, the next morning, after an hour or so through featureless island channels, the naturalists who were aboard the boat announced they had sighted the Orca pod.

The naturalists/marine biologists, used this sightseeing boat to monitor this pod in a symbiotic relationship with its owners, who got a more reliable sightseeing trip, there was no mistaking the six-foot high dorsal fin of the alpha male, which along with the rest of the pod, had been given a name, don't think it was Nemo, but these biologists had learnt where to find these marine mammals, identify individuals from fin and back profiles, and knew their feeding habits, well enough to take us to the right place at the right time.

It was not a very close encounter, the Orca were closer to another boat when one of them leapt clear of the water right in front of it, but we were less than 100 yds away, and as it is not something you see every day, we were well satisfied with what we saw. The location of this pod's feeding grounds must have been well known to the local sightseeing boat community, as though we did not go out in a convoy, radio communication with a binocular network from a few boats ensured a much better chance of someone spotting the pod more often, sharing this would be good for the local economy, so although we were first on the scene that day, within 15 minutes, it was like sightseeing Land Rovers grouped on the Serengeti view points within 15 minutes.

Next morning a road trip of nearly 200 miles stretched before us, to Tofino, halfway up the West (Pacific) Coast of this large island, where we were booked to stay for three days. Looks a lot, but I, enjoy the occasional long drive, especially if it's in countryside and the roads aren't too busy, we could have shortened this considerably by catching the "last train to Parksville" (sorry, but not really) this town being our later destination, and somewhere we would have to pass close by before turning west across the island.

Our route that day took us north along highway 1, the main east coast road, passing Nanaimo, (where we would eventually catch the ferry back to just north of Vancouver) from here, we continued north following the east coast, along Hwy 19 past Nonoose bay, then passing the turn of for Parksville, before reaching the turn off for Hwy 4, opposite the Qualicum Beach road, Hwy 4 taking us north west, where I was hoping for some wilder country, a fair chunk of what we had passed on the east coast looking quite tame retirement areas, with lots of bungalows, and residential estates, more populated than we had expected.

As we drove along the west side of Cameron Lake, apart from a railway running along the opposite side, the countryside became just that, much less busy, we continued on to Port Alberni, though I forget where, we would have stopped at some point for coffee on the east coast road.

Port Alberni is situated in the middle of Vancouver Island, about a third of the way up, set at the head of Alberni Inlet, which if in Scotland, would be a very large Sea Loch, snaking around thirty miles in from the pacific coast, past an abandoned pilchard cannery set near the coast called Kildonan, bought by the Wallace Bros in the early 1900s who named it after their home town in Scotland. Kildonan also being a Steamer stop where the canned fish would be picked up for distribution.

By the time we got this far, it was well past midday, and time for a rest and some food, we had covered around two thirds of the route to Tofino, and so could relax for a while. The most striking place in Port Alberni, is the fish smokehouse and cannery there, painted pink and green, I photographed this as it was unusual, hoping that Sarah might paint the picture, which she subsequently did, though it just looks odd as it did where it was, probably an attempt to brighten the pier up, the bottom half being pink, the top green. After admiring a giant wood carved Eagle situated on the boardwalk, we found a cafe/bar.

I think we had fish and chips that lunchtime, before setting off west on the Pacific Rim Highway (4), past the Kiehoot Indian Reserve, then along the north shore of Sproat lake for at least ten miles before turning south west past Clayoquot plateau park, then on to the south east shore of Kennedy Lake, before meeting the Peninsula Road junction, which would take you to Ucluelet at the base of the peninsular of that name.

At this junction, we did a more or less 90 degree turn from a south west to a north west heading, on the last leg of this day-long road trip, with only food and drink breaks, we were now in a heavily forested area, still on the Pacific Rim Highway, we knew when we were on the Tofino peninsular, as we started seeing signs, warning of Tsunami risk, with regular little roads of the highway, promising high ground if a Tsunami warning was broadcast, presumably from a hidden speaker network.

Set at the base of the Tofino peninsular, which sticks out into the Pacific, hence the tsunami risk, we passed the perimeter of Tofino Long Beach Airport, serving those with deeper pockets who would prefer a quick journey to the nearby golf course and wilderness Lodges, no doubt able to pick up a hire car there.

Chapter 83

Our hotel was on the south side, about halfway out on the peninsula, on the Tin Wis Indian Reserve, it now shows as a Best Western, had nice gardens, and you could see the sea from our second-story balcony, the weather was sunny, but Best Western might have arranged that to get you in, as the next morning, and following two days were wet, not a temperate rain forest area for nothing then! Blissfully unaware of the weather to come, we went out to stretch our legs on Mackenzie Beach and walked to a high rocky outcropping on our left, glad to get the sea air and legs moving after the long trip up from Victoria.

That evening we drove into Tofino on the western tip of the peninsular of that name, a small town, well spread out, and after a walk around, had a meal in a small wood-built restaurant, name now lost to us but Sarah says posh and expensive. In the morning the rain had arrived, though not heavy, so we went into Tofino where we booked a bear hunting (photo) "boat Safari" for the following day.

The weather dried up a bit in the afternoon, and one of the local natives told us a good place to fish from, as I had bought my telescopic Rod and a few spinners. After spinning from some rocks for a while with no luck, we moved on to the other location, which was at the dead end of a track near an inlet, there were sunken branches close to the shore, and as Sarah sat in the car reading, as it had started raining again, I tried a few casts out with a fairly large silver spinner.

It was the proverbial One That Got Away, for about ten seconds I got hooked into something quite powerful, vibrating the small rod quite hard, but as I tried to turn it, the line suddenly went slack near one of the many large sunken branches, I assume the line got snagged. Encouraged, despite the rain, I tried for a while longer, but no more bites, I gave up, quite soaked by that time, we went back to the hotel.

That evening we decided as is always our plan on hols, to eat somewhere less expensive alternately, we had spotted a large place called "The Docksider" in Tofino, it had wall-to-wall TVs in every direction, with baseball, ice hockey, and American Football, all silent thankfully, accompanied by mainly country music, we had a giant mixed meats, chips, onion rings platter, which we had seen passed out, this was meant for one, but we decided would do for both of us, washed down with beer.

The hotel dining room did a good breakfast, too much for every day, but nice for a holiday treat, bacon and muffin stacks, complete with maple syrup – well it was Canada after all.

Then it was time to go to the small dock area in town and catch our bear photo-hunting trip. With there being lots of long narrow inlets and a few large forested islands, close in to Vancouver island, especially on the western pacific coast, it made looking for bears from a boat a worthwhile proposition, with so much forested coastline to patrol, what was not so good was the weather, which as time went on, deteriorated from light to heavy rain, and we found ourselves glad we were in a covered boat, unlike some who were out in bright orange hard hulled ribbed dinghies, the passengers being issued with waterproofed coats and hats, but still looking pretty forlorn.

The setup was similar to the Orca watching off Victoria, several boats roaming a larger area than one could cover, keeping in touch so as to report any sightings for the others to converge on. When the rain was at its worst, seeing any brown bears through rain streaked closed windows was virtually impossible, no matter how close we were to the shoreline, those in the ribbed boats with their sou'wester on stood a better chance with nothing to impede their view, though I suspected that any self-respecting bear would have retreated from near the shoreline deeper into the woods for shelter, and the bright orange coats and boats, safer as it was, was not the best of camouflage for creeping up on an unsuspecting bear, having a back scratch against a tree, or else doing what bears do in the woods…

After four long hours moving from one location to another, with only one supposed sighting that neither of us saw, the boat took us back to Tofino. Not sure where we ate that night, Sarah had been able to put some of our clothes through a hotel laundry room washer and dryer, while she sat and read.

A fair way along the Mackenzie Beach away from the hotel we spotted a huge upturned tree stump, complete with roots with a span of at least ten feet, all somewhat whitewashed, that must have been washed up some time ago, as we saw a drawing of it somewhere local before we left the region.

On that same walk, I took a photo of some tracks on the beach that were so large, I speculated they might have been from the cougar that had been reported in the area, and no, not the older woman type! Sarah thought the prints could have been from a large dog, prints spread out in the wet sand, I preferred the cougar option, I have never since seen tracks so large, apart from tractors…

Chapter 84

On our last day there, we went to a national park temperate rainforest boardwalk, which was very dark and gloomy under the canopy of mixed ancient forest trees, the boardwalk was quite extensive, periodic descriptions at junctions and observation points named the various flora and fauna known to inhabit the area, but with drizzly overcast weather, the thick canopy and the brown forest floor, you wondered if there was a bear hiding in the gloom just round the back of some of the bigger trees, waiting in ambush to step out from cover – to sell you surplus Cushelle toilet paper! Sorry, I'm on a roll…

The boardwalk ended at a place called Wickaninnish Beach, which had at the end of the beach where the boardwalk came out, was a wooden lodge hotel and nature museum and Barebum cafe, all this on raised stanchions, overlooking the long, log-covered beach, the recent storm responsible for most of the timber, surfers were braving the slightly better weather, that being a bit of sun peeping through the clouds, with plenty of white surf to go at. I seem to recall a rainbow there.

Lunch was partaken of whilst there, Sarah says there was a Totem pole just outside, her memory being better than my grey mush. At the hotel, which was run by the native population, on one side there was an older guy hollowing out a kayak in the old traditional way using a pick scoop, though it was for show, it was still interesting to watch. That was Tofino. Nicer in good weather, just our pot luck.

The next destination on this pre-booked tour was Parksville, back on the east coast, we were due to stop four nights there. The drive back the way we came was uneventful, Sarah not seeing any bears whilst leaving the Tofino peninsular, as I have forgotten to mention she did whilst we were driving there, the car in front slowing to let it cross the road, it was on the wrong side of the road for me to see as it climbed over the banking into the woods, Sarah says it did not have a roll of Cushelle under its arm, so it did not need to go (the company pays the bear minimum for these adverts).

Stopping at Port Alberni as we did on the way over, we ate at the same cafe/bar as a few days earlier, must have liked it. As mentioned earlier, we past the turn of to Parksville on the way up from Victoria, and was not far down the main west coast highway 19 from Qualicum Beach where we joined it from the cross-island road.

Parksville was a disappointment, a very suburban boring looking place, our hotel near the seafront, no real beach there, looked like a quite retirement town.

In our room we found one of those books on the local area, we decided that we wanted to see a little more of the wild woods before we went home, so we found a small log cabin resort north west of Campbell River listed in the book, phoned them and managed to book an overnight stay in a cabin on Campbell Lake in two days' time.

We let the hotel know we would not be there that night, but would be back for our last night's stay on Vancouver Island. Took the hit on the lost night at the hotel. Apart from a guy playing weird synthesised music through his guitar on a bandstand along the seafront, my memory logs little of interest in Parksville, we ate at a quite Chinese restaurant one night, the highlight was when we went to a river inlet out of town up the coast, the day before we were due to set off for our overnight at the log cabin.

The weather was overcast, Sarah stayed close to a bar restaurant, with a coffee, reading, whilst I tried spinning in the estuary of the little river Sarah says was called French Creek, after several casts, I caught a small Sea Trout, about a pound, plate-sized, I was stood on large breakwater rocks, after a while I caught another about the same size, though this looked a little different, and may have been a small salmon, the fish dropped off as I was about to take the hook out, falling in a gap between the rocks, I nearly shredded my hand and arm reaching down to retrieve it, took several tries, but I got it up in the end, determined and pleased to have something wild to take to the log cabin to cook for tea.

Sarah's jaw dropped a little when I walked back from the rocks with two edible fish dangling from my fingers, last thing she expected to see I think, we found a plastic bag to put them in while we had lunch at the bar, before going back to the hotel, putting the fish in the drinks fridge in our room – at least the hotel would not smell a rat…

For the third time, the next morning we passed the crossroads heading north on Hwy 19 that had Port Alberni as the left turn destination, or Qualicum Beach if turned right, only a few miles east on the coast, as the name suggests, but never destined to be visited by us, as we were heading up to Campbell River, 75 miles up the coast from Parksville before turning inland to Campbell lake, another ten or so miles to the small log cabin resort whose name we can nether recall or find now. It was good weather on that drive up, passing the only place big enough to be called a town about halfway up called Courtenay, in the Comox Valley, this having a small airport serving the region. Neither of us can recall stopping before Campbell River, we did pass a district called Headquarters, though only the locals know what of.

Chapter 85

Campbell River is set at the northern end of the Strait of Georgia, and is the last major town heading north, even though it is not much more than halfway up this large island. The last outpost, another eighty or so miles further north on the Inland Hwy (19), being Port Hardy, on the Queen Charlotte Strait, this being the limit of major roads north. Food supplies were bought at a shopping centre, asparagus, sauce and potatoes to accompany the fish brought with us, plus something for next day's breakfast, we had coffee and a snack at a Starbucks, had a walk along the seafront, not for long, as we wanted to get to our log cabin.

The road out of Campbell River up to Campbell Lake was the Gold River Highway (28), the settlement/resort of Gold River being the only place signposted on our quite empty road inland, where we reached the west side of Campbell lake, by this time we did feel we were out in the wilderness, which was the idea.

By the time we reached the turn off for the log cabin camp, which was not far of Hwy 28, it was mid-afternoon, we checked in at the reception house, where we bought some wine to go with our fish supper, then were shown our cabin, set close to the lake shore, it was nicely isolated, the nearest other cabin not being occupied, it was what a log cabin was supposed to be, complete with wood burner, old leather settee, and a great view over the lake.

There was a small jetty about eighty yards away where some kids went out in a few canoe's, with supervision, I tried a little fishing, nothing doing, I didn't mind, I had already caught supper yesterday. Not often I could say that, not since my Hebrides visiting days many years ago. We were leaning over the wooden veranda rail with a coffee, when I spotted a small snake curled up in the vegetation, no idea what species, but uncoiled it would be less than 18 inches, we left it alone, it had gone later.

We had a coffee, some biscuits, and discovered that not all the wildlife here was that wild, in the shape of a very tame blue jay, that arrived first on the rail, but was soon on the veranda table eating biscuit crumbs, before long on Sarah's knee, it must have been well used to the occupiers of these cabins feeding them at close quarters, it was so tame. We got the photos, along with the snake, and unusual cabin, which had the double bed jutting out in a side bay window arrangement, strange to sleep in, almost like being outside.

After our coffee, we went across the highway, no more than what we would call a B road this far out, to a small, marked trail for a short walk in the woods. When we got back the biscuit packet that we had left on the table with one or two biscuits in it, had been emptied by one of the blue jays at a guess. Sarah cooked the fish supper, and we ate it sat on the veranda with the white wine bought from the reception, admiring the wild view. Nice when what you envisage actually turns out as imagined. The wine was bought there, not at the Campbell River supermarket, as you could not buy alcohol at supermarkets in British Columbia at that time, may have changed now.

I then proceeded to turn our cabin into a sauna that evening, putting too many logs in the wood burner. It was well after we had climbed into the windowsill bed as I called it, before it cooled down enough to sleep. It was properly dark, as it can only be with no streetlights and well away from the nearest town. Plenty of stars to see that night.

I think breakfast was croissants and scrambled eggs, not rushing, but after coffee, packing up and paying up, we retraced our steps back along the Gold River Highway, Gold River itself is a lot further west than we reached, but after the logging markets forced the Pulp mill closure there, it reinvented itself as a tourist destination for sports fishing, kayaking, climbing and hiking, whilst also being the closest village to where Captain James Cook landed and met a local Native chief during his endeavours…

On our way back we bypassed Campbell river, we had no reason to stop so early, but both of us liked the town, remarking that it would be a nice place to live near, big enough to have most facilities, but right on the edge of true wilderness, though from what I read about Gold River, it also attracts retirees, as well as young families, with its low priced housing, and multi-events tourism job opportunities, not sure Sarah would like the winters though, not liking snow, which is all white by me.

Heading south on Hwy 19 again, we stopped at what looked like a junk shop, a mix of old books and oddments, don't think we bought anything, literally, a bit further down the road, looking for a drink stop, we entered a petrol station that had a cafe, with decking overlooking water round the back, river or lake, can't recall, but Sarah remembers it as it was the first place she drunk caramel coffee, which she much enjoyed.

It must have been late afternoon by the time we reached Parksville, and our last night on the island. Fairly sure, we went back to the Chinese restaurant we ate at on our first night there, three nights ago, too tired after our long drive back to go looking further afield for somewhere different, the hotel restaurant being too expensive for more than one-night meal.

The travel agent we booked this trip with had said that we could use the ferry ticket at any ferry location crossing back to the mainland, and so we headed for the port of Nanaimo, which was only a quarter of the way back down to Victoria, from Parksville.

At the ticket office for the ferry in Nanaimo, the guy we spoke to must not have been used to tourists leaving from a different port from their arrival, as he had to make a call before he OK'd our pass from there. The crossing took us to Horseshoe Bay at the top end of Vancouver, and the top end of Hwy 1, it was a half-hour drive back onto Granville St and our hotel, where we dropped off our bags before taking the hire car back to its depot, walking distance back to the hotel, that was it, down to the corner Chinese Cafe/Takeaway that evening and again for breakfast, the lady owner recognising us from ten days earlier. Then it was the Skyway train, plane, and automobile home.

Chapter 86

Back at the Smart Meter Production factory, from time to time, other jobs other than line and cell production work became available from time to time.

I was not the fastest at some of the more repetitive operations, (getting old) and my concentration would let me down occasionally, leaving something set not quite right, usually spotted and corrected, so when a job in the refurbishing dept was brought to my attention, I jumped before I was pushed, not sorry to leave the high pressure, high speed production line. I had to wait a while to take my place on the Refurb Line, waiting for training, meanwhile doing sorting work in the transducer room, getting rid of damaged or defective units.

A guy called Lee was in charge of the Refurb Line, and it was he who showed me, in stages, how to process the various different types of gas meter that came back from customer companies, in many different states of disrepair. This job had one big advantage over the production lines, you had a sit-down work station, this was not to say you spent all your time sat, but it was not all standing in one place all the time either.

There were many reasons a meter might be returned, and it was our job to find out what was wrong – water damage of the circuitry was a common fault, green blotches being the indicator of this. You had a computer terminal and receptor plugs to fix the returned meter onto, and a set sequence of IF, THEN, GO-TO type operations to follow in the diagnostic procedure to find the less obvious faults.

Faulty circuitry, leading to current overload, battery problems, some meters had batteries replaced anyway, even if OK, some were burst and a right mess, the whole meter then being bagged and scrapped.

After testing for blown fuses, and removing these integrated fuses from the circuit board by heating the soldered wires and replacing with new fuses, some meters were fit for sending back out as refurbished units, depending on their production date.

There were two lines of workstations with a manually feed roller line on a slight downward gradient, meters fed from a tub at the top end, so the idea was grab two or three at a time, so while one was on a test that took a little while, you could be checking, and opening up others ready for further processing, having in effect your own mini production line, a branch off the main feed.

Though there were nominal targets you were expected to reach, different numbers, depending on the type of meter, there being four types, some needing much more processing, some with a much higher instance of scrappage, this being a good thing from our point of view, as soon as a fault was found that was not correctable, this info was entered onto the process software, and you moved onto the next, cutting a lot out of the checking time per unit. The unspoken idea generally being, that you went full pelt in the early two thirds of the shift, then as you approached the target for that type of meter, you slackened off, relaxing and chatting a bit, so as not to overshoot the target by much, as it was always the same everywhere, if you overshot the target regularly by much – up went the target.

On the new meter cell production operations where I used to work, there was no chance of getting away with that, you were one cog in a clockwork machine, the only relief being when one section of the assembly process had a breakdown, or was found not to be testing accurately, soon as everything was backed up you stopped.

The only other stoppage was the "Just in time" policy, the factory floor being that full of production cells and lines, that you ordered new meter cases or other components so as to arrive in the holding area, not long before you ran out, the warehouse operation having to bring these from the other building, so if by chance several production lines ordered new material at roughly the same time – you guessed it, someone was not going to get their stuff before it ran out. You could try ordering early, but as the holding area had limited space, the warehouse would not bring you order over until there was a slot.

This bottleneck called "lean manufacturing" in management speak, had not been sorted out long after I transferred to the refurbishment dept, from the point of view of the operators, this was a good thing, as if bought some relief, though as targets were more prominent, the cell supervisors started recording the downtime and reasons for it, as it was they would take the heat from management for lower output without explanation.

Where I now worked in the Refurb, targets were nominal only, to my knowledge no one was disciplined or brought to tack for being below the target expected, there being about a dozen of us, if we were all below, it was usually due to the type of meter. As mentioned, we made sure the target was not so high that we had to go full speed all day to reach it, the trick was not to make it obvious we were slowing down by messing around and talking too much, to the point where the Manager of the floor noticed, as Lee, our supervisor would then be in trouble. A good guy, he knew the score. The rest of us would come down on anyone who attracted unwanted attention.

No one works at the same speed on independent processes, unlike the assembly lines, so now and again some youngster usually, would get near the target so fast, that he did one of two things, neither of them good for the rest of us.

He would start talking with others, leaving his station for long periods, making it obvious he was near finishing, of worse still, as it was recorded on the computer, he, (we were nearly all male on this dept) would keep going way over the target, without letting on, Lee would sometimes notice this, and ask how many he had done, sometimes able to slow him down and pointing out why it was in the common interest, not always obvious to some.

If a major overshoot was not spotted in time, this was spotted by management and the target upped, we coped with this by making sure the person concerned did not repeat his transgression, we would all go a little over the old target for a while, gradually dropping back to the original target, nothing being said. Lee would explain to the manager that a lot of errors were later found on the meters the "fast" guy had processed.

Depending on your point of view, you may find this mode of working lazy or offensive, I agree with lee's view, that as long as we pushed hard when we were fresh in the earlier part of the day, then slowing a little when we were tired later on, produced fewer incorrectly processed meters, and gave us a bit of wriggle room when we came across a batch of nearly all repairable meters, these reducing the number we could get through, as fewer scrappers as we called them, much increased the average time per meter. So regulating the flow to a reasonable level overall was OUR policy, as we were given no incentive to work flat out, no bonus, instead the EU open immigration policy was used as the unspoken threat of my way or the highway, by ours and many other production companies, as previously mentioned.

Chapter 87

Though not married, Sarah and I were coming up to twenty-five years together, and we decided to mark this by going somewhere special, as you have read if you have got this far, we have been fortunate enough to already have had some good trips to some of the nicer parts of the world, by me meeting Sarah, and being given the option, and choosing not to reproduce, therefore not having the cost of bringing up children, for a combination of reasons already discussed, some of which you may think bizarre, some of which even I, a fully qualified Oddball, think stretches credibility, only the *lack* of uniqueness, if looked into, and the end result, my stressful childhood and adolescence added to slightly reduced mental capabilities, mainly memory and concentration compared with my siblings, there probably being nothing more to it than that aboriginal original, the boomerang, i.e. – a throwback, that being me.

Though I stand by my unusually sharp recall of my early childhood events as not being fiction, parental abuse, or standard dreams, read up on the subject and you will find this is far from unique to me, (my jury is still out). The upshot as I have said, being that we are able to take more exotic trips away than many of those of my contemporary workers on the reproductive normal cycle of what used to be two point four kids, I must have been one of the point four. So after that digression, this somewhere special this time was Australia, hinted at above with the Throwback half joke.

A company called Flight Centre were offering a ten night, three centre holiday at a pretty good price, you may think going that far for only ten days is a long way to go for that amount of time, and it is, there being one constraint on us, that if you have no pets you may think daft, but if you have cats or dogs, who have no way of knowing why they are confined somewhere for days or weeks for some unknown reason as far as they are concerned, and you are witness to the fuss they make when brought home, cats as much as dogs, for the next two or three days wary of leaving your side, all this makes you feel guilty about putting them through this for any longer that you need to.

The flight there involved a twenty-one-hour journey, including a changeover stop at Dubai, on one of those double decker planes, us being on the lower (cattle truck), sorry I meant economy class, though to be fair, the leg room was better than short haul flights, me being just over six foot at the start of the day, gravity reducing that by at least a half inch by flattening spinal cartilage by the end of the day.

The seat entertainment screen, offering a choice of film, music and games did help pass the time. Dubai Airport seen from the air or a distance to me resembles a giant semi-transparent slug, with its undulating glass covered internal train-linked terminals.

Somewhere over the Indian ocean, in the hours of darkness, (calling it night is subjective when on the move west or east for any significant distance) I decided while it was quite and most were asleep, to sneak up the spiral staircase at the back of the plane to catch a glimpse of what first class looked like, how the other half lived, though I do realise that I live in the top quarter of this planet's "well-off" strata, just being on this flight evidence of that. I only got to the top of the stairs, enough to see the hardwood lined drinks bar at the back of the top deck, I then decided discretion was the better part of valour, as I had not yet been challenged in the semi darkness of the planes "official" night, so not wanting to push my luck, I retreated downstairs to steerage, sorry can't resist, despite the evident privilege of even being on such a flight.

A pre-arranged taxi took us to our hotel in the Kings Cross area of Sydney, our hotel must have been on the edge of this area, as it is known for its red light district, strip clubs, and other salubrious entertainments, none of which were in evidence where we were, and as the whole package was relatively cheap, the location was not bad, being a half hour walk from the Botanical Gardens, with the Opera House situated at its southern tip. Breakfast was in with the package in this hotel, but while the food was OK, it was a bit of a shock to discover we were probably the only Westerners staying in this hotel, all the rest of the guests being Chinese, so we stood out like a sore thumb. Not a problem, just a bit of a surprise, guess Flight Centre found it good value for money is the best way of putting it.

We had two full days after our arrival day to take a look at Sydney, part of the package included a half-day boat trip round the harbour, with a meal included, but that was tomorrow, for today, we decided to walk down to the Botanical Gardens, having been given a good map of the city with the package, the walk was fairly easy to the Botanical Gardens, the time of year being May, early autumn down under, so the temperature was nice for a walk, not too hot, tame White Ibis wandered the park, looking for food from the tourists sitting drinking coffee and eating snacks, us included.

We ended up chatting to a New Zealander girl also on holiday, who overheard our English accent, she was from Christchurch, we exchanged e-mail addresses, for the purpose of me sending photos of our impending excursions north, which she requested, her going home the next day.

Whenever we go, TO some iconic building anywhere in the world, it always seems to be undergoing repair or improvements, whether its Gaudi's Cathedral in Barcelona, though to be fair it's been worked on for about a century, or Duat Castle (if where? Google) in the Hebrides, which I was looking forward to photographing on the way back to Oban, only to see scaffolding over part of it, and so it was with the Sydney Opera House, though it was partitioned off at the back, I was able to get photos as good as any postcard of the front, from the ferry we took round to Darling harbour.

Chapter 88

Before we got on the ferry at Circular Quay, we spotted two buskers along the front, one being a hippy type, playing the aboriginal Didgeridoo, with some competence, with occasional variations on the core rhythm, while a true aborigine clicked the sticks in a steady rhythm, dressed in very little, white painted stripes covering most of his body, one leg up periodically with the sole of his foot up against the side of his other knee, in a classic stance, last seen by me when Ian Anderson of Jethro Tull was playing the flute, but this guy would also have his painted palms turned outward, tongue out, striking a perfect pose for the tourists that included us.

After watching and filming for some time, we contributed to their cash tin, before catching the ferry round the built-up shoreline to darling harbour, partly to find the spot where the following day we would get on the luxury boat for the harbour trip, which was a feature of this package, as well as to make the most of our short time in Sydney.

Having found our departure point for the following day, we wandered along the built up front, before setting off to what on the city map promised was a Chinese tea garden, which we found eventually, protected by a high wall, not a large garden, but with its pond, and little bridge across to the tea pavilion, it was a peaceful haven from the noisy city surrounding it, it was lunchtime, can't recall what we ate, nothing exotic, but it was a nice place to rest, as we had walked a fair distance that day. Then it was back down to the Darling Harbour ferry that took round to Circular Quay where we had come from earlier, the Opera House on your left as you approached the Quay.

After getting off the ferry, we noticed the two buskers were still performing, this being at least three hours later than when we saw them earlier, I went over, and spoke to them between performing, saying they had put in a good shift, as we had seen them some hours earlier, the aboriginal guy say they had to make the most of the tourist season, asking us where we were from, after telling him, he said he remembered getting stuck on the M25, some time ago, I said that was some walkabout, that got a laugh, whilst adding a bit more to their pot.

We started to look for a bus that would take us back to our hotel in Kings Cross, as having eaten, I would have suffered chest pains that two sets of tests say are not angina, trying to walk the uphill road we needed to follow. Having a detailed map of the city that included bus routes led us to the right place and the right bus, the route being fairly straight, a short dip, followed by a long uphill run, our hotel being only a short walk from the junction we got off at.

After eating in the hotel on our arrival night, we followed our usual practice and found a burger joint to eat not far away that night. In the morning we had the (package included) luxury boat trip with meal to look forward to. A four-hour trip around some of the more exclusive nooks and crannies of the extensive Sydney harbour area, where people such as Russell Crow and Nicole Kidman had houses.

The boat, which I think we got on at eleven, was a smart motor yacht of about forty feet, there being no more than a dozen passengers, a party of Americans, I think some French, Sarah talking to two older English ladies, while I listened to a conversation two Americans were having about working on the undercarriage of a secret US aircraft, when I joined in the conversation, asking innocently if it was the Pulse Jet known as the Aurora, I was met with slightly stunned consternation.

I knew I had hit the bull's-eye, letting on I had a keen interest in the latest aviation innovations, careful to keep the subject of UFOs out of my conversation, the Aurora is speculated on in aviation magazines I explained, I did not ask this guy about the TR- 3B, the 600-ft long "aircraft" better known as the Black Triangle, regarded by some as an alien ship, the nuts and bolts version US built, possibly using handed over, or back engineered tech, from crashed or captured ships. I did ask this question on a later boat holiday in Croatia, of an ex-RAF logistics Officer, who talked of setting up "Airheads", advanced landing sites for setting up a new base of operations, when asked if he had heard of the above-mentioned craft, his response was "I'd rather not say", this could mean he had, or it could mean he hadn't, but didn't want to say as much.

If he was in service for a long period, I think he would have caught at least a hint of it, as compartmentalised UK forces share in this Black Budget, Special Access Projects stuff, at least to an extent, but speaking of such things was not good for a career. I said I was careful to keep on the fringe of such things, implying I knew more than I did, but he did not take the hook, though giving me what Pooh Bear would describe as a "Hard stare".

Chapter 89

Anyway, back on the Sydney harbour tour, after having been offered canopies and drinks of our choice, we came to a quite cove where we were invited to have a swim in the harbour, the water looking a bit murky, there were not many takers, myself and two or three others jumping from the back or using steps into the quite cold water, it was deep, and not having mask or flippers, I was soon back, Sarah opting not to have a dip in what was quite uninviting waters.

A buffet followed this dip, quite a good selection from what I can recall. Either on our way out or coming back, I got more photos of the opera house, with the required perfect blue-sky background. It was a pleasant trip, with an unexpected but interesting turn of conversation, though I tried to pump the American for more info on the propulsion of the Aurora, he deflected, saying it was not his area, he would have been required to keep anything he did know to himself, possibly a little worried he had let slip anything on the subject, though to be fair it was me who said the word Aurora, he not confirming it in words, only the look on his face when I said it.

After returning to Circular Quay, we got the bus back up to the hotel. That evening, our last in Sydney, we headed downhill, turned right up to a parallel street to our hotel and continued to where we had spotted a Chinese restaurant (as we always seem to do) eating a meal without alcohol, as you were supposed to bring your own, it was a bit of a backpackers district, younger than us more at home, but we went to a bar after the meal, where Sarah said we had conversations with locals, I do not recall this, though we had only one drink, as I needed a clear head for driving the next day, but we came to no harm, so it must have been OK.

The next part of this three-centre holiday involved driving up to the Hunter Valley, the wine producing region north of Sydney, but first we had to get out of Sydney. Our car hire pick up depot was an uphill trek from the hotel, so with the cases in mind, we took a taxi, which had to meander round a one-way system to get us about half a mile. Again, not knowing I would ever be trying to write anything down, I can only tell you that this car was bright red, and the only reason I recall that much is because of a memorable event later this day where a paler colour might have helped prolong that event.

This time we did have a satnav, which helped us find our way out of Sydney in the direction we needed to go – always a good start. As Kings Cross is in south Sydney, there was no practical alternative but to pay tolls on the way north, first on the Harbour tunnel, onto the A1, then onto the M1 Pacific Motorway, all this we prepaid at the pick-up depot, as when returning, it would not be to there, but an airport drop-off for the flight north to Port Douglas, north of Cairns.

Passing districts such as Crow's Nest, Willoughby, and native-sounding Ku-ring-gai, we eventually reached what became the M1 at the north edge of the city at Hornsby.

Travelling north westerly until then, we turned slightly east of north at first on the M1, having roughly 120 miles to reach our hotel in the Hunter Valley, (we had decided not to risk a possible inland route) that would take us west through Windsor and Wilberforce, (someone was homesick!) and up through the Comleroy State Forest and the Parr Conservation Park on the "Putty Road", that would turn north east and bring us on an arc that would add about thirty – forty miles into the Hunter Valley area.

After a small town near the Colo River, there did not look to be any habitation through fifty or sixty miles of "bush", so being novices of the Australian wilds, we decided not to risk taking off into the wilds in a standard car, and so reluctantly, stuck to the main roads for a while, though with enough courage to head off the motorway well before the satnav wanted us to.

Heading north past Brooklyn, and the Mooney Creek, up past Gosford then Cooranbong, recalling little, we decided a turn off inland this was a must, as it might be the only chance to get off the beaten track under our own steam, the B82, Freemans Drive, named by the ex-convicts who first built it and only about forty miles short of where the satnav wanted us to turn off, looked like a good compromise between recklessness and playing it too safe.

It turned out to be a good choice, the road was OK, getting a little dusty in places, but just after we had crossed a small creek bridge, we caught sight of a few Big Red Kangaroo's, some a good six feet tall, near a stand of trees about thirty yards from the road, I stopped maybe a bit too quick, as it spooked them, being in a bright red car as was mentioned earlier probably didn't help, but then more than we first saw trooped out from under the trees and headed uphill away from us, six to eight in all, all bigger than we were to see again, we would see many Wallabies, and other larger Roo's in captivity later, but nothing like the Big Reds we saw then, that two minutes sticks in my mind as special moments do. It must have been well past midday by then, and knowing we were three quarters there, it was time for lunch, the town of Cessnock looked to be not far away, so we decided to stop there.

Chapter 90

Finding an outdoor table at a cafe/bar there, that looked like it had a mix of locals and travellers, we had some large bread roll sandwiches filled with Wichita grubs, or maybe not, (as far as we know) we were not yet that far out, so not fresh enough, BLT then, or something like. At least one guy there had the dangling cork hat, so no flies on him then, apart from lower down… Right next door was a tack shop, full of a things horsey as you would expect, a full size plastic horse just outside, across the road was an agricultural machinery depot, quite a lively little town, with obvious similarities to American rural towns.

However, travelling north of Cessnock, the countryside became more genteel, with neatly planted vine, and other crops, interspersed with horse paddocks, all very green, like areas of Cheshire, or south east England, where the money is, this was estate country, very different from south of Cessnock, if you look at a map of the area, there are a lot of small lakes and ponds, the water table must be close to the surface here, with a river a bit further north, that, and fairly flat land, makes a good combination for the pleasant, but intensively managed agriculture in the Hunter Valley.

It looks good, due to the field size not being too large, and the white picket fenced meadows for the expensive looking horses intermixed with the agricultural and vine plantations. Sarah described it as little England, I would, with a touch of France in the mix. After passing between the Hunter Valley Golf and Country Club, and the small airport on the other side of the B82, now called Wine Country Drive, we started looking for road names, as our hotel was set out on its own, near one of the innumerable small lakes in the area.

Unaware I would be writing this, we did not keep any bumf on this hotel, but it was set atop a small hill, surrounded by lush grassland, with a few well-spaced trees, the hotel was a green and white wooden, Colonial-style building, single story, with veranda surround, pool and sauna in a separate building, a central reception area, with a small, too quite restaurant/breakfast room off from this. A little stuffy, too genteel. After dumping bags, we swum, Sarah then going for a Sauna, I tried in vain to get the hotel Wi-Fi, as I was looking for specific Emails, can't recall why, but seemed important at the time.

It looked to be a distance from our hotel to anywhere, so we ate in from a limited menu there, it was quite a sleepy place, but we were only there for two nights, breakfast was included in the package, but after a drive around the area, including a visit to one of the many vineyards, where we ate lunch as well as tasting the local wine, we came away with nothing, not inspired enough to add to our case weight.

The area around the hotel was like parkland, there was little in the way of wildlife other than a few White Ibis dotted about. We headed up to a small town called Singleton as it had a river running through, in the hope there would a nice riverside walk to be had, not so, just an old-fashioned wood facade, veranda side walked street, but otherwise a nondescript one horse small town, Australia style.

If there longer it would have been possible to book a hot air balloon trip, but to be honest, the view would have been of a neat agricultural patchwork quilt, with mountains a suggestion way off in the interior to the west. It was only a two night stay there, that was enough, I suppose the holiday company were trying to provide a contrast at each stay, but this one was just not our idea of Australia, and we were glad to be moving on. This meant heading down to Kuri, onto the M15, Hunter Expressway turning right and south at West Wallsend onto the M1, so not into Newcastle, which was straight on, well in Aussie it is!

The trip back down to Sydney Airport was uneventful as it turned out, saw plenty of Wallabies, some eating planted crops, so must be a real pest from the farmers viewpoint. We were warned that a Marathon taking place in Sydney that day might delay us, but maybe bypassing the centre allowed us to miss the route, as we saw no sigh of it. With the airport set in south Sydney, we left the motorway further west, bypassing the centre, as stated, turning south to the airport, which is situated at Botany Bay, so a good landing point then, must have thought this a fine spot for an Airport, first English here, good bit of forward planning that!

So now for the last, but most eagerly awaited part of this trip, five night in Port Douglas, north of Cairns, and just south of the Daintree Forest, one of the oldest virgin rainforests in the world.

Chapter 91

It was a three-hour, 1200-mile flight from Sydney to Cairns, on a domestic airline, then a forty-mile transfer to our duplex in the southern hotel strip of Port Douglas, the main town a 15-minute bus ride away. At the reception/restaurant of the resort, you could phone order food to be delivered to your door, and as ours was a fair walk away, set on a partially residential internal road, tired from a long journey, we did just that the first night, fast food – burgers and chips and some beer.

You don't go all the way to north Queensland and not go out to the Great Barrier Reef, this was the other excursion in with the package holiday, but not due for two days. That evening, sat out on the balcony at the back of our corner duplex, we were quite startled, at dusk, by the first of quite a few large Fruit Bats flying along the tree line that followed a stream separating the communal grassland from a golf course on the other side. I tried, in vain to get a photo of these over the next few days, I am no specialist with camera's, and the lack of a fast shutter speed, combined with the fast flight of the bats, left me defeated in my attempts.

Like most reception areas, there was a wall with all the information leaflets for things to do in the area, and here, they were legion, we intended to make the most of our time there. On the transfer bus in from the airport, just after the turn off from the Captain Cook Highway (44), onto the Port Douglas road, we both spotted a complex called the Wildlife Habitat, and remarking that it looked worth a visit, together with our other wish list priority, getting an excursion up into the Daintree National Park.

For me, as well as for many people, half the value of an exotic holiday, booked well in advance, is the sudden incentive to research your chosen destination, for places of interest to visit, so as well as the Daintree and Barrier Reef, one other place of note took our interest, well before we went, this was a place called Kuranda, inland, north west of Cairns, even though it was a tourist centre for Aboriginal art, and innumerable other artefacts, plus wildlife attractions, bars, and restaurants, getting there looked interesting…

Its main interest for us was that it had one way of getting up there, and another for getting back down, both good, so that was on our bucket list if possible. We decided to mine the extensive leaflet wall in the hopes of finding trips to match out bucket list, after having the first of our included breakfasts in the bright and airy restaurant, this opening out to a central garden/pool, surrounded by hotel rooms on the other three sides. We struck gold with that leaflet wall, everything mentioned above we found leaflets for, took them back to our duplex, I called them up, booked all of the above, leaving only the rest of that day and one other free to find the local beach and have a look round Port Douglas.

As mentioned, the resort was situated on the long approach road with most other hotels, we caught one of the frequent buses into town. This town is purely a holiday resort, the last major resort town on the Australian Coral sea coast, with Cooktown being the most northerly town on that north eastern peninsular, not counting a few remote settlements. This Cook guy seemed to have followed us from west coast Canada, maybe he got there first…

Wandering around Port Douglas, it was impossible to get lost, we had looked on Google Earth at the resort, intending at first to find the tourist information office, before finding everything we needed on the hotel reception wall. Even though we were to be picked up for our Quicksilver catamaran trip out to Agincourt reef, (our bit of the Barrier Reef), we thought we would find the harbour, as you do on coastal resorts, when we did, we could see ours was a big boat, more like a fast ferry, easily the biggest boat in the harbour, though a few private yachts were a fair size. I fancied a go at fishing the local inlet, not a large river, so finding a small hire boat company, I booked a little motor boat with a sun canopy for the one remaining free day.

On the harbour boardwalk, on stilts, we found a restaurant where Barramundi and chips was our lunch, washed down with a beer, then wandering around, finding a supermarket, deciding we would eat in at least one night, as the duplex had a cooker. Nothing took our fancy as a souvenir, and looked around for a likely eatery for an evening visit into town, they all seemed much of a muchness, a bit like in the U S, variations on steak, burgers, or fish, and didn't settle on anywhere to book, deciding there were enough to choose from that we could pick on the night.

Next morning was a fairly early pick up, not crack of dawn, it was our trip into the Daintree Forest. An outfit called Billy Tea bush Safaris, named after the Aussie bush tucker version of tea making, they were our hosts for that day, looking at the photo on the back door of the truck, they operated as far afield as Tasmania, Alice Springs, Kakadu and Fraser Island, so a national network, picking us up in a 4 x 4 raised chassis minibus, along with about ten others picked up along the way to the Captain Cook Highway (44), where we turned north, following it to its end, then following a B road equivalent to a small town called Mossman, where we met up with another Billy Tea truck, and this really was a truck, with wheels half as big again as ours, built to travel the rough roads right up to the sparsely settled northern end of the Cape York peninsular that we were at the eastern base of. The top-end of Cape York being the closest mainland bit of Australia to Papua New Guinea.

Chapter 92

We were not going quite that far; the rainforests of Borneo having sated our desire for extended jungle wilderness expeditions (Uncle Tan's camp). So while our young driver/guide chatted with his fellow guide, we were given time to stretch our legs and buy a coffee, before heading out towards the Daintree River.

Before reaching the main river, we turned off an hour later for lunch at the side of a tributary river, there was a professional-sized barbecue in full swing, along with a small wildlife sanctuary nearby, with parrots, kangaroo's, can't recall what else, but I don't think they were used on the Barbie, as the giant steaks, sausages and burgers were of familiar tastes. It was a good job we were not going on a hike anywhere, as whatever ails me after eating, would have had me as immobile as the crocodiles we were about to go out and observe along the riverbank.

In a canopied boat, the local wildlife Ranger took us along the windy, steeply mud banked river. Before long we saw the first crocodile on the muddy bank, six or seven feet long, after seeing several baby, one to two feet crocs, we then saw a second larger, eight/nine foot croc, the guide explaining that these were territorial females, spaced along the banks, and that males visited these resident females, we also saw a small tree snake, various birds, the guide was looking out for "Queen Elisabeth", the dominant female in the area, I know David Ike had said the royal family were reptiles, but this was Aussie humour. Queen Elisabeth was not at home, to be seen, I could have told him that, as there was no flag flying…

Several more crocodiles of varying sizes were seen on the banks, none in the water, at least on the surface, the boat being big and noisy enough to keep anything swimming submerged, we returned to the jetty and trooped back onto the Billy Tea truck and continued to the Daintree River proper, after our tributary croc excursion. We were to cross this bigger river on a small ferry, then following the Cape Tribulation Road, into the forest where we stopped at another much smaller loop, further up river of the same Daintree we had crossed on the ferry earlier.

Here the river was only about twenty odd feet wide, with a small tree and moss-covered island in the middle, this island and surrounding area, having an unknown (to us)yellow flowering plant in a carpet over the moss, a unique looking area, surrounded by rainforest, this location photographed by me, then painted by Sarah at home. At the small clearing by the river, our guide (whose name escapes both of us) prepared refreshments Aussie Bush tucker style, employing us tourists to fetch twigs for the fire, while some of the younger people in our group went swimming in the deeper section near the crossing point. No crocs here I assume.

Billy tea is made with centrifugal force, as once the metal bucket shaped can had the loose tea leaves boiling over the fire, our guide picked it up with the handle – and spun it round and round at full stretch at least a dozen times, this being his party piece, before dunking mugs in and handing the tea round, ready to drink, a few leaves in each, not quite Earl Grey…

To go with this tea, was some pre-mixed "Damper", a dough baked on the fire in a tin container, added to this were plates with chopped custard apple, kiwi fruit, and other locally grown fruit. After this we climbed back in the truck, which was driven across the river, less than two feet deep at this crossing point, we kept going then until arriving at Cape Tribulation beach, the Cape itself sticking out at the southern end of the beach.

This being where Captain Cook in 1770, hit and got stuck on a reef, several cannon and other weighty objects were jettisoned before HMS Endeavour was re-floated, in his log, Cook said 'Here began all my troubles,' hence the name Cape Tribulation. Whilst on this beach, which was deserted apart from a hut, with a plaque explaining its historical name, a bird looking like a black turkey with big tail feathers and a red head came out of the forest, not in the least bothered by us, by now dispersed up and down the beach, clearly a wild bird, if not a turkey, then something close – it seemed to know Christmas was long gone, crackers, I know, I am.

Somewhere on the return journey, after crossing back on the Daintree ferry, we stopped at a forest boardwalk, our guide warning us to avoid getting cut on the razor-sharp vines wrapped around the vegetation, these having small reverse hooks, that could tear your skin, I saw and photographed an exotic wild bird with a large yellow beak and a frilly necked lizard about a foot long that looked like one of those that were used in old dinosaur movies, magnified a thousand times. There was an ice cream shop at the car park, with a myriad of flavours, I would have had mint choc, or coconut, or rum and raisin, Sarah tried a local fruit flavoured delicacy.

Then it was back to Port Douglas, probably around 6 by the time we were back. If you're ever up there, I can recommend Billy Tea Bush Safaris, they pack in a lot in one day, Cook included…

Chapter 93

Pretty sure it was that night we ate in the Hotel restaurant, being tired after a trip out like that, we would not have wanted to go far to eat, or have Sarah cooking either. Not sure what I ate, Sarah recalls she had a Seafood Pasta. I could see food and ate some.

Having given up on trying to capture the twilight flight of the giant Fruit Bats in one's and two's, as they followed the tree line that lined the small stream marking the boundary between the resort and the golf course next door, I was pleased to photograph a Kookaburra posing nicely on a post at the back of our duplex that evening.

The next morning was a fairly early get up, which I like on holiday, Sarah not so much, OK when she gets going, if the day has something pre-booked in store for us, it will be me getting us up – with a brew if it's not sparrow fart early, so as to give Sarah a chance to come round. Only once in all the years we have been away together, have I failed to get us up on time for an excursion, that being the Thailand trip out to "James Bond Island" of Man with Golden Gun fame, as mentioned earlier in this narrative, my excuse being one of those genuinely rare occasions where we had been drinking heavily the night before as recounted earlier.

The reason for this get up was the package included a Quicksilver catamaran trip to the Barrier Reef, in particular the Agincourt Reef. Having already found the docking area for this giant catamaran, we were up early enough to grab a quick croissant breakfast before being picked up at the resort gates.

There are many smaller operators all along the Queensland coast that will take you out to many different locations along the vast Barrier Reef, but as with Billy Tea Bush Safaris, Flight Centre, the package operators, had picked out one of the larger operators that cater for tourists like us who by and large have only a short time in the area, and need a dependable operator to deliver consistently on something that is included as a feature in their adverts. Quicksilver is one such operator, the 45-meter Wavepiercer, Quicksilver's aptly named flagship's torpedo shaped twin hulls power through, not over the waves, making the trip out to the reef in fairly rough conditions, much smoother that it could otherwise have been.

The boat was almost like a seagoing ferry, though not big enough for a car hold, its passenger cabin was large enough to have its own restaurant area, and it had one similarity to an aircraft passenger cabin, it had the equivalent of Air Hostesses/Stewards. There was a good reason for this…

As this trip out was in quite choppy conditions, though the boat's design reduced movement to a slow rise and fall, these steward/esses, were stationed at the side of the stairs leading up to the open-air deck, equipped with boxes of sick bags, for the inevitable few out of the up to 450 people capacity that succumbed to sea sickness, not bad for a boat capable of cruising at 32 knots, using four water jets to manage this.

Agincourt Reef is nearly 40 miles out from the mainland, but the speed of the catamaran meant that it was less than 1 ½ hours before we arrived, I had been hoping to go out with the marine biologist snorkelling, one of the many activities available out there, but with the swell of the sea, I could not see that happening. As we slowed, the large floating platform that quicksilver keep out there came into view, situated in shallow water, and nearly surrounded by reefs almost reaching the surface, I realised the ocean swell here was only a quarter that of the surrounding open sea, though still a little rough, with flippers on I would be able to cope.

As we approached, a crew member gave us an overview of the options available to us when we boarded the two-story platform, there was even a helicopter for those wanting a top-down view of the surrounding area, as I was going out on an extended swim along with a half dozen others with the marine biologist, I asked Sarah if she wanted to go up, I got an emphatic no thanks, so I found something we could do together first. This was a half-hour trip on a semi-submersible, yellow of course, with portholes three feet below the surface. A gangway with two seats either side, holding about thirty or so all told.

Mostly small fish were on view, as well as some colourful coral, the highlight being a small turtle coming into view for a short while, a crew member provided a commentary on what was seen.

After re boarding the platform, Sarah went for a swim in a buoyed off safe area, next to the platform, while I struggled into a wetsuit, along with the others going a bit further out.

There was scuba diving available, but this, like the helicopter option was a bit more time than I wanted to spend away from Sarah, and another expense only I would benefit from, so with my last diving trip way back in Thailand's Phi Phi Islands, and the sharp pain in my head in mind that bought my second dive there to an early end, I was happy to go out with a snorkel, mask and flippers, with someone who could show us anything of interest nearby.

Chapter 94

With all of us in the water, the marine biologist called to us to follow, then she set off with us half dozen following. As we left the platform behind, the sea became a little choppier, but still swimmable with flippers, head down to cut through the swell, using the snorkel.

About a hundred yards away from the platform, our biologist guide stopped to point out various different corals, including a large Brain Coral about fifteen feet down, immersed in its own convoluted thoughts, at least that was my take, (as you might expect by now). Moving on, seeing small but colourful fish Nemo like among the Anemones. A bit further out we saw a small turtle, about three feet long, a little further out, our guide stopped again and pointed down, asking us what we could see.

With there being a bit of a swell out here, visibility was a little hazy, so with the bottom around twenty feet down here, it took a moment to see what she was pointing to, it was a giant clam, about four foot long, with the characteristic wavy shaped mouth, of the type seen in old films with the diver's leg trapped, and running out of air. If it was me, and I survived to tell the tale – you guessed it, I would be so embarrassed if anyone asked me about it, I would clam up, then get legless after all…

We were invited to follow her down to it to take a closer look. Ten years earlier, I might have tried it, not now, me being about twice as old as the rest of our party, with an asthmatic's lung capacity, I didn't feel so bad when no one else went down either. We were all tired I think, just getting there, unlike the biologist who probably did this swim five days a week in peak season.

After returning to the surface, she released a telescopic rod from her belt, extending it to about two feet, she dived down again, putting the rod into the jaws of the clam, with the expected result, proving it was alive, no one put their foot in it by asking her to, not even me. That was it, we returned through the choppy, shark free water, back to the platform, the sharks, we were told, staying nearer to the five hundred meter drop off at the edge of the continental shelf, not much more than a mile further out than this reef.

Meeting up with Sarah after returning, I was only now able to turn my attention to food, as usual only able to eat *after* any strenuous activity involving use of legs, able to get away with arm work if not on the move. Sarah having a wander round while waiting for me, before we crossed back over to the moored catamaran ferry to attack the extensive, mainly seafood buffet now laid out, with wine or beer also included on this excursion. With it by now being mid-afternoon, and only having a light early breakfast, attack it we did, myself especially after that long swim, knowing we had only the walk from the resort gates to our duplex after returning ashore.

The following day we decided to find the nearby beach. From Google Earth, we could see that after crossing the duel carriageway outside the resort gates, there was a residential area to walk through, with a public park near the beach, we expected to find a beach cafe somewhere along the seafront, so off we went.

It took at least half an hour through back streets to emerge at the small municipal park, the beach visible on the other side. Sarah as usual being the one to recall details such as there being bottles of vinegar set on posts at regular intervals along the beach, with notices saying "for use if stung by jellyfish" or words to that effect.

After a long walk down the beach, we were disappointed to discover the only cafe shack in sight was shut, this not being a tourist area, there were few people around, local kids being in school at that time of day. The walk back through the smart residential streets to the main road seeming longer as we were pretty thirsty by then, it was straight to the pool bar when we made it back to our resort complex.

That evening we caught the bus into town, looking for somewhere to eat, there being plenty of choice, I forget its name, but in the Rough Guide book, there was a place set on stilts near the harbour where a large Grouper was supposed to turn up most evenings to be fed. We found it, more of a big hut kitted out as a bar, only burgers on offer, we decided that as it was our main night out in town, we would look elsewhere, after a long wander around, we settled on a place called "The Iron Bar," a Gastropub with a twist, as for a small fee you could go out back and bet on Cain Toad racing. These being the giant non-native species that have devastated the local native smaller frog and fish ecology, as is often the case with introduced species.

Though a good laugh, trying to get these things to go anywhere in a straight line would be impossible without a bit of a prod, not for the politically correct brigade, and though we are not really a member of that club, were not keen on animal poor treatment, we contented ourselves with staying in the restaurant/bar, leaving that bit of Aussie culture for others, while we contented ourselves with a meal and a drink or two, making sure neither of us ordered the "chicken" from the menu. Not sure what I had, but Sarah had that other Aussie delicacy, no not crocodile, though it was an option, but Kangaroo, whatever I had doesn't spring to mind, most likely walked, not jumped. Next day would be a lively one, so we did not drink too much before returning back to base that night.

Chapter 95

Another early get up, but with this day trip, breakfast is available at our first stop which is only ten-minute drive away from our resort gate pickup, heading south towards the main Captain Cook (HWY 44) but a few hundred yards short of this, is a place we made a note of as looking worth a visit on our way in, and I had managed to combine a visit here, in with another trip all in a one full-day excursion. The name of this brilliant place is the Port Douglas Wildlife Habitat, to call it a zoo would be doing it an injustice.

If like us, and many tourists, you have only a fairly short time in Australia, unless you are able to spend a lot of money and time out in the rainforests or other remote areas, you are not going to see a fraction of the wildlife that's out there, we considered ourselves lucky to catch a glimpse of those big red kangaroos on our drive up to the hunter valley. In this habitat, you are able to mix in with almost every animal in there, with the exception of the at least twelve foot Estuarine Crocodile, and if you are there at the right time of day you get to see that fed.

But first, breakfast, if you can imagine eating breakfast inside a giant aviary, that's where you start, you order your food, sit down, briefly, for you are soon up, gawping at just about every type of parrot, hornbill, weird jungle owls, that are to be found in Aussie, they are all tame in there, so of course I spent more time taking photos of parrots on Sarah's arm than I did eating my by now half-cold breakfast.

After this treat, we started our walkabout, Sarah getting to cuddle one of the koala's, I got the photo, then walking round feeding the Kangaroo's, large (ish) four to five feet, and numerous wallabies, some with Joey's sticking out of their pouches, plus some tree kangaroo's. Sarah would have stayed there all day, but there was more to see, and we still had the main part of this trip to get to yet. But for now, there were walkways over enclosures with Cassowaries below, this being the third largest bird in the world, quite rare now in the Daintree Rainforest, there is also a wetland area, full of pelicans crossing flamingos, and the world's only captive breeding pair of black necked Storks, all of which you are walking round with. Everything from Snakes to Flutterbyes, I mean butterflies, are all there, but 90% of the wildlife here is not caged off, so interactive. To look at the entrance driving by, you would never guess the area this place spreads out to, and is also well managed, allowing much close access to its residents.

From an 8 am pick up, we stayed at this habitat until around 11-ish, then it was off to Kuranda, billed as the village in the rainforest, set inland, northwest of Cairns, so south from us, the most interesting way to reach there from the main highway, is to climb aboard the Skyrail Rainforest Cableway, which takes you a considerable distance up the steep escarpment, in a six person bubble, past waterfalls, just above the forest canopy, over the Barron River Valley, and eventually up to the Kuranda Heights where you alight.

To call this a village is a misnomer, it is a resort, Aboriginal craft centre, scattered zoo, foodie paradise, all rolled into one, I bought a well painted boomerang from a choice of about fifty, that were genuine Aboriginal art, indeed in this craft centre there were locals doing the painting nearby, the significance of the dots, representing time and distance explained to us, this green and red decorative version now sits on its stand atop my aquarium. A remainer the natives over there learnt how to recycle their throw – away items early. They know – What goes around comes around…

There was a large tourist market there, especially leather goods, we ate dinner there, (not leather) had a beer, wandered around for a couple of hours, there was a lodge resort there somewhere a little way off you could stay at, do river cruises, and many other activities, but for us it was time to head back, this time on the Kuranda Scenic Railway through the world heritage listed Barron Gorge National Park, this 127-year-old railway is considered a huge engineering feat, and is also heritage listed, passing as it does around and over the gorge, with its many waterfalls, built on massive stilted bridges for large sections, as well as through fifteen hand carved tunnels, this journey can, and was experienced by us in Gold class, vintage green carriages.

Gold class just meant a steward came around with light refreshments, and you were sat in lounge seats, in a cedar wood carriage, a taste of luxury for a couple hours, as you watched the dramatic scenery roll by. But all good things come to an end, and so after leaving the train at Freshwater, which continued on to Cairns, we were run back to our Port Douglas resort. Between that trip and the Wildlife Habitat all in one day, not a bad way to end our unofficial 25th anniversary special holiday.

Chapter 96

On the whole, Flight Centre had organised a pretty good itinerary for what was a fairly short holiday considering it was on the opposite side of the world, cattery guilt making this the maximum we would stay away from home. There was only one part of the schedule which had concerned me a little from the start, that being there was only ninety minutes between landing at Sydney on our return flight from Cairns, and our take off time for the UK. I had to assume this allowed enough time for us to change terminals, along with our luggage transfer – Sarah said I was worrying for nothing, they must have done this before, mmm, OK.

As it turned out, I think this must rank as one of my personal records for being at continuous risk of heart attack that I have experienced to date. I was too used to years of everything going pretty much like clockwork on all the holidays we had been on in the last twenty-five years, the worst we had experienced was a few half hour or so delays, quite lucky for such a period, or being turfed out of lodgings with your luggage with hours to go before airport pick-up – in short, the usual, nothing dramatic.

From about half an hour after the minibus pick up at the gates onwards, it was a building nightmare for me, who has always been perhaps overly concerned with time, always early for everything.

Space cadets Hawkwind (got you scratching your head now), made an album called "Warrior on the Edge of Time", well, I can at times be the "Worrier on the edge of time", and this turned out to be me that day, as the guy driving our airport feeder minibus could not seem to find the address of some of his other pick-ups, then had to double back for one, to be fair I think that was a radio instruction to go back for someone who was not there on time.

Anyway the upshot was that I could see we would be late to Cairns Airport, and not just a bit late, Sarah was getting annoyed with me as I was making my concerns known, all I could think of was that if we missed this flight, the tight schedule at Sydney meant we would miss the flight home, and not having even experienced that in Europe, I imagined that from here, we could be days late home, cats, and missing work both playing on my mind.

As it turned out, our plane from Cairns was delayed by an hour, (first bit of luck) so we were able to get on it, just. But of course, that did not alter the take-off time for the Sydney to Manchester flight, so I spent the flight to Sydney still as the "Worrier on the edge of time", the 1 ½ hour gap between landing and take for home almost wiped out by the Cairns take of delay (that had allowed us to catch that!).

It was only after landing at Sydney and discovering that our homeward bound flight was also delayed ninety minutes, again – pure luck again, not a coordinated delay as far as we know, as it was late landing. So twice by sheer luck we were fortunate to catch our planes home, I was going to give Flight Centre some earache when I got home for the tight scheduling that made no allowance for delays.

The homeward journey went OK, if four hours kicking our heels at Dubai instead of six for a plane transfer can be called OK, but again to be fair that would have been factored into the package price – that was good overall, with the Sydney Harbour luxury boat trip, and the Quicksilver reef trip, Hunter Valley car hire included, it was up to us to make the most of the rest of our short time there, with the Daintree, Kuranda and Wildlife habitat, we did that alright.

Apart from my blood pressure skyrocketing that last day, only to get lucky with flight delays, which is ironically what allowed us to get home on the day we were meant to, the rest was all good.

While it is usually nice to be proved right, the shine is taken off when to do so involves going through the above on the last day, I would rather kick me heels for a while(between flights), Flight Centre take note, than spending time before and during the holiday concerned about the tight scheduling, only to have to go through exactly the scenario I feared, with only the ironic fortune of twin delays saving the day in the end.

Chapter 97

Shift work, as most people who work it know, is bad news, very few do it by choice, extra money, baby-sitting rotation with a partner, all are necessary reasons, not ideal if regular days were an option, which it is not for many. Such was the case where I was working, though it was only a 6-2, 2-10 rotation, with a small, separate permanent night shift, it was my working the 2-10 shift that was the final straw in the end for us.

Lack of a proper garden was also making Sarah in particular feel claustrophobic, and I realised that despite it being a hill, I was beginning to miss our spacious garden at Gee Cross near the canal. Spending every other week on her own in the evenings was depressing for Sarah, to the point in the end, of taking anti-depressants from the doctor.

The special twenty-five-year Australian holiday now in the past, we had returned to long weekend trips to our caravan near Caerwys, and with this, a plan that had been forming in both of our minds – that eventually it would be a nice idea to retire somewhere in North Wales. Sarah being already retired, this move was meant to happen in a few years, nearer my retirement, but I made up my mind that with Sarah clearly becoming less happy by the month, something had to change.

I put it to her that with the money we had in the bank, I was prepared to move there as soon as possible without a job, spend a few weeks getting straight, registering with a Council, doctors, dentists, redecorate, that sort of thing, but with two overriding objectives ONE – house must have a decent sized back garden, away from a busy road for the cats safety, and TWO – I would only work a day job, no shifts, possibly part time if I could manage it.

Although it would mean moving a distance away from her family, Sarah agreed, maybe a little surprised I was willing to take a bit of a chance with work, but realising we were in a rut that needed addressing. Our trips to the caravan had a new purpose, it became a base to scout out first local estate agents, and then getting to know residential areas along the North Wales corridor between the A55 and the coast. Though we at first considered as far along the coast as Conway, we had decided that as we were supposed to be grow old with this last move, a bungalow would be a good idea.

With this in mind the seaside resorts of Towyn and Kimmel bay and Abergele were given a good looking at, all full of bungalow estates, but it soon dawned on us that likely having to get to work on the A55, especially in the summer months, coming off resort roads would be a bit of a nightmare.

The back residential areas of Rhyl and Prestatyn became target areas, though after a few months of looking, I became aware that the coastal A548 road was home to a significant number of small industrial estates where I might find work, and although Deeside industrial estate was the monster in the area, it was not as far west, indeed not even in Wales, though commutable if it had to be.

A favoured small town and its surrounding areas was starting to look a good idea, off the tourist beat, being not on the coast, it was quite central to small industrial areas, we knew its layout fairly well and it had nearby larger supermarkets and other essential amenities. So we zeroed in on this, our favoured town as a good place to relocate.

This town was also close to the A55, handy if work turned out to be a bit of a distance away, it was also good for Sarah, being not much more than an hour and a by bit by car to visit her Son and Daughter's homes in Stockport. I did not see much of her son or his wife, who (tangentially now) had many years ago, whilst staying on Anglesey in a towed caravan, filmed a very strange metallic object that changed shape as it moved from a long cylinder to a circular blob and back again to cylindrical, looking almost like liquid mercury, with nothing close to wings, this thing was not flying as we know the term.

She being aware that I had a certain amount of interest in this type of thing, via Sarah, she sent me an email of the video, which I sent to the current BUFORA director, no longer Jenny Randles, hoping for some feedback.

I got none, but that video is the closest in terms of me knowing that a witness has not had any previous interest, and is defiantly a no-nonsense person who would not have sent this to me if she had any possible explanation for what she saw, and for that I am grateful to her, my only regret is that the video file is now lost to me. Though not unknown, this type of shape changing is rarely filmed as clearly as on this video clip. UFO digression over.

Sarah tends to see her daughter more often, though she did once go with the above-mentioned daughter in law on a short trip to a holiday park with the kids, though only once.

Chapter 98

Our search then crystallised down to house type, bungalow favourite, but a modern two bed house if near to our favoured town, with a decent garden. Our Modus Operandi would be to find three or four interesting looking prospects using national database property sites, these giving you the contact details of the local estate agent, which I would call and book viewings with, careful to space them out to avoid time pressure, unless with the same agent, no more than two in the same day, in this way we combined caravan-based sightseeing and house hunting, trying not to get too stressed by overdoing it.

It took us most of a year before we came across what was to become our current home. Set on a back road bordering a farm, but screened off with trees and a public footpath, this bungalow had what we were looking for, though on a hill of a road, as is much of north Wales housing stock, not on a main road, this bungalow was of seventies construction, but with a large, flat back garden, lawned, as was the front, groaning inwardly, I resolved to have the front paved over if I ended up working full time, Sarah agreeing to that, as there was plenty of border space for plants.

But first was the little detail of buying and moving into the place, as well as selling our Hyde house…

This turned into a bit of a nightmare, though we made an offer that was accepted, having soon found a buyer for our Hyde property, the matter of our house being leasehold soon became an issue, (as recent headlines have pointed out) for the solicitors of the young lady buying our house in Hyde.

It became evident to our solicitors, that our buyer had hired solicitors that had little experience dealing with leasehold issues, such as maintenance fees for gardens and car parking, then her solicitor went on holiday, passing on to someone we seemed to want to start from scratch, all the while, our vendors were a couple who had bought a large camper van, and were itching to drive of into the sunset, complete with dog and cat to sunny Spain, where they would find and buy a house at their leisure, with our cash from their sale.

They were hoping to be gone before the end of May, before the busy summer tourist season, in the event, it was the end of July before our buyer's solicitor, got their act together enough, with much chivvying from our solicitors, (who were acting for us buying and selling) for the exchange day to finally materialise much to our vendors relief.

Chapter 99

Therefore before this move took place, the most important democratic vote in over forty years took place in Britain on the 23rd June, you already know which way I voted in this, but no one was more amazed the next morning than I, when I switched the telly on (which I never normally do on a workday) to discover vote leave had actually won, despite the government and complicit *BBC* propaganda, known as "Project Fear" that had spent a taxpayers fortune sending out "government advice" in the form or remainer leaflets, *just* before the four week moratorium from which spending is counted, as well as complicit *BBC* blanket coverage of ministers virtually telling us that an asteroid would hit us the next day if we voted leave – or so it seemed, plus an *immediate* sharp downturn, followed by *massive* job losses, yet despite this, enough people had had enough of EU Directives.

Many working in countless mid-sized factories half filled with migrants that were there to make sure the rest of us dare not ask for a modest wage rise after years of none, as well as the older generations who remember self-determination, in the days when, if mistakes were made, at least we made them and were able to hold those responsible to account, not had them forced on us by unelected Commissioners, who hide behind the thin veil of democracy that is the European Parliament, where MEP's are deliberately given ridiculously short periods of time to scrutinise proposed legislation before having to vote on it.

Lo and behold, as I write this (mid 2018), unemployment here is half the EU average, with southern areas of Europe having catastrophic numbers of young people out of work, mainly due to the "one size fits all Euro", even when it clearly doesn't, ask Greece.

It is here then, that I will give a back handed thank you to David Cameron, who was foolish enough, and so out of touch, that he thought he could win a referendum, albeit forced on him by an MEP called Nigel Farage, to whom I give real heartfelt thanks, who almost single handed until the very late stages, led this country back on the road to self-determination.

Trying not to generalise, but vast swathes of senior civil "servants" who thinks of themselves as the exact opposite, mainly in the Treasury, (led by a complicit Hammond) and Foreign Office, who have for years just had to nod through EU laws, hastening our countries decline as a world power, (less work?) loosing influence where they might better have helped steer former colonies to stable democracy, unlike the French, who have kept hold of their choicer territories by the simple expedient of turning these into overseas parts of France, got to hand it to them, a great idea, though the Yanks led the way there.

As alluded to earlier, these people, if they fail in their plots to thwart Brexit, or so water it down as to be meaningless, will suddenly be called on to respond to the democratic will of ministers who can no longer cry "My hands are tied by EU rules", and instead have to actually work to enact laws that reflect the interests and will of the British people alone, or face the consequences of failure.

As I write this section, the government majority is now so slim, due to someone listening to too narrow a selection of advisors, that the more diehard Remain MP's (despite some of their constituencies voting Leave), have become bold enough to show their true regard for democracy, trying every trick in the book to prevent us returning to self-government, which is what Brexit is, many of them with vested financial interests.

As with a lot of the chattering classes, the ones with access to the *BBC*, who have deluded themselves into thinking if they can engineer a dumbed down government like they had in the Blair years, so they can manipulate that government to further their own influence, as they have been public funded for so long, they appear to think themselves the arbiter of how we are all supposed to think, in their arrogance, fortunately, the silent majority are still able to filter out their brand of politics, though we are sick of having our own money spent trying to influence those of us who bear the brunt of their policies, not the champagne socialists, who by and large, live well away from the results of their cynical politicking, and no, I am not blind to the other end of the spectrum, where some try to influence according to their commercial interests, it is the impact on the majority who have little media clout to which I feel aligned, those who were finally *given* a "meaningful vote".

Before the 2019 Leave date, the (effectively) two party system of politics we have had for so long May, and I use that choice of word ironically, fracture under the strain of achieving Brexit, with (at time of writing) all four top Ministerial Jobs now in Remain hands after the Chequers coup, despite rear-guard amendments just making the vote to steer clear of a customs union by another name.

Dominic Raab would have had an enormous responsibility on his shoulders, if Mrs May had not just days after I wrote the original draft for this section, pulled the rug from under him and given him a subservient role. Now taking direct control of the "Negotiations", Ollie Robbins a known remainder civil "servant" Mandarin as the puppeteer in charge, completing the coup.

Chapter 100

I am sure then, I am not alone in thinking (and wanting) a realignment of political parties based on Leave and Remain constituencies, I am told seven out of ten Labour constituencies voted leave, and if Corbin does not jump of the fence soon, many of these might be forced by political self-preservation to form an unholy alliance with Tory Brexiteers, with Nigel perhaps, after leaving the EU parliament, just maybe returning to lick his unruly party back into something that might be fit to add some backbone to the chaos our countries parliament might find itself in, though I suspect that political preservation on both sides of the channel might well bang some heads together enough to avoid the alternative, though many "Power by Stealth" experts in Brussels, especially the new EU Secretary General, Martin Selmayr, determined to try punishing us to deter others, would have to go, or be bypassed, to manage that.

In the end, the Brussels Sprouts may be forced by German and east European governments into practical arrangements they are terrified other countries are waiting in the wings to emulate, or to then demand similar from Brussels, either a totally reformed truly democratic EU, which is all *we* ever wanted, run by consent, not diktat, or the disintegration back to a Franco-German collaboration rump.

By the time this is published, if it ever is, then what you have just read, or persevered through, though I doubt any but Brexiteers and family are still reading this, will have played itself out, unless we are in for a truly massive political earthquake not seen since the Civil War, which is what happens to a country whose electorate sees its democracy reduced too much to be responsive.

As to a second referendum, I suspect many who thought leave had no chance of winning, succumbing to project fear, did not vote, but having seen the silent majority stronger than they thought, would join in this time – if push came to shove.

Ironically, the one big thing the EU got right as mentioned earlier, but must reiterate, was the proportional representation system it used to elect its MEP's, this allowed UKIP to gain representation and funding, beyond the control of the cosy cabal of our outdated, vested interest system, to gain the four million votes that forced Cameron into the Referendum, despite those votes in the UK not resulting in a single MP, highlighting our system where you can come second in a hundred constituencies, and gain no representation.

If our political earthquake is big enough, you never know, it might just change the system to truly reflect our wishes, though don't hold your breath, as power, combined with self-interest in maintaining the status quo will not relinquish its hold by choice, it will have to so fracture and realign itself along Leave/Remain lines, that both major parties can no longer hold together over, this would not happen gradually, but like a Dam, sizeable cracks would appear first (as they now have) before one large faction makes the break, appealing (maybe in secret in advance) to like-minded Leave / Remain opposing MP's to join them, with smaller rumps of the original parties still there, a general election would then have to ensue to determine the future destiny of our country.

Depending on when, if ever I get this published, or more to the point my last chance to edit the contents, I will try to use the above chapter to update my take on Brexit developments, as I have done with Raab's downgrading (and subsequent resignation), unless something major happens before this goes to print that might warrant a further chapter, the above to be read as a historical snapshot of events as I saw them at the time.

At this point I wish to remind any remaining! readers, that none of my political or other more conspiracy minded views are representative of my partners (Sarah) or family members views, so their lives are left out of this, so as to avoid any flack I may take, this is about my life and my take on issues beyond my control, hence the false names, just in case this is read by more than a very few.

Chapter 101

Back to our house move, we used a guy we had used before to move the bulk of our furniture and worldly goods we had not discarded, this being a lot easier than last time, the Hyde house being so small that we were leaving.

The caravan we still had in Caerwys would play a useful role in this move, though we had agreed for the site to buy it back from us, (at a much reduced price), we would retain it until after we moved house, and so on the day Sarah took the cats to the caravan, out of the way, whilst I took myself, our large TV, computer and other delicate items to a supermarket car park near our new location, in advance of Dave, our removal man, where we would wait for word from the local estate agent handling our purchase, that the sellers had handed in the house keys. The supermarket car park was the nearest handy rendezvous spot, less than a mile from the bungalow, where we could both get in the vicinity before the bungalow was vacated, which turned out to be the case.

I spent a nerve-racked hour, while the estate agent twice told me they could not reach the vendors. Of course I imagined all sorts, but it turned out to be nothing more prosaic than the sellers final loading of their mobile home taking time, ignoring the phone until they we ready to depart (my guess).

First letting Sarah know at the caravan, where she had the cats indoors, that I had finally got the call that the keys were at the agents office, I walked up to the estate agents, where the seller still was when I got there, we exchanged a few polite words, wishing each other well, before taking the keys back to my car, where Dave and mate nearby had finished a late lunch, before following me to the bungalow.

Won't bore you with details, save to say bed and settee went in, but much else went in the detached garage that came with the bungalow, so we could sort ourselves out gradually, Sarah able to bring the cats without much delay after our removal men had gone. There was some painting to do to brighten up the place, get registered with the local council, doctors, dentists, all the usual, I helped decorate, then start work on the somewhat neglected big back garden, then I got registered with local work agencies.

I was soon offered agency work, a few miles away at a site reclaiming and breaking down old TVs, this was very hard work, and though I stuck with it for a few weeks, my iffy health forced me to look for better work, it being handy that I was working a 6-2 day, no late's, so I had afternoons to look elsewhere. As for the Bungalow move, we had gone from virtually no private outside space, to a back garden with a seven-foot high hedge on one side, backing on to a public green on one side, with a drive that could fit four cars if needed.

On the other side of the back garden was a mixed hedge, if you can call it that, which was around eight foot high, the neighbours having abandoned the back half of their back garden to what is best described as jungle, though this might seem a little alarming, the up side is that we got a large back garden with total visual privacy, though we would need a hedge fund to maintain it…

After a few weeks, one of the work agencies I had registered with sent me for an interview with a small industrial company situated just off the coastal A548, not too far away from where we now live in Flintshire.

Keeping equipment clean, some basic recycling, and van driving was to become my job, not exactly inspiring, but what sealed the deal was the boss agreeing with me that if I could do this on three days a week basis, though it was advertised as five, as far as he was concerned It would save him money and I was happy to have found a part time job, able to spend more time with Sarah. After a probationary period of three months I was taken on by the company and off the agency books.

With the small private pension, and income from investments, this became what is still my current situation, though my work was gradually to become more varied as time went on.

Having found work that looked stable for the foreseeable future, though It was now September, we both agreed we needed a holiday after such a stressful move and transition, nothing too grand, just a week somewhere warm before winter.

Chapter 102

After due consideration, this turned out to be a place called Opatija, pronounced with a silent j.

Opatija, is in northern Croatia, on the coast where the Istrian Peninsula's south-eastern edge joins the coast that turns south towards Split. Having only decided in September, this trip was for the last week of October, so the weather was only a little warmer than home, but not being that much beach people, a change really is as good as a rest.

Opatija, once upon a time, used to be the resort of choice for those running the old Hapsburg, latterly Austro-Hungarian empire, so there is some quite imposing nineteenth century architecture along the main road running through this town, and along the seafront, including the Grand Hotel, split into four buildings, one of which we stayed in.

As usual, you will know by now, we had booked a package that included a few excursions to see the local, and as this trip turned out, not so local sights. Having mentioned we are not beach people, it did not bother us that most beaches in Croatia are shingle, and in Opatija, not even that, just a rocky shoreline, a small harbour, with a few concrete sunbathing areas dotted about.

What there was however, was an endless tree lined coastal path, through the town seafront, and off in both directions for miles, which we explored when we were not on an excursion, the first of which took us west into the Istrian Peninsula with Pula and Rovinj respectively being our destinations for that day, the first of which we would not forget in a hurry.

Pula is the largest town in Istria, and is known mainly for its extensive Roman architecture, of which its amphitheatre, one of the best-preserved outside Rome, was to be on our itinerary, weather (not misspelt) we liked it or not. Upon arrival, our group were handed over to a local guide for the walking tour, of which the arena was to be the main feature. Within five minutes of starting the guided tour, the heavens opened, and stayed open. As a group, we had on light jackets or similar, but our intrepid guide ignored the rain, sticking to his prepared historical info script, as if the sun were shining, making no attempt to find sheltered areas to deliver his no doubt worthy historical oration, despite the increasingly heavy rain.

We were glad to enter the underground sections of the arena, where exhibits of old Roman artefacts made an interesting respite from the rain. However this guide was on a timetable, and soon marched us off, back into the rain, by then most of us were soaked, I said to Sarah, that as soon as we knew where we were in relation to the coach pick up point, we would leave this guy, who seemed determined to drag us round, stopping nowhere near shelter to deliver his speech, regardless of the continuing rain.

In the end he realised he had stretched our patience to the limit, as just as we were about to desert to a nearby cafe, he curtailed his not quite finished tour of the old walls, as others of our group followed us to the large cafe.

At no point of this walking tour did he give us the option of finding shelter, he had his brolly, and sod the rest of us, if I had a clue how to find our way back after the first half hour of rain, we would have done so. It was likely that if he didn't deliver his full tour, he would not get paid, and he was not going to let that happen. The next stop of this day's excursion was the delightful town of Rovinj, set some miles north of Pula, halfway up the Adriatic west coast of Istria.

The weather was kinder to us there, though not at first, so we opted out of the available guided tour, and decided we would first buy a brolly, no sooner had we done this, than the light rain here stopped altogether, and the sun soon came out – Sod's law. Rovinj is a mainly medieval town, with a very pretty round almost island, attached to the mainland by a short, narrow isthmus, in the centre of this almost island, is a Venetian church, with a tall steeple.

Either side of the isthmus were picturesque pleasure and fishing boat harbours, one of which Sarah has since painted from one of my photos – as she does, if it merits it. Just of the coast were several tree covered true islands, the whole vista lifting our spirits after the Pula debacle.

The countryside of Istria is of small, neat vineyards and farms and olives orchards, as in most of the north Med, what we saw looked well-kept and fairly small scale. The major roads are pretty good, the traffic flowing quite well in the crowded coastal tourist hot spots we saw.

Chapter 103

This package included half board, the hotel's dining building was a modern largely glass add on situated near the seafront, overlooking the small harbour off to one side, the food was OK, buffet style, usually one or two hot choices in the evening, with plenty of fish, cold meats,, salami dominated as in much of eastern Europe, with plenty of vegetable alternatives, breakfast was of a similar standard, the holiday company had a deserved reputation for value for money, catering in the main for a late middle age with a few younger and older people in the mix. Unlike Spain, Greece, and France, there were few alternate eating establishments away from the hotel if you are not in one of the tourist hotspots, such as Pula, Porac, or Rovinj.

There are some, but not back to back, nicely spaced among other commercial outlets, so not giving you the feeling of being a walking cash cow, as when walking past a dozen restaurants with tables ten deep and someone in your path paid to try and drag you into theirs.

Being late October, well past the high season, we were initially put in a room on the first floor, overlooking a garden that was being dug out with a mechanical digger, no doubt going to look good by next year, but noisy for us, we asked to be moved, and were rewarded with a room facing the sea four floors up, a good result. I think others asked to move, we may have been the first, as we heard some grumbling about their alternative room, pot luck for us, if you're going to complain, get in quick before the crowd, as there will only be few better options available.

As mentioned, like many tourist coastal areas, seafront paths can run for many miles, here was no exception, the next day was a little overcast with spots of rain, but the clouds was not that dark grey that promised much rain, we had a tourist map of Opatija and surrounds, so armed with that, the brolly bought in Rovinj, big coats, mid-teens degrees C, we set off for a coastal walk, we knew there was a public park not far away, soon finding that not far along, pleasant, with a few drawings of locally famous poets and writers, the greenery as always most pleasing for me, beyond the park was a long, crazy paved sunbathing area, where you could in warmer days, jump straight into fairly deep water, so not child friendly. After a bit more walking, we found a cafe, had coffee, not cheap, but not as bad as Italy, but also not as cheap as the early years of east European independence from the then Soviet Union, now in the EU, let hope Croatia doesn't go the way of much of southern Europe.

Still retaining its own currency, the Kuna, though linked to the euro, and fairly stable at the time of writing, Croatia may need the flexibility we in Britain enjoy, to react to its own market conditions, unlike Greece, with Spain and Italy in almost as bad a state with mass youth unemployment, not the one size fits all that suits German and French interests, let's hope for Croatia's sake they retain this vital currency freedom to revalue if needed, seeing what's happening elsewhere (as above) I for one hope they have the savvy to do so.

As I recall, the price of coffee set the tone, but in general the Croatians seem to know they can make more from their tourist industry if they avoid over development, and concentrate on maintaining their beautiful old towns as cultural masterpieces. After finding a kiosk for a local water taxi, we took note of the timetable, deciding that on another day later in the week, we would catch this to visit a village called Lovran, where we were told there was to be a chestnut festival.

Istria, the peninsula, is not quite all Croatian, the top north eastern area being part of Slovenia, the bit of old Yugoslavia that managed to break away with the least trouble from Serbia, Croatia shielding it from Serbia being the main reason, thus avoiding the war that followed the break up. A small north-westerly tip of Istria is in Italy, not much more than a buffer zone for Trieste.

Lake Bled, in Slovenia was to be a full day excursion, part of the package, it looks so pretty in the brochures, but from Opatija it is a heck of a way by road, almost the entire length of Istria x 2 and a bit more besides. The amount of time spent in the coach that day had a direct bearing on what we did next day. After crossing the border into Slovenia, held up by a coach in front carrying Chinese tourists, a passport problem we were told, we eventually passed the outskirts of Ljubljana, the capital, soon after stopping for coffee, then heading north west, reaching lake Bled after well over three hours.

It is smaller than it looks in the brochures, you could walk round it in an hour, we didn't as it was raining for most of our two hours there, though only light, not enough to stop us having a wander, the island in the middle, with its pretty church is picturesque enough, though an overcast sky takes some of the charm away.

The castle, perched above a white cliff face across the lake was quite a picture, painted white with red roof, complete with red topped turret plus moat, so we were told, as the steep climb up the hill was no longer an option for me, having eaten something with coffee on the way, but still able to walk around half of the lake, stopping for coffee, and eventually lunch in a pub like establishment.

Chapter 104

After wandering around the trinket shops dotted along the shore, it was soon time to head back on the long coach trip back. While not quite a disappointment, perhaps the dull weather, combined with what seemed a smaller scale lake vista than we were led to imagine from its description, add that to the long coach trip, and we came away a little underwhelmed.

There was an included trip to Krka national park, with its multiple waterfalls, and several lakes, meant to be quite spectacular, but due to the local weather forecast, the holiday company had decided to make this trip a day earlier, and move a planned boat trip out to nearby islands back a day, when the local forecast was better, good idea in theory, but on the long trip back from lake bled, we both decided we could not endure another long coach trip the next day, Krka being even further away, in the opposite direction, not far north east of Split, which is a long way down the Adriatic coast

We had been told of "Marunada" a chestnut festival at a village called Lovran, a few miles down the coast from Opatija, and having been told of the excursion trip swap, and that this chestnut festival was now on the same day as the long trip to Krka national park, we decided to take the water taxi to Lovran, and forgo another, even longer coach trip, however spectacular the waterfalls were promised to be.

That morning was quite cool, but not wet, we were the only two passengers on the boat, which could have carried a dozen, it was only between nine and ten am. Part way to Lovran we were given a drink of some spirit that was close to brandy by the driver of the water taxi. It may have been a local hooch, but it wasn't bad on a cool late-October morning on the sea, he received an appreciative tip on arrival at the small pier in Lovran, it was a short walk uphill to the village proper, which was not a problem, as I had had no breakfast, as I do when I know I have some possibly uphill walking to do that day.

Having taken around forty minutes to get to Lovran, it was still only between ten and eleven, we wondered if it was still a bit early, and were quite surprised to see hundreds of people thronging the village centre, there were various choirs, in competition as it turned out, musicians, stalls of all types, with quite a few – wait for it, roast chestnut vendors for some strange reason…

The star of this festival as far as I was concerned was dead, but still held centre stage, it was a whole roast pig on a spit, though not fully cooked yet, it looked good. We bought a bag of roast chestnuts, not bad, if a little dry after a few, so had some lager to wash then down, sitting in the communal eating area that was surrounded by vendors. Not often I have lager for breakfast, though by then it was not far-off midday.

The day turned out to be sunny, despite trips having been swapped due to supposed bad weather locally, a cool start turned into a nice day, after our unusual breakfast we wandered the stalls, buying a small black olive picture, and an almost matching tile clock, both for the kitchen, which both still look good in there. Sarah also bought a ceramic apple, and pear, to go with the jade like grapes, so we now had a fruit bowl full – that never over-ripened! I also bought a woolly hat for the coming winter.

After listening to a few of the competing choirs for a while, we meandered down towards the jetty, just above which, we had spotted a nice-looking restaurant/cafe, Sarah says it was German owned, no longer accessible in my corrupted memory banks, I'll go with that, we had posh (priced) fish and chips – apparently, I do recall sitting outside to eat, it was quite warm by then (around two pm).

Then it was a hop across the coast road and a wait for the water taxi to take us back to Opatija. The taxi back was the same one, but being full this time, there was no hooch handed round. On the way back it stopped at a small village called Icici, that was host to quite a large marina, I took note of this, thinking it might be worth a look round in a spare few hour. We got off where we boarded a good half mile short of Opatija, not realising we could have stayed on to Opatija harbour, which in hindsight should have been obvious, but I think the kiosk there was closed when we looked around the harbour two days earlier, being flat along the coast walk, I was OK, if a little slow, after fish and chips.

Chapter 105

Along the main coast road running through Opatija's high street we had spotted what looked like a lively but smart modern bar, so a couple of nights that week, after dinner on days without long trips out, we walked the short distance to the subtlety lit neon blue front aged bar. This place had a mix of age groups, with comfortable chairs, and music that was complementary, not dominating, all in all a nice spot to spend a couple of evenings in. The barman mixed Sarah one or two fever tree flavoured – Med versions of G and T, her preferred tipple, though very rarely in excess I would add. I even ran to a couple of double Glenmorangies on the rocks, the first as a beer chancer, the second to savour, we were on hols after all, and it was only a short walk back to the hotel.

The main group that went to Krka National park, were so late back that evening, that they were told in the hotel restaurant to get their buffet food quick, as a wedding reception was set up there for not much later, if I had endured that sort of journey, only to be told "bolt you dinner" and get out of the way, I would not have been happy to say the least, I would imagine the travel company paid for that in the reviews.

Close to Opatija, in Kvarner Bay, are the two main islands of Krk and Cres, the day trip to these were swapped with Krka NP, as mentioned, so next day was now this trip, the weather all blue sky. the first stop was a quite harbour village, to wander then coffee stop, a beach walk, then a ferry across to the other island, where we were split into makeshift minibus and taxi groups, taken up to a Vulture rescue centre, where chicks were reared then released back into the wild. First I knew there are wild vultures outside Africa. They are rare here, conservation a late effort – as always.

We had walked round the back of the very large aviary and had a good look at the two adolescent vultures before most of the group had arrived in the makeshift transport, we got back to the main group, just in time to hear that contact with humans was kept to a minimum to maintain their best chance of survival, as shepherds would kill any they came across in the mountains to protect their flock, this talk was indoors, we were then led out to a spot about thirty yards from the aviary where we could not actually see the vultures, that was as close as the main group got to them. We did not show our close-up photos to anyone, or let on we had got close, feeling guilty that we had violated the vulture's privacy, though no signs warned us off, us just a bit quick off the mark.

There was a cafe nearby, selling local honey and lunch. Set near the top of a hill, there was a valley, with on the other side, a picturesque red roofed village perched on top of the next hill, with the traditional church at the highest point as always, the sea visible behind, good enough for a zoom photo, painted by Sarah later.

On the last day, it was late in the day before our trip to the airport, so we got a bus in the morning to Icici, had a look around the marina, took a few photos, had coffee and pastries, then back on the bus, Icici being only half the distance to Lovran where we had been to in the water taxi two days earlier.

P.S. we got the Lovran "Muruanada" chestnut festival fridge magnet whilst there. Always nice to see a bit of local culture, something lacking at home in large areas these days if football is not your first love. Not a bad holiday, good value, better if you don't mind very long coach trips, but for a late planned trip after a tough house move and a new job to find, Croatia is a good destination if you want to go beyond just sun and sand.

Chapter 106

After any house move, then comes the redecorating, having taken the late holiday just described, we set about brightening our new home up, mainly Sarah's province, with me helping where I can do the least harm, so where I was likely to get more on the wall than on me…

Lighter colours were the main order of those days, done gradually, living room first with some coving added to add softer lines, then the dark main bedroom, the kitchen, a much needed clean of the older conservatory, both inside and out took place. The back garden was in need of much revamping, you could tell the previous occupants had had enough, though to be fair one was disabled, and once they had made up their mind up to move to Spain, I do not blame them for only keeping minimum maintenance going, indeed I will admit to sometimes needing a good shove from Sarah to get going, at other times ideas do take hold, in short, I can be a bit on the mercurial side.

As this sort of thing is the same as most people go through periodically, I will not go into every detail. One of the few things I will mention is that I reverted to form, in that I found a way to get a large (55-gallon) four-foot long aquarium, complete in its own Pine cabinet stand, into our living room. It came at a price in the New Year's sales, too good to miss, and to my surprise, Sarah agreed to getting it after I had worked out how to fit it in.

The large two and three-seater settees that had moved with us, was separated, the two-seater moved into the conservatory, thus making room for the tank set on its own pine cupboard unit as mentioned, this matching the coffee table and a nest set in similar shades.

With room underneath for the large filter unit needed for such a tank, this makes for a colourful alternative, especially in winter, to the sometimes "57 channels and nothing on" tyranny of the telly, where we find that TV companies have found it much easier and cheaper to put out UN reality TV, instead of intelligent entertainment, so much so, that when decent drama is made, it's shouted from the rooftops, it is so rare these days, you would think most people at the end of a hard day would prefer to be taken to somewhere beyond their usual experience, as in a good book, but now even mainstream channels have discovered there is a large enough percentage of the human race that takes delight is seeing others make a fool of themselves.

I will admit to watching *Place in the Sun*, though for looking at the regions of those brave enough to make the move as much as the properties on offer, having had a small place in Crete for a while, but this sort of programme is not about making people look foolish, it is about their hopes for a better life, at no one else's expense.

As winter approached, we settled into a life of going out at least one of the four days I now had off from work, going to locations such as the Lleyn peninsular, or Anglesey, if we planned in advance to get up early-ish, though more often much closer to home, along the coast if it was dry, this being the general idea of moving here, close enough to reach a variety of flat-ish countryside, not eating, as previously gone into, until the walk was done, then a hearty brunch, though cutting my meat intake to a minimum on these late breakfasts, though not to nil, though I will eat scrambled eggs without any pig quite often these days.

My work had settled into a mix of keeping the place clean and tidy, oxygen bottle decontamination, and going out on a mix of short or sometimes longer runs taking an average of three large containers full of product of various sizes, sometimes full, sometimes empty, to our other main depot, sometimes as part of a relay to distribution bases further afield. At that time these trips were quite frequent, though not at set times, as the least skilled person on the shop floor, it was a regular occurrence to be told at a moment's notice I was to go on the road, something I did not mind, as the job I was doing could usually wait, that being the whole point, I was backup when needed.

We both enjoy a quiet life, interspersed with occasional livelier times, unlike some of the generally higher achieving people who usually have an interesting enough life, often overcoming great adversity at some stage, this being the driving force to gaining public recognition for actions of note in later life. I can claim no single event that put me on course to writing this book, only a gradually growing unease, now I have enough downtime from work, to realise that as I amass all I have learnt about the *lack* of uniqueness of my strange (repeat – not imagined) early childhood experiences, *not* misremembered interference of a nasty but conventional type, as some would infer, and add to this the resulting compulsion to find out about possible correlating events, learning to categorise the fake, the deliberate disinformation, the grey areas, (sorry couldn't resist), as this is the largest section, along with the thousands of witness sightings, radar reports and contested reports of covert Secret Access Projects that may still be ongoing.

Chapter 107

Back to the winter of 2016, little to report, we went to my brothers just after Christmas, stayed over, as a few drinks were of course involved. Periodically, Sarah would visit her daughter, I would go occasionally for the odd Sunday dinner.

Gradual work on the house and garden, that and walks followed by brunch on one of my four days off, usually Fridays as it is quieter than weekend, when the weather was up to it.

Van driving trips continued out to my work's other main depot in the West Midlands, around 80 miles away, in the winter – if clear – is a drive straight into the low winter sun on the way down, as it is a generally south easterly run, sunglasses were essential, but the route I take, as do most, avoids the dreaded M6, instead following the A41 off from the A55, down past Whitchurch a very agricultural, but scenic route, getting stuck behind the occasional tractor that soon turns off, usually a pleasant change from my fairly boring plant cleaning.

I am being deliberately vague (as you may have realised, about the exact nature of my current employment, as I am also about where exactly we now live, as I wish to be an Oddball representative of my peer group, I do not wish to be recognised as an individual, even if this may turn out to be detrimental to sales of any book this script results in.

Several times over the years Sarah had voiced an interest in my teens and early twenties trips to the Outer Hebrides, so I decided to take her there, in April of the new year 2017, hoping spring would have took the edge off the cold weather by then, this took some planning, booking B&Bs along the way, including a motorway lodge heading north in England, stopping there again on the way back five days later, this proved to be one day less than would have been ideal, as three days to cover the whole of the Outer Hebrides, from Stornoway on Lewis, down to the southern ferry on South Uist, proved to be too rushed.

I had decided that as we were going all the way up there, we might as well see the whole island group from top to bottom, minus Barra, as I had only been to South Uist and Benbecula, as you may recall on my report of earlier up days there.

As this was such a long road trip, an overnight stop was needed, North Wales to Ullapool in one day is not doable unless I get my pilots license (not got around to that), so a coffee break on the north M6, followed by an overnight stop at a basic travel chain hotel short of Moffat on the A74 was our first day on the road,

I won't go into much detail at this stage as many of you will have travelled these roads.

I decided, as it was still a long hop from just north of the English border to Ullapool, to head for Perth and the more direct A9 route north, rather than the fifty miles longer, but more scenic A82 western route up to Fort William and through the Great Glen to Inverness, a decision I was to regret, as not far north of Perth, we encountered an endless succession of road widening works.

The time it took us to get through that lot meant that we got to Inverness no quicker than if we had gone on the longer more scenic western route. Sarah, ever practical, had bought a crusty stick loaf at the shop near our overnight stop, so after crossing the Moray Firth, a ham, cheese and tomato sandwich, and coffee in a small park on the northern outskirts of Inverness was very welcome, as was a leg stretch on a cool, breezy but bright day.

Soon after resuming our journey, at a roundabout in Tore, we parted company with the A9 and forked north west onto the A835 which would take us all the way to Ullapool, crossing the north of Scotland on that north easterly road at its narrowest width, through pine forests, passing a few lochs, a scenic route that Sarah had a better look at than I, having to keep my eye on the road, that last section was the best part, the weather bright, with only sparse traffic, guessing that much of this traffic heading the same way, could well be catching the ferry the next day with us, the only onward road alternative taking the route to the top coast of Scotland, as we did last time we were in this neck of the woods.

By mid-afternoon we reached Loch Broom, and knew Ullapool was only about seven miles away. Last time we were there, on our version of "Billy Connolly's *World Tour of Scotland*", it was wet and windy, this time bright and breezy, if cool. I had booked us in at the Anchor Inn, close to the ferry terminal, and after signing in, we went for a much-needed stretch of legs, calling in at the ferry terminal to find out where to queue up in the morning. That done, it was time for a rest and a read, until a nice meal of fish and chips was had that evening at the Anchor, accompanied by a beer and a wee dram.

Chapter 108

The Caledonian Macbrayne ferry took us on a slightly choppy crossing of the Minch to Stornoway on Lewis, arriving early afternoon. We planned to drop of our cases at the B&B we had booked a little out of town, then do a circuit of the north of Lewis. No one was home when we reached the B&B, so we headed west up the A857, across the flat landscape of the north of Lewis, turning north and running up to Port Ness, on the Butt of Lewis, Port is a bit of a stretch, it is only a tiny harbour, and a small village. What we did find near a field wall, were some highland cattle, I had standing orders to photograph one – a head close up, which I duly did, for Sarah to paint later on, which she has.

We retraced our steps (so to speak) staying on the north coast, following it around, where we eventually reached our intended "Must See", the Standing Stones of Callanish.

When we got there, a coachload of tourists had beaten us to it, and so it was some time before we were able to get a decent people free photo. Your guess is as good as mine as to why these and many other stone circles were erected, but a lot of effort was involved, ritual is the standard explanation, if there was something more they tapped into, it is lost, or kept from Joe public now.

After tea and cake at the visitor centre, we completed the circuit of the A858, down onto the 859, turning northeast back to Stornoway and our B&B, where our hosts were now home and ready for us, it now being late afternoon. The B&B was a good one, rosewood dining table, big windows, with a view of more hilly, varying landscape than most of north Lewis has, the rest being a fat-ish tussock grass landscape for much of the interior.

From the big window of the B&B, the view is towards Stornoway, on a small hill halfway to town can be seen a large stone monument, asking our host about it, when told, I realised I had vague memories of being told about it whilst on South Uist around forty years ago.

It is a very sad tale of a ship, HM Yacht Iolaire bringing home Lewis and Harris men from WW1.

As with many man-made disasters, there were warning signs of the potential for what happened here. Too many men had boarded this ship, to the disquiet of its Master, the ship had never docked at Stornaway before, it had only two lifeboats. It was around Two AM on the 1st of January 1919 when it approached the harbour, so pitch dark, gale force winds, a lack of experience of this harbour, all must have played a part in what happened next, it has never been established exactly why, but instead of turning into the harbour, the ship ploughed into the rocks beyond, capsizing the Iolaire, killing 174 Lewis men, and 7 Harris men, only forty men managed to get ashore.

Having already lost around a thousand men already to the Great War, for soldiers to get so close to home, indeed in sight of waiting family, it must have been unbearably heart breaking to all concerned. As usual, Search online for the full story.

We bid our farewell to our overnight hosts, of what turned out to be the best B and B we stayed at on our over hurried trip to these islands, not before mentioning that we had heard reports of possible snow heading their way, they discounted it saying it was rare for then to get snow there…

I then took a small gamble and lost, it was Sunday, so I should have known better. Years ago many places, including pubs up here were shut Sundays, I was not sure where petrol would be next available, so after a good breakfast, we were ready to set off south by around 9.30, and were told that the petrol station in Stornoway would not open until 10.30, so having done the A857 / 858 circle for Callanish Standing Stones the previous day, we had spotted a small shop with a petrol pump on the A858/9 junction back up to Stornoway, so rather than waiting an hour, I risked the twenty-minute run down to this shop, only to find that shut, a local guy saying it was shut all day Sunday, so it was back up to Stornaway and the petrol station there, I had wasted a little petrol on the speculative scout south, but not time, as we still had to wait another twenty minutes before this station opened.

Having filled up, we set off south on the A859, heading for Harris, if we had another day up there, the Uig area of West Lewis, with its Blackhouse village and Caloway Broch, would have been worth a visit, but this trip was not meant to be a major holiday, as we had one such due in only a couple of months.

As it turned out, it was a good job we didn't hang about, we thought we would put some miles behind us before turning of the main road on North Harris to take a look at Amhuinnshidhe Castle, now a Hotel and B and B, with shooting and fishing available.

Chapter 109

This stretch of the B887, only a single lane with passing places, is one of the most winding, narrow, bits of road I have ever driven, with sharp drop off either side for much of it, the rocky landscape was a wilderness. The rock in this area is said to be billions of years old, I would not like to get stranded on this road, as rescue would be very awkward, but after a challenging few mile, we reached the castle.

If you wanted to really, really get away from it all, but in a bit of comfort, this is the place for you, built in 1865 for local nobility, it was built as a hunting lodge, but the estate owner, the 7th earl of Dunmore's mother, Lady Catherine, set up an embroidery school to encourage the then fledgling Harris tweed industry, so the local economy was also helped to develop.

On this trip I knew vittles' might be hard to come by, so we had bought a flask with us, which as well as being used at Inverness, we had refilled at the B&B in Stornoway, with Sunday closing the norm out there, I had bought something sweet at the petrol station, Mars Bars or some such, we did not enter the hotel/castle, but stopped at a nearby viewing spot opposite what looked like a small primary school, and had coffee and snack there, the weather by then getting colder, with bits of snow in the air.

Resuming our way up this assault course of a road back to the main road, not far short of it, we came across on odd sight, two shepherdesses, putting bright orange coats on new born lambs, aware as we were of the imminent cold snap catching up with us as we headed south, it was a good idea, as the new-born lambs would probably not survive this late March winter snap without help.

Back on the A 859 heading south, we soon came to Tarbert, where North Harris is joined to South Harris by a short causeway, we took note of a small hotel there, as though we had booked a nights bed and breakfast further south at Sorrel Cottage, just north of Leverburgh, where we would catch the ferry to Lochmaddy on North Uist the next morning, I was a bit concerned as to where we would find somewhere to eat that evening.

Continuing along the main road that veered west to the Atlantic coast, we came to a point where beyond a pristine white beach, we could see the Island of Taransay, which I was to learn later, was the location of the *BBC's Castaway 2000*, where several people were left to see how long they could survive, not long, as far as I know the island remains uninhabited.

By now the wind was strong and very cold, coming straight from the Arctic, I had picked the worst week of that year's late winter/early spring to visit an old haunt. A little further down the coast we stopped at a vantage point lay-by to view a pink and white beach set below Harris Golf Course.

What we saw next was quite surreal – a young couple were attempting to play golf in the gale force, freezing wind and snow that was now blowing in the air, when they saw us they laughed, probably at the expression on our faces of disbelief at their presence out there. We smiled at their antics, but did not wind our window down to attempt talking in the howling wind, instead finishing the last of our coffee, before continuing south towards our next B and B. As last time at Stornoway, when we got there early afternoon, no one was home, so we continued on to Leverburgh, two miles down the road to see where to catch the ferry next morning, and also to find something warm to eat, as Stornoway's breakfast, though nice, seemed a long time ago in this cold weather, Mars bars notwithstanding.

There was a small supermarket as we entered the village that we were lucky enough to find open for a few hours on a Sunday afternoon, I wolfed down a pasty, Sarah a sandwich. We soon saw it was obvious where the ferry would run onto the concrete ramp and drop its car door, white painted lines for lining up to board, we would return for our crossing in the morning.

It was now late enough in the afternoon that we hoped the lady owner of Sorrel Cottage would be in to allow us to install ourselves in our booked room, she was, though we had to remove our shoes and put special slippers on in the porch. I think she was used to cyclists and hikers turning up in mud covered boots, so we didn't mind. Our room was the attic bedroom, light enough with front and back windows, and warm enough with the electric heater provided, it was needed as the weather remained cold and wet with mixed snow and rain.

Over a welcome cup of tea in the breakfast/sitting room, we met three older guys, also staying, whom I am afraid, almost instantly in my mind, Christened "Foggy, Compo and Clegg" from *Last of the Summer Wine* fame, such was their similarity to those three characters, right down to their dress, which were outdoor cords, old jumpers and heavy jackets.

After a chat with them, we asked where they were going to eat that evening, the more outspoken of the three, "Compo" (in my mind), telling us of a small bistro, not far back up and off the "main" road half a mile on our left, heading north, we asked as advised, the owner of the B and B for the phone number of this Bistro, she told us that she had advised them already they might have two more customers, a fair guess, as it was the only eatery for miles around, and that she would call them herself now confirm we would be there, she told us it would have to be at eight PM, as they were booked up till then, we said fine by us (like we had a choice!), but at least we were going to eat that evening.

Chapter 110

It had emerged that the last of the summer wine trio were from just north of Manchester, not Yorkshire as were their namesakes, whose real names we cannot recall, but in the unlikely event that one of them reads this, they will recognise themselves, as the inevitable happened that evening…

They were booked in the same small "Temple Cafe", but at seven pm.

This renovated old stone circular building with walls around three foot thick, not sure of its history, but the name might be a clue, was owned by a young couple, the guy a trained chef, judging from the quite sophisticated menu, his wife, the Maître D, come waitress and everything else in this small cramped bistro.

How the guy managed to cook all he did in the tiny kitchen, which was a small hallway off the round eating room was a minor miracle, but the place was jam packed with about a dozen of us, we of course were plonked next to Foggy, Compo, and Clegg, who despite being there an hour earlier, were still eating when we sat down.

The Temple cafe did not have an alcohol licence, but you could bring your own bottle, we had none, so we had soft drinks with our meal, not so the trio next to us, they had brought a wine box with them, so by the time we had virtually joined them, they were in full flow with the banter, it emerged they were bus drivers, and had got up there on discount passes by plane, train, and no doubt automobile, and were heading north towards Stornoway, and had been told by the Sorrel Cottage B&B owner that they had snow up there, I could not help thinking of the warning I gave to the B&B people we stayed with up there that we had heard snow was on the way, them doubting it, as they very rarely got it there, this would turn out to be that rare time.

The three guys were throwing banter about, some at us to the point that I could no longer contain myself, and asked them which one was Foggy, which was Compo, and which was Clegg, this produced the first silence from Clegg, who was leading the banter, but not for long, though I think he saw the funny side, he was more used to giving it out than receiving a direct hit like that, his remaining conversation a little more muted.

I would not normally have dreamed of coming out with something that might have caused offence like that, but "Clegg" in particular had wasted no time in telling us where we had to go and what we had to see, saying we should spend more time up there, us explaining we only had limited holiday time available as we had another longer trip away in a couple of months, though right, he was also a little mocking of our rushed schedule, and that gave me my opening. You could tell my comparison had hit home, and I could not help wondering if I was not the first to compare this trio with their more famous counterparts.

Not sure how they got back to the B&B, though we had seen them on hired bikes from the B&B earlier in the day, before we knew they were staying at our digs. We never found out as they left before us, having got there earlier, it would have been a wet ride back to Sorrel Cottage, as the weather was that and windy. They had finished breakfast the next morning as we sat down for ours, which was had quite early, the proprietor used to this as many were catching the ferry, if not just arrived from it, those heading north, like our "Summer wine" trio.

Our intrepid trio were at the nearby bus stop heading north as said. South Harris has a circular road, the east coast, unexplored by us, looks to have a few small settlements along its Minch facing coastline, so a bus no doubt comes down from Stornaway, circles South Harris before returning north. Our trio having a timetable, being bus drivers, were quite literally on a busman's holiday, at that point.

That morning Caledonian MacBrayne had sent me a text telling us the sea was too rough for the morning ferry, and it would now be nearer midday before it would arrive at Harris from North Uist, even that depending on the weather. We decided that as this ferry was likely to be small, we had better park up in the queue lanes, to make sure late arrivals would not be in front of us, with not knowing if Cal/Mac's policy was first come first served or not, though they were on the ball enough to keep us informed of changes, and after a coffee at the nearby cafe, now open, we got another text informing us the midday ferry would be sailing, much to our relief, mine in particular, as I knew it would now be a very rushed drive over North Uist, Benbecula and South Uist, to reach our booked last B and B in Lochboisdale before evening, wishing now I had allowed an extra day for this trip.

Chapter 111

(ADD) – ROOM

I considered phoning this, our last Island B&B, and asking if they had an extra night available, but this would also involve trying to put our mainland ferry crossing back a day, in the end I decided to make the best of it, especially with the weather being so inclement.

Soon after midday the ferry arrived from Berneray; a small island joined to the top of North Uist by a causeway. A bit of blue sky and whiter clouds gave us a break in the rough weather, though it was still cold and windy, the sea choppy, but the crossing now doable by the ferry skipper's judgement.

It was a relief to see it, as though we had a text saying it was coming, a worsening of conditions could have seen it cancelled. A small, Ramp Drop ferry, with no more than for a dozen cars and a couple of small trucks, it took about an hour to cross from Harris to Berneray, just time for a coffee and snack in the seating room/cafeteria, the weather looking ominous by the time we disembarked and drove across the short causeway onto North Uist which is circled after a short B Road south, by the A865 with the A867 leading to (or from) Lochmaddy, a small ferry port on the east coast, where, on some of my thirty five to forty years ago trips to these islands, I had sometimes docked, when making what we called the northern crossing, driving to the north of Sky to Uig and crossing from there, and driving down to South Uist from there, Lochmaddy being the farthest north I had previously been on these islands until now.

With the three-hour ferry delay, we now only had from around 1.30pm to get all the way down the Uists to Lochboisdale fifty odd miles south, hopefully making a little time to find some of my old stomping grounds from yesteryear.

With this in mind, I chose the eastern shorter route of the circular road across North Uist, we were not far into this tussock grass and small loch landscape, when the bad weather from the arctic caught up with us, the sky turned black, and we were hit with a mix a hailstones and snow, driven by gale force winds that almost brought us to a stop, but we were following another car and despite struggling to see ahead, buffeted by the wind, we thought it a good idea to stay with the other car, likely off the same ferry as us, if he could keep going, we would.

If I had more time, and the weather better, I would have turned off onto the mile or so road to have a quick look at Lochmaddy on the east coast, little more than a few houses, ferry terminal and a small shop when last there, I don't expect its changed much, but time was pressing even though the weather had not yet got really bad when we passed the sign for it, I had not allowed for ferry delays, and so we saw very little of North Uist other than very dark looking loch water, made this way by the peat seeping into it, black skies enhancing this impression, a lot of this islands east and south is made up of a hundred small lochs, sparse habitation, a few small hamlets or Townships as some are called up here.

In continuing snow and hail, we reached the mile or more long causeway, which while crossing to Benbecula, Sarah says the weather was so bad you could not see far in any direction, the causeway exposed to the worst of the howling wind, we kept going, slowly, but wanting to get of this exposed stretch quickly. After reaching Benbecula, I had to again regretfully make the decision to continue down the main road south.

If I had allowed for one more day, we could have turned west soon after the causeway, and headed for Balivanich, indeed I should have found a B and B there, as it is the largest township for miles, with its own airport, once used in the days I was there forty years ago by the RAF for ground to air missile testing, old Canberra jets towing targets behind.

I had been there once, with the "Wild Bunch" to a Ceilidh, pronounced Keyligh to us Sassenachs, invited there by the younger members of a South Uist family we had got to know many moons ago, to see what were the superstars of the West Highlands and Islands in the late seventies, they were a group called Runrig, later to achieve passing fame on Top of the Pops a few years later, as I mentioned in my account of my earlier visits up here. There is also a large beach near this west coast large village (by island standards), but I never saw it then, and due to bad planning and false economy, not now. There is no point in going somewhere unless you make enough time to see all you want to see, and I had not done so here, even with the bad weather, we should have seen more of these places.

So due to lack of time we continued south to a place called Creagorry at the southern end of Benbecula, where I hoped there was still a shop I recall from years ago, as though we had bought sandwiches at Leverburgh ferry terminal on Harris, we had nothing to drink, having drunk the flask of coffee we made at the B and B before setting out, nothing hot to be had at this small Spar I remembered from donkeys years ago, so only orange or some such to wash down our sandwiches.

Chapter 112

As we drove across the smaller causeway to South Uist, the weather started to clear somewhat, so I thought at least it would be worth turning off to try finding my old camping and rabbit shooting grounds on the West Coast Machair, the nearly twenty miles of grasslands and sand dunes running along about a quarter mile deep strip along the bottom two thirds of the west coast of this island.

I took a turning a little south of Ormiclate Castle (a ruin) which I recalled seeing in the distance to the north of where I and the Wild Bunch used to roam the Machair. We passed what I was fairly sure was the Macmillan's house where I stayed for two weeks of the four in the first year up there (for me) in the late seventies. The house was situated on a hillock where few others were, this house now looked modernised, with a conservatory added, I briefly thought about calling there, but as Euan and Morag, were long since passed away, with no children I knew of, I thought it pointless in the end as I would have no connection to the new owners.

I was making for what we used to call "The Point", a bit of land sticking out into the Atlantic on Bornish Machair, Rudha Ardvule on the map, where we used to make campfires, and where we set off on our canoe/ trip down to bottom of the island, described earlier.

Though it had brightened up, it was still blowing a bitter gale, so after a brief wander around, me thinking we should have come of the main road a little nearer Ormiclate to find our camping area, but there would be nothing to mark it now, and as I had told Sarah, it is not a scenic island, unlike Sky, but she had still expressed in interest in seeing these islands, so here we were.

It is often said it is not a good idea to revisit your youth, and as I had not made enough time to revisit old haunts like Loch Skipport on the west coast, and could not be sure of where we used to stay in the old builders caravan, they had now built a golf course on part of where we used to wander and camp, so I would agree with the above saying. If Sarah had not shown an interest, and me thinking the islands to the north would be new to me as well, I would not have returned, with hindsight, as the Lewis, Harris and North Uist, that we saw are not much to look at, unless you like tussock grass and peaty water. You had to be there with a much younger, different perspective, to still find this place of great interest, even with better weather.

We returned to the "Main" road, stopping at a war memorial on a hill a few miles further south, for no other reason than it was on a hill, so there was a good all-round view, and I thought I would let our last B and B know we were less than an hour away, being as it was late afternoon by then.

Again, an extra day would have let us drive down to the southern tip of the island, called in at the Pollachar Hotel, where we had dragged our canoe's out after our twenty-mile paddle so long ago, we could have crossed the short causeway to Eriskay, if this and if that, but this was not meant to be a main holiday, so it was what it was.

As you might recall, I did mention on my earlier narrative of my times here, there was a pub/hotel called the Borrodale at the township of Daliburgh, where the junction for the southern tip (Pollachar) meets the main road as its swings east for Lochbosdale, I spent quite a few nights getting drunk in there, and it was from there we once risked our lives in the pitch dark walking miles north whilst drunk, to meet one of the older Wild brothers who was supposed to be picking us up, one of the local girls he was "seeing" finding a way to delay him somewhat…

This time around, apart from a brief look at it – I could see it had been extended for more accommodation, we followed the road east to our last B and B at Lochboisdale, where we would now be catching the ferry early the next morning to Oban, not Mallaig, as we had booked for, as Caledonian MacBrayne had again texted me to say the weather was too rough to dock at The small Mallaig Pier.

Though we would not now revisit Fort William on our way south, this alternate route through the Sound of Mull would save us fifty miles of driving, and as we had booked to stay in the same motorway lodge down past Moffat near the border, this longer sea trip, but shorter drive was OK by me.

The elder member of the family at our Lochboisdale B&B was the closest lookalike I have ever seen to Uncle Fester of the *Adams Family*, the house almost as dated, but it was a roof over our heads when the weather was still blowing a gale, with squally showers, the walk to and from the Lochboisdale Hotel only two hundred yards away was an example of walking at a thirty degree tilt into the wind.

The curry we had there was out of a tin, but it was hot food so found the spot, that and a beer with my (hols only) Glenmorangie chaser, Sarah on wine this time. Having disparaged our last B&B host, they did let us have a bath, which was very welcome after the freezing winds outside.

Up at first light, we had a six thirty ferry to catch, having paid for our room the previous evening, we let ourselves out, the owners being used to early ferry sailings. As usual, I got us there a little early as is my wont, we were second in the car-boarding queue.

Chapter 113

Breakfast was had before long, once we were heading back to the mainland, on this route we past the Islands of Rum and Eigg, which were covered in snow from halfway up, dry and bright now, it looked like we were in the Arctic passing those two snow covered islands, I knew we would soon be in the Sound of Mull, where I wanted, at its southern end, to get a good photo of Duat Castle, dating back to the 13th century, and the Seat of the Clan Maclean, standing on a rocky promontory, it looks quite a sight from the ship, if I could get a good photo, Sarah would likely paint it – which she did. We had passed Tobermory at the top end of the Sound, but not close enough to get a photo of the colourful houses. Our earlier "Safari" visit to Mull was recalled on our "World Tour of Scotland" trip. I had passed this castle going the other way on my first (very rough) trip to the Outer Hebrides, recounted earlier.

I had switched "location on" in my phone, so the map showed when we neared the castle, we passed a smaller Cal Mac ferry heading somewhere as we passed the castle, but it did not obscure my photos, the scaffolding on the castle did, but Sarah edited this out of her picture.

It was still dry and bright when we docked at Oban, sheltered now from the north wind, with its hill that the faux coliseum (McCraig's Tower) sits atop behind the town. The seafront was pleasant enough to have a coffee sat outside a cafe there. It was ironic that the two best spells of weather we had on the whole trip was just before we left the mainland, and just after we returned.

We then headed first north east five miles to the inlet of Loch Etive, before following the south bank east on the A85, then south east to Loch Awe, where at the top end of the Loch you pass the picturesque ruined, but impressive Kilchurn Castle set on a promontory. This fifteenth century castle was built for the Campbell Clan to dominate Glen Orchy, which they did for over 150 years. We continued east towards Tyndrum, somewhere along this road we stopped at a large shop that looked interesting, next to a cafe for coffee.

In the shop there, I could not resist buying an expensive "Isle of Lewis" chess set, so named after some figures that were found in the north of that Island. Then it was south east to Crianlarich, where possibly because we stopped at a pub off the main road for lunch, I took a wrong turn afterwards, continuing east along the A85, instead of turning south on the A82 towards Loch Lomond. We followed the A 85 where it turned south to Lochearnhead, not noticing that we had switched onto the A84 until what I thought was Loch Lomond appeared next to us, which made Sarah look at the map and tell me it was on the wrong side of the road!

We then stopped and puzzled over the map before discovering we were on the banks of Loch Lubnaig, way over in Strathyre Forest. It had crossed my mind that it was taking a long time to reach Loch Lomond… must have been distracted at Crianlarich, so we picked out a route to get us back on course, down to Callander and the turning just past Rob Roy's grave site onto the A81, heading through Aberfoyle, then down only as far as the A811, turning south west towards Balloch Castle at the southern tip of Loch Lomond, deciding we needed to stretch our legs somewhere nice before Glasgow and the motorway.

We did not go in the castle, just had a good walk in the gardens, and another tea or coffee, before heading down the A82 into Glasgow, literally, as in my/our second navigational blunder of the day, we missed the Erskine Bridge turn off for the M8, and so crawled through the middle of town in rush hour before finally reaching the M74, so it must have been gone eight by the time we reached the motor lodge south of Moffat we had re booked on the way up, for this return stop on the way home.

Getting caught in the worst week of weather after a mild early March, and the Harris ferry delay, made for a mad dash of a holiday, me having in mind a major trip less than three months down the line, this making me skimp, not allowing for any hold up, so it was a rushed experience, Sarah saying at least she had seen some of where I used to talk of enough to peek her interest, me regretting I had not added an extra day, to see a bit more, but that was that, breakfast, and a M6 Tebay coffee break, as on the way up, with its duck pond view, saw us home a couple hours or so later.

Chapter 114

If you have no interest in board games, you might want to skip this section, though it will show some more of how my mind works – if that is a good idea…

As a youngster, I used to enjoy military, or strategy games, often making up my own, games of chance holding little interest for me. I was taught chess by my dad, and used to enjoy occasional games with my step grandfather, who encouraged me. For some reason in my make up, I have never enjoyed being in a chess club, I seem to resist without knowing why, being in anything too organised, like artists in a way, I have to feel like playing, not on demand, I suspect partly I probably don't wish to find my exact level, as I know it is not too high.

I could maybe improve with constant training, but apart from not being that committed to any sort of rat race, chess included, my memory would not let me learn the multiple set piece classic move variations that seem to be required learning. In the end, I have got more enjoyment for tinkering with the rules of chess to produce variations, this, to most serious chess players, is sacrilege, chess rules are sacrosanct, and so very few variants ever see the light of day.

Chess, as it stands, is unforgiving of mistakes, at a lower level you can get away with one, if the loss is not your queen, but club level players, if wanting to win in a safe but lazy and boring way will, if you lose a knight or bishop without reply, play the rest of the game as a constant simplification, forcing equal exchanges of pieces, knowing that eventually three major pieces will face two, making victory most likely just by following this tenant, so the result has effectively been decided back when you made that early mistake.

So I came up with the idea of introducing some additional moves to most of the pieces on the board, not extra taking moves, these remain as normal with the rooks, knights, and bishops. However, after playing chess/war game crossovers, and modified early Persian and Indian versions of chess on the internet with a guy from New York who had developed these, and had also shown me the value of short-range pieces, I had decided to give normal chess pawns some extra *umph* in my new variation.

I have developed other variations, but an amalgamation of two of these is now for me the best example of what I wanted to create – a game that intends to do two things to chess, the first is redundancy, in that if you make an early mistake, the remaining pieces are now powerful enough to compensate, so the result is not yet a forgone conclusion, the second intention, with the additional optional moves, is to create a board with so many possible combinations of moves, that the normal advantage of a better player in seeing more moves ahead, is negated somewhat by the sheer number of options available, so a small element of luck in seeing moves that have been overlooked amongst so many options is intended in this variation, that I call Xtra-Noble Chess, described below –

Xtra-Noble Chess

DELETE

Introduction

Xtra-Noble Chess adds extra mobility and a little extra firepower. Differing from standard chess in that the three Wing pieces and Pawns on each side are given an alternate move – but not piece taking option, (shown in diagram) these remain the same as in standard chess, apart from Kingpawns (described below). Standard chess can also be played using these pieces on the standard 8 x 8 chessboard. Major pieces are given higher noble ranks, (hence the name) to reflect their increased power. Pawns are also renamed to reflect their new strength in this game.

Pieces

Both Bishops become – **Archbishops**
Both Knights become – **Barons**
Both Rooks become – **Earls**
All Pawns become – **Kingpawns**
King and Queen – remain the same as in standard chess.

Setup – all pieces start on an 8x8 chessboard, in the standard chess pieces start positions.

Rules – alternate moves as described below, optional moves to empty squares only.

King and Queen – move and take only as kings and queens in standard chess, with no alternate move, or piece taking options.

Archbishops – move and take pieces as standard chess bishops, but with the option *instead* of moving but NOT taking pieces, one square as rook in any direction – thus able to move from one colour square to another, and back again later if wanted. *Check and Checkmate* are valid as a result of taking this move option – but only resulting in diagonal check as standard bishop.

Barons – move and take pieces as standard Chess Knights, but with the option *instead* of moving one square in *any* direction – diagonally or as rook, but CANNOT take pieces using this move option. *Check and checkmate* are valid as a result of this move option – but only as in a standard knight check.

Earls – move and take pieces as standard chess rooks – but with the option *instead* of moving from one to four spaces diagonally as bishop in any direction, but CANNOT take pieces using this move option. *Check and Checkmate* are valid as a result of taking this move option – but only as in a standard rook check.

Kingpawns – move and take pieces as standard pawns, BUT can also move one space only like a rook, so moving one square in any of four directions, or instead, taking pieces one square diagonally in all four diagonal directions. Two steps forward start option allowed as with standard Pawns.

Pawn promotion and en Passant – both of these options are NOT allowed in this game.

Check and checkmate – as in standard chess – with the inclusion of the alternate move options resulting in orthodox Chess Pieces, check and checkmate.

0000000000000000000000000000000000000000000000000000000000000
0000000

There it is, for anyone who feels like a change from the usual game, kingpawns, especially used in pairs, with their new found mobility and bite, can become a powerful force working together or on their own, allocated to attack or defence, combine this with the new fluidity of movement of the "noble" pieces, and it becomes quite a different game – using the same basic framework, which is the general idea…

Chapter 115

Sarah continued with her art club membership this spring, learning new techniques from some, but having a different set of people to talk to, in my mind is as important, as with retirement, can come relative isolation, weekdays and weekends all becoming the same if not careful, a change from shopping, cleaning, cooking, reading and the occasional rare chat with neighbours, is not always enough, so on the now four days I am not working, I try to make sure that on one of these at the very least, we go for a walk or trip somewhere, then brunch, then art or reading for Sarah or me, or writing this for me, preparing tea, (Sarah) telly filling part of the evenings, reading for both of us often finishing off the day.

I have ongoing games of chess via the internet with one of my workmates, this same guy Rhod, also has included me in intermittent games of doubles badminton, with two of his mates, they like him, in their mid-thirties, so when I say intermittent, I sometimes have to decline a session as my feet, right ankle and heel especially, will sometimes become painful and swollen if I overdo it, I have played enough over the years, so I can hold my own with these lads, twenty odd years younger than I, but landing very badly on this foot years ago has weakened that ankle so that it gives way if not looked after.

I have never been quite sure what Sarah thinks of my interest in, to keep things simple, the UFO enigma, she seems to blow hot and cold on the subject, she is a no nonsense person, so when I am watching one of the minor channel programmes on the subject, some of them poorly made to the point of endlessly repeating the same things over and over, or making extra-terrestrial connections on the most spurious of evidence, she will sometimes ridicule the presentations, often rightly so, though sometimes she does seem to agree that some, not all ancient carvings, depictions of flying machines, and strange looking humanoids may have some validity, that often expressed by a *lack* of criticism to what is displayed.

Sarah saw something as a seven or eight-year-old while she was on her way home from school with a friend, she says she saw what looked like the planet Saturn in the sky – in daylight, quite large, a fuzzy disc with rings round it, she knows Saturn is hundreds of millions of miles away, but at the age she saw it, she knew enough from school to relate what she saw to looking like Saturn, I have not been able to find out any more, other than she recalls telling her mum she saw Saturn when she got home, who said the equivalent of "of course you did" now go wash your hands for tea. She does not recall being told off for being late…

So despite a general scepticism as default, what she saw as a youngster may leave her in conflict on the subject, due to the sheer amount of reasonable witness testimony she has been exposed to through my interest.

If she sees anything in the paper on the subject, such as the revelation that the Pentagon has after all kept a small UFO evaluation department going long after it had supposedly lost interest, she will bring it to my attention. When I am watching telly stuff on the subject, sifting for anything that I have not heard before, and she is reading the paper or a magazine, seemingly not paying attention to the telly, she seems to know when something new and interesting crosses the screen, though this is rare.

I think she sometimes thinks me unable to sift rubbish that is displayed or spouted, from the possible true witnessing of unexplained events, I then have to occasionally remind her that I am not taking all I see and hear as literal truth. Like most people who have been busy bringing up kids, and had no conscious reason to think that the world and its history is not exactly as portrayed on the "News", or standard education. I cannot fault healthy scepticism, especially when I see a little doubt surfacing from what she has been exposed to in my interest of the subject. Sarah has become a useful barometer to see how new information stands in terms of plausibility. The less she says, I have found, the more there might be something to it, as I am soon told if something is less than plausible, often confirming my own serious doubt.

At the end of this book, I will try to present a linier time line of major events, real or disputed, and try to break down the logic of what might or might not be true, and my reasoning for this. I will refer again to those who have investigated and written on the relevant area of this vast subject, and ask you to decide, as in a court case on the balance of probabilities, not for a guilty or innocent verdict, but if you have had little interest in the subject, due to a full and busy life, or especially if you are a high achiever, and therefore more invested in the world view as it stands, whether the information and arguments drawn together here and in my Addendum is enough to leave you with a more open verdict than you might have expected.

Chapter 116

For someone who presents himself as an oddball, the word average is also important in the title of the book, as there is little to see in my home and work life apart from the impact on my confidence of my early life to the point of being happy not to produce offspring, other than that and my interest in the UFO subject, which I have left alone for long periods, so a recurring or sometimes dormant rather than all-consuming interest, as unless you are prepared or obsessed enough to devote your life to it, there are long periods where nothing new comes to light, I just keep an interest, fairly sure that unless I keep imputing keywords such as NSA, CIA, NASA, Special Access Projects, or other such into my internet browser or emails, I will be left alone to speculate.

Working full time until recently, keeping out of trouble, is not oddball, my brother and sisters family take my interests with a pinch of salt I think, me being the least successful in life, I am humoured, but with no kids, side-lined by choice from mainstream life, bit of a dud, by choice partly, but harmless enough. I know myself well enough to realise I am not a very sociable person, not a man's man, no great interest in football, or pub crowds as those of my station are expected to partake of, probably seen as a little cold, I try to come out with witty remarks that sometimes gain the expected moans, but I don't seem to fit in properly at any level, and so may appear a little aloof at times, when in fact I am wary of making a fool of myself, unable to recall many things of common interest without prompts, or my poor hearing unable to pick out words in a noisy background, so just giving a nod to god knows what sometimes.

I try to make up for this by coming out with carefully pre-thought out unbidden comments on conversations that are not directed at me, trying to show an interest.

The above to the point that I sometimes wonder that the autism my brothers lads grew up with might have surfaced a little in me, not bad enough to gain attention, especially when I grew up in the sixties and early seventies, but if dyslexia, (had to use the spellchecker for that) is a part of it, then a poor memory and concentration that is my bane, is the opposite of what I have seen in my brothers autistic lads growing up, as any interest they have is followed through with concentrated encyclopaedic thoroughness, one of the few benefits of that condition.

Not something I am capable of, is that, and as I am not a complete loner either, enjoying quite company, the average part of an Average Oddball, reflects the fact that I am not an extremist in my commitment to anything, without proof, however much circumstantial knowledge I acquire, does not mean unconditional belief, as is my being unable to commit to, as I see it fanatical support for a football club, knowing that the clubs players is irrelevant to its name these days, only its spending power counts. I have a lingering interest in watching the team my dad used to take me to see, MUFC, but my disgust in seeing many "players" use underhand methods, and deception of referees to make up for losing control of a situation, limits my interest in this "sport". My brother had the right idea in getting involved in the grass roots setting up and supporting of FC United of Manchester, in protest, by MUFC fans after the Glazer take-over of that club.

The only abstract thing I can say I feel strongly about is that my country should be run from here, hence a Brexiteer, but with no commitment to a current party, only a realigned future one that avoids extremes of Left or Right, or only as Right as is required for self-determination, in the old belief that charity begins at home, not with those whose self-interest coincides with their professed politics. Average in that I have not a very clever mind, but able to see enough not to follow all conventions regardless, unless I have subjected them to analysis, and found in favour of them.

Thus it follows that my analysis of such a complex thing as Leave, can never be totally right, and Remain, totally wrong, there being a multitude of close cooperation projects that were facilitated under the umbrella of the EU, I and other Brexiteers are not blind to this, and it is with a heavy heart that I and it seems many others realise that free trade and these closer ties, have been used as hostages by those bent on central political control by decree, or "directive" as the price to pay for this. Not for us.

That then is my favourite pastime, analysis, probably why I like chess, but being too scatter brained to have ever pushed myself to find work in that area, not having realised until too late, this maybe could have given me a living which I would have found more rewarding, as my brain seems to like looking for connections that are not immediately obvious.

Chapter 117

Unfortunately for me, two things would have been needed for me to have found a career involving analysis, the first is luck, someone would have had to have seen any potential in me to have pointed this out to me in time to have given me pointers to the right subjects at school, such as maths, which were seen at that age as of no great use beyond simple arithmetic, though I did pick up on percentage as useful.

My interest in history was mainly on large scale demographic events, such as invasions and mass movements of people, such as the east European tribal expansion west, causing pressure on those in the west of Europe, thus helping to trigger the Angles and Saxons push to find new land and so invade Britain, it is the causes of these events, as much as the events themselves, that interest me.

The second thing was to feel comfortable in my learning environment, as I have gone over early in this narrative, I was under constant threat from bullying at school, being tall, but stick thin, and not socially adept enough to evade the wrong sort of attention, it left any chance of being calm and collected enough for planning future learning at the back of my priority list, in the early seventies, you were fourteen before being able to choose subjects to study or drop, so History and Geography, of most interest to me, came too late as classes where the thug element were no longer present in the last two years of school to give me any chance of improving my academic achievements, though I did get a grade one in history CSE, the equal to an O level, due to my interest in the subject and being able to learn in an environment without menace in the background.

My spelling in this exam was probably as bad as it still is, (only able to write this now with the aid of the spellchecker function), but whoever read the content of my answers and essay must have seen beyond my spelling to the content, for which I was grateful, giving me a little bit of self-belief on seeing the results of being allowed to learn in peace and express my interest and understanding somewhere, if too late for future benefit.

Enough navel gazing, though the sight of the first of our new aircraft carriers was good to see, or will be, when it gets aircraft to fly, if the Treasury is not allowed to further emaciate the prime responsibility of government, which is to safeguard the nation's security, which can only be done by being strong enough to deter those who look for weakness, though this might not look good on a spreadsheet.

As a trading nation, once again, soon able to trade without EU shackles with old (and new) friends, we need to be able to protect our shipping, as for instance, we only grow enough food at home to feed about a third of our crowded population, having a similar population to France, but much less than half the agricultural land they have, theirs being subsidised by us for the last forty years, so our basic necessity imports should cost us less, now we will not have to buy solely from the countries we have subsidised to grow it in the first place, will need ta navy with the wherewithal to protect our major shipping routes, and as I have seen, intimidation from lack of defence is often as effective as direct force, we dare not rely on the fickle US, as Europe does to maintain our freedom.

The only thing stopping Russia from moving west is the billions it receives from the cash cow that is Europe, especially Germany, for its gas, to prop up its regime, a tap that he can turn down or off at any time if it becomes strategically useful, as the Ukraine has found out.

At home, our shameful dithering (or worse, foreign manipulation) means a lack of effective new energy production has left us dangerously dependent on gas and electricity imports, with storage for that being dangerously small, so we have got to be able to look as though we can protect these imports. I have already touched on this subject, but it bears reiterating, history will not end, as some seem to think, with our current status quo, we have to be ready and able to respond to unwelcome events.

As in the slightly misquoted, but apt saying, "Those who ignore history are doomed to repeat it," some of our current politicians regard robust defence as wasted spending, gaining no political payback in the short term, this being the curse of democratic European countries, leaning on the crutch of a US who are now less committed to a Europe these days, who dare to challenge US tech giants on tax evasion, inviting tougher tariffs on steel and other imports in retaliation, European democracies for so long, by their nature, not having long-term policies, being subject to re-election, spend as little as they can physically protecting their borders, whilst erecting trade barriers with the rest of the world.

When we see the alternatives to democracy around the world, (current example – Venezuela), unless we are not being given the whole picture, as I allude to in my other main Oddball subject matter, Britain, and the continent we are still geographically, if no longer politically chained to, should not be seen for too much longer to be a soft target, (my view).

Chapter 118

Equally, as we are belatedly waking up to, our politically naive younger generation are being manipulated on social media, by hard left, tech savvy, domestic and foreign operators, who would hijack our democratic voting system by promising unsustainable but attractive sounding policies, such as scrapping university fees, unwittingly abetted by the abuse of many in the hierarchy of these institutions who charge the absolute maximum allowed, in order to pay themselves many times what they are worth.

In my humble opinion (whilst I am putting the world to rights), it would make sense to me, to charge most for those courses that will help our economy least, letting the rich who are so inclined, pay more for their offspring's classical education, whilst subsidising scientific, engineering, mathematical medical, Biotech and other technical and business oriented courses that will retain for our country the necessary knowledge base needed to keep and sustain our reputation for innovation and quality at the top end of the market, as we can no longer mix it with those emerging countries taking their turn in flooding the mass market place.

This will be made harder while successive domestic governments lean too far in free market "enlightened liberal" lack of patriotism, (Patriotism is looking after your own people, not a dirty word) ignoring foreign takeovers of key tech companies, such as the recent sale of Arm holdings, to a Japanese Bank, that has close ties with China, thus letting our hard-won silicon chip expertise find its way to a country whose long-term policy towards us may be less than friendly. Countries such as France take a much more proactive and protective stance with their own key industries – credit where its due, we ignore this to our detriment.

Already a Chinese company, currently promoting themselves with the phrase "Active intelligence" might just be *gaining* exactly that, having secured commercial access to British Telecom's network infrastructure, a move that has been disallowed by America's and Australia's comparable infrastructure on security grounds, a move that I hope our own GCHQ were allowed a good look at before allowing it here, as though a commercial enterprise, no large Chinese company operates without state oversight, which may include furthering that states strategic interests, which unlike western democracies, is not hindered by short-term re-election considerations, let us hope that the vast younger new middle classes emerging there – might want to change that, that state becoming a victim of its own success, though it has *so far* been very clever at reconciling capitalism with communism.

Reading this, knowing the low levels of success I have reached in my own life, you might think it pointless in keeping myself aware and caring about things beyond my "little people" life that I have no control over, but like many, less able to grow their work/social station, it does not stop us keeping a weather eye on the world, mostly silent on the media, but much to the chagrin of the "Chattering Classes" who have control of the TV and Digital media, though not yet the most popular (not populist) papers, such as the Daily Mail, though the Mail on Sunday is a cuckoo in the nest, as readers of the Daily Mail will know, I digress, but the chattering classes ignored the rest of us as our views don't count – until they did, with Brexit, (thanks again to Nigel, who I have heard may resurface soon).

Chapter 119

Rather than use the word Popular, which they (Remainers) cannot stomach due to the reality of it, they had to pervert it into "Populist" something they could use as code for "Dumb and unthinking", anything but the reality that the silent majority in Europe is asserting itself, fed up of being kept poorer, whilst the pay gap widens by use of cheap labour imports, and wilful ignorance by some in government as to what the senior fat cats of the media "Intelligentsia" (I use quotation marks with great emphasis here) are able to get away with.

There are hopeful signs at the time of writing this, that this "May" be being addressed, with reviews on Vice (appropriate) Chancellors salaries, and possible new laws to prevent unscrupulous businessmen from tapping into, then walking away from collapsing company pension funds, so much for the Robert Maxwell inquiry. There will be as much resistance to this as always, vested interests are powerful, looking after each other as always, so determination must be the order of the day for genuine long-term success.

Use of TV and other media, as in the very successful promotion of PC policies, some good, some not so, must be used in order to make exploitation as unacceptable as drink driving, smoking in Non-smoke areas etc. though use of soaps on telly, that are currently being used for "awareness" of all sorts of personal problems, by the supposed independent producers of such programmes. Public image, such as charity contribution, (tax deductible), must not be allowed to hide dubious business practice, such as short selling, leveraged buyouts for short term gain, at the expense of jobs when a company is bought to gut or stifle competition.

What would be a **very** good idea, though unlikely to ever see the light of day, is to introduce a law that prevents government ministers, and high-level civil servants, from taking up posts with companies after their term in power, that have anything to do with the departments they had power over whilst in office.

Likewise any payments to the above, including relatives or partners, received from relevant companies should be illegal *after* leaving office for many years, so as to prevent the promise of future reward from influencing current policies as may have happened in (for example) climate change related energy policy. I am not short sighted enough to realise that being a politician can sometimes be a short term career, so I would rather use public money to look after those leaving office,(good pension) who cannot find an income from their original profession which most will have had before gaining high influence in government, or in any field *other* than where they controlled policy whilst in power, than getting away as some have, with directing policy in favour of those promising future secret reward, from home or abroad. This would mean financial checks and even extradition for any of the above who try evasion of this policy. Not going to happen, I know – Those in power are not going to tie one hand behind their backs.

Back down now from Cloud Cuckoo land – after our return from our rushed, wet and windy Hebrides trip, life settled back to a steady enough routine, most of my free days of helping to bring our gardens, front and back, to life after the patchy spring. After removing a potted apple tree, set against the garage wall, and planting it in the middle of the back lawn, digging a small plant circle around it back in the autumn of 2016, seeing a good blossom flowering the following spring, we decided to remove the other three fruit trees from their pots, these also set next to the garage wall, and plant these in dug over planted areas in our back garden, the Pear, behind the conservatory, the Peach in the triangular patch on the right at the top of the steps on the right as you go up, just past a wooden arch I had erected there, and the smaller Cherry tree back nearer the apex of the same triangular planted patch, in the hope they would all do better with room to spread their roots.

While I was working, Sarah painted the second bedroom a light grey, though no bed, apart from an inflatable double, stored ready for use in there, this room having a dressing table and double chest of draws, a unit with my printer and other stuff in the corner, to make up for two small wardrobes, the only storage space in our bedroom, apart from under bed draws and cramped bedside tables.

One of Sarah's paintings that I particularly liked, a view from a hotel, set on a hill looking down, on the coast of Sweden, north of Gothenburg where we had visited one new year quite some years ago, overlooked a frozen bay with a tree in the foreground, a standard lamp further down, and a small jetty disappearing into the mist hovering over the water, vague hills on the far side, all looking quite oriental in its beguiling simplicity in this painting, having gone there looking for snow after a few years without any, we only encountered -12 degree frost there, this looked like snow, it was that thick on the pine trees.

A framed Led Zep poster, with a happy 50th birthday, hand written by Robert Plant, from my brother and his wife, whose workmate knew a former girlfriend of Plant's, also adorns a wall in there. Three framed photos of Weaver birds in various stages of nest building currently adorns another wall in there, not quite a box room, but multi-purpose, being a little short of space in this bungalow.

At that time, I was currently doing two five-hour return trips, Tuesdays and Thursdays to our other main depot at work, travelling down the A41, then the A5, avoiding the M6, to the west Midlands, which broke up nicely the tedium of site work, taking product and picking up empties in one of our three ton vans, trunk route work, for further distribution.

Chapter 120

Before very long, in June, it was time for our next long ago booked trip away, the Hebrides an almost spur of the moment thing, taken after we had booked this holiday, which was again to Croatia, but hopefully quite a different experience from last year's Opatija trip, as we were booked to travel on a sixteen cabin motor yacht, setting off from a small coastal village near Dubrovnik, at the southern end of Croatia, to visit many of the Dalmatian Islands, where we would meet 101 locals, and spot a few more before eventually calling at Split, tacking back on a different route to visit Dubrovnik before flying home.

We flew from Manchester, arriving early evening, the transfer to our boat taking about an hour, well into dusk when we boarded, after dumping our bags in our cabin, (set on the port-side main deck as you look for'd), we entered the main dining/breakfast room and small bar, to a round of applause, the already installed guests for this trip having nearly finished dinner, we were not the last to board, but almost.

As just mentioned, we were made welcome, offered a drink, served dinner from the set menu, this always having a vegetarian alternative, whilst being gently interrogated by the more forthright of our fellow sailors as to from where we hailed, our work – or not, as most but not all were recent retirees, the most interesting for me being an ex RAF "Airhead"(forward base set up) officer, the one mentioned much earlier in this book in context, concerning US (and, or Antarctic built) triangular gravity amplification capable craft, the TR3 B's, (as discovered by (*BBC* Newsworthy, Pentagon hacker – Gary McKinnon,) to this query, the ex RAF Officer replied, "rather not talk about it", when asked about the above, if not knowing of them, then he did not look mystified, or amused at my "daft question", Airhead officer being the RAF officer in charge of setting up a new airstrip/base in advance of planes landing, so reasonably senior, I did not ask his rank as he did not volunteer it, my above query coming later in the trip, after some general conversation.

We also had an elderly gent in his eighties called John, apparently a published author, his books set pre and during the WW2 era, though not directly about the fighting. I am ashamed to say we cannot recall book names, John liked to regale us fellow passengers with anecdotes and short stories, behaving as though he was a bit of a celebrity. A younger couple our age seemed to be there to look after him, were a little in awe of him, we had to assume he had sold enough books to make a living from them, though not an "A-lister" there must be several thousand in the category just below, comfortably off, without being millionaires from their book sales, we assumed John to be in this category.

Most, but not all of our remaining fellow passengers appeared well heeled, ex professional, one or two from academic backgrounds, all but one or two, whom we had more in common with, used to a higher social station than us. We have encountered this quite often when abroad, or even on domestic trips, as my lack of having to bring up kids enables us to take holidays aimed at those of, shall I say a slightly more refined type than the average beach goer, some more amiable than others, on discerning us to be of a lesser social station than themselves, depending on their open-mindedness, minding our manners, sufficiently used to this, so as to be able to pick up the right set of knives and forks when required, I hammed up my work position to something a little more akin to what I used to do, than I now do, able to talk a little technical from my production tech days, to those on board who did not look down on anything industrial as a way of making a living.

Our boat cast off from the small inlet village north of Dubrovnik the morning after we boarded, one more couple boarding later than us the night before. Our crew numbered six, including the captain, sadly, at the time, as with most of the people we met on our travels, we cannot recall our crew names, however, if you can picture the ruggedly handsome actor Jurgen Prochnow, who played the U-boat captain in Das Boot, (though I hoped to remain mostly on the surface for this trip) he also played Duke Leto in Frank Herbert's Si-Fi blockbuster *Dune*, one of my favourite films, among other major roles, then our captain was very similar both in looks, and in his brooding no nonsense demeanour, not inviting general conversation, but happy to talk about his ship, the MS Mendula, which he told me he was involved in designing, pride evident in this.

Alone of all the motor yachts that I saw plying the tourist passenger trade among these islands, this ship actually had a couple of sails, though only used a sparingly, when the wind was favourable, it gave our small ship character the others lacked, with their faux masts, I told him this, which was well received, as he then told me he had to argue hard to have sails added to this ship, for just the reason I had said, added character, so I was glad to have added a little extra wind to his sails…

Chapter 121

Some mornings I would get up quite early, leaving Sarah asleep, wanting to take in the activities of the crew preparing to cast off, persuading the bar steward, who was setting the breakfast table, to let me have an early coffee from a brewed pot, then up on the deck if not too windy, keeping out of the way, me complaining later at breakfast (with a sly look on my face) to him that our coffee pot was nearly empty – getting the hoped for grin that told me of his amusement of my one time only joke.

After a breakfast choice of cold meats, croissants, and cereals, we sailed north, cruising through the Elaphiti isles, dropping anchor eventually, as we did most days around midday, in a secluded bay, with about fifteen to twenty feet of water under our keel, one of the younger, fitter lads in the crew then performing his party piece, which was to dive from the from the prow with a thin rope, swim ashore, usually around fifty yards away, find the nearest stout tree, then pull a thicker rope, attached to his thin swimming rope, ashore, securing this round the tree, so that between the anchor and this shore rope, there was little movement of our ship, enabling easy diving in for those like myself who wanted to and for re-boarding at the side ladder.

After we had an hour or so of swimming, (long enough after breakfast for me) for five of our seven days afloat, soon after, lunch was served, this being a three course affair, of soup, then usually two choices, or pasta variations with many pickled vegetables and other options, quite often fish, with as you would expect in this region, olive oil to dip your bread or pour over your salad, this followed by something sweet, we would not starve…

A reverse performance by our own Man from Atlantis, retrieving the "shore tree" rope, up anchor, then a leisurely afternoon sail, now replete, us picking our spot on the front deck, if not too windy, some setting deck chairs for the sun, others heading to the chairs and tables set on the aft deck to read, chat, and/or drink, most of us paying a visit to the little bar set at one side of the entrance to the dining cabin on more than one occasion in the afternoon. It was on one of these lazy afternoons I had the above-mentioned conversation with the ex RAF officer, talking amiably enough, but bringing about a brief enigmatic look on his face before his "don't want to talk about it" response to my previously mentioned query on the TR3B craft.

We sailed, not literally, (without enough wind) towards our first overnight stop at a small village, on the long and narrow island (as many here are) of Mljet, where after tying up, we descended the gangplank to wander the few seafront shops and stretch our legs, with an eye out for a nice restaurant to settle at after a good wander, the late June weather sunny, with a sea breeze keeping it not too hot.

No joint recollection of what or where we ate that first evening out, must have been a fair number of options as we dined without meeting any ships company, re boarding Mendula mid-evening, still dusk in June, joining those already back for sundowners on the aft deck, where cliques were already forming, a Jeff and Lindy, Sarah recalls, were more our cup of tea, unpretentious, plus a Gay couple, and another pair, who had just sold a pub (one of three), and very much liked their products, we both recall, but could hold it (from much practice I think), these people were all not above mixing with us.

A museum curator and his also academic background wife were, I think, a little surprised at my interest in history, and overall, if not detailed awareness of many events relevant to their subject matter, though when they learnt I had not attended university, they could not disguise a little condescension in their conversation, my lack of formal education, and my letting on that many of my historical facts were gleaned from fictional writers that wove characters and story lines around major events, gave them cause for this, though to be fair, they seemed pleased that one of the great unwashed took such an interest in past events.

With such a mix of characters on board, it seems almost a shame no one died in suspicious circumstances on board, as it would have made a great version of *Murder on the Orient Express* meets *A Slow Boat to China* type mystery novel, though we had not quite enough passengers, or quite that much tension aboard, but did have just enough caricatured types to imagine such a scenario…

With all aboard still alive, more or less, for breakfast the next morning, we weighed anchor, (and yes, it was heavy), continuing on a meandering northerly route, stopping at a small island called Scedro around midday, after a quite morning, Sarah chatting a little with the two gay guys, at ease as she had worked alongside a gay couple for some time in Stockport Town hall restaurant a few years back, these guys a little relieved I think, that someone was willing to say more than a polite hello to them. I joined in a little, then setting us up a pair of recliners, as most did on the fore deck, from which to take in the passing scenery, as we were never far from one island or another, or with the mainland mountains in the distance, that and reading, with the occasional coffee for us in the mornings, one or two others not waiting for the sun to gain the yardarm, afore partaking of grape shots or Juniper juice, forgive me waxing a little salty. Scredo is home to a few small vineyards, but little else as far as we could see, a small cove, our anchorage for swimming and then lunch, setting off for Korcula Island, not so far away.

Chapter 122

Korcula town, the island capital, is a medieval walled town, set on a circular isthmus of land jutting out (as an isthmus would) from the largest of the Dalmatian Islands. Inhabited from before the tenth century, it was eventually incorporated into the Venetian trading empire, indeed the explorer Marco Polo was reputedly born in this town, his (reputed) birthplace a visitor attraction.

Our on-board female guide, a partner of one of our crew, informed us that we would be dropped off on one side of town, Mendula then berthing overnight on the other side of the Isthmus town, our disembarking jetty here only used for brief stops. Medieval it may have been, but the original town planners were very clever in creating a unique (as far as I know) climate controlling design for this town, if Venetian, then not blind, but farsighted!

As stated, the town sticks out into a channel, subject to winds, cold in winter, stifling in the narrow streets in summer, with this in mind, some genius set the main street down the centre of the slightly raised centre of the town, with side streets running slightly curved, off each side like a fish skeleton, the curves in the side streets providing shelter from the cold winter winds, and creating a cool micro climate in summer, as we experienced when set loose on the town.

After a short-guided tour, which included a visit to where Marco Polo was likely, though not definitely born, and a pointer to an interactive museum dedicated to his travels, plus an orientation stop to the quay where we would find Mendula that evening, we were free to roam. After refreshments somewhere, we wandered back to where I had seen what turned out to be one of a chain of Marco Polo themed, mock maritime antique gift shops, a sucker for this sort of thing, I duly bought a small brass, wood mounted Astrolabe, the shop girl seemingly surprised at my knowing what it was, overpriced as everything was in there, I resisted the mock sextants and olde-worlde globes, also the larger astrolabes, which were a small fortune, which thankfully would not fit on our mantelpiece, where my memento still resides, Sarah then navigating our way out before I spent any more.

We came to an intersection where a guy was making wire names to order which would attach to a chain making a necklace, Sarah ordered one for her then 12-year-old granddaughter, we watched whilst this was made using tiny pliers to bend the wire into a joined-up name, considerable dexterity needed to make a neat job of it, which he did, this was not that, but ideal for a young teenager.

Having the rest of the late afternoon to fill, we found the Marco Polo Museum, one of the places where you donned a pair of earphones, (like our

Norman Wisdom Bayeux Tapestry tour), and followed a passageway interspersed with a series of tableaux depicting key stages of his journey to China, his stay, and return journey, at each tableau, a monologue with background music would be fed by Bluetooth presumably, through the earphones, telling that part of his story in your chosen language.

Not so well known perhaps is that his father had gone east before him, but not recording in such rich detail his adventures, this must surely have been Marco's inspiration for his own trip east. This was an enjoyable experience, the elaborately depicted scenes adding context to the story of his many experiences, well worth the entrance fee and the time in there.

The walk and earphone story (mentioned) around the U-shaped Bayeux Tapestry being a comparable experience many years earlier, that depiction being an original treasure, the Marco Polo story, for me was still a very well depicted story of a life that served as a catalyst to bring about east-west trade in the renaissance era, so a story of equal stature in history for me to the Norman invasion.

By the time we came out of this museum, it was heading towards evening, so after a coffee, we started to look out for somewhere nice to have our dinner, there being a multitude of choices, we wandered around for a while, before choosing a restaurant on a side street of the main spine, that was just wide enough to have a few tables on each side with room in between to pass through, it was busy, and it was after sunset before we had eaten and drunk the white wine accompanying our fish based meal, in an atmosphere that can be found around much of the Adriatic, as well as the Med, though being situated on a narrow, gradually down sloping, medieval, slightly curved street where you could see the harbour about fifty yards downslope, this made for a pleasant end to the day, or almost end of the day, as there were still the aft deck sundowners and recounting our various wanderings before turning into our main deck cabin.

Chapter 123

After a few days, routine sets in, no matter how pleasant your surroundings, and so not having written anything down at the time, details are forgotten, we all have holidays, so I will try not to bore you with repeat experiences, recalling little of the following day apart from one highlight, that being the raising of the two for'd mast sails, the wind blowing the right way to push us for a few hours towards our next destination, this occurring in the morning before our midday swim and lunch. There was no discernible tacking needed, the wind within a few degrees of being right behind us.

Our captain telling me earlier, that sails would only be used when we would not need to tack, which explains why they were only used twice on our weeks tour, deck movement under sail was more pronounced, the higher winds necessary to make using a for'd rigged sailing ship practical, this contributing to the swell under our keel, it was an exhilarating novelty, as it was intended to be for most of us, not used to genuine sailing, as opposed to the more sedate movement under power. Whilst sails were up, passengers were forbidden from the upper foredeck as the boom at the base of the mainsail could sweep the unwary off the boat, another reason to restrict actual sailing time to a few hours only, apart from having to maintain a schedule.

Our captain was right in my opinion to have argued for sailing capability, as it added an extra dimension, if only as a novelty, for us tourists. This captain was of the old school, so along with his successful inclusion of sail, also was his evident authority, while being relatively discreet, his crew were not allowed to be idle, the wooden deck, all brass, and railings were given constant cleaning. Jurgen, the captain (as we cannot recall his real name), explaining that sea salt would soon rot or rust anything not constantly cleaned, you could see the intense pride he had for his ship, I might be being unkind here, but to an extent, passengers might be a necessary evil, to be tolerated in order to pay "his" ship's way.

His ship being not just by virtue of being captain, he was also a part owner, along with the fleet company, of which Mendula was the only sail rigged example, so he might just have invested his life savings into this vessel, to get it part sail rigged. True commitment then.

Our evening port of call after our "Sailing day" was the chic old port of Hvar, the party capital of the Dalmatian islands, where we were warned to expect high prices for everything, and as we pulled into our mooring berth, several boats sideways out from dry land, with open central hatches to pass from boat to boat over gangways before stepping onto the quayside, you could see a few of the playboy super yachts you might expect to see in Monte Carlo or St Tropez.

The old town had walls dating back to the thirteenth century, but there was nothing old about the average age of the visitors here, almost as soon as we were ashore, a white toga dress themed party of more than dozen well-heeled youngsters, none looking older than twenty-two or three, passed near us, before heading up steps into what looked like an exclusive private disco party, the place was living up to its reputation.

In the main square there is a well, dating back to 1520, with a set of channels at the side of the square reaching back beyond St Stephen's Cathedral, set at the back with its Venetian bell tower, the channels there to drain off potential flooding from the surrounding hills from what we were told by our tour guide. The first public theatre in Europe built in 1612, is located here, above the Arsenal, where historically, boats were built and repaired, as well as armed from, presumably.

Set above the town is a fortress originally built around 1278, when the town requested protection from Venice against the Turks, too much of a climb for us, we passed on that, as we also did on visiting the Caepe Diem bar, set above the beach of the same name, it is this club that made the chic reputation of Hvar for the "in crowd", so we are told, with prices to match I'll bet, we found a quite restaurant and had the local equivalent of a Tapas type meal, bits of this and that.

Had a couple of drinks with our meal, strolled, noting that as advertised, the average age in town was about thirty years younger than ourselves, though in winter as in all tourist hotspots, those living here would be older, with the bar staff stripped back to family members as much as possible. We re-boarded Mendula, having only one drink (more) before turning in.

Not sure now of where we stopped midday-ish, but from Hvar, we would have turned from a generally north western route to the north, through a gap between islands, heading for Split, our most northern port of call, before a route back, closer to, and including mainland stops.

Chapter 124

Split is a fascinating city, though a modern tourist-oriented town, it is still dominated at its centre by Diocletian's Palace. Though now called a palace, when built at the turn of the fourth century A D, it was built with one thing in mind, the Roman Emperor Diocletian intended to survive his abdication into retirement, no mean feat, as few Emperor's lived beyond their rule.

This palace then was much more than luxury living quarters, though part of it was, most of it was built to house his personal guard, indeed the whole complex was built as a grander version of a Roman marching camp, a square with a central crossroads dissecting the interior into four quarters. Diocletian's history, one of stabilising a vast empire that was falling into chaos, by raising subordinate emperors in order to make regions more manageable, plus other reforms to standardise economic, and trade laws, restoring the military, that had lost its iron discipline, and increasing military numbers, whilst reducing to twenty years the time required to serve. So looking after his power base then.

This background, after being raised to the Purple from being a cavalry commander, by his troops, during a time of chaos, must have left its mark on him, so with the foresight given to few emperors, he had this vast fortress of a palace built as a city within a city – that still largely stands today.

He alone among emperors, managed to abdicate, and retire for eleven years within this palace, with presumably very well paid and so loyal troops, to safeguard his retirement. Around him the empire gradually descended back into civil wars without his overall control, only to be restored one last time by Constantine, after which only the eastern Byzantine Empire persisted. Diocletian's only dark shadow was a persecution of Christians, but as an unfettered ego was part of the job description, and he was much more disposed towards Jupiter, he must have seen them with his usual foresightedness, as a threat, which as Constantine not so long after made Christianity the state religion, to Diocletian, they were.

Back to our visit there, upon stepping ashore, we were given a short orientation tour, which included pointing out a large seafront restaurant, whose chef had won "master chef" at some point, (so priced accordingly, no doubt). What must be the West gates to the palace were pointed out, (near the seafront, on a north/south coastline) these now woven into the fabric of modern Split, but were a useful way of orienting yourself. Much of the vast imposing ruins of the old palace are preserved and incorporated into Split's old town, set on a short peninsular two thirds of the way down Croatia's coast.

We could see, across the busy main coast road, the entrance gate facing the sea, so in we went, ancient arched stone roofed galleries greeted us. Modern, expensive jewellery and other gift franchises lined the first few yards, we loitered and viewed, but did not buy, before climbing a few ancient, well-worn stone steps, through another archway onto a cobbled street, this led us to what is now a cathedral, converted from what was Diocletian's mausoleum in the seventh century, with what looks like a bell tower added in the twelfth century, the tower there looking Venetian, controlling much of the Adriatic later, so probably not the original bell tower, but impressive just the same, if a little out of place from the older surroundings.

Wandering around within the old palace complex, I could feel the great age and strength of the place, so well-integrated now as to not just be its backbone, but the whole town's skeleton. At one point this atmosphere was comically (for me) ruined, as an unearthly musical drum and cymbal beat preceded the amusing (again to me) sight of a troupe of Hare Krishna devotees in bright orange, marching through one of the towns small squares, I of course having forgotten this, but as usual, Sarah reminding me of events.

After a few hours wander around, having already eaten on the boat before docking at Split early that afternoon, Sarah said she did not want a big evening meal, so after returning back to the boat for a short rest, and to change, we went back ashore looking for somewhere low key for a snack-ish tea, ending up with a burger and salad bite somewhere in the back streets, a lager/beer to wash our food down, it was a clean, modern bar, I have vague memories of tall black bar stools there.

On the wide approach to the stepped area opposite a big archway, were two guys, doing the Legionnaire dressed trick of freezing like a statue, (as can be seen in Barcelona's La Ramblas,) only to move when approached by the unwary, well kitted out, they had spent some time there, as we saw them a few hours earlier on the tour, local government funded to promote the location. Parts of this impressive palace/fortress, that had survived so long, were used in filming *Game of Thrones* scenes, only the dragons were missing while we were there...

Chapter 125

A small square, with an ornate ancient archway at one end, next to a church, which we had been taken through on the earlier tour, was our last destination of the day after eating, as we were told that live music of one sort or another was performed on the steps to one side of the "Luxor" Restaurant, strange name for somewhere in the middle of Split, restaurant it may be, but it did a roaring trade keeping everyone in the vicinity supplied with beer, sat, and some standing on the steps, about six high, set on two sides and the far end of what was effectively a shallow forum, with the Luxor at the end of one side.

Sturdy cushions were distributed around the "Forum" belonging to the Luxor, in a bid I suspect, by the Luxor to control who sat watching the performers next to the Bar/restaurant, the bar "waiters" who delivered the ordered beer, were also seen to move people on, who did not order drinks when approached by them, which you were, if you did not have a drink. We drank very slowly.

Whether this was legal or not, is not known, as they would have had to own the whole "forum" area, which I doubt. A lone performer with an amplified acoustic guitar, sang well-known, mostly dated pop songs, Simon and Garfunkel, Beatles, that sort of stuff, pitched for an international tourist audience, so in English mainly, with the odd local ditty interspersed.

After an hour or so, with numb bums, despite the cushions, we'd had enough, and headed back to Mendula, having the usual nightcap and note-comparing session with other returnees before turning in.

Some mornings saw us having breakfast after weighing anchor, the morning after Split being one, this usually happened when we had a "busy" day ahead. No trip on the high seas would be complete without mention of pirates, and today was the day for that, we hugged the mainland coast, as we would be calling in to the town of Omis, situated at the Cetina River mouth. Dominated by spectacular cliffs, this is a pretty little port, picture postcard now, but used by pirates in the past to raid passing Venetian merchant shipping, then retreating in their shallow draft vessels up the Cetina river, beyond the reach of deeper draft Venetian warships sent to catch them.

After docking, at a Mole (Adrian maybe…) at the end of a pier, our live aboard, sometimes guide, whose name we cannot recall, led us ashore along the south side of the river, passing the busy shops and cafes to the bridge, I stopping briefly to buy a few peaches, from the archetypal old woman in a black shawl, it was hot that day and needed to quench my thirst with such on the go.

After crossing the river bridge, we came to the jetty where a canopied tourist boat was waiting to take us up the river, where a young steersman/guide got us all aboard, older John helped by his attendant couple, we cast off, heading for the interior, our steersman on the tiller, recounting the pirate story mentioned above, ending with the inevitable, the Venetians having had enough, sent shallow draft boats packed with troops with a merchant convoy, who followed the pirates up the Cetina River, an unexpected and unpleasant surprise, "destroying" the pirates, details not gone into…

The scenery along this river, that after a short run inland, turns south, almost parallel with the coast, is stunning, with cliffs on both sides, one or two people could be seen climbing these cliffs, set well back from the river. At a wider side pool, turtles were spotted, sunning themselves on branches, ducks and other waders, large iridescent dragonflies, wild uncultivated wetland and woodland, along with a clear blue sky, made for a pleasant run up this river.

Talking with the guide/tiller man, he told me he was a student, studying to be a teacher, this being his summer job, he was born in Omis, and was proud to be part of conservation work along this river valley.

Along the cliff top, on the side dividing us from the coast, a fish eagle's nest was pointed out to us, not currently occupied, the young having flown the nest. Eventually, we came to our turn around point which was a large restaurant, with lots of outdoor tables, a separate ice cream vendor and toilet block, the river at this point reachable from a road, us having already passed a cafe at a wide section of the river, the one we stopped at was at the end of the navigable section of the Cetina river.

A path followed the river beyond the cafe area, after an iced coffee, we walked along for less than a quarter mile, some, from other "younger" boats, moored near ours. Other people from cars parked near the road, locals I imagine, were swimming in the river at a point with a shingle beach on a bend in the river.

We were given an hour, which after our iced coffee and short walk, gave us just enough time afterwards for coconut flavoured ice cream, for Sarah, she recalls, I would have had, Rum and Raisin, or Choc-chip Mint, at a guess. Then it was back on the boat for the return to Omis, at a point where the cliffs were set back around 100yds from the river, I, having a small pair of binoculars with me, spotted a cave ¾ of the way up the cliff side, that must have had at least a six foot opening, drawing the attention of our guide/pilot, whom I was sitting next to, I lent him my binoculars and pointed it out, expecting to be told about it, he surprised me by telling me he had never seen it before, despite doing this run many times.

As without binoculars it is fairly inconspicuous, just a darker area, I suggested to him that he was too busy steering the boat to see it, I could see mild consternation on his face, and knew he would ask about it back at Omis. I recall being mildly pleased with myself at spotting something new to a local guide. Set in a sheer cliff face, this cave would only be accessible to climbers, who may find it easier to abseil down to it, rather than make a harder climb up to it. Not able to discern its depth with the resolution of my small binoculars, it was big enough for a person to enter, able to compare this cave with the size of climbers seen further down river. I would be very surprised if no one local knew of it, so I could delude myself I had found it, even though on another day climbers might have been there, but it was new to our riverboat guide, I will never find out, which, depending on what was known of it, is a shame. Then we were back in Omis, all ashore and back over the bridge of this small but pretty town.

A coffee was had at a cafe in sight of Mendula, moored alongside "Adrian's Mole" as I had dubbed it, then it was back aboard. Omis was a nice place, with its cliffs behind, a small keep set above the mouth of the river, beaches either side of the river mouth, with small hotels set back from the longer beach on the other side of the river.

Chapter 126

We "sailed" across for the island of Brac, beginning the return leg of our trip through the southern Croatian islands and coastal towns, a sleepy village our late afternoon mooring stop. Here we would be staying overnight, as it was the "Captain's Dinner" that evening, the only time apart from the arrival evening, we ate dinner on the boat. A short shore "Liberty" ensued, a complete contrast to busy Omis, a quite stroll along a short beach front, a light snack and more iced coffee at some point, after wandering around the few tourist shops in this otherwise quiet village, before re-boarding for a short rest on deck.

Then it was Sarah, and no doubt the other ladies back to the cabins for a head start in the scrub up for the Captain's Muster, sorry, Dinner. This being the only occasion I wore a tie all week, with other clothes saved for the occasion, Sarah in a classic black dress and silver belt.

There were about four large tables with six to eight of us spread around these, our Capitan (right letters in continental order) did as captain's are supposed to, plastered a smile on his face all evening and moved from table to table, finding something to say to all of us, not I think his ideal evening, but the more impressive for that, talking about his beloved Mendula and the islands tourist trip a safe subject, the evening livened up by John, our aged raconteur author, making a speech about our trip, including referring to earlier in the day when Jeff, a fellow passenger, lost his cap on the river trip, the riverboat turning back to retrieve it.

Along with other anecdotes that had our ships master saying at the end of it, that this was the best speech he had heard on his ship, his normal serious demeanour banished for that evening, which for a guy who, when his young children boarded at one port earlier in the trip, had them polishing the brass work along with the crew, quite good to see, he normally the old school professional, knew when to let it slip, required, but still able to appear relaxed when deemed appropriate, having to for public relations, but made easier with characters like John aboard, who seemed to think it his responsibility to maintain moral aboard ship, it felt like stepping into a film from a bygone age at times, but pleasant for all that.

I must have slept with my head, or neck, at an odd angle that night, as I got up the next morning with a deep seated "Crick" in my neck, which did not improve as the morning passed, on a quite rough sea.

After a few hours with no improvement, though not in agony, the ache was enough for me to make, in retrospect, a bad decision. As mentioned a while back,

I used to suffer from gout, but since being put on permanent prevention tablets, I no longer suffered this painful experience, however before being put on these, I used to take some powerful prescription only, anti-inflammatory pain killers, to mitigate the symptoms.

I still had quite a few of these, which on occasion when suffering pulled muscles, back strains, or the like, I would take one of these tablets, as they worked well on anything like this. You know where this is going – I took one of these "atomic weapons" as I called them, as they worked far better than Ibuprofen or Paracetamol for serious aches and pains, only taking these stronger tablets when something was persistently painful and debilitating and could no longer be ignored.

If I had thought a bit more, I might have thought twice, as the side effects for me with these tablets was slight dizziness when turning quickly and a slightly drunk feeling, both only mild, but lasting up to six hours, taking about an hour before starting to work.

Now if you recall, in my defence, a few days ago, we had the sails up while there was a good wind in our favour, and a fair sea swell to go with it, to which I suffered no ill effects, so although aware of the side effects, I did not link these to the slightly rough sea we were on at the time, giving us a slow rolling swell…

You guessed it – in spades, the next few hours were hell, I shut myself in the tiny on suite bathroom to our cabin, and all I will say is that it was small enough in there to sit on the toilet and lean over the sink at the same time, this one tablet magnifying its side effects a hundred-fold when combined with a moderate sea swell.

The sounds coming out of there in-between frequent evacuations were probably similar to a humpback whale giving birth in full song. Even crossing the "Minch" to the Hebrides that first time as recalled early in this book, when the ferry was nearly swamped, the seasickness then was as nothing to the perfect storm of mixing one of these tablets with a moderate swell on that day, Sarah having to listen whilst reading on the bed through the two to three hours it took before it was worth me leaving the bathroom. Fortunately, there was no next-door on the bathroom side, the midship gantry way being on that side, so no one reported hearing a sea monster aboard…

Chapter 127

Hours later, when we docked at a small town called Sobra, on a nearby island that evening, where the few seafront restaurants served Pizza or similar, I could eat nothing, Sarah saying she was not really hungry having had the big lunch always served on this boat, (mine now recycled for the fish). We talked briefly to a couple of fellow passengers we saw eating near the seafront road we walked around, explaining we were not eating due to my iffy stomach, sparing details, before walking a little longer just for some air, before regaining our boat.

Next day was our last full day aboard Mendula, I recovering from my tablet induced seasickness. Calling again at Mljet, our first island port of call, where I have forgotten to mention that on our outward route, we had an excursion into a "National Park" with a small lake, that had a little island we went across to, a ruined small monastery awaiting us and of course a cafe, not memorable, or worth a visit, but included anyway, so you do it unless you knew any better.

Then it was back to Zaton Bay, not too far north of Dubrovnik, where we had first boarded Mendula, again, me only eating plain food ashore that evening, then a quite hour on the aft deck before bed, a coach trip awaiting us into Dubrovnik the next day, the finale of our tour.

We followed the main coast road, the Jadranska Magistrala across a river bridge, passing docked cruise ships, into the old town area of Dubrovnik, where we were given a guided tour.

This was a hot day, and after a little while we noticed people peeling away from the tour, we were getting thirsty, in the end (Split)ing off from the tour, looking for a watering hole, which we found in one of the small squares of the old town, at last, slaking our thirst. Apart from wandering around the back streets, and Sarah finding some earrings she fancied, we headed back to the area overlooking the old harbour, used for some scenes in "Game of Thrones", found a cafe there, before re boarding our coach at the allotted time, having forgone the uphill trudge in the heat up to where you could catch the cable car for a trip above the town.

That evening after walking along the bay front, we found what turned out to be a German restaurant, with a fish barbecue set up, so a fish meal was had by us that last evening, followed by a last night on the aft deck, chatting with our mixed group of travellers over a nightcap, most of whom were going early the next day to the airport, us and a few others not leaving until mid-afternoon, those of us that arrived late evening on the first day now getting an extra half day in the bay, including lunch on the boat.

We spent the morning after breakfast walking around the bay inlet, a good half mile round, whilst the crew changed the cabins, ready for the next batch of island hoppers to start boarding for another week, which, after our return from meandering along the quite village waterfront, they had started to do.

It had been a good trip, with Korcula, Split and Omis being the highlights for me, though most of the quiet, well-kept harbour towns of these islands were great to relax in, a good mix of the peaceful, with the contrast of bustling Hvar and Split, making a well thought out tour of this southern region of Croatia.

P S, never did find out who didn't kill anybody aboard what felt like a great setting for maritime Cludo, if the boat had been just a bit bigger, with a few more nooks and crannies, the genuine characters aboard just a little more desperate, someone sailing a little closer to the wind, the nearest port not always quite so close…

A "Novel experience" of this nature is probably not so much fun when had for real, especially for the target! We are a strange species, something in our nature keeping a whole book, film and gaming industry churning out countless such scenarios that keep millions entertained, as we seem fascinated to become embroiled in make believe or historical re-enactment, of people suffering – but all from a safe distance.

In a utopian world, with no crime or war to draw from, where would many find their entertainment?

Would it be such a surprise, given the above, if we were actually in quarantine as a species, not yet ready to be allowed to mix with more mature races, for me, that would explain a lot. (Average Oddball moment…)

Chapter 128

Back then to Groundhog Day revisited, me on my three-day working week, spent van driving or doing simple maintenance and cleaning, Sarah looking after our house, going to her art club, visiting her daughter in Stockport every few weeks – who then threw us a curved ball soon after we returned from Croatia in early July.

Sue, Sarah's daughter, is not a great one for holidays, she prefers home life, however her son Ben, a young teenager must have been getting peer pressure from school about never having been abroad, and passing this on to Sue, as we received a fairly desperate call from her asking us to find somewhere all four of us could go as soon as possible, Sue being aware that we were seasoned travellers, she having only rarely been abroad, probably at the instance of previous partners, given her general reluctance for travel, preferring to get her tan from a sunbed.

I was not told what Ben had said to his mum to bring this about, might have been just constant pressure, or threatening to go live with his dad, whatever, I had to put my thinking cap on.

Left to ourselves, we would likely have gone away somewhere for a week late September or early October, as last year, now we had a young teenager to factor in, I started looking on the net for south of France or Spain holiday camps, somewhere that catered for teens as well as us – that would not cost a fortune.

After some net searching, I settled on a static holiday caravan site set on the south western French coast, a Taxi ride south of Beziers, ironically twinned with Stockport. This site, called Le Castellas, is sited on a narrow strip of land that seals off the Thau Basin, a large brackish Salt Lake, from the Med.

On the seaward side of this strip, is a miles long beach, a road down the centre of this long isthmus separates agricultural land bordering the Etang (Brackish Lake) from a few holiday camps, well separated, on the south side of this road.

This camp appeared to cater for all ages, including teenage parties, with various water-based activities, in short, somewhere Ben as well as us would not get bored. At the east end of this strip of land is the picturesque town of Sete a 10 km bus ride away, much closer, about 3 km to the west is the small resort town of Marseillan Plage, the beach resort extension of the town of Marseillan, set at the western end of the Thau Basin. The other key reason I recommended this place was that Ryanair flew to Beziers Airport, which is situated west of that town, and so close to this Holiday Camp.

Whilst I do not like Ryanair's hard-nosed profiteering activities, such as wheedling extra money just to let family sit next to each other, it is the fact that it flies to so many small European airports, that no one else does, this is what allows it to cash in on its monopoly routes.

Once Sarah agreed with me this site looked a good prospect, we called Sue and told her the Website to look at, soon after she called us back after showing it to Ben, much relieved I think, that she had given him something to look forward to, agreeing with us it looked good, but the prices during school hols was too much, so she decided to phone him in sick for a week, as many others do, and risk a fine, still much cheaper than paying summer prices, and we would go in mid-September, hoping it would not have wound down too much by then.

All in agreement, I booked a static caravan with two bedrooms, a roof terrace and a barbecue, only one line in – from the beachfront side of the site, the sea visible from this roof terrace. I decided we would pay the extra for this, not something I have seen in this country, so a worthwhile novelty.

Sue had to renew her passport, which only took a few weeks, Ben apparently much looking forward to this holiday, not surprising, as his dad only ever took him to his grandmothers living not far outside Wrexham, sometimes leaving him with her, but he was getting to the age where spoiling him as grandparents do on day trips was not enough for him, he now knew there was a bigger, wider world out there than he had so far seen, still mentioning to his mum about his toddler trips to Crete, and the water park we took him to many years ago.

I had forgotten, but now recall that two years later, he went back with his mum and dad, still together then, staying at our holiday home, at around seven years old, so no wonder a lasting memory then.

Little other than routine must have occurred for us during the remainder of the summer of 2017, at work, our company was taken over by a larger, related, but thankfully not directly overlapping concern, (as we all know what happens in that scenario), they in turn owned by a multinational. An injection of capital resulted in extensions in our operating areas, so good news as far as I know, for the stability of my little part time job. With my boss Phil, I have developed a tradition of sending daft texts to him just before he or I are going on holidays, one example I sent just before I went to Croatia – "A Serb, Croat and Bosnian all walk into a bar – Should I move it? The jury is Split! While there I met 101 Dalmatians, spotted a few more…"

Another example I sent just before Phil went on a long weekend in Amsterdam – "Find the Wakybaky Cafe on Double Dutch Street – get STONED, only then might you enjoy a duo of *Two lips from Amsterdam* as sung by Max By graves and Mick Jagger accompanied by Jules Holland on Piano".

Phil was also the guy who mentioned Iceland to me as a possible short break, which as you will read later, we did. A year later, Phil went himself with some old Army mates. Just before he went, I sent him this warning – "Watch out for the Polar bears, if you do, have to kill one – at least you can have Bear Grills for dinner…" So not a bad boss if he can take those. OK, I think you might have had enough of that for now.

Chapter 129

We went on a trip to the Lleyn Peninsular in August, on one of my long weekends off, staying in what turned out to be a scruffy, noisy pub in Porthmadog overnight, noisy – as in a thrash metal band playing all evening, not right under us, but noisy enough, no wonder it was cheap – do look like a gift horse in the mouth! Using Porthmadog as an early start base, we continued down the coast to Pwllheli, where I photographed a group of sailing dinghy's in competition, chasing round a couple of buoys, (no girls) complete with judging boat, which soon after our return and after enlargement, Sarah transposed into a painted scene on the bathroom wall, this already a pale blue in colour above the tiles, looking a T refreshingly clever good addition.

Continuing our whistle stop tour, Abersoch was our lunch stop, this being where the money is in this area, so apart from a blue and white matching boat-themed trinket for the bathroom windowsill, we headed back to just short of Pwllheli before turning north on the A497 for a brief stop at the beach of Morfa Nefyn, where on a previous visit, Sarah had picked up a couple of spider crab shells among others, still in a basket with shells on the kitchen table today. A coffee, then along the north coast, re-joining the A499, the 487, the 55 and home.

August turned to September and a few more weeks of work and late summer gardening, the odd Sunday breakfast out on the small patio when the weather was up to it, work, more slight variations of Groundhog Day…

The time came for our family trip to the south of France, Sarah and I staying overnight at Sue's house, as we were flying from Manchester Airport. After parking in a nearby long stay car park, *not* your keys hand over meet and greet, with too many horror stories reported as to what happens after you hand over your keys, though my aged, but reliable car would not likely be a candidate for "joy" riding, as there are not enough horses under the bonnet, paint job and lines not winning any style awards either.

After noting our location in the vast car park, took the bus to terminal three, and the long walk to Ryanair's end, checked in, ate, waited for the pay through the nose brigade to board first, who had to wait for us to board before taking off…

After Manchester Airport, I warned Sue and Ben, Sarah already aware, that Beziers would likely be very small in comparison, guessing that on the basis that only Ryanair flew there from England. And so it proved, it did have a concrete runway, but little else, just a very small check in, and snack shop, that was it. It was hot that day, Sarah, Sue and Ben sat outside whilst I went looking for our pre-booked taxi that would take us to Le Castellas.

Our travel broker, that had our accommodation static concession at the camp, had provided a list of recommended taxi operators that frequented this site, so I had booked one of these, after a bit of confusion, I found the older lady whose taxi company it was, and with my limited French and her bit of English, contact was established, and off we went, me in the front, Sue apparently taking phone photos of the French road signs from the back seat, this being a novelty for her, first time in France, apart from a booze Super Marché ferry run with her ex many years ago so I am told.

Passing a Go-Cart circuit close to the turn off for the camp road which I said I would look into for Ben, we passed south of the town of Adge, which we see more of later, travelling on the D612 up to Marseillan Plage, just beyond which the one mile or so wide spit of land that leads on the south side of the Etang (brackish lake) to Sete, and where a third of the way along, wider at its western end, with planted fields of Maize on the north side of the road, now the N112 down to the Etang, after Marseillan Plage there is Le Castellas Camping, the gates around fifty yards south of a small roundabout, where bus stops was set nearby, west and east.

After passing a manned barrier, we bid Au revoir to our taxi driver, having already sorted our pick up for a week later, the other three waited with our cases whilst I went into the reception to get us logged into the site, and find out how to get to our caravan, that done, mostly in English, as my French is fairly basic, I went and told the others we would be picked up by a guy with an electric cart, which we soon were.

On the way down, we were given "zone" security wristbands, the whole site fenced off from the road and beach, with periodic keypad locked gates, hopefully to keep the uninvited out, not us in, I noted there were no corner towers with machine guns either, we were told the current gate code as we were delivered to our Static, so we were allowed out! The other good news – there was no tannoy system, not sure what Hi de Hi is in French, but I did not want to find out…

A large decking area, complete with benches and table for four, with gas barbecue off to one side as advertised, with at one end, stairs up to the roof terrace, a fenced square around 8'x8', enough to fit four plastic chairs and small table, looked good outside, the inside was clean, and fairly new looking, the central kitchen area cupboards bright red, bright and modern-looking I thought, Sue not so keen, though everywhere would be purple, as her kitchen was, if she had her way, Sarah seemed happy with it, apart from the microwave being set too high up, three bar stools were set around a breakfast bar, with settee and single chair in the living area, two bedrooms, shower and sink room, with a separate toilet at the other end, us taking the double, Sue and Ben with the two singles room, we could work with this for a week!

Chapter 130

After some unpacking, we studied the site plan we had been given, and worked out where the main shop was, set on a small precinct not far from the reception block, not sure how late it stayed open, we thought we had better go get some food in, before heading for the beach.

It was at least a good ten-minute walk back to the reception/precinct area, up near the main gate, the small precinct had a small super Marché, a chemist, patisserie, a small boucherie, a snack bar, all you needed for a week, Sarah, bought chicken, sauce, pasta, I would have bought something sweet for afters, milk, eggs, tomatoes, other bits, we had bought sausages, bacon, coffee, earl grey and normal teabags, even a little sugar with us, Sarah found some tinned Cassoulet, so that was another night's food base, we of course got a couple of baguettes, though we found out there was a small patisserie at the far end of the site, nearer to us, after seeing a guy on a bike with a large baguette, complete with striped blue and white tea shirt, beret, only thing missing were the onion or garlic string around his neck!

We were definitely in rural France, this site looking to be about ninety % French occupied – funny that! I am guessing there were a few more English and others there during the school holidays as we had booked through an English site.

Unfortunately, there were much fewer teenagers than hoped, only a few doing the same as us and defying the out of term ban, but Ben seemed in good spirits, spending every spare moment in the caravan on Snapchat, thank God the Wi-Fi was included in our top of the range van.

After returning with our supplies, we headed for the nearest gate, someone keeping it open for us as they came in, a narrow road to cross, a cycle path really, as we never saw any cars on it, then we were on the beach, which was quite windy, being September, I expected the sea to be still quite warm in the September Med, as in Crete, it was not.

Nevertheless, Sarah in her cut-off jeans and tea shirt took the plunge, much to Ben's amazement, he then followed, which was Sarah's intention, making a big thing of shivering, but staying in for quite a while, more than I or Sue did, neither going in further than ankle deep. After coming out, we wandered a distance savouring the endless, if windy nearly empty beach, before returning to the caravan, after struggling with the gate code, needing to keep a letter depressed a while before it worked.

Behind the Statics nearest the fence it was less windy, so being sunny, it was still warm enough to eat our cooked chicken and pasta first meal outside on the decking, along with some cheap wine to wash it down. Having flown and taxied, got settled in, we had a little more wine on the top deck, after another half an hour, by now quite cool and getting dark we retreated indoors. After a bit of music and chatting about ideas for the rest of the week, and finishing off the wine of course! Ben getting half portions, we took turns in the bathroom for bed.

Next morning, after Sarah and Sue returned from the small Patisserie concession at the end nearer us with two large baguettes, which were chopped in half, on top of which our locally bought eggs and tomatoes were added to some of our bacon and sausage brought with us, made a fine first English breakfast – eaten French style, sort of.

As you do, we thought to spend our first day finding out which facilities were still in use on site, in this transition period to the low season, first to look for was the water park, much featured on the website, we followed the site map, reaching it after a twenty-minute walk, still barely mid-morning, we were in for another shock, the main pool was not heated, though there was a large Jacuzzi pool that was heated, a little. Ben could not wait to have a go on the enclosed water slides, whilst after Sarah and I first having a brief swim in the large cold pool, we joined Sue on sunbeds in the as yet fairly quite park.

Ben decided he wanted me to join him on the enclosed helter skelter plumes, after the other two joined forces with him, I was forced to oblige, emerging a little dizzy, I had two runs, after which Sarah had a go. We let Ben wear himself out on the slides, after which I took him with me to carry back some hot drinks from the snack bar, a short walk away from the park, we settled in the sun for a while, Ben and I having a brief sojourn in the luke-warm, shallow Jacuzzi pool, before settling for a while reading, Ben having yet more go's on the water slides before all of us headed back to the snack bar for some lunch. After which we went over to one of the gates on the beach side for a longish walk down the beach, the afternoon a little warmer, later heading back to a beach bar we had spotted in the distance, all slaking our thirst, after a longish walk in the warmer – less windy than yesterday's sun.

Chapter 131

After returning to the caravan, it was tea or coffee on the top deck and a book or magazine for a while, watching the local world go by on the main drag, site workers trundling up and down on their electric carts, heading for vans vacated, readying them for next arrivals, some at least. Quite a few continental plated cars coming and going from Belgium, Holland, and Germany, as well as French, some, such as the one opposite us, owning Static vans there as holiday homes, after a halting mixed English/French conversation, giving us a card, with contact No, for if we wanted to rent their van in the future.

Not far away, a five-minute walk was a Pizza Hut, not the chain, literally a hut, with outdoor tables we decided to get take-aways from, with some chips, having bought more beers and wine from the super Marché, along with cheesecake I think, not two ambitious on our first full day there.

After a conversation in the reception block earlier in the day, I had found out that bikes were still for hire, so after unsuccessfully trying to persuade Sarah to join us, she not happy on bikes, the one time She did come with me, also in France, mentioned earlier, getting drowned when the heavens opened miles away from our base, so I booked three bikes for the next day, for half a day.

I had started to develop a head cold, going to bed fairly early after pizza and beer. Not long after, I started hearing howls of laughter coming from the other end of the van, unknown to me, Ben had gone out, giddy, acting the fool in just his shorts, hiding behind trees when people were walking by, then running from tree to tree, doing a Mr Bean like run when no one was about, Sue videoing this on her phone, he eventually returning, me getting up to find out what all the fuss was, but I had missed it, they all laughing at the video for some time to come. He did a repeat performance, acting like Mr Bean, I think for my benefit the following night, egged on by his mum and Sarah.

Next day, despite my cold, hoping it would clear my head, we three, sans Sarah, who said she was going for a beach walk, picked up our bikes, I having to return with mine within five minutes, as it must have had a not very slow puncture. Supplied with another bike, we set off towards Marseillan Plage along the cycle track that ran past the camp, next to the beach, Sarah saying later that she waived to three people on bikes from near the sea, not sure if it were us, we never saw her if it was, though we would not be looking that way.

It took us no more than half an hour to reach the edge of town, crossing a small river bridge, on the other side we could see a multi-story small motor boat storage facility, could not see how they got up and down, specialised fork truck or some such, but we decided to turn left, following the coast road, as I had seen on the website that there was a jet ski operation somewhere in town, and had promised Ben I would take him out on one if at all possible. We eventually came to a small harbour area, low and behold we spotted a small building, in front of which were parked a few jet skis, but the place was all shut up, I think it was Sunday, so I said we would come back tomorrow with Sarah – on the bus.

Cycling along the town beach front we came across a cycle parking area, leading into a market area, and other shops, mainly shut then, but hopefully open in the week, Sue saying Sarah would like it there, they would have a wander around the market and shops while we went to see if the Jet ski outfit was still operating on Monday.

After having a drink at a cafe somewhere, we had a quick look in one or two gift shops, where I bought some mugs, as the cups in the van were small. Then we headed back to Le Castellas, arriving back early afternoon, we returned the bikes, found Sarah on the top deck, reading. She told us she might have seen us from the beach. We broke out that day's two-footer baguette, chopped into four, with ham, cheese and tomato, or gherkins, this became our in camp staple lunch for the three days we were on site at midday.

Chapter 132

Apart from a walk to the super Marché, where we bought burgers and other bits, including more wine of course, intending to make use of the gas barbecue our decking came equipped with, we spent that afternoon resting after our bike ride, me still with what was now a chest cold, Ben retreating to his duvet for another Snapchet session, us three up on the top deck for a while, enjoying the scenery, though there we about half a dozen "Premier Statics" with top decks, most were unoccupied, so we had the view to ourselves most of the time, the vans being well spaced apart.

I was a little wary, as I was expected to do the barbecuing, but not having used one like this, I needed to get used to it just being one big hotplate instead of grill bars, the plate lifting off to reveal two rings to light, Sandra and Sue getting the trimmings, including crushed garlic mixed with olive oil, spread on bread and lightly toasted on the plate, making home-made garlic bread, to go with the sausages, some cut lengthways and burgers, along with salad and coleslaw, wine and beer, mixed with lemonade for Ben, getting us gradually slightly merry as you do, without overdoing it.

Breakfast on Monday on the decking included the ritual of dropping morsels through the gaps for the pair of lizards that must have claimed the sub terrain of this deck as their own, living of "gap" scraps all season to supplement their natural diet.

After picking up a timetable the day before from reception for the buses running past the top gate, both to Sete, Montpelier to the northeast, the same distance again beyond, though we never got that far this trip, Marseillan Plage and Adge to the west. We decided to catch one to Marseillan Plage, so Sue could take Sarah to the market and shops we reached on the bikes, whilst Ben and I would see if the jet ski company was open, I had my doubts, but was hoping it was, as most of the camp facilities were winding down, and I wanted to give the young lad something to remember this trip for, plan B was to look for a scuba diving centre near Sete, but that was for another day.

The bus was on time, taking us to the centre of the small beach resort, the bus station close to the pedestrianised shop and restaurant area. Ben and I left Sarah and Sue, agreeing to meet back there in a couple of hours if we did not see each other before, mobiles the last resort. The two of us knew if we walked to the other end of the paved area, not far past was the cycle parking we used the day before, turning left along the beachfront to the small harbour.

Much to my surprise, the Jet ski outfit was just opening, two young gents setting up, so I paid up, we got kitted out in short wet suits, much to Ben's dismay, he would be passenger, as under sixteen's were not allowed to drive, we would be escorted out by one of the instructors, me replying to the query about previous experience, saying once, in Clearlake, California, many years ago, recounted earlier.

Easy enough to drive, right hand throttle, with a dead man's cut out, attached to your wrist, so if you come off, it stopped. Ben on the back, we followed the instructor out through the twisting breakwater rocks built channel, then turned right out to an area beyond the beach, marked by buoys, having been told not to go inshore beyond these. The instructor then idled, indicating for us to go…

So I did, soon accelerating to near full speed, having told Ben to hold on round my waist, I let rip, soon we were bouncing off the slight swell, Ben clearly enjoying the ride, shouting "faster, faster!", so swinging round in an arc, I turned back towards shore, having headed out to sea, eventually I turned in too tight of an arc for the speed we were doing, and over went the Jet ski, flinging us off, we had float jackets on, I looked round for Ben, who was Laughing, I regained the side on Jet Ski, pushing it upright was easier than I anticipated, I climbed on, putting a hand out to pull Ben on the back, the instructor approaching, but Ben climbed on without help.

Waving we were OK to go to the instructor, off we went again, at one stage I started to try to stand, as you might on a galloping horse to mitigate the buffeting, before realising it was not possible with a passenger hanging on round your middle, Ben telling me later, he nearly fell off when I started to rise. After what seemed quite a while, but was not much more than forty minutes, our instructor, having had a couple of fast runs himself, signalled it was time to follow him back in, so we did, both happy with the experience just had, told to accelerate just enough to beach the Jet Ski, we changed back, both of us with a grin on our face as we walked back along the front, knowing we had another hour before we were to meet Sarah and Sue.

Chapter 133

I suggested we stop at a bar on the way up to the precinct, got Ben a shandy, I had a beer, the bar having barrels as tables, we sat outside near the walkway, my hands I realised, were shaking now, the adrenalin had worn off, (getting old) I told myself, my chest feeling rough from the cold I still had, ribs aching a little from being held on to for dear life for half an hour, Ben quite, as teenagers are without peer company, but still with a grin on his face, then out of nowhere Sarah and Sue happened along, Sue asking Ben, with a smirk on her face If he had been on a Jet Ski, to which he replied "No", with no conviction whatsoever, all laughing, they told us they had seen two Skis out, one with two on board, too far out to see who it was, but able to see us come off.

Must have made an impression on Ben, as he said he was coming back next year when he was old enough to drive his own Jet Ski. Sarah introduced Sue to the drink "Kir" the French blackberry liqueur.

I was just relieved that I had delivered on at least one promise of possible things of interest to the young lad. We got the bus back, noting one or two not too posh looking restaurants to eat out at one day soon, another item on Ben's wish list. When we reached Le Castellas, we spotted on the way to the van, that a mobile seafood shop, set not far from us on the site, shut up the last two days, was open that day, an instant decision was made for a seafood Barbecue, returning to the van briefly, to drop stuff off, we went back to the seafood stand, where all sorts of fish, octopus, shellfish, crab, lobster and white fish, which were all well presented on piles of crushed ice – awaiting our choices.

We bought large crab claws, salmon, large prawns and chunks of fresh tuna, crusty bread and asparagus were bought from the shop, possibly other stuff, wine most certainly if we had none in, with a plan to send someone for hot chips from the "pizza hut" when everything else was almost ready.

Ben found a suitably sharp rock near our van with which to crack open the crab claws, "So we are back to the stone age then," I quipped, as I do, the rock just right for the job, not to heavy, or light. I had an extra allopurinol tablet, to counter the threat posed by the prawns and crab, to my susceptibility for gout, shellfish being amongst the highest in purines, the cause of gout, as I was not about to abstain from this treat. I suffered no consequences from my indulgence that night, I will never know if that extra tablet was needed, but I was taking no chance of ruining the rest of this holiday for me.

We got the chips to add to our feast, I was now used to the Barbecue, we shared the preparation and cooking between us, liquid refreshments of the alcoholic kind added to our feast, we ate and drank our fill, salmon almost always on Sarah's menu when seafood is involved. Everything must have cooked well enough, as nobody suffered any ill effects the day after. No night-time antics followed that night from Ben, having run its course the last two nights, I think he and I were tired from our sea excursion and bed soon followed after a few more drinks.

After perusing the leaflets in the reception block, I had a couple more idea's to keep us from getting bored, as with me suggesting this place as a holiday, Ben being the main reason we were here, I felt it was down to me to keep things interesting, even if he reverted to Snapchat on his phone when anywhere near usable Wi-Fi.

The following morning, lizards as well as us fed, we caught the bus again, this time in the opposite direction, to the outskirts of Sete, where a diving school was located, hoping to book a training dive for Ben and I, so we got off the bus at the approximate location of this school, which turned out to be a Portakabin in a small locked park, with no signs of life, oh well, the best laid plans of mice and men and all that…

If we had been able to book a diving session, it would not have been that day, so the plan was to then walk into Sete centre, though it was overcast and spotting rain. Sete was advertised as a picturesque small town that includes a central canal area, indeed Sue thought she had seen this town in a film not so long ago, turned out to be Amsterdam, but it was a pretty little town, with many oyster bars, gift shops, interesting old waterfront architecture, the main waterways shaped like the letter T, with the vertical leading out into the Mediterranean, the cross of the T being the main mooring basin, the far end of which is called the Basin Du Midi, as it marks the bottom of this great canal system, there being an inlet in the top left corner of the T in Sete from the Thau Basin, where, from a unique three way lock at Adge, beyond the western end of the basin, where the Canal Du Midi splits, the easterly route eventually entering the Thau Basin at its western end, effectively the end of the canal, but navigable through the Etang into Sete.

By the time we reached the town centre, it was brightening up, our spirits lifting after the half-hour walk, as Sete's pretty centre de la ville revealed itself to us, we strolled alongside the Canal Lateral, (the T cross) on the Route de Cayenne, as far as the Basin du Midi, walking past the stem of the T, the Canal Maritime, (guess where that leads…), before turning back – looking for a snack – oops poet and I didn't know it. Though my idea of poetry being Pam Ayres on the toilet, quoting peristalsis, poetry in motion (Google if required) …

Brief poetic corruption over, we found a small snack bar where we had crepes, mine with orange liqueur drizzled on it, Sarah Recalls, (my memory beyond such detail) as you know. Coffees were had, then it was off to find a bus back, this time not far away, as we now had no need to look for the dive school at the edge of town.

Chapter 134

On the return bus, one of us, could have been me, must have accidentally pressed the stop button set halfway up whilst holding on the rail bar, a snooty looking woman not far away was heard to groan "Dans tout le Monde", which brought a few giggles from a couple of young girls who looked a little younger than Ben's age, who had been whispering to each other whilst glancing at him, not for me to say what was going through Ben's head…

That evening the two large tins of Cassoulet, bought at the camp shop, along with crusty bread, with other vegetables added to the haricot beans, made for a hearty dinner. All of us quite tired after our trek into and around Sete.

The following day was a quite one spent partly in the water park, the weather a little warmer, with plans to address one of Ben's requests for this holiday that evening, while I spent some time in the camp reception/HQ, which resembled a bank with three counter workers, always fairly busy, asking one of the young woman if she could book us a taxi for the next day to Le Grau-D' Agde, where Herault River reaches the Med from the more direct main route of the split with the Canal Du Midi just north of Adge, as from what we could see, it looked like two different long winded bus trips to get there, as I had found a leaflet offering a boat trip up the canal, turning right at the three-way loch mentioned above, so passing through Agde before the turn.

Le Grau-D Agde, was the sea front extension to Adge, to which I paid a taxi a fair bit to take us there, as it would not have been fair for Sue to stump up half for a trip that was my idea, but only practical by taxi as mentioned, we arrived in brilliant sunshine, dropped in sight of the canal side commercial tourist boat jetties. First things first, we bought tickets for the next trip, which was near two hours away, so we walked the hundred yards or so to the sea front, sat on stylish concrete benches, set on fancy paving with decorative lamp posts, a bit of a focal point, set next to a small beach, with shops across the road, at the base of a longish mole, (not Adrian) that was more a breakwater for the River Herault estuary, as there was no moorings there, just large rocks on either side of a concrete path, the moorings on the river side further in.

Sarah, knowing this day out would cost more in taxi fares than the boat trip itself, had prepared a packed lunch, cheese, ham, tomato and gherkin on buttered baguettes for our delectation, which we enjoyed, bottled water washing it down, then meandered through the gift shop strewn back streets, before sitting at a cafe with iced coffee, at least for Sarah and I, not sure about Sue and Ben, but drinks, as it was a hot day, before heading for the boat, one side street away.

This boat was your typical tourist boat, all on one level, but with little in the way of refreshments, selling only bottled water. Seats for about fifty punters, (not literally) but it would get us around for a few hours. Heading north, towards Agde, a commentary was delivered in French, which I am sure was very informative, Sarah and I understanding one word in ten, with Sue and Ben totally in the dark – in the brilliant sunshine of that day.

The Town of Adge was pretty, well looked after old river front architecture on view as we passed by, under the Pont Des Marechaux, sat at a crossroads branching either side, with roads with names like Avenue Victor Hugo, on one side, Rue Richelieu joining the Avenue Du General De Gaulle on the other side, you might be forgiven for thinking you were in Paris, town planners with national pride, understated as normal in France…

Then it was north another mile or two to what is called The Round Lock, which was built back in 1676, since expanded to allow larger barges to turn, connecting the upper Herault river to the lower, the Canal Du Midi entering the lower Herault just south of the lock, the third gate continuing the canal east, which after our boat entering the lock from the Lower Herault, we joined, the experience from a boat perspective, of lock gates being opened and water level changes new to us all at the time.

I pointed out that the Canal Du Midi west of there, then went through Carcassonne, the biggest intact walled town left in the world, which I hoped to visit (remember I said that), before eventually joining the Canal Lateral north of Toulouse, where it enters the Bay of Biscay at Bordeaux, thus providing water navigation for boats from the Med to the Atlantic coast, without having to go around the Spanish coast.

We headed east alongside Reserve Naturelle Bagnas, with Cranes and Egrets both in evidence, passing to the south of Marseillan town proper, before entering the Etang called the Thau Basin at its western end, this being the same large brackish lake that borders the northern side of the long spit of land that starts at Marseillan Plage and includes Le Castellas, our site, among others on its seaward side. I for one, wishing I had bought a hat with me, as my bald patch was beginning to feel the scorching sun of that day, with no breeze up to that point to cool us down, the big Etang providing a little relief breeze, being such a large expanse of water.

We reached a commercial oyster farm, the Etang evidently salty enough for their liking, one of the crew, I am sure with pre-agreed permission, pulling up one of the ropes they were growing on to show them to us. Not seen by us at the time, they must have taken some from the line, as just in time, on the way back, as we were all getting a little bored by then, the crew came round with a couple of large plates full of oysters, along with a glass of white wine

Chapter 135

Now if you recall back to where Sarah and I had stayed north of St Nazaire and the Loire estuary in the Briere Nature Reserve in a thatched cottage, we had happened upon oysters on the cote Sauvage, on Brittany's south coast, we took back so many we had them cooked one way or another, for the next three days. For me, bolting them down raw was a different proposition, three out of us four declining, perhaps one in four on the boat having one, cockles and Mussels I can eat and enjoy, oysters raw that you bolt down, no thanks, too big to chew, (not meant to, I know) I preferred mine cooked, as we had, some years earlier. However, Ben became the star of the show, wolfing down not one, but four of the big slippery molluscs, astounding us, and half the boat with his bravado, he must have been bored and hungry, the rest of us just had the wine, while Ben lapped up the praise from nearby French passengers, the tone conveying this…

He suffered no ill effects from his oyster feast, this episode livening up what was becoming a boring trip, apart from the round lock river/canal connection, after arriving back we started looking for a taxi rank, but there were none in sight, the one we came in was from miles away, so we headed into the town, thinking to find one nearby. After walking half an hour, with no idea now where we were, with a vague plan to head for the seafront, we decided we were in the words of Bonny Tyler, *Lost in France*.

Just starting to get dusk, I was getting a little concerned, when we spotted a group of young people, who it turned out, were on a break from working in the small hotel they were stood near, Sarah went over, asking '*Parles vous Anglais?*' Most of them did, so we asked if they knew a local taxi number, one kitchen worker very obligingly phoned a guy, who said he would be there in ten minutes, which he was, we thanked the young lad, the taxi taking us back for a fair bit less than the one we came in, I should have looked on my phone, recalling the site girl at the desk, could not get hold of the first two she tried, anyway we got back to the site, picking something up from the "Pizza shed" near our caravan, as it was a bit late to shop and start cooking, we were all tired from our wander around town, after being baked on the boat we settled down after that, with one more full day left on site.

Our last day there was spent relaxing at the on-site water park, with the promise to Ben that in the evening we would catch the bus into Marseillan Plage and eat out in a local restaurant, as by now we had seen several to choose from not far from the bus station. After a quiet day, we packed later in the afternoon, so as to only have minimal left for the morrow.

Bussed it into town, had a wander passed the precinct restaurants, checking out the menu's, which were all much of a muchness, selected one, got sat, ordered wine, perused the menu, which was geared up for tourists, with pictures to match the choices, we ordered a Charcuterie Board for starters, Sarah having her beloved Moules frites, myself and Sue on Ribs, so says Sarah, not sure how cooked, but probably barbecued, Sarah not sure about Ben, fried squid rings a bell.

Our waiter was very amiable, unlike the reputation of some Parisian waiters who look down their noses at Les Rosbifs, if we cannot speak fluent French, ours encouraging Ben to attempt some French pronunciation, but with a smile on his face, hopefully leaving a favourable impression of the "French meal out" he had requested, he seemed happy enough, quite chatty for a teenager not in his peer group, likely posting about it, along with his jet-ski ride on Snapchat…

Then it was time to go home, not due for pick up by our pre-booked return taxi, till two, we spent the morning at the caravan, trundling our cases to the cafe near the water park, coffee and snack, the day dragging like it always does on the last day of holidays, eventually parking ourselves where we could see arrivals at the gate, picked up ahead of time, back to the smallest airport I have yet to visit, at Beziers, more coffee, before Ryanair flew us back to Manchester, stopping at the local Morrisions, for chicken and rice to cook and eat at their house, before we left them, hopefully satisfied with their French hols.

Sarah told me later Sue was impressed that I had engaged with Ben, she was not sure how well we would interact, Ben told his mum I was better company than he thought I might be, so Sarah told me, a good time was had by all it seems…

Chapter 136

Returning to work was not so bad, boring at times, trips out in a works van delivering product to our Midlands depot for onward distribution, the highlight of my three-day week, being a change of scenery, if living the Groundhog Day life, as most do, there being three main alternatives to that for most of us, holidays, day trips/event visits, or trouble, so avoiding the later as much as possible, as you do, we resumed our routines.

Where we live, we have a long deep, high hedge bordering a grassed open space, I keep our side trimmed, but the outside, on a downslope so the top takes most of a day, with a heavy duty extendable pole cutter, with a couple of trailer loads to remove when all done, so we have a guy, Rob, come and do this for us once a year, around the end of October, not cheap, but not OTT either, maybe a little lazy, but not sure I am fit enough these days to tackle the big cut, or want the cost of the necessary ladder, long pole cutter and harness gear needed, I will continue the summer monthly internal snips though.

Our life therefore continued after our French holiday, with little to write about other than us going along to Tier Prince near Towyn, to watch the special starting "Special Stage" of the 2017 World Rally Championships, whilst not a fanatic, I have had an interest in the sport since the days of Colin McRae, so could not pass up an event taking place so close to home, Sarah taking the opportunity to pick up Ben, who like most lads his age enjoys speed close up.

In the event it was a bit of a wet afternoon and evening, and so not quite as much fun as hoped, having a sit in a simulator, and eating rough burgers, a little beer taking the edge of two long a wait for action.

Some car jumps, turbo fire and lots of exhaust noise livened things up before eventually heading home, Ben, sleeping on our spare room inflatable double bed, spending a couple of hours on Snapchat as far as I could tell, before he took the hint when I turned off the broadband around midnight. Like most teenagers he pushes, but knowns when he has had a fair deal, not to be outdone, his dad later took him to another special stage in Deeside.

Not planned, but two days later Sarah and I went to Brenig reservoir, west of Ruthin, where the surrounding forest and Dam made for a spectacular finale "Power Stage" of the same event, though the walk, well downhill from parking, to a good viewing area up at the dam nearly killed us, (slight exaggeration) the visitor centre being used to stage the presentations afterwards.

We have since returned there for an enjoyable walk along the dam and a bit more on the far side, then brunch in the Visitor Centre with a good view of the reservoir, plenty of hardy folk out on hire boats, fishing, despite the weather going downhill into drizzle and fog, our view enhanced by the sight of a Great Crested Grebe diving for fish close to shore, no great twitcher I, but seeing such a bird, not something I have seen since holidays on the Norfolk Broads, helped make up for a day of deteriorating weather, so a pleasant day out, able now to park at the visitor centre, instead of a mile downhill for the Rally.

What keeps me going is the thought of somewhere different to see, so with winter approaching, we did what we usually do, and found somewhere to look forward to (again, remember I said that) next spring. Harking back to our previous domestic boating holidays, I had pretty much given up doing any more, as neither of us liked the idea of canal boating involving lots of lock gates. But after our south of France hols, including the Canal Du Midi southern end day trip, I hit upon the idea of killing two birds with one stone, feasible I discovered, after a little research.

The two birds being (1) visiting the walled city of Carcassonne, as mentioned a while back, (2) doing a canal trip without having to work lock gates. The Canal Du Midi, in common with most French canals, have manned lock gates, which are electronically operated, this canal being twice the width of most English canals, internet research telling me that a company called Le Boat, hired out cruisers small enough for two from their base in Castelnaudary, south of Toulouse, from which you could cruise down into the centre of Carcassonne town and back in a week.

Ideal would have been to continue a little further down to Trebes and leave the boat there, as is sometimes possible, as from there a taxi to the nearest airport near Carcassonne was closer than from Castelnaudary, alas, even in October 2017, such was the demand for the smaller cruisers in May 2018, that only a return cruise was available, so we booked it, something to look forward to…

Chapter 137

About a month later, Phil my boss at work, who knew of my fondness for travel, asked me if I had ever been to Iceland, as he was considering it, adding that he liked cold weather. Putting it as politely as possible, he (at time of writing this) is currently well insulated of build, so I could see where he was coming from. He suggested I look at the Reykjavik based short breaks on offer with Icelandair.

Out of curiosity, I did, fatal, what with geysers, volcanos, glaciers and a giant waterfall, not to mention the famous Blue Lagoon, along with the Northern Lights, who could resist, unless you are a dedicated beach and sun worshipper to the exclusion of all else, which we are not. After searching out a three-day package, that included a Blue Lagoon visit, as well as the "Golden Circle Tour" where, in one long day, you are taken to much of the above, Blue Lagoon saved for the next day, I persuaded Sarah that May of next year was a long way off, and so I booked us on the above trip – for late January, usually a fairly good time to see the Northern lights.

That booked, there was Christmas and the New Year, a time for family, before either of the above trips, Sarah's daughter Sue had invited us for a Christmas Dinner (Boxing day), I think partly as a thank you for organising the French caravan trip, not sure now, but I don't think I had to book any additional days off work, with the only bank holidays I get off from work being at Christmas and or New year, if they do not fall on a Friday or Monday when I am off anyway, not getting any days off in lieu if they do, being a part timer, not daft are they, making sure my working three days do not include Monday or Friday, the only days where all other bank hols fall the rest of the year…

The winter of 2017, as you know, was a hard one when compared with most recent winters in north Wales, most of the snow coming in early 2018, us having no problem getting to both Sue's house on Boxing day, or to my brother's house for an overnight stay in Poynton, Cheshire, early in the new year. For us (at least), this included a rare walking pub crawl around a few of the local public houses, eventually settling in one for some live music, before sleeping it off at my brother Rick's house. We had not gone there on new year's eve, as Cheryl, Rick's wife, had just suffered the loss of her sister-in-law from cancer, so Christmas and new year celebrations were somewhat muted this year, us having attended her funeral in late November.

Late January saw us off to Iceland for our short winter break there, you would have to be well off indeed to spend a long holiday there, as otherwise a mortgage would be needed just to eat out up there. Scandinavia in general has a reputation for being expensive to eat or drink out, but with our package, we were booked into a relativity inexpensive hotel called The Cabin, though a cabin it was not, being a five or six-story concrete building, the only concession to a cabin being the large rounded rectangular windows, similar to those on some larger ships.

It was early afternoon before our transfer from Keflavik Airport, which is set near the end of a peninsular west of Reykjavik, arriving in the city, which is well spread out, mostly low-rise buildings due to the risk of earthquakes, our hotel was set a little out of the centre of town, which was reachable from a bus stop set right outside "The Cabin". We found our small room, set a couple of floors up, dumped our cases. The view from our rounded window (no, not the Play School one!) was bleak indeed, we could see the sea, but between us and the seafront were two busy roads, walking on the pavements looked as though you might need crampons (not the monthly sort!), sorry, Miss Spelling uses these on poetic license… but anyway, we decided to get togged up in our heavy coats and navigate our way across to the seafront – before it started getting dark, which this far north at this time of year would not be much past three, the light already fading.

Out we went, it was about two below zero, looking out for the transparent two to three-inch thick ice that had built up in places at the edge of the pavement, the sort you see in icicles, in windswept sheets here, two-foot icicles visible on building overhangs nearby.

We hung on to each other for balance as we avoided the worst, taking each step carefully. In this fashion, it took us nearly a quarter hour to cross two roads normally crossable in five minutes, waiting for lights to change on the coastal dual carriageway. We made it to the rocky seafront, the sea rough but not wild. What was wild was the view, at least to those of us not used to it, the coast to the north east of us curving past an inlet, round to the north west, so opposite, off to the right appearing to us like a vast flat-topped glacier, but with rock striated vertically through it, so not a glacier then, but seemingly more ice than rock, at least this time of year, with a couple of islands to the left of this, from our point of view, white enough to be icebergs – though not.

Walking along the seafront for ten minutes, we crossed back where it was less busy away from the intersection opposite our hotel, it was getting dark by then. looking in a petrol station shop opposite our hotel, but not seeing anything we wanted for tea/dinner, we deciding to risk the hotel evening meal, not in our package, but apparently considerably cheaper than eating in town, which we planned to do the following night, having taken out the appropriate mortgage…

Chapter 138

The lower of two hotel restaurants was set out like a diner, with bench seats, with one hot meal available, plus a smorgasbord buffet of cold meats and vegetables as in the Scandinavian manner. You paid on entering, a set price, then had as much or little as you wanted, the hot food welcome after our outdoor wanderings, not thinking to tell the reception we were "Just going outside and may be some time..."

Heading to the hotel bar a little later, we noticed quite a few people boarding a small coach just outside. Didn't know it at the time, but we had missed our only chance of seeing the Northern Lights on this trip, only being seen rarely from the city, you needed to get well out of town to stand a chance of a good viewing, reports the next morning saying they had good sightings that Wednesday night.

Up early Thursday morning as scheduled, this was to be our "Golden Circle" day, as this tour is the most recommended if you are only here a few days as many are, though for those who wish to do more, there are a multitude of options – for those prepared to pay for it, from snowmobiling, to whale watching boat trips, ice cave visits, lava tunnel excursions, volcano tours, glacier hikes, horse riding, helicopter tours, you could spend a couple of weeks and a few thousand pounds and not get bored on this large, but thinly populated island.

After a cold buffet breakfast, with the option of making your own toast, a feeder coach picked us up at The Cabin, along with others from here, before continuing its no doubt well-travelled circuit around Reykjavik picking up others for this most popular of tours, before arriving at the main tour bus station. Everyone from all the feeder coaches were mixed and matched at desks with a tour name and number they had booked, not all doing the ubiquitous Golden Circle. Registered, we boarded our tour bus and off we went.

Passing through a stark rubble strewn landscape, we entered Thingvelir National park, I have used "Th" at the start of this park name, as that is how it is pronounced, the Icelandic letter not available on my discombooberattor (to my limited knowledge). As we progressed through a greener area, with a few pine trees and small ponds scattered here and there, the guide told us something of the history of this area, where some of the earliest settlements were located, including the original parliament, called the Althing established back in 930 AD, the oldest in the world, still used even after its union with Norway in 1262.

Situated about thirty miles east of Reykjavik, this continued right up to 1800, discontinued for forty-four years, (infighting) before being re-established at Reykjavik in1845, the Christian Church gaining a tenuous hold, but with a widespread Norse Gods tradition remaining, lip service paid to Christianity as and when required, as with much of Scandinavia for many centuries beyond "official" conversion. They continued under Norwegian rule until 1944, declaring independence whilst Norway was itself occupied by Germany.

Passing through one village, a building was pointed out, that housed a geothermal pump. As I understand it, the first guy in the area with the wherewithal to fund the pump, and the network of pipes to the nearby houses, is paid by the heat recipients to pump the hot water round the system, this is repeated over much of rural Iceland.

We stopped at the Fridheimar greenhouse cultivation centre, where tomatoes and cucumbers are grown using geothermal heat to maintain growing temperature, reducing the amount of imports needed, with other smaller similar greenhouses dotted around the country.

After pushing their green credentials, I was somewhat dismayed to discover that in order to achieve pollination, and thus a crop, they have to air fright in boxes of bees as we were shown, that are periodically released into the greenhouses, with no native insects, this being only way to maintain pollination, but with the bees dying of starvation after a short period, as the nectar from tomato and cucumber flowers are not enough to keep them going. I suggested they plant rows of nectar rich flowers alongside the tomatoes, but how much longer they would live and work with this extra food I don't know.

They may have looked into setting up a hive colony, but it would have to stay under a heated glass space, costing money, so presumably not commercially viable, a side effect would be native honey…

After buying coffee from an urn they had set up, we wandered outside over to where, in the same complex, show horses were to be seen in small paddocks, not to be fed by tourists, this area had a few deciduous trees, of which there were precious few in the areas we saw that day. This south western loop the Golden Circle comprises being not even a tenth of the circumference of Iceland, but the most benign and relatively fertile, hence the population concentration there, though one third of Icelanders are scattered outside this area, around the 800-mile coastline.

Chapter 139

Our journey continued inland up to Gullfoss, which to me is the most majestic waterfall I have seen. I have seen Niagara, but when we were here, in late January, Gullfoss was half frozen, two tiered, the top tier angled away at roughly forty five degrees, spread out into the snow and ice covered flat landscape, before converging opposite our vantage point for a mighty, half frozen, roaring drop, I with my camera, determined to capture the raw majesty of this place both on video and still photograph, braving the coldest, bighting, gale force wind I have ever experienced, to get this photo, now up on our dining area wall as a 12 x 16 inch print.

Though kitted out in thermal everything, we could not stand that wind chill micro climate for long, heading into the nearby cafe, declining the long queue for hot soup, opting for a quicker hot coffee instead, a toffee crisp from home supplying quick energy.

Haukadalur was our next destination, less than half an hour away, this is where the name Geysir originally came from, Geysir itself no longer erupts at regular intervals, due to geological shifts in the earth, but its next-door neighbour, Strokkur puts on a stunning show every six to eight minutes, you see the hot steaming turquoise pool convulse, then sink a little just before it spouts anywhere from 60 feet to 130 on occasion. The whole area covered in bubbling hot mud pools and Fumaroles, with little shallow steaming streams running between them, microbial algae growing in different colours along the streambeds.

Needless to say, tourists have been coming here for a long time, able to get coffee and refreshments since 1928, we were no different, it was lunchtime, us having brought foil wrapped sausage roll, from home (still only yesterday), along with another (for me) toffee crisp, saving our Krona for our planned trip into town that evening, though we bought a puffin bottle opener and Guysir fridge magnet there, (last of the big spenders…)

From there, it was off to our last excursion of a long day out, back to a different location in Thingvelir National Park, this place was billed as where you could walk from Europe to America in a few steps. Iceland being so geologically active, with more than twenty volcanoes, due to two tectonic plates, the Eurasian and North American, very slowly drifting apart right across the middle of Iceland. We were taken to the great rift of Almannagja, where we were dropped off to take a guided walk along and between the fissure rock, up to twenty feet high in places. The Oxara River cuts across the western plate, running off in a series of cascades. Probably due to its good acoustic reflecting location, the speaker of early parliaments would use this location to read out periodic law-giving, trials of witches and others there – resulted in drowning in nearby pools. Up there though, not often a summery execution…

In any group large group there is always one, or two, who know better, in this case two young American tourists that left our coach, and so counted in with our group, went off on their own at some point. Our coach, having dropped us off, drove off in a big horseshoe of a drive, around to the visitor centre, to await our arrival there from our guided walk. After the inevitable coffee upon our group reaching the visitor centre, we boarded the waiting coach, and as many of you will know, the familiar head count commenced, after two or three of these, it was established we were two short (I am six foot!), sorry… People sitting near the empty two seats told the guide who was missing, though everyone knew by then, it was decided by the guide to wait a while for them, still no sign, so our guide had to do the walk-in reverse, so our coach driver had to drive back to the original drop off point, to pick up the guide, and hopefully the Americans.

Our guide was there, no Yanks, so off he went again, saying he would check other paths back. So back we in the coach went to the centre/cafe, again. When the guide reappeared, he was still alone, then out strolled the Yanks from the cafe, we never got the full story, but they had delayed our return by over an hour, stony silence reigned on the coach, no apology from these yanks, many of us were itching to question them, no one did, they would have heard many comments pitched for their hearing, but wisely, kept their mouths shut.

With all the coach excursions we have been on, the odds of this happening on one of ours must have built to the inevitable, they were lucky our guide probably had to follow a search protocol before having to alert search and rescue, with the location being remote, whatever the reason they missed the original pick up, only injury would have been a good reason. They should have had to pay a financial cost for their arrogance, don't suppose they did, so I rather hope they end up on the receiving end of something similar, but without anyone else suffering with them. What goes around comes around.

Chapter 140

Some people on that coach had meal bookings and were worried they would lose their bookings, but the guide said they would try to make up time returning to Reykjavik, I think some was gained, but we were still quite late back. Fortunately, though we planned to catch the bus into town for a meal, we had not booked anywhere, having been told by The Cabin reception there were many choices of pubs and restaurants if we got off the bus at Hafnarstraeti, the stop being opposite a pedestrianised area with at least a dozen choices close by.

So we did just that, not sure what time, but knowing the last bus back was about 10.40, giving us enough time to wander around, reading the window and outdoor menus. there were French, American fast food, a Hard Rock cafe,(more burgers) but after the best part of a half-hour wander, on a cold, icy under foot night, we settled on an Icelandic Gastropub called Saeta svinid, no translation available, the menu was extensive, but for the price we knew we were about to pay, we wanted a good choice, and this place was very busy, wood beams everywhere, cosy style well lit, all sorts on the walls, and a good mix of all ages, locals being younger, more of these just drinking, as you would expect at these prices.

Stating we wanted to eat, we were shown upstairs, a small table found for us, it was as packed as downstairs, wood beamed as downstairs, an olde-worlde theme, pictures of old Reykjavik, the music older pop, but not too loud, I ordered an Icelandic beer, which had a good hop flavour, Sarah chose white wine, as she had ordered Cod, cold with all sorts of flavours and juices added, along with a salad, which Sarah said was very good.

Being sentimental Brits, we decided we would not try the puffin or minke whale on offer…

I had lamb rump, that and all the vegetables expertly cooked and flavoured, followed by Skyr, which is classified as a cheese, but is more like a cross between yogurt and porrage to me, it was sweet, with blueberries added, very nice, I know we both thought this was the best meal out we had eaten out in a long time, and it needed to be, as the only other time I had paid this sort of price for a meal, we were at Rick Stein's restaurant in Padstow. But I had planned for this, in for a penny…

When we asked our waiter to complement the chef, he told us they were aware how high the price was, and so did their utmost to serve as good a meal as possible, I told him they had succeeded.

We met other English people at the return bus stop, Brummies as I recall, who had also paid a fortune for a good meal, it was a cold wait, but the last bus was on time, and were soon back at The Cabin, in our small but warm room. Friday was to be Blue Lagoon day, our last here, this was pre-booked in with our package and we had vouchers from Icelandair, printed off the internet that included the return journey to the Blue lagoon, which is out in the middle of the Reykjanes geothermal field, on the peninsular of the same name, west of Reykjavik, in the same direction as the airport, but with a turning south, a few miles short of Grindavik to where this cleverly crafted place is located.

Though there are as many as twenty geothermal spas dotted around Iceland, though none as famous or as large as The Blue Lagoon, it is a clever piece of engineering, as sea water is mixed with the hot water from the spring, to maintain a fairly even temperature in the large blue painted pool, with vents pumping the mixed fresh and seawater up through the bottom.

The pool complex is run from a large building with turnstile entry and exit. Changing rooms, showers and lockers upstairs, a cafe and gift shop downstairs. It *was* worth the visit, you were issued with a waterproof wristband, that acted as a debit card, as there was plenty to spend on once through the turnstiles. Essentials such as a large thick white bathrobe, more of a wearable bath towel really, were for hire, towels were free, there were hanger racks at the pool's edge to leave your gown, but no guarantee the same one would still be there when you climbed out, as I found out. Meeting up with Sarah after striping to swim wear in our respective areas, we met up at the main pool steps.

The pool was large enough that at times you could not see the other sides of the curving irregularly shaped pool through the steam rising of it. Surreal is the word that best describes this experience, the water depth about four and half feet, with a shallow pool for kids, the whole place surrounded by rock and large boulder groups, to give a wild, if early *Star Trek* set look. Up to now, I could be describing any of the large Med hotel pool complexes in appearance, apart from the steam rising of the water, there was even a pool bar.

This is where it gets surreal, you go up to the poolside bar, sunk to waist height, to order beer or wine, you being in swim wear, the bar staff are in multi layers of clothes, topped off with heavy fur lined coats, hoods up, as the temperature when we were there in February, out of the pool, was below zero. Think Japanese Macaques in geothermal pools on Hokkaido, that was us, but with a bar handy, of no use to Macaques – as they did not have wrist debit bands to pay for beer and wine…

Somewhere off in the mists, was a facial treatment hut, from which pool staff wandered round the Lagoon with tubs of sludge of different colours for you to try, wrist debit receivers at the ready. Sarah plastered some white facial mask before eventually washing it off, I had to assume the filtration plant was up to this, the water itself being a milky blue/white due to the mix of sea and fresh water, (as well as the bottom and sides being painted pale blue), the whole lagoon volume being replaced over forty-eight hours.

I would estimate there were well over a hundred people in the Lagoon, hard to tell when the steam stopped you seeing the whole pool at once, but it was not quite overcrowded, the booking system probably preventing this, though the only time constraint once you were in, was being out and ready to catch the bus back, the latest at 5.30 pm, though we left on the 4.30, after spending nearly three hours in this almost hot water, some of it sat on the bench ledges set in the lagoon wall opposite the bar, feet over feed vents where the water was warmest. For a while, it was like being *in* cloud nine…

Chapter 141

All good things come to an end, out we got eventually, meeting up at the out turnstile after retrieving my mysteriously shrunken bathrobe at the steps, to settle up the debit bands, heading into the cafe for coffee, and a sweet snack for me no doubt. Then it was back along the peninsula, through Reykjavik, spotting the Hallgrimshirkja Church tower in the middle distance, not having time to visit this striking building, one of the tallest buildings in Iceland, named after a local poet and clergyman, this church tower looking like a cross between a giant pipe organ and a rocket launch gantry, but graceful for all That, grand and original in its modern expressionist-architectural style.

Then it was back to The Cabin, and a second in house restaurant evening meal, Roast Chicken being the hot choice on offer. After splashing out the previous night, there was no point going out far, as we had to be up in the early hours, to catch an eight o'clock flight home. So before eating, we went for a longer walk along the sea front, braving the icy pavements, noting the local equivalent of mini, one man council leaf sweepers, that here were mini ice scrapers, breaking up the sheets of clear ice that built up at the roadsides, marvelling at how these hardy people lived much of the year in almost continuous darkness, children and elders needing vitamin D supplements to stay healthy, while we take our mild climate for granted…

Early morning and time to go home – in the dark. Keflavik Airport being so busy is the reason they packed us of so early on a Saturday morning, to make room for the next influx. Another region of our planet now experienced, if only briefly.

I did just say "our mild climate", didn't I, we in north Wales had already had a larger dose of snow in early December 2017, than I had seen in a long time in the Manchester area, and soon after returning from Iceland, where we saw lying snow inland, but little falling, we were deluged at home in February, at times eight to ten inches of it accumulating, I had some rock salt, it was needed most to get onto the drive from the road, though if I had not got a 4 x 4 crossover car, I would not have been able to get up the hill to the main road for several days at a time.

Not sure if he is paid by the council, but the local farmer was the first to turn up with grit on our street, his tractor better than any 4x4 or standard gritter wagon for getting around this hilly area.

Just after we, and the rest of Britain, thought we were past the worst of this relatively hard winter, then came the Beast from the East at the end of February, after the big heavy snow we had just seen the back of, this stuff was small spots, but driven by a cold east wind, it soon piled up on the roads, especially roads exposed to open farmland, as I found out on the return of a trunk run at work to our Midlands depot.

At this time, there are usually three large van "trunk" return runs a day from North Wales to our Midlands operation, one soon after six am, another at eight, the third taking the van that has returned from the early run. On the Beast from the East week, one of our engineering staff went with the 8 o'clock run to do weekly maintenance work, probably on a Wednesday, that being usual, with the expectation of being taken back by the guy doing the late run, that sets off from North Wales around eleven fifteen-thirtyish, getting to our near Midlands base around One thirtyish, depending on traffic.

We had seen the forecast for this bad weather, though the east of England was supposed to get the worst of it. I was on the late run at that time, on the run down, small amounts of windswept snow was starting to pile up along the agriculture lined A41 route that some of us use before turning west onto the A5, but nothing major, I hoped I would be there and heading back before it became a concern. I delivered our goods, picked up three large boxes of return goods, and our engineer in fairly good time. There was space for one more box in the long wheelbase van I was in, so I checked with the fork truck loader, there was no more to go, and set off, we were about half an hour into our return journey when we got the call from our base, can we go back and pick up another box!

The snow was getting driven a little harder by then, a little deeper at the side of the road, I was still on the A5 leg, out in the sticks, so I managed a three-point turn, with the aid of our engineer's eyes, and back we went. I couldn't prove it, but I think the loader was coming to the end of his shift at 2 pm when he said carefully (in retrospect) there was nothing else ready to go, when I checked before setting off, but product was still being processed that was needed that evening for the night shift at North Wales, the loader might have had to wait, so he took no chance, finishing his shift on time.

We were not told this, but it was what happened, a supervisor loaded this last box when we arrived back, now an hour behind schedule. We set off home for the second time, the sky leaden, the roads getting noticeably more snow covered then an hour earlier, it was now a case of following the two furrows made by the light but steady traffic ahead of us, the snow building on the roads where the hedges were thin or non-existent on the eastern side of the A41 heading north, after initially heading west on the A5, with the wind behind us, so not building up more on one side there– mostly.

Another hour later, I don't think we would have got through, as it was, the further north and slightly west we got, out of Shropshire and into south Cheshire, the less snow there was, we had just made it, though it was well past our usual knocking off time by the time we got back off the A55 to our base in Flintshire where the snow was thin, if blowing hard.

Chapter 142

I should have taken the hint in February when our boiler, situated in the attic of our bungalow, temporarily froze up, ice forming in its pump, but just as a guy we called had ordered a new pump, it defrosted. I was able to call him and get the order cancelled before it was sent, having used a hair drier to defrost the pump, after which it started working, but it was an old boiler, with no automatic cut in at a low temperature to keep it from freezing again. Within a month it was malfunctioning again, the water pressure in it all over the place, eventually blasting water out of the relief pipe sticking out the sidewall, to the point where I had to shut it down altogether.

No hot water, but at least our shower was electric, thankfully. It took a week before we had a new boiler installed, one with an optional regular half-hour firing option lasting two minutes, to leave on in the winter so as to prevent freezing, heating up a small quick tap supply, to reduce waiting time for hot water, this Combi boiler costing half what British Gas wanted for their main advertised equivalent. At time of writing this. When the old one was stripped out, a circular relief tank was full to the brim with water, so it had probably been gradually filling each time the pressure was too high. Our boiler guy telling us the make we had replaced was regarded in the trade as poor, but we had inherited it. I think it will be the washing machine next, I can hear the bearings starting to sound louder on the fast spin…

Easter came and went – I, not working Friday or Monday anyway, had no extra time off, as mentioned. Not being religious, in any recognised form, I do sometimes wonder about the Intelligent Design theories put forward by some scientists, pointing at the perfect twenty-three degrees tilt of the earth, without which there would be no seasons, the perfect size and positioning of the moon for moderate tidal action – arguments for and against rage. I do have a problem with God, if anyone knocks on our door pushing this idea of one God, I always ask them "if you can tell me *who* created God, please let me know". Our Solar System is only five billion years old, and the current universe we know of, is around thirteen billion, so there has been plenty of time for civilisations to have been around for so long, that to us, for all intents and purposes – some would have godlike power.

So by Intelligent Design, I entertain the possibility of entities or civilisations millions, if not a few billion years old with enough power to reshape and then seed solar systems, perhaps using lower level, but still vastly beyond us, entities to intervene in nurturing life in this current universe. Depicted by *all* old cultures, legends and stories of the creator "Sky people" were here to teach us the basics of civilisation.

At the end of this life storyline, (not quite yet) I will stop at the most recent notable event, before any attempt at publication. Then based on the above world view, that to me seems more likely than the chance evolution of life on just one only, of billions of planets, this view, logical to me, and shared by many, begs one question – *Where Are They*. To answer that, after my little story, as stated earlier, I am going to write out an Addendum – a timeline of most of the major salient, key events I know of, with names of authors, or other key people, for those still reading this – to search out online if interested. I am definitely no expert, but I have read enough from people who have spent their lives researching different aspects of this biggest of all questions, also having had those early life experiences, tenuous, I admit, but compelling enough to generate a lifelong interest, especially after gaining retrospective knowledge.

If even one person reading this, questions our apparent world and its presented history as complete, with no other major causes behind any of it, as described by our establishment, I will be the happier for it. Open-minded people, without accepting all read as fact, like me, but curious enough to follow up on some of the searches I mention, who have not previously done so, often busily absorbed with life, content with their lot, then I will have done my bit towards raising awareness of possibilities beyond those visible to casual view.

Notice given then, those with firm other beliefs, but still interested in the life of one of the little people, can skip the above-mentioned end of book Addendum/summery. Countering all of the information collated, with more than just "Not Proven" answers, might prove an interesting exercise in testing your own world view, bearing in mind that if *any one* of the events I mention *is* true, then some governments, "Black Budget – Special Access Projects" deception at the very least, is being perpetrated to levels the general public will not forgive, and so the need to perpetuate this deception as long as possible will continue.

Chapter 143

Meanwhile, in the spring of 2018, the last of that long, extended winter finally behind us, it was May, (not Teresa), and our usual time of year for a foray out into the wider world, otherwise known to most as a holiday, this time, as touched upon earlier, not too far north of where we, plus Sue and Ben, spent some of last September – the south of France, but this time it would be just Sarah and I, something we would rue, the reason for which will become evident…

Having already concluded there was little of Britain's waterways that we had not visited, that did not need endless lock gate working, I, as mentioned earlier, had booked us for a week's cruise on the Canal Du Midi, the southern end of which we had already encountered, as recalled, at the "Round Lock", just north of Agde, the previous year. This time our trip would start some distance west of there, at a town along the canal called Castelnaudary, where "Le Boat" hires out canal cruisers at their marina situated on "Le Canelot", a wide basin near the centre of this small town.

First though, we had to get there, as with last year's trip, we were forced to rely on Ryanair again, they being the only airline that could get us to Carcassonne Airport, the nearest to our starting point, Toulouse, the next closest, being half as far again away, set at the top end of the Canal Du midi.

The best return flight I could get was not a perfect fit, they were on Fridays, the boat trips were Saturday to Saturday, this meant returning to Castelnaudary a day early, but this was much preferable to the alternative of a channel ferry and driving, with the extra cost and four days return travelling time plus overnight en route stays, set against one Friday night's accommodation, and the return taxi fare to Carcassonne airport, which while not cheap, was still a lot less than the above alternative, not having checked a rail option, like driving, too much extra travelling time, and highly unlikely to have been cheaper than flying – even with Ryanair charging extra just to sit together, along with anything else they can get away with, it being an example of "better the devil you know…"

We landed in bright sunlight, looking for a taxi rank, not seeing one, I was about to ask at the information desk, but an older English expat overheard us talking, and very kindly offered to call a guy he used, he had no sooner done this for us – than he stepped back and went flying over Sarah's suitcase, landing hard. We got him up, he was shaken and a little stirred, (though not Mr Bond) but otherwise OK, probably wishing he had ignored us, though he had done his good deed for the day.

Castelnaudary is at the centre of the region renowned for the duck, pork and Haricot Blanc stew called Cassoulet, a tinned version of which we ate last September at Le Castellas. Our taxi took us to the main square in Castelnaudary, thirty yards from our overnight stop – the Hotel Cassoulet, it was locked up, but a guy from the restaurant next door, pointed us to another restaurant directly across the road, it turned out this was owned by the same people who ran the "hotel" opposite, which was just rooms, and a breakfast room on the ground floor, with no reception, we were given keys to our room, and the code to enter the building, our room was two floors up, no lift, so we lugged our cases and bags up the stairs. Thought it was a good price on the net – you get what you pay for, the room basic, but with an on-suite bathroom, so OK.

Cases dumped, the weather still OK, but clouding over after a blue-sky landing, it was mid-afternoon now, giving us time to find Le Boat's Marina on the Canal Du Midi. I had turned on location on my phone, (not something I like to keep on all the time), we are already the most surveilled country in the world, but zooming in on my phone map, with my location marked as a bull's-eye, and Le Boats location called up, made it easy to find, following the main road back to the bridge we crossed over in the taxi. Turning left downhill onto the canal aide road, a boat restaurant, and several smart looking "Dutch" barges, the giant versions of our little Narrow boats, plus larger cruisers, were moored on our side of the canal, a mix of small shops, a Bank and a few larger terraced houses on our left as we walked towards the next bridge about 200 yds away, this being a smaller humped bridge, cars only able to get over this from one side at a time.

The canal opens out a short distance past this bridge, which we crossed, turning down off the far side to our left into a park like area alongside a narrow channel, this being due to there being a wooded island on this side of Le Canelot, the wide basin where Le boat's local base is located towards the other end of this large basin.

Chapter 144

A lone white duck swam this channel. Opposite, just down from the bridge we had crossed, at the neck of Le Canelot basin, situated on the Quai de la Cybele, is a squat, two-story round, now scruffy white building that looks very old, now in a dilapidated condition, roof part caved in, looking as though it could have been a mill, with a large opening on its upper floor, I could imagine a block and tackle pulley set up, with swinging beam, being used to lower large bags of flour onto barges in a bygone era.

I thought it a shame the locals, be it counsel, entrepreneur, or just a well-off individual with some capital, had not been able to convert it into a smart canal side house, it not being that big, two rooms downstairs, a spiral staircase to a large upper room with a balcony, if rich, I would be tempted…

We walked two-thirds the length of the basin, finding Le Boat just the other side of a covered boat repair yard. Looking along the quay, blue and white cruisers of various sizes were moored, back end on, from the largest smoke glassed modern family-sized boats, down to what I was fairly sure was our "Capri" class boat, with its French window backed upper steering cabin. We entered the main office, the lady in charge there noting our arrival, but not willing to allow us an early departure the following morning, despite my offering to pay extra, telling us we would have to wait until late tomorrow morning as booked, presumably, too many others setting off earlier, Saturday being the main change over day.

Before leaving Le boats office, I asked if there was a cafe nearby, a building on the other side of the basin was pointed out, with a few large umbrellas outside on decking. Upon us reaching the far end of Le Caneot, before crossing the bridge there, we were able to see down the flight of four locks we would be setting off through on the morrow, this whole flight controlled and operated from what can only be described as a control tower, painted over in green and beige camouflage, the upper story with control tower windows, giving the operator a commanding view of the four locks which as mentioned, are electronically, remotely operated.

So we would then, be straight in at the deep end, with little time to get used to the boat before traversing this flight, but that was tomorrow, right then, I was spitting feathers as they say, we crossed the bridge, turning left to follow the "Avenue François Mitterrand" and the terraced houses that lined the other side of the basin, a short distance along which was L'Escapade, a patisserie come cafe, entered from the street side only. There was a gorgeous selection of pastries, I chose a large slice of glazed Tarte aux Pomme, Sarah having only coffee, me with a Cappuccino to wash down the tasty apple slice, sitting out on the decking on the basin side, the cafe having indoor and outdoor tables, the blue umbrellas we had seen from the marina set up here. After a pleasant half hour here, the sky now white over, though still warm, blissfully ignorant of what was to come, we retraced our steps and re-crossed the bridge, the road on the patisserie side turning at a tangent away from the basin.

We backtrack the same route to the town centre, re-crossing the bridge at the other end of the basin, where the Quai du Port is just wide enough to justify its name, before the canal narrows on the other side of the main road bridge, meandering northwest towards Toulouse. Passing our "hotel", we walked along the tree lined road the short distance to the town square, on the far side of which there was a building in the middle that looked as though as it served as a public meeting place or civic function room, probably both.

At the far end of this square we spotted what we were looking for, the local Spar, after checking it out that Friday tea time, I don't think we bought anything then, unless some non-perishables, but knowing it would have everything we needed to stock our boat the following morning, then back to our room for a rest, before crossing the road for a meal out at the restaurant we got our room keys from.

Both of us having something there that involved lamb, not sure beyond that, I promising we would eat out next when we reached Carcassonne, which by then we had worked out was as far as we would get before having to turn round, if we wanted to stay a full day there, which we did. Not expected at Le Boat until 11.30 next morning, we were not up that early, having time to eat breakfast served on the ground floor, (on a table), before heading to the Spar, buying enough food to last us the couple of days or so it would take to reach the walled city.

Having bought with us from home a packet of bacon and some sausages, coffee and Earl grey teabags, we bought eggs and tinned tomato. For lunch, two large baguettes, in case there was non-available en route (which turned out to be the case). Added to this, we had cooked meat, cheese, two large fresh tomatoes and a gherkin. For evening, a tin of the inevitable Cassoulet for one dinner, Confit of duck legs, plus a chilli con carne tin and rice, also some tinned veg. Whatever else happened on this boat – we would not starve…

Chapter 145

Two big shopping bags full then had to be lugged up to our room, stopping of for a coffee on the way back, with some time to kill before the fun of dragging cases food bags on top, along the half-hour walk route to Le boat, I gave us plenty of time for rest stops, Sarah agreeing with me that a taxi would have to take a very out of the way route to reach le Boat, bit of a slog, but we made it, stopping twice on a bench at the basin start, opposite that roundhouse, or what could be if renovated, and again halfway along Le Canelot, the gravel path making dragging cases harder.

When we arrived at le Boats office/depot, we joined a small queue, registering before depositing our cases and bags in racks, set up for those like us waiting for boarding, then it was lunchtime, in France, everything stops for lunch for about 1 ½ hours, the staff all leaving the building, locking up, so everyone's gear in the racks was safe, some of the staff playing Boules nearby, nothing for it but for us to wander back around to L'Escapade, the cafe we visited the previous day. This time Sarah filled her boots, with a Brie and Walnut baguette, (hard to clean out?), think I had chicken and bacon.

When finally Le boat opened for business again, we sat down round a large low table with half a dozen others, in what is best called a briefing room, a detailed map of the canal was spread on the table, but first we were told a little on safety, not to jump ashore when mooring etc. and what time the lock keepers stopped for lunch, what they did not tell us, and what took us a painful while to find out, was the use of the boat hooks, unless that bit was told only in French, these not necessary for boats manned with three or more people, this snippet would have saved us two days of near chaos at some locks, but on this large, wide canal, boats with only two aboard was rare, so the boat hooks were not mentioned then, at least in English.

While this briefing was happening, we could see that the overcast sky was starting to release rain. Then we were told our boat was ready for us, a boat worker showing us quickly around the boat controls in halting English, before leaving us to it.

Off we went, a simple forward and reverse throttle and a wheel to work with, no side thrusters as they have on larger cruisers, within two minutes, we entered the top lock of four, leaving Le Canelot basin, heading generally south east, the guy in the "control tower" must have seen us coming, the lock gate opening as we neared, we did not know it at the time, but going through on our own was to be a rare event, most times, between two to four was the norm, the lock keepers in radio communication, letting each other know if it was worthwhile waiting for a boat that might be just out of sight round the next bend.

It was to be a gradual introduction to the assault course that two older people, inexperienced in lock operation, were to encounter from the start, it was a mixed blessing having the large, four lock flight to ourselves, Sarah, with forward and aft mooring ropes in her hands, paying them out around the mooring bollards as we descended, letting go when equalised, dragging the remainder quickly round the bollards so as to keep them out of the water, coiling them up ready for "stepping" ashore with them again when I had steered us through to the next lock, securing them round the bollards before the guy in the tower opened the next gate down and we started descending again.

It very soon became evident that I would need to leave the controls of the boat and take charge of the aft rope, I just aimed the boat very slowly to a mooring spot, a brief reverse thrust to stop us, and very quickly threw the aft rope to Sarah to grab before I drifted out to pay out around the posts, she standing midway between fore and aft posts as we descended, keeping the lines just tight enough to keep our boat alongside the oval, slightly inward angled sides of these old locks, Sarah throwing me the remainder of the aft rope when equalised again, holding on to the forward rope walking with the boat as I slowly eased it through the gates into the next "Ecluse" as the French call their locks.

This is *not* how two people should navigate between locks, Sarah hanging onto the forward rope as she clambers over the lock gate, having to move away from the bank, lifting the rope over the gate railings, no one there to tell or show us the correct method, which included vital use of the six-foot-long mooring spike, that we initially used only to fend us of the canal bank when setting off…

By the time we had cleared the last of the four "Ecluses" the rain had turned into a steady downpour, the next lock, a single, we think, certainly no more than two, just in sight, Sarah, her anorak already soaked, we decided to get through this lock, then moor up, the rain not letting up, again, the gate was open, so in we went, thankful we had been seen, reported on our way by the tower no doubt, or just lucky the last boat through was heading upstream, either way, when we were through, we motored a couple of hundred yards to the next pair of wood mooring posts on our left, these sometimes few and far between, we were to discover, though we had a pair of mooring spikes aboard, Sarah having to do the majority of outside work, was as I said, already soaked. Good start…

Chapter 146

We were just about to "Batten down the hatches" against this terrible weather, when the lock keeper, a young woman (the majority were) from the next lock down, not far away, appeared, her in proper waterproofs, asking us if we would want to go through her lock, with the downpour still raging, we told her we would spend the night here, little more than a mile from where we had set off from, a little incredulous she had come out to us, but realising she must have no more traffic reported on her radio, so hoping she was finished for the day in this weather, with only a few lock keepers living in lock side houses, most, as here, finishing at 6 pm, then going home, starting again at nine am. Though only just past five, she knew she could now go home.

After Sarah had dried off, changed out of wet clothes, the boat heater drying us out and warming us, I think we had the tinned Cassoulet that eve, though we are not sure what order we ate our evening "rations" (hand to mouth?), tinned food being the quickest and easiest, this is a fair bet, plus a hot drink. We ate this accompanied by a local French radio pop station; our boat equipped with built in stereo speakers for this radio. Both tired, Sarah with the beginnings of rope burns from the last hours lock work, we read for only a short time, the rain still pouring down as it got dark, we went to bed early in the small forward cabin.

Sometime a few hours later, the aliens came to abduct us! Within a few moments of being awakened by a bright, rapidly flashing light, I got up with only underwear on, to tell them to sod off, seriously though, I had no idea where this bright flashing light was coming from, until I opened the French doors at the rear of the steering cabin, it was then I saw that a powerful light attached to the red and white lifebelt, (hooked on the wall behind the driving station) was the source of this flashing, a sensor setting this off due to the amount of driving rain hitting it, fooled into thinking it was immersed in the Canal du Midi, I saw another of these going off on another boat a few days later. Mystery over – no aliens.

For now, I put this light on its lead in a black heavy-duty black bin with the lid on. There it stayed, next to the lifebelt for the rest of this "holiday", as every time I moved it, it set off again. I had to dry myself off before returning to bed, almost wishing it had been aliens – as long as their ship was warm and dry, I soon revised that thought after warming up next to Sarah…

The next morning found the weather little improved, still raining, though not with yesterday's intensity, but not what we had pictured either. We started on our English sausage and bacon, with local bought eggs, mushroom and tomato, breakfast cheering us up. But motoring along in spring sunshine tackling just the occasional lock was not happening yet, the detailed map book issued to us, telling us otherwise anyway, locks in twos and a few threes, with only the odd single, would be appearing every half mile to a mile it looked like. You don't get to see this detailed a map till your there – wonder why…

It was rare to spend more than forty-five minutes lock free, most times we would share these large locks, always with larger cruisers, some of the largest carrying with up to eight, the average four or five, poor Sarah having to do the lion's share of rope work, I needing to steer the boat, before abandoning the wheel at the last moment to throw the aft line up to Sarah, the lock keepers not hanging about, opening the next gate to drain almost before the boats were settled, we resolved to buy some gloves when we reached Carcassonne. At midday, the locks stop operating for an hour, so after we had cleared any locks after 11.30, we would moor up in sight of the next lock. Ham, cheese and tomato or gherkin on buttered baguette our default lunch, me also on biscuits or a kit cat with my coffee or tea.

It was whilst moored at lunch here, we were told by a party of English from a large boat, that as a result of last night's stormy weather, a fallen tree was blocking the canal after the next lock. With it being Sunday, we feared no one would clear this until Monday, stranding us here, putting our aim of making it as far as Carcassonne before having to turn back in doubt. Half an hour later, two men from this large cruiser got on bikes, hired at Castelnaudary, to go and investigate this blockage, they returned within an hour saying the tree had been pushed to one side of the canal and that it was now passable, the next Lock keeper confirmed this by allowing us through, relief all round, thankful our tight-ish schedule had not suffered too badly, we would still reach Carcassonne with time for a short respite from this assault course of a "holiday".

Unlike most English waterways, there was little in the way of habitation along this canal, at least not on the section between Castelnaudary and Carcassonne, the few villages were all a good walk away from the canal. Eventually, near three pm, we moored up just past a little cafe, not far from a village called Bram on our map, though we could not see it a quarter mile or more away. This cafe, the first and only c one on our route, little as it was, a couple of tables outside, coffee, tea, wine, or bottled beer, all orders taken in the little shop, that also sold honey, jam, bottled wine, little else. Drinks, and a slice of meringue for me, I recall on our way downslope (to Carcassonne), were brought out from a private side room in this small house, an older couple running this little cafe/shop as what was likely a supplement to their pensions.

Chapter 147

Eventually we caught on to the main use for the mooring spike, after spotting others hooking the rope on the end, and holding it up to a crew member to grab on the lock side, much better than trying to throw an often wet and heavy rope up, as you were often on your way down within seconds of lining up at the lock side, you still had to be quick, but at least the chance of the thrown rope not being caught first time (as happened once or twice) was eliminated. We got more practised at this, I would have the coiled aft rope hooked, ready to offer up to Sarah to grab the second I could leave the wheel, after she had the fore line set against the post or bollard. Whilst this sounds more organised, it was all a mad rush at times, lock keepers, especially those on triple locks, opened gates so quick, two of you barely had time to set up, though sometimes "spare" crew from larger boats would take our lines, the more astute aware we were short-handed at times.

This was not the relaxed cruise I was hoping for, lulled by the thought of electric manned gates, I thought we would have plenty of time for securing our lines once in, not so, if you were the last boat in, you were doing this as you were sinking, the plug pulled out (so to speak) at the other end, the moment the gate was closed behind you, most keepers were OK, but you did wonder whether it was just efficiency, or if some secretly enjoyed watching the boat tourist being pushed hard…

I was starting to feel guilty about how much work I was effectively forcing on Sarah, she was being pushed to her limit at times with the rope work. She would not swap jobs though. I had said the electric gate system would make gate transit easy, it was not a deliberate deception to encourage her agreement to this trip, it was ignorance on my part, lulled by the electric gate system, I was also unable to find out just how many locks were involved, which turned out to be more than I had thought, only realised by me when I saw the detailed map at Le Boat's base at Castelnaudary. Prior to booking, I had looked on the net, but no maps with this many locks showed up – not good for business?

While the rain had lessened, it drizzled on and off, no sign of any blue sky, I was to learn in Carcassonne that this region was prone to bad weather, not something mentioned in the holiday brochures either, I'll bet!

After 5 pm, we decided that when we reached the next lock, we would moor up for the night, this was near a small seemingly deserted village called Villesequelande, closer than most to the canal, we decided we would stretch our legs and have a wander around, as there was finally a brighter sky that early evening. We saw no one, though no doubt we were observed through latted windows. In the small triangular village "Square" there was a monument to wartime resistance. This far south would have been in Vichy France after the "accommodation" with the Germans, but there was an invasion in the south after "Overlord" in the north, in July 1944, call operation Dragoon, opposed by Churchill, who thought the Balkans a better option, but pushed through by the Americans, though much less publicised than the D-Day landings, it went in near Toulon, supported by air from Corsica, the French resistance playing a major part in this event, thus the likely reason this village commemorated their part, and loss of life as a result. Little else there apart from a church and a small hotel near the canal– no food advertised for sale, or we might have indulged ourselves, instead of the Chilli and rice we had that evening on the boat.

We knew from the map it should only be a couple of hours boating the next morning to reach Carcassonne. After breakfasting on our home and local bought supplies on the Tuesday morning, there were only a few locks to navigate before we entered the Carcassonne basin. We followed a large cruiser into the basin, this cruiser tried several times to moor up on the left or Port side, relative to us, me cutting my speed to a crawl to keep out of his way,(and maintain mine) eventually I spotted an empty berth on the opposite side, just wide enough for our small boat to reverse into, which I managed to do without any drama, Sarah tying up on one side, a guy on the boat on our other side taking our line, tying it along with his, after watching us back in without bumping his posh boat. We then watched as the large cruiser we followed in finally managed to get moored across the other side, with help from shore parties pulling them in with their lines.

Chapter 148

As this was a major (as canals go) dock, there would be a fee for overnight mooring, in return for this, we hooked up to a power line set on a post, that also had a water feed port, something I had never seen, and needed the assistance of the female harbour master, whom was called Le Kapitan here, to explain the linkage to the unusual pressurised coupling to our hose connector, me not sure how much water we had left, but judging by the ten minutes it took to fill up at a good rate, not so much.

Our batteries charging, our water tank full, there was the most-prized thing of all still to come at this basin, a shower. Both of us wasted no time once we had paid our mooring fee, which was fourteen Euros I think, Le Kapitan, first showing us – in what looked like a much-practised routine – in English, on a town map, where we could catch a bus in the morning that would get us up to the walled city, high on a hill over a mile away from this canal basin, which was in the middle of the newer, lower part of town, not far from the railway station. After thanking her in our limited French, we returned to our boat for our shower gear, the code for access given to us by Le Kapitan to our respective shower halls, all in the same old building as Le Kapitan's office, the showers were in old white tiled cubicles, and you had to keep pressing a button to renew the flow, but it was still heaven after the last two days of basically hard work in mainly cold and wet conditions, amphibious assault course, mostly…

At the time we were there, right next to the basin, contractors were busy constructing a paved pedestrianised area right next to the basin, so getting to anywhere in lower modern Carcassonne from the Basin on our side involved negotiating temporary walkways to reach the nearby streets. Even after our showers, it was still only mid-afternoon, and feeling a little better by then, we had decided to find the large supermarket/department store Le Kapitan had marked on our Council issue map she had provided us with, whilst on the way scouting out potential eateries for the meal out I had promised Sarah for our overnight stay in Carcassonne.

Once again lightly raining, with a little sun trying, we noted a few restaurants from burger joints to posh steak houses along the route we followed, reaching Boulevard Jean Jaures, we found where we would catch the bus the next morning on this main thoroughfare, for the walled old town, we had battled to reach, (felt like) also finding the shop marked on the town map. Top of our shopping list were some gloves for rope handling, none were seen, so we ended up with rubber washing up gloves – better than nothing. Return journey food, such as diced chicken with a sauce of some sort, another large baguette, other bits and pieces, including a whisky flask sized bottle of that spirit, intended for fortifying tea and coffee on the return run, as cold and wet seemed to be the prevailing conditions around here in late May…

Retracing our steps, back to our boat, we stopped at La Rotonde, a mid-range restaurant set on a corner off our main route back along Boulevard Omer Sarrut. It was an inviting-looking place with huge, curved windows following around the corner of the intersection, (the clue being in the name). You could see a buffet selection lit up beyond tables lining the windows. We booked for 7.30, this place less than ten minutes a pied from our boat.

For the first time since arriving, it would be time to dig out decent clothes, rather than the one set of warmer clothes we had bought just in case it was not warm and had not changed out of in the last two days, such was the weather! After a hot drink fortified with a tot from the whisky we had just added to our stores, a short rest, listening to the pop station and reading a little, we pulled out from the little wardrobe our Sunday best – for this Tuesday evening's meal out, for now feeling a little more like we were on holiday, not an endurance test…

Off we went about seven, glad rags covered by our coats against the cool weather and drizzle of light rain persisting into the evening. La Rotonde was half full when we arrived, we were shown to a window table, the waiter gesturing to the buffet stand, where starters of all kinds including large prawns, pate, various vegetables including corn, which I seem to recall eating with prawns, you could fill your plate with anything from this buffet stand, Sarah having soup of some sort, followed by her French favourite Moule Frit, eaten using a Mussel shell to dig out the Moule from the rest of the shells. I had a boeuf Wellington, with vegetables added from the buffet stand, French crusty bread and butter on side plates, a bottle of the house red, a Merlot, washing this down, crème brûlée plus a slice of meringue (comfort food) selected by me from the sweet stand for desert, Sarah having just the crème brûlée.

Chapter 149

While not exactly posh, this mixture of buffet and ordered mains made us feel like we were on holiday, if tempered a little with knowing we still had the return journey to tackle, while more organised now with the mooring spike, which we now knew was most useful in proffering the rope from the boat to lock side hands, at least travelling down, where you started on the same level. The same number of locks were still to come, this time from the bottom up, so offering the rope from the end of a six-foot pole above my six foot would be a stretch, just barely reaching Sarah at the top of an empty lock, she having to kneel down, wary of falling in, to reach the pole offered rope.

All this having to be done very quickly after I had abandoned the wheel and throttle, before the boat started drifting out from which ever end of the boat I sent up the second rope, even if this small boat had had side thrusters, we had no one to operate this, you really do need three people, preferably four, one at the controls, one for lock side, one for forward and aft rope, as we saw operating on most larger craft, we had our work cut out, to say the least – but they had roped us in with no loopholes…

Before all that, after a nice meal out and a good night's sleep, so recovered somewhat, after spending only a couple of hours and having only a few "ecluses" to negotiate the previous day, we forwent an early breakfast, just imbibing hot drinks, and were ashore by Nine am, heading for the bus stop on Boulevard Jean Jaures, the bus I think due about twenty past.

The lower town of Carcassonne, on the left bank of the River Aude, is called Bastide Saint-Louis, and it is from here on the above-mentioned boulevard, we caught the No 4 bus, which took us across the Aude right up to its terminus, close to the Narbonnaise Gate of the upper Walled Town we had come to see, where we entered between two massive towers, but not before I took the first of many photos here of the inner and outer walls, these added in the 13th century. Originally built on the hill as a Roman fort back in the 1st century AD, since then occupied by the Visigoths, Saracens, Cathar involvement resulted in a siege by Simon de Montfort leading a Crusader army, which took the city, then to be handed to the French king in 1226, Saint Louis then turned it into a Royal Fortress, at the forefront of a defence line on the Franco Spanish border.

In 1355 The Prince of Wales (the Black Prince) burnt the Bastide or Lower town, when rebuilt, it was encircled by ramparts. After the Treaty of the Pyrenees (1659) now further behind the border, it lost its pre-eminence as a border crossing, woollen cloth production, followed later by viticulture, kept the city going, but by the nineteenth century, the city was being plundered as a stone quarry, but was saved by a far sighted local, and restored to its present architectural glory by Eugene Viollet-le-Duc. Both the City and the Canal Du Midi are listed as UNESCO World Heritage Sites, so, two birds with one stone, though the second is best not mentioned to Sarah without earplugs in…

After wandering around Carcassonne's cobbled streets, which these days is mainly inhabited by a tourist or heritage related small population, these working in a few hotels, gift shops, museums and a few eateries. Still in a light rain at times, we had a good breakfast in an oak beamed atmospheric eatery, then wandered some more, I took more Photos, one or two of which Sarah has since painted, (can't get it off). Architecturally, the Basilica of St Nazaire, with its impressive stained glass, and the Château Comtal, with wall sections dating back to Roman times, are two highlights among many other historical features and museums contained within this restored and well-preserved medieval marvel, some things the French do well.

This being Tuesday, we had got up early to catch the first bus up to the old city, so we could do the rounds, have breakfast, and be back down at the boat in time to get some of the way back that afternoon, as we needed to be back at Castelnaudary by Thursday evening, ready for a taxi back to the airport on Friday. Having discovered there was little in the way of home comforts to be had on this section of the canal other than where we were or Castelnaudary, we indulged in the luxury of a shower at the Basin when we made it back from the walled city, before disconnecting the battery charging line, then it was off back the way we had come, making it as far as the bridge at Villesequelande mentioned earlier on the "downslope" with its WW2 memorial.

The return "upslope" of this canal meant that making good use of the mooring spike was vital, as you now started at the base of a lock, Sarah ten foot or more up on the sloped lock sides, unique to this old passage from the Med to the Atlantic, sometimes able to walk up the side of the lock, alongside the slowly advancing boat with the forward line in hand, me trying to aim our boat to a suitable spot below bollards set above, ready with a quick reverse thrust to almost stop – so drifting in while I quickly grabbed the aft rope, put it on the spike for Sarah to haul in slowly as the boat rose in the filling lock, keeping us close to the side, which was wider at the top due to the aforementioned sloping sides.

Chapter 150

I hoped for one advantage of returning a day earlier than most, who would have their boats until Saturday, not having to catch a Friday flight as we did, was that there would be fewer boats heading back with us, most having that extra day, so hopefully less crowded locks than when we descended, the more amiable lock keepers more often able to either assist with our lines, those less so, at least paying more attention to when we were both ready for the powerful current that hit us when the big gates were opened from the lock or canal above. With only us or one more boat in the lock at once, we were more often able to moor further back from the gates, lessening the impact on Sarah having to hold the boat still against the inrush from wider opened gates by some lock keepers apparent rush to fill the lock very quickly – when faced with boats waiting their turn from both ends at times.

Not sure when we moored up that Tuesday evening, or even what we ate, not straying far from the boat knowing there was nothing worth a revisit at the local village, not needing to stretch our legs, having spent the morning wandering the walled city. We must have brought plenty of bacon with us, as Sarah handed a pack over to a German crewed boat, the crew of which had helped us at the previous lock. Wednesday was the brightest day we had on that trip, good news, as we made good progress, stopping near Bram again at the one cafe on our route, having our lunch on the boat before making our appearance once again for Cappuccino, greeted by the owners two amiable dogs like long lost friends, though they must be very used to seeing everyone twice, maybe recalling who fed them a treat on the way down a few days back.

A hard slog, but by the end of the day we were close enough to Castelnaudary to decide to stop just after our penultimate lock flight, well short of the big four flight up to Le Canelot, our base, not wanting to be crowded, so moored where there was room only for our boat, I did not want to be in a mad scramble of boats on Thursday morning to climb that last flight, as we would have the rest of the day there. We had made it back faster than going down to Carcassonne, where we could have spent the rest of that day there, setting off the next morning, but we had seen what was of interest to us, the Walled City, and there was no point in going a bit further east. I decided we would both need some down time on reaching the top and base.

So the return was a no brainer then, instead, push back up as we had, that Tuesday afternoon, then Wednesday to break its back (and ours), then give ourselves a rest, somewhere quite, within easy reach of Le Canelot basin, a plan

I'm glad we stuck to. The weather had improved, we moored up in sunshine for the first time that Wednesday mid-afternoon, sitting on the aft deck, reading, eating and drinking with the French music station on, later, I walked the thirtyish yards back to the locks we had just climbed, took a few photos as it was quite picturesque, (I had time to actually notice for a change), as was the reed bedded view from there to our moored boat, if only the rest of this trip had been this relaxed, instead, heading off on that first Saturday with many others in the increasingly worsening weather was like Wacky Races on (and in water), as was the also wet Monday up to Carcassonne.

It was only the fact that most others had another day to travel east, probably as far as Trebes before turning back, some not having to return to Le Canelot at all, able to hand the bigger boats in at Homps, another Le boat base, (not an option for our boat), which would have been much closer to the airport for our taxi back there, one way traffic from the east mostly also not needing to be at Castelnaudary until Friday night for Saturday hand over, all this making for a less crowded scramble at the locks heading back, though still hard work for two, so not sure Sarah will ever set foot on a boat again…

Thursday morning we took it easy, a slow breakfast, before setting off after ten on the half hour up to the four-lock climb at Castelnaudary, with its control tower at the top, a short wait for down cycling boats, then in with two others for the up run, getting a little help from other crew with our lines, then at Le Boat, a convenient space for me to reverse into (as at Carcassonne), and we were back, with the rest of the day to relax, not handing our boat over until Friday morning.

Chapter 151

First port of call, showers, which despite half the lights being out, was still a luxury after a couple of days without, needing some heat on tired muscles, then a stroll into town, where we booked an evening table at a Vietnamese restaurant we had spotted down a side street before setting off, though the surprised and over eager look we got gave me pause for thought, something not quite right there…

Sarah bought a bottle of red wine at the small super Marché of the same brand her daughter Sue had liked last autumn to take back for her.

Not much to see in town, but some nice big Dutch barges to see moored up on the way back, some looking like permanent houseboats there, on the wide strip beyond the western end of Le Canelot basin, me still imagining as we past it, buying and converting for living in, the historic looking, round squat half ruined tower at the junction of the above waterways, though too nearby association, to the hard grind of our undermanned boat trip for Sarah's taste, however nice the setting.

By the time we got back it was lunchtime, the weather bright sunshine now we were back, so back across the far bridge at the top of the locks to the Patisserie/cafe L'Escapade overlooking Le Canelot from its back decking for one last BLT or similar, enjoying the sun, after which I called in at Le Boat to ask them for a local taxi Number for Friday, to the Airport, the guy on the desk took the unspoken hint and called one up for us, for 11 am.

That done, we rested, read and watched the boat cleaners and other Le Boat employee's going about their work for the rest of the afternoon. Once again we put on decent cloths for our third and last meal out that evening. When we entered the Vietnamese restaurant, we were shown to a table in a nicely furnished room at the back, we were alone, at first, we put it down to being early evening, but after ordering our food, we heard several people picking up ordered food from the front reception, as we ate our food, slight variations on Chinese, it dawned on us that probably 95% of this "restaurant's" business was take away, unless, still May then, it picked up later on in the summer, the room looking forlorn now despite some nice oriental decoration, I understood then the look we got when we booked in, we may have been the first eaters in this year…

Friday morning, and our boat inspection, prior to handing it back, was a brief affair, I had slight concerns that some paint scraping near the bow on the port side might have happened on our watch, maybe scraping against a stone lock side whilst descending, we took over the boat, prow facing out with boats either side, so would not have been able to see if this scraped paint area was there then or not, but after a quick inspection, nothing was said to us, indeed we received a small fuel rebate, likely due to our early return due to Friday flights, we then had a relaxed wait for our taxi, cases on the dock behind our boat, which we did not have to leave until twelve, so were gone by then, not a cheap taxi run from there to Carcassonne Airport, but far cheaper than car and ferry, and the overnights stays that go with that.

This trip will have to be put down to experience, two not being enough crew for a boat trip involving multi locks. Norfolk Broads out of season, or even the Caledonian Canal, with its few locks at Fort Augustus is fine, but we won't be doing multi-lock canals again, not unless we are on a bigger boat with side thrusters and four crew minimum, even then too many locks defeats the object of relaxing for hours between locks. Some plans don't survive execution – with too much rope work and rain, this one did not. Con Tours, or was it Tiger Moth Airways, or maybe Ryanair got us home from tiny Carcassonne Airport. Not one of my better ideas, though Sarah was now a true sailor, with the rope burns to prove it, but not by choice, press-ganged sailors of old at least got paid…

Chapter 152

Routine once again took over, welcome after that trip, at least for a while, work was same old slog, as it is for most, this early summer turning into a drought for our grass, especially at the back as in places the soil is thin, full of stones, as I found out when I planted the apple tree in the middle eighteen months or so ago. As we are on a water meter, we decided to water our many plants only, though three buckets a week were added to our bin turned water butt from my aquarium's weekly water changes, the black bin and brown, now with the garage roof drain fed into it, soon ran out with no rain to feed it as June passed with no rain, the longest spell of unbroken sun since 76, as older readers may recall, mid-July before turned back into our usual mix, raining more at night round our way.

Soon after getting back from France, it was Sarah's birthday, celebrated with a meal out a posh country Hotel near Mold called Plas Hafod, last visited by Sarah with her art club on their annual do. Set on a hill in woodland it was a sunny, pleasant day, food OK but not special enough to recall, the big Orangery setting quite grand though on that sunny day.

I could have brought our boat's anchor back from France as a memento/birthday present, but I had not had gout for some time, and did not want it again after Sarah dropped this on my foot, the chain already wound around my neck, me then invited down to the nearest Dee estuary harbour wall for a swim…

A hairdo paid for and some minor presents were bought instead.

Not long after, before my birthday at the end of July, I had thought about the fact that next year was a decade birthday for Sarah, being a little older than I, and after the last trip that was too much hard work to be called a holiday, I decided to plan something special for next year, we had just received the brochure (being on their client list) from the holiday company we had done both Croatia trips with. In amongst their more exotic options I spotted something that might just appeal to Sarah.

Wilbur Smith used to be on Sarah's extensive list of regularly read authors, those who know him will be aware most of his books are set in Africa, Sarah liking the wildlife background in these stories, and wildlife in general. Denied the Safari trip years ago after her whiplash injury, when we settled for Thailand, older as we are now, I hope I have found us a less arduous, but still interesting trip she seems to like the idea of. Hope so, as I have now paid a deposit for next May – for a Cape town and Garden Route escorted tour, incorporating a stay in a Game Lodge with four Game drives included, so wildlife from penguins to elephants all being well, this book hopefully done by then, if I find a publisher.

Meanwhile, I had spent less of my time on the road at work this last summer, instead, after some basic training, spending more time in the repair room of our base. Having demonstrated that I will always be found working, my boss Phil lets me determine my base work schedule, leaving me to get on with it unless he wants something specific doing at any time, this a good idea as I cannot always get access to some operational equipment due to production work, so I juggle this work as required.

I have to remain vague as to my exact workplace, as with relatives, I do not want intrusion or media contact here, in the unlikely event that this narrative reaches sale in any numbers, due to the perceived Oddball content of some of the book. Should it become one, however logically I try to state mine and others observations, many will not consider beyond what is not easily seen. Others may use ridicule to hide their fear – that we may not be top dog. Still others use ridicule or worse due to knowing we are not.

On politics I will stay linier with my observations, the summer of 2018, providing little beyond the ambush of Boris and other Brexiters, forcing him to resign, the craftier of this camp "remaining" in cabinet, signed up to Chequers to try to mitigate the depth of surrender to the EU, though they must know this will not pass the commons, the EU as always ignoring what "negotiate" means, as long as it thinks it has enough witting or unwitting fifth columnists in our ranks. Using the Irish government to forestall any agreement is a blessing in disguise for Brexiteers, though the EU does not think so. I will update my take on major unfolding events of Brexit until such time as this narrative goes to print.

At time of writing, I still predict a realignment of political parties along the lines of Cavaliers and Roundheads if May fails, or does a Chamberlin, as is looking likely, to do a deal with an EU elite who does not want one without our surrender to their laws. The reason we voted out in the first place, they don't care about continental job losses, ours they want, only their removal by a radical new German government would see any change there, though present EU policies are making the current French, as well as German governments look increasingly fragile, next year could well be very explosive, a No Deal being the trigger…

Chapter 153

Back with my little life, and though next year's South Africa booking meant we would have no week-long holiday late this year, to help save for this, we decided on a trip to Southport, in August, with a one-night Bed (not breakfast) at the Captain's Table, located near the pier, which we enjoy walking down.

We got up early, to make the most of the day, the weather looking good, we decided to stop at Scarisbrick Marina, where the Leeds Liverpool canal meets the A570, not to far short of Southport, and have breakfast there, in the Bridge Tea Rooms, stopping there again for the following morning's breakfast on our way back, such was the pleasant location, sat looking at dozens of narrowboats moored and passing through there, chatting with someone with a boat there, who had also done the Canal Du Midi, though I think with more crew than two, Sarah listening, saying little, beyond brief comments, now set against canal trips a little, this spot being a world away from that trial.

Soon after we had got together, many moons ago, we did a day trip to Southport, walking miles down its massive beach in the baking sun, I could swear I saw a camel train in the distance, such is the expanse of sand there when the tide is out, might have been a mirage, I may have mentioned this earlier, but memories of that day left us with a wish to return from time to time, this time only walking the pier, not the beach, giving us time to walk the majority of Lord Street, with its many book shops, and a massive Junk/Antiques emporium that seemed to go on forever, loads of fun, feet aching, we rested at the Captains Table late afternoon before eating at the Empire Restaurant on Nevill St, a Chinese restaurant that also does buffets (Dim Sum), this time sitting down to a proper evening meal there. So an enjoyable, if brief change of scenery for us at the height of summer.

A week is a long time in politics, as I write now, in mid-November, Teresa May has agreed a Draft deal with the EU, Fisheries, Agriculture and Immigration, looks OK, but having no unilateral say on leaving EU customs union rules, transition trade or the Northern Ireland "Backstop" border, means we will pay, but have no say, so I very much doubt this will pass the Commons vote. Dominic Raab has proved honourable, quitting, not able to rubber stamp this "Deal" without a get out clause, not sure what Mr Gove is up to, refusing to do the same, but staying on the inside as I write this…

We *have* to be prepared to play tough, to get the EU's attention on self-determination, the silent (little people majority) the people, media pay no attention to – except when *they* finally *had* their people's vote, people like me, I will update my take here on developments as long as possible, until (publication?).

Dropping back to late August, and the drought we had in the first half of summer meant we had to buy and spread about ten bags of compost soil over the worst of the dead patches of grass where the soil is thinnest, put fresh grass seed in. After a month, most of the back grass is green again, we will finish small patches in the spring.

One more trip to mention, unless it takes a very long time to get this to print, so then, knowing we would not be doing any winter trips like Iceland, whilst saving for South Africa, Sarah agreed a two-night stay in Pembrokeshire, a part of Wales we had not seen. Having watched a mini-series about Tenby, I had thought it a good idea for a mini break, in the end booking two nights in the Fishguard Bay Hotel, which sounds grand, but was no more expensive that most B&Bs in the area. This hotel is situated in Goodwick, not far from the terminal for the Rosslare, Ireland ferry, which we saw once as we arrived. The hotel, is a Victorian mock castle-looking building, set up on a hill in its own woods above and back from the terminal approaches.

Booked in early September for the end of the month, it was soon upon us, set for a Friday and Saturday night. I booked the Thursday off work to cut front and back grass, water change three buckets in the aquarium, also not wanting to do the long drive without being a bit rested. A friendly neighbour agreeing to put fresh cat food and water out on Saturday, to go with the large amount of dried food also out. Cats you can leave for a couple of days, with a cat flap in the conservatory, so in and out as they please.

Chapter 154

All packed by Thursday night, we were ready for an early get up and go, with just a hot drink to wake us up, planning to eat breakfast on the way down, the first of two stops I expected to have to break the journey. Starting not bad, the weather deteriorated as forecast as we headed south on the A494 towards Bala, where we hoped to Breakfast. Passing Bala lake (Llyn Tegid), we found a cafe on the main road in town, still only 9-ish, it was chucking it down, but was only a short hop across the road, a medium cooked breakfast, for me, small for Sarah, a cuppa fuelled us up for the day, the cafe at that time – catering for mums having dropped their kids off at school, infants in tow while we were there. Back on the road then, with more than ¾ of our journey yet to do.

Bad as the weather was, it was forecast to be sunny the next day, our one full day down there, which I planned to make the most of, for now it was convoy traffic, something I was used to by now on my A41 work runs down to the West Midlands. A Brief left turn at Dolgellau onto the A470, then south, joining the A487, which stretches along much of the Welsh west coast, with thoughts of stopping at Aberystwyth for a coffee break, but after following the winding road, passing through Machynlleth, before eventually reaching the coast at Aberystwyth, we decided not to leave the main road, so not reaching the seafront, as the 487 turns south before then.

Not wanting to lose that much time for a pit stop there, we carried on along what was soon the coast road of Cardigan Bay, past a few holiday caravan and camping sites, the weather slowly brightening up, until we reached Aberaeron, which has a small, pretty harbour, here we bought coffee from the take-away on the car park, strolling round to the toilets a hundred yards away, the rain almost stopped now, still very breezy, us needing to stretch our legs anyway.

Refreshed, windy as it was on the coast there, we continued, now south west, the road leaving the coast heading now to Cardigan, the last major town before Fishguard, crossing the Afon Teifi on the Priory Bridge, Cardigan Castle away to our right, Sarah now had a sore throat, coming on since breakfast at Bala. We reached Fishguard Bay, crossing the small single passing Afon Guaun Bridge at the lower town, a small picturesque harbour village, with our destination hotel, impressive looking, set high enough up on the hill to be in sight across the bay in Goodwick, well above the ferry terminal as mentioned.

The ferry was docked as we arrived, after driving up through Fishguard proper, then down along The Parrog, the coastal strip between Fishguard and

Goodwick, out from which a long mole reached out into the Bay, likely used in the past for ferries, not big enough for today's Rosslare bound larger ship.

After rising up from the Parrog, we turned right, entering the wooded approach road and car park of our hotel, grand looking in its Victorian mock castle style, but as I said, no dearer than most local B&Bs, so why not? It was around Two PM when we checked in, our room on the first floor overlooking the Bay, which I admit to paying a little extra for, going the whole hog as it was too nice a setting to not have that view. Sarah's sore throat, that and the journey had made her tired enough that she wanted a rest.

Surprisingly, probably to it now being clear blue skies, I felt I wanted to get some fresh air, despite the long drive, so decided to go back as far as Fishguard Lower town, Sarah, having a kip, for an hour she said, I left her to it, driving back through the main town, down to the Bay inlet where the Afon Guaun, little more than a stream, ran into, a car park right next to the bridge, which I turned into, buying an ice cream, such was the weather here now, strolling along Quay Street, a few houses and a cafe, with a ramp into the inlet which was home to a few small boats, our hotel visible set in its woods across the bay a good mile away.

Wanting to stretch my legs a little more, I walked across the narrow bridge, turning onto a path leading upstream alongside the Afon Guaun, walking around two hundred yards or so, admiring nice gardens of houses opposite, before turning back when I reached what looked like a recently fallen big tree straddling the river, I had stretched my legs enough, returning to the hotel, finding Sarah awake in our room, we went down to the bar, ordered tea, and sat outside in the late afternoon sunshine, the ferry now gone from the terminal below.

We talked of our plans for Saturday, planning to drive across Pembrokeshire to Tenby, then Northwest from there to St Davids, before completing a rough triangle back to Fishguard, assuming the weather turned out bright and dry as forecast. It did, after a buffet breakfast in the hotel, we set off in sunny weather around half nine, on to the A40 south towards Haverfordwest, as we only had this one full day down here, we had to pick out "highlights" of the peninsular we could visit in one day. Tenby was first on our list, so starting farthest away meant crossing from north to south, the A40 covering most of this, pleasant rolling countryside, past a few villages and holiday parks, took us to the outskirts of Haverfordwest, where we followed the A40 on its turn east, as far as short run on a B road to Narberth, where turning south again, the A478 took us down to Tenby, passing close to a small village called Stepaside, which we side stepped...

Chapter 155

Tenby on TV shows little more than the seafront, a quintessential pretty holiday harbour town, the likes of which are much more prevalent in Devon and Cornwall, not so much in Wales, so there it stands out a little more, much painted and photographed, I took a few from a good vantage point myself, we wandered down around the harbour area, before doing the main shopping street, picking up no more than a fridge magnet, Sarah finding an art shop, having a discussion with the self-important sounding owner (her view as well) over background painting techniques, me finding one not bad sunset picture that was well overpriced, Sarah saying afterwards she would not have been happy if I had bought it, the rest of his shop full of fields of flowers type paintings, I was not impressed, we came away with nothing.

Finding our way over the other side of the quaint old town, down to the beach, and a cafe where we sat out in the sun with a coffee for a while, before window shopping our way back to the car, heading out of town about two hours after arriving along the coast on the A4139, which took us up to the county town of Pembroke, situated on one of the inner arms of Milford Haven Waterway, leading to the short Pembroke river, the impressive castle of that name visible on our left before we turned north to cross the river there, the much larger toll bridge crossing the main Milford Haven Waterway at Nayland next, exploring that vast waterway network would be nice week on its own, from a boat or car, though not for the time we had here, but filed away for possible future reference…

So we pressed on back up to the western side of Haverfordwest this time, the signposting a little lacking at times on some of the roundabouts, not keen to point the way to St Davids, until we finally reached the bottom end of the A487, the road that had brought us all the way down from Dolgellau where we had joined it, reaching all the way up to Caernarfon. Down here it would take us via St Davids, on the western peninsular of Pembrokeshire, back up to Fishguard.

By now it was early afternoon, and having had an early breakfast, we decided in advance we would have a good lunch somewhere, rather than a heavy evening meal, so we initially picked out Newgale on the map, as the first place the road reached the coast, but when we reached it we found it well named, somewhat windswept, the one pub not looking inviting, we had spotted Solva on the map situated at the neck of an inlet a few miles on, so we carried on, reaching this village around half one. Here there was a busy pub called the Harbour Inn which specialised in fish and chips, which is what I had promised Sarah we would have on that full day out, and so we did, large fish, Sarah on mushy peas, me on un mushy, chips OK, sitting outside, the inlet sheltered from the wind that swept Newgale, not a cheap meal these days, but enjoyable in the sun, with a small craft beer for me, cider for Sarah.

Now well-fed, we headed on into St Davids, officially the smallest city in Britain, the Cathedral responsible for that status, the city's actually a small town, pleasant enough to wander around in the sun, I managed a good photo of the Cathedral, with its gold-painted window arches and tower spires, the Bishops Palace in the background, having not long since had lunch and a little beer, we did not stop long, not being religious, just as well, as we had no rugby ball available for conversion, which we Mitre kicked into touch (my idea of a hat trick)… and so headed back to Fishguard Lower Town – where I had gone for a walk while Sarah rested the previous day. It is pretty if very small, a hamlet really, we were ready by then for a cuppa in the cafe there, after which we walked along the little river I had strolled alongside the day before, before returning to the hotel, I took a photo of the inlet with its few boats, zoomed so our hotel looks quite large, visible in the background across the bay.

Having had a hearty fish and chips lunch, neither of us wanted a large dinner, so we stopped off on The Parrog on the way back to the hotel at a small supermarket and bought sandwiches for later, after a rest and a read in our room, we had our sandwiches, a cuppa, watched a little telly, then later went down to the hotel bar, Guinness with a Whisky chaser, for me, a couple of G and T's for Sarah, no more for me, as I had the long drive back in the morning, which, as with the trip down, in reverse, turned progressively wetter the further north we went, so we only stopped once, a few miles north of Machynlleth, more than halfway home, at King Arthur's Labyrinth, for a coffee, and a wander around the Corris Craft Centre also located there, on the A487, with its underground boat ride, it is an attraction in its own right, but not for us that day, a walk around the craft shops stretched our legs enough to resume our drive home. A good break. Bracketed on the way down and back by rain, but dry and sunny on our whistle stop full day trip around what I will call the Pembrokeshire Triangle of Fishguard, Tenby and St Davids.

Chapter 156

Back to work for me, though three days a week is hardly purgatory, the first being the worst, if I am not on the road for most of it, just being on my feet all day after four days off is enough to remind me I am starting to get old, though many will tell me deservedly, it could be worse, five day weeks and or shifts being the norm for most until sixty five plus these days, no kids being the price paid for opting out of the above, but a chance of more of anything like my childhood is not a risk I was willing to take for any child of mine, being as I had been given the choice, for reasons gone into earlier.

There is an antiques shop/cafe on the A541 at Afon Wen between Mold and Denbigh, just south of Caerwys where we used to have our static caravan, which we make periodic visits to, months apart, making the occasional purchase, buying a set of eight small painted engravings of Welsh scenes of the time, dated 1830, which was bought to hang on our caravan walls, but which now hang in our conservatory, I have no interest in trading antiques, but have an eye for anything of age that will look OK in our small bungalow, where space for such is very limited, as I am cautioned by Sarah, who does not like clutter.

However, having bought with her a nice brass fire grating that fits in front of our modern electric fire (not used) on a nice marble plinth and surround, I had a while back, since bought at Afon Wen, a pair of brass "Fire Dogs" that stand in front of said grating, the purpose of these, in times gone by, is to lay a fire poker and tongs across these, ready to stoke or add to your coal fire, I found brass tongs at Afon Wen, after a brief search, found a reasonably matching poker in Denbigh to make the setup, or so I thought. But on a recent, visit to Afon Wen, just for a look around on a wet day off, not on the lookout for anything, upstairs amongst the furniture and tea sets, I spotted a large decoratively made brass fire guard, not wanting trouble, I said nothing to Sarah, but noted the 47-inch length written on its ticket, upon returning home, I measured the length of the lintel sides, 46½ inches, so the sides of the guard would not quite fit down the sides, or would they?

One of our engineers at work might be able to cut a quarter inch of the sidepieces to make a snug fit, so I bought this fireguard. Like the firedogs, poker and tongs, I do not know its age, but all are pitted, looking well used, so a mixture anywhere from Victorian up to early 1970s bought from house clearances at a guess. That night I had a thought, (I do occasionally), this fireguard has no supporting spars connecting the front to the sides to hold it rigid! So I got up in the middle of the night to test my theory – that the length of the guard might give enough play in it to stretch the sides enough to reach around the lintel sides, yes it did! A snug fit, a couple of inches down each side meant the front fitted a perfect ½ inch short of the plinth edge, the tension now holding it in place, so no need to take it to work…

Whoever made this guard was either an apprentice or drunk, as the central decorative section was welded on at an off angle to the line of the base section, but this just added character to it, Sarah, now a little worried that I would (in her words) have the place looking like *Steptoe and Son's* house by the time I was finished. I had to assure her I will buy nothing else of this nature, as I can see we have no more room. But with a Brass Neck like mine…

I have also promised I will clean all this brass once a month, as I knew her ex had her cleaning brass he used to buy, and I am not going to bring back those sort of memories for her. I have, and will stick to that promise, just having done so this morning.

Almost up to date now, November Brexit latest having the EU leaders rubber stamping the "Deal" that would keep us permanently in their customs union, until they say otherwise, and us paying for the privilege, but it is the N I Backstop, which they have no interest in solving, as it keeps us under their control, that should see it defeated in the Commons, unless Project Fear Two, works on all the various factions in parliament, the DUP, Scots Nat's, Labour, plus Brexiteers, an unholy alliance yes, but it looks like an almost impossible sell for their various different reasons, this deal, OK *but* for the Backstop, which will not get voted through, despite all the fanfare in Brussels, with warnings from there the deal is complete, with no more amendments.

We will see, if no deal is on the cards, and if as likely, it is voted down in *our* Parliament. As usual, the "impartial" *BBC*, in its "analysis" of the agreement, made sure not to mention this Backstop tie in on Sunday, neither did Mrs May's open letter on this "deal", so disingenuous to say the least, but no one in parliament is fooled by this crucial "Achilles Heel" section of the legally binding *draft* deal, as that is *all it is* until we agree to it.

Chapter 157

Back to more domestic matters for now, and whilst leaving my house less than two weeks ago, I saw a Council work crew starting to chop a big pine tree in someone's front garden that was becoming unsafe, or too near street lights. When I returned less than an hour later, I could see a pile of four foot long log sections, I went home and told Sarah that if they would let me have a few of those sections, I would hollow them out and make planters of them, lining them up along our hedge, where the ground is too rocky to dig a soil border. We had put three plastic planters there, to take the bareness off, but had moved them up to the Arbour corner, to add to the three already there, making a continuous line behind the low border fence there, while I cut the hedge some time back, and had never moved them back as they look better behind the low corner border fence.

Sarah, looking a little dubious, agreed. My first thought being I would need an axe as I walked back down to the tree felling operation, just in time, they had a large shredder wagon, and were in the process of feeding chopped sections into it, I asked the guy in charge for three of these four foot sections, telling him of my plans for them, and a little to my surprise, he agreed, instead of quoting some council regs that prevented him. If you don't ask, you don't get!

I nipped back home, brought my hatchback back down, and was helped by a younger man, to carry three heavy logs into the lowered back seat section of my car, thanking them, I got a surprised Sarah to help me carry them the short distance into the garage. But everything comes with a price, even if it is not immediately obvious, the price for these came as we were putting the last log into place, I said to Sarah, 'Drop it there,' meaning her end, blocked from our view, "there" turned out to be my right big toe! Which was duly squished, over a week later I am still not sure, now the blood had dried, the bruises fading from black, whether I will lose my nail or not, as more than half of it has dried blood underneath…

Undeterred, blooded but unbowed, this last weekend I bought a small chainsaw, as cheap as hiring one for a day as it turned out, meaning eventually to go back to Texas to mop up any survivors from the chainsaw massacre there, in revenge for my toe mashing, (anyone's fault but mine) as long as they tell me where to plug in my lead, and then stay still for some armless fun, before then getting legless…

But for now, I spent two hours of Saturday afternoon, with the garage door shut, to minimise the noise for neighbours, digging out the first of the planters, cutting a line six inches in from each end at an angle in, so that when I cut the same line in about eight inches across the top of the log, also at an angle in, the two cuts eventually met, two thirds deep into the log, taking out a long triangular wedge section, plus lots of sawdust, after also cutting into both ends, leaving a space big enough for daffodils, then summer plants. Hard work for an older, fairly unfit man, so I plan to do one more log next weekend, the last the weekend after, then logoff…

Sarah tells me January/February is about right for Daff bulbs to start growing, and so give off some light in the dark winter months… where do you put the batteries?

Update, early December now, logged on and off twice more, meaning I have now hollowed out all three logs I rescued from the shredder, one each weekend as planned, as it is quite a workout for an old man. All I have left to do on my next "Log on" is to chop the wedge-shaped sections I have cut from the logs into six equal-sized pieces, turned bark side down, a shallow V-shape cut into each section, two of these under each planter will raise them slightly off the ground, giving them a look a shade less Rufus Roughcut hopefully. (A *Wacky Races* character – for younger readers, if there are any…)

Chapter 158

Meanwhile, Sarah's art seems to be on an upward curve, though she will deny that, but since joining a local art club, new perspectives (pardon the pun) in different techniques has seen her branch out from acrylics, into collage and latterly, pastels. Benefiting from interaction with other members and occasional tutorials from visiting artists, Sarah has just recently sold her first work on display with other club pictures, at a local coffee tasting room/lounge. This picture, a collage of a harbour scene, with a subtly clever 3-D effect added. Not a surprise it sold to me. Now able to work with pastels, she has just finished both a portrait of her granddaughter, and a strikingly colourful picture of some hens she keeps.

Also in her recent portfolio of pastels is a seasonal (autumnal at that time) drawing of her own composition of teasels and trailing ivy, in an earthenware jar, with a red berry sprig, a chestnut and pine cones laid out in front, another, to me, easily saleable picture I would want to keep here.

Along with this, she has done a classy pastel rendering of a display set up at her club, of a wine bottle and glass with strawberries in front, all set to a blue background, this to be offered to my brother and his wife, who is fond of the odd glass, when we meet at Christmas. To my untrained eyes at least, she is fast becoming, what Sarah would describe underwhelmingly as "a competent artist".

December 8th, the eve of the "Meaningful" Brexit vote (that backfired spectacularly on those who dreamed it up, didn't it) and as usual the EU and their fifth columnists, (witting and unwitting), here, are up to their expected tricks, confident that their propagandists, the *BBC* have and will give maximum airtime to these. All their alternatives from "Norway Plus" the worst of all options, to the European courts (who usually take forever) who are suddenly and conveniently able to come up with a ruling the day before the Vote, that we can revoke article 50 if we want to, still don't get it, do they…

When our MPs reject this deal, which from what I see is OK without the backstop, I get the feeling Mrs May might actually be wanting this, despite appearances, as she can then go back to the Brussels Sprouts, and tell them, "Drop the backstop, or get No Deal, and no 39 Billion – that ought to do the trick… Going to be an interesting week – watch this space. Unbeknown to me, even as I was writing the above Mrs May had pulled Tuesday's Vote, certain to be defeated, by Friday as I continue writing after my three-day working week, the above-aborted (for now) vote was enough to push the No Confidence letters above forty-eight. She then won her Vote to remain in charge, her majority mainly from those MPs in government jobs, so vested interest votes, but the Brussels Sprouts will not budge on the backstop until forced to. Our prime Minister May have been too trusting of her senior civil servant negotiator, who might want to collaborate and remain too close to the EU, she will now have to steer a steady course close to the wind and be ready for No Deal, if the EU entity tries (as usual) to put its interests above those of its member states, which it has a track record of doing."

Writing in mid-February 2019 now, and all the usual suspects have tried all the tricks they can to derail Brexit. The one Ace Mrs may has with her rebels MP's – is to threaten them with a general election – the nuclear option, and they know it, many betraying their own constituents Brexit wishes, maybe now a little in fear of this comeuppance, as now are some Labour MP's, also inviting deselection.

Monday 18th February, and what many including myself have been predicting for months is finally starting to happen. Seven Labour MP's have left the party, and with many more facing deselection, I expect more to rid themselves of the yoke of the hard left bullies that now control this party. Some from the conservatives may even join them in a Remainer alliance. Writing again on the 22nd February, three now ex-Conservative MP's (at last count) have now joined the Dodo Alliance. I am sure Mrs May misses Anna Soubry already… At least their constituents will know what they stand for at the next election…

Meanwhile, we are looking forward to our next adventure – South Africa in May (2019). Getting near the end of this story now – waiting for publisher responses, got to stop somewhere, thought it might be Brexit result, but that is being dragged out, just as the EU intended – got to set an example for others… Just thought I would mention that “Sarah” has now sold her second painting – so that is two sales in two exhibitions, if my writing does as well, I’ll be happy…

Chapter 159

Brexit break now – If I were to make a post-apocalyptic film – all the letters & parcels would go to the wrong addresses. No joke this – when I get my boat, from sails of this book, it would not have sails, instead it would have two masts set up like those rural road signs – one with solar panels & one with a ribbon wind turbine. The power generated going straight to big enough batteries to include overnight wind power storage to drive an electric engine. No tacking sailing for me, bought a garden sundial today, thought I would wait until British summer time so I did not have to adjust it. Not very good though – only works when not cloudy, should have got one with a battery. I recently watched an Indian rope trick – invited to climb the rope, now ten foot high – they had to call the fire brigade when I got stuck at the top. Late March 2019 now, Mrs May is still unable to get her tied into customs union Brexit deal through, might try next week if she thinks it will pass under pressure from the EU – who have reset our leaving date to April 12, if deal not passed, May 22nd if passed. MP's still trying to get control of leaving terms. Be interesting to see how inflexible the EU remains if April 12th approaches and no deal looms. I for one cannot wait to finally escape the European Onion (not misspelt) as like an onion, the more you peel away the layers – the more tears! Of course by the time this gets published these events will all be history – though if no Brexit is delivered, or we are still tied to the EU with a soft Brexit, the nation will give its verdict in the next general election, (it had not yet happened) at the time of writing this, Mrs May's position is looking more fragile than ever. Rather than being forced out early, she may yet go to the country, despite or because Boris has asked her not to – with her in charge. As I said, this will be history by the time it is read. As I and many have said – re alignment of political parties is long overdue, I for one will be surprised if it has not happened by the end of this year, I expect now to not be adding to this narrative beyond the end of March 2019 – but you never know. Many readers will have a very different view on this contentious subject, which I respect – but as the writer, I can only give my view, born from my experiences, as your views might remain your own, from your perspective.

I was at my local barbers the other day, he chatting with the guy before me, telling him he used to work on road maintenance when younger – repairing pot holes. A bit later with me in the chair, he told me he was in a choir – like many in Wales. I pointed out to him that his earlier work must have given him perfect pitch – expecting a cutting remark, he said he would give me that one. Meanwhile, we are looking forward to our next adventure – South Africa in May 2019.

Turned out OK – though not impressed by the shanty towns still surrounding major cities. Many years after majority rule, it seems corruption at the top is still stifling progress for many. Saw a bit of wildlife, cheetah chasing impala, hippo and a pair of elephants, but it was two people on our coach that stopped this trip from being a little boring, Dale & Suzanne having the same sense of humour as myself – EG, when asked by our guide how we found the Cango caves near Cape Town, I piped up – "just at the top of the steps", got a few laughs, from those not yet fossilised on the coach. So much for the land of penguins & elephants... (saw a few of both).

Getting near the end of this story now – waiting for publisher responses, got to stop somewhere, thought it might be Brexit result, but that is being dragged out, just as the EU intended – got to set an example for others... Just thought I would mention that "Sarah" has now sold her second painting – so got that is two sales in two exhibitions, if my writing does as well, I'll be happy. On a recent work van run, I heard a road traffic warning on the radio of an accident several times at the junction of the A380 & A38 in Devon south of Exeter, genuinely called – Splatford Split! Hope this was not named after a previous accident. Mid-April now, it seems Nigel Farage has come back as he said he would if a real Brexit was not delivered. Polls suggest that if we are not out of our EU shackles by May 23rd, his new Brexit party will wipe the floor with May & Corbyn's MP's betrayal of the referendum result. Unfortunately, I suspect the top priority of our current parliament majority – self-interest, terrified of the EU elections, could well see a soft Brexit pushed through before then. If that happens, I hope Boris, if in power, maybe with Nigel's help, will find a way of correcting this – unilaterally if necessary, or by means of an early general election, with hopefully re-aligned parties. I told Andy, our works engineer, that whilst working in his Machine room, I was inspired to come up with a faster than light drive – or FLT, I said they almost had it right on Star Trek, my version was "Swarf drive", this got a LOL from Andy. (Swarf being the name given to metal shavings). 17th April 2019: I must be a bit psychic – I had a hunch there would be a fire at Notre Dame. It was The Bells, I should have stuck to Glenmorangie, sorry Esmeralda, but you got my back up. The Ramblers Association talk too much – and yes I should have been a founder member. Walked into that one. Not yet got the first proofs of my manuscript back from my publishers, who have said until this is returned by me, I may still add a small amount – at their discretion to edit, to the end of my book, so – politics again – Farage, as I hoped, did wipe the floor with established parties in EU elections we should never have been in, and now holds the sword of Damocles over the Conservative party, to elect a leader that will take us out – or face destruction at the next general election. This new leader MUST be perceived by the EU to be genuine in the threat to leave under WTO rules if they try to stick to May's dead con of a deal, indeed no effort should be made to talk to them until they come to us – or not, in October, that would be my stance, with 39 billion Euro (That could be used to bail out worst affected businesses) withheld until they want to talk. Bought & knocked together a large raised planter for the rough hedged side of the back garden, now full of fuchsia's & other flowering plants, the ground so full of stones as mentioned before, so raised a planter being the only way forward. Good to see Gove got his comeuppance for pulling the rug on Boris at the last leadership election, and the subsequent result of an attempted cave in to the backstop trick – and has now been put in the front line of any no deal Brexit by Boris, who seems to be saying all the right things to date, put some good people in the right places – lets hope enough Labour MP's in strong leave continuances are too scared of an election (where a significant number of voters might vote Brexit Party under the current Labour leadership's sitting on the fence policy) to not back a no confidence vote – though the date of any election is of course down to Boris. Wrong time of year I know, (October now) but for a winter garage project, I bought another flat pack, this time a 6' x 3' two foot deep raised wooden pond, which when finished, I managed to lay fairly even with the aid of my spirit level (with a new bubble of course...).

Mainly for plants, next summer, but may put about four small goldfish in, not wanting to install pumps & filter – just rely on a large solar fountain for water movement, and plenty of oxygenating plants to keep it healthy.

Chapter 160

Mid November now, Boris has managed to remove the backstop, though with complications not acceptable to the DUP. He has also got rid of the remainer hard core in his party, and has at last brought about the inevitable General Election. If only Gove had given Boris his chance three years ago, and spared us this pain, maybe he was not ready then, but all the signs are he is now. After all Nigel Farage has done to get us out of the EU, he now finally had the sense to pull out of the Tory constituencies at least, but should now concentrate only on Labour remainer MP's whose voters voted leave, but would (I thought) never vote Conservative, these are his core opportunities, so not hurting the chances of a strong majority being returned for Boris, who now has a strong committed team to work with. This will all be history if & when read, but at time of writing I am hoping for the will of the silent majority to return to this country its referendum choice, despite all attempts to hold it to ransom by an unholy alliance of self-evident anti-democratic parties. We will see within the month... And so it came to pass – Nigel having done the decent thing withdrawing all candidates from Tory held seats, enough to give Boris a commanding majority, and leave the Brexit party with none, a sacrifice I hope will be recognised sometime soon. This 2019 Christmas will be remembered as Brexmas, by all those like myself breathing a huge sigh of relief that democracy finally put the reds back under the bed, and the BBC and the EU on notice. Lets hope he can deliver on his promises and justify the lent votes he has been entrusted with, go for it Boris. Got shunted on a work run, hit at the back by another van, not quite hard enough for whiplash, but enough to give me a headache for a couple of days. Other driver's insurance soon owned up, so work OK about this, just left me looking at my mirrors a little more often... One of my work colleagues went off to visit family in Australia just before Brexmas. Unlike me & Notre Dame, he does it seems – have a burning ambition, as soon after he arrived, all the raging fires down under joined together to make bigger firestorms, it may just be coincidence, but lets not beat about the bush, he is returning as I write this early in the new year, I expect with no suntan, a little lighter – if you know what I mean. If convicted by a kangaroo court, he would have been sentenced to hard labour in the UK, so not scot free then... Booked a trip to lake Garda for this July with an excursion to Venice included, before it sinks hopefully. A bit of sun, but not enough to make a Venetian Blind. Finally, for those not appreciating my dafter bits of narrative in this tome, as above, I offer up in my defence an incurable condition I am cursed with called – Humouroid Author-writeus of the funny bone...

2020 – Lockdown, I leave to many others to describe...

Adrian Lincoln

As promised, at the end of this narrative, for the more inquisitive, I have compiled a timeline of events in this world, in an Addendum, that mostly have never made it to the mainstream news, or briefly, long ago, this is also the Oddball part of my narrative. I have chosen these events from many as they have stood the test of time, all have multiple witnesses and or have left physical or other evidence such as radar logs behind. If just one of these events is true, then heaven help us, as so much else must be kept hidden from the general population of this planet. Revealed over the years by painstaking investigative work by many, some mentioned in this selection below. I salute them all (except the hoaxers, who muddy the waters), including the myriad brave witnesses able or unable to testify, who are not mentioned here, to a world that may be far stranger than is publicly acknowledged.

I only compile a summary of the above here – to help further the cause of those who have unearthed or witnessed any of the events listed below. These are only the bare bones I point out – for you who have busy lives and had little time for such, but might wish to look a little deeper…

Addendum

A TIMELINE OF STRANGE EVENTS

Before I go into the highlighted summary of what I have learnt over the years, first I want you to consider the logical progression that guides what I think may be possible from the collated reports and testimonies I highlight below –

> We, our current "visible" civilisation, have had electric-based technology for less than 150 years.
> What will we be doing in 1000 years if we survive that long, let alone 10,000 years, or 100,000?
> Where will we be in terms of space travel on the above timescales?
> Many millions of stars in our galaxy similar to ours are older than our own sun, so also their planets.
> Unlike popular Science Fiction, the odds against a nearby civilisation being at almost the same level as us is highly unlikely, given the eons of time difference in Steller development.
> For this reason, I fear SETI is barking up the wrong tree…
> Therefore – logically – many civilisations, if only one in a thousand of these stars produce one, should have a head start on us measuring thousands, if not millions of years in some cases.
> So the real question to me should be, not what might we be doing by the above timescales, but – what are some of them likely to be doing, and why not here?

A table, at the end of the following "highlights", outlines known facts followed by scenarios extrapolated or recounted as claims from "whistle blowers".

You and I must try to make sense of what is known and what might be known…

Some of the following events have verifiable documented evidence, most are a result of dedicated investigative work by many authors over the last seventy years. I will below recommend books or just the names of interesting people to search out online, some of which I have mentioned earlier, but collated here along with others. If, after reading and verifying online some of the events highlighted here, you are still convinced there is nothing to any of them, at least you will then have more data to come to that conclusion.

What you chose to believe is up to you, some of the "facts" or events claimed are tough to swallow, including by me, but events early in my life have been enough it seems, to generate a lifelong interest in this subject, and I have read and heard enough to come to the conclusion that the sheer volume of testimony, good photos as opposed to fake, plus video, and radar logs, some multiple of the same event, adds up to something more than meets the casual eye, and is being hidden from the general public. If it is just our military, it is way beyond "next generation" hardware, so the question is – how was it developed or obtained?

Or, there is an extra-terrestrial presence here and or on our moon. Our military (mainly, but not just US) benefiting from a dubious treaty, with either a possibly Antarctic based, German WW2 remnant /alien alliance – those certainly not with our best long-term interests in mind. Might explain why we have not gone back to the moon, told to keep off the grass, then there is Phobos, a very strange satellite of Mars, with possible artificial structures photographed on and near its surface.

If there are any aliens here, you have to go the whole hog and realise there is likely many species, this would fit the variety of observations over time. There could also be various secret human factions involved.

If any of this was true, it would surely have leaked out by now, no secret this big could have been kept this long? It hasn't, but a combination of ridicule and dire threat has kept the lid on enough to deter mainstream acceptance. If you are a success in mainstream media or science, you don't want to jeopardise that do you…

Depending on the true nature of any contact, a selected small "Breakaway Civilisation" (search Richard Dolan) of humans could be managing our contact – if some stories are true, it would take a dedicated organisation such as Majesty through the appointed MJ 12 or successors, working for the heads of intelligence agencies such as the NSA, CIA, all threatening witnesses and especially their families with dire consequences if they don't shut up or stay quiet. NASA, a partly a military organisation, though keeping that side quiet, is in collusion with the above. Most employees there are in complete ignorance of their photo doctoring section for instance, or the people that cut the live feed from the ISS whenever something they don't want us to see shows up. Many others are only aware of public projects, there doing useful work but also there to provide plausible deniability, if they don't know, they can't tell can they…

There are stories of nuclear-powered subterranean craft that have a drilling end so hot, that they melt the rock in front, able to create smooth-sided large tunnels below US territory, over vast distances, linking many underground bases, though why is anyone's guess, if this sounds far-fetched, which it does, it would also fit the "Breakaway civilisation" theory. Authors, claimed witnesses and verified technical data, such as radar logs, all infer that something beyond your daily newsfeed is going on.

Below is a relatively brief synopsis (compared with all that is out there) in general, oldest to newer order, with names of book authors to search out, that deal with different aspects of this vast subject, also individuals that have contentious claims, including a former government defence minister, plus major events that seem to include strange elements.

All of the witnesses mentioned, authors, investigators, all have spent much of their lives, often starting from respectable careers, then alienating themselves from the establishment they were often part of before some event or other led them down an investigative path they could no longer ignore. It is the sheer volume of this data in the public domain, if you have a reason to start looking, that convinces me, we as a general population are being kept from world-changing knowledge, maybe for a valid reason, but possibly for short-sighted, dangerous and selfish reasons.

If, up till now, you are unaware or vaguely aware of some of the ET stuff that is usually banded about in a derisory fashion, only fit for kids, that sort of thing, then I suggest that if you search the net for a few of the stories, books and individuals I mention below, some of which I have already talked about earlier in this, my storyline, and are in your own mind, satisfied that ALL of it is pure fiction, with no room for doubt, perhaps thinking there is no way something of this magnitude could be kept under wraps. Please bear in mind that as recounted above, if many of you have not experienced real, serious fear, for yourself and, or, your family, many of the people with first-hand experience of this subject, are often subjected to just such threat by MJ 12 or their proxies, this organisation set up in the 1950s, or their successors are there to oversee the suppression of any leaked knowledge of crash retrieval, reverse engineering of such craft, close encounters, serious sightings and anything else that does not fit in with established knowledge.

Pilots, radar operators and other military personnel are debriefed and told to not to talk, easier than civilians to control, until very late in life, when many do start talking. Civilians, including police, are usually ridiculed if they persist in talking publicly, films such as *Men in Black* have been made, deliberately comical in order to further discredit the subject as something to be taken seriously, though witnesses have often been visited by real strange, Men in Black, or military, and warned to stop talking.

This section is dedicated to the *genuine* investigators and authors, first-hand witnesses, military personnel, both junior and senior in rank, one ex-defence minister and all public figures who dare to speak out.

I list below, as promised, in a roughly linier timeline, some major events, some of you may wish to research further.

Starting with historical background data that suggests this is not something new, but has been here possibly longer than we have. This is aimed for those too busy with their normal lives, to be more than vaguely aware of this subject, so please forgive me, those of you with more knowledge, I claim no original knowledge of my own, beyond a few strange very early life experiences and a lifetime of accumulating the knowledge of others, and with such, I could not write a book of my very average life without including something, the tip of an iceberg only, from a world that might be stranger than at first sight… so from older to newer.

Ancient Civilisations

Without reading any books on the subject, it is possible to pick up from TV Channels such as the *H2* Channel, the *Discovery* Channel and *National Geographic* and, to a lesser extent, these days on *BBC 2*, that most major older civilisations, the Egyptian and Mayan in particular, the Hopi of North America, the Assyrian of ancient Mesopotamia, all speak of "gods" who came from the sky, imparting knowledge which was of great assistance in developing their civilisations. Characters such as Imhotep, who in ancient Egypt came from nowhere to seemingly impart high levels of mathematical, medical, agricultural expertise and other advanced know-how without any apparent prior development. The Pharaoh Akhenaten, depicted with a strange, elongated head, abandoned all previous gods, making the sun the only deity, what prompted this?

> In Bolivia, South America, near the temple site of Tiwanaku, which the natives say is human built, in honour of a nearby site like no other on earth, in that the precision built stone H blocks there are unadorned, looking like they were used for construction in a modular form, which the local inhabitants say were put there by "the gods", the blocks are now scattered around the site due to an unknown destructive event there, Search – Pumu Punku.
>
> For data of many other ancient Central and South American anomalies, such as the Nazca Lines, of Peru, which were bought to international prominence by the pioneer of this subject, search **Erich Von Daniken**, who made a few early errors but has unearthed much valid knowledge in this area, including highlighting the (search) Lid of Palenque, the Sarcophagus lid of the tomb of Lord Pacal, a Priest King of the Maya, the lid depicts what looks like a space capsule interior, with Lord Pacal operating with feet as well as hands what appears to be complicated machinery.
>
> In front of the Great Pyramids on the Giza Plateau (which are now beginning to reveal strange electromagnetic proprieties to scientists) is the Sphinx, this edifice is supposed to have been built around the same time as the Pyramids, but two investigative writers, (Search) **Robert Bauval,** and **Graham Hancock,** known for their discovery of structural ruins of lost offshore cities off the coast of India and Japan, also claim the erosion around the base of the Sphinx, could only have been caused by water. Last time substantial water was in this area was ten or twelve thousand years ago, around the same time many civilisations put the time of the Great Flood featured in the Bible, but not exclusive to it. So if the Sphinx predates the Pyramids by many thousands of years, who built it? And why, when ground penetrating radar investigation revealed voids

beneath it, Egyptian antiquities authorities suddenly stepped in to prevent any further *Public* investigation into this anomaly? What do they already know…?

Last but not least, we have the modern church distancing itself from The Old Testament, why, could it be that there are too many accounts of events such as Ezekiel being "taken up in a fiery Chariot to look down upon the earth", or the Nephilim, giant offspring of the "gods and the daughters of men", or Methuselah – living for 900 years – something the Church would rather not explain, along with many other anomalies to be found in these texts.

Interestingly, the Assyrians, among others describe their "gods" the Annunaki (search) as like the Nephilim, giants, according to the translations of Zecharia Sitchin.

Speculation: These giants may come from a lower gravity environment, interbreeding with locals – producing offspring such as Akhenaten?

Sanskrit Mahabharata and Ramayana Texts

Considered by most but not all mainstream local scholars as myth, these ancient texts tell of "War in the Skies" between various gods, including Shiva, in "Fiery Chariots" fought with weapons, which if described in modern terms, would include Pulse lasers and atomic bombs, maybe fantasy, but desert areas of vitrified sand, created under very high temperatures such as found in the New Mexico desert after the atomic bomb tests there, have been found in the Indian subcontinent…

Mysterious Maps

In more recent history, maps of two locations stand out as worth a mention, the first an island known as Hy Brasil, (search) derived from Celtic, and meaning High King, said to be located 200 miles to the west of Ireland, found on maps as early as 1325 by the Genoese, later in the Catalan in 1375, again in 1436 on a Venetian cartographic map, still later in 1595 in the Europa Mercator Map, roughly circular, with a dividing waterway running across the centre, it is mentioned in Irish legends.

In 1480 and again in 1481, expeditions from Bristol went out looking for this island, returning without success, though in 1497 Spanish diplomat Pedro de Ayala reported to the King of Spain that John Cabot had "discovered in the past by the men from Bristol who had found Brasil", so as always, contradictions, but reports all concur this island was inhabited by advanced people. Comparison with Atlantis is obvious, but what I find interesting is all along the western coastal fringe of Europe, there are a seemingly separate groupings of peoples with related languages, Cornish has much in common with Breton, as with the Basques, as though they have a lost common ancestry, survivors of a lost land to the West.

The second mysterious map is that compiled by Ottoman Admiral and Cartographer Peri Reis in 1513, said to be a compilation of earlier, mainly Portuguese maps and even Egyptian scrolls, the map depicts the west coast of Europe and Africa, much of the east coast of South America, but what is most interesting is that it depicts quite accurately the coastline of Antarctica, not the variable ice-covered coast, but the land coastline beneath the ice, only now mapped by satellite and radar, how could this be seen in earlier times, just another anomaly… (Search) Peri Reis Map. Charles Hapgood (search) may provide one possible explanation for this (Pole Shift).

1897 "Airships"

According to researcher Jerome Clarke (search), in the late 1880s and 1890s, "Airships" were reported in newspapers in the western United States, as well as worldwide, these are not verifiable but represent the earliest modern sightings of something in the air unidentifiable at the time, dirigibles were not around until the 1930s, so not the lights in the sky reports here, *The Ships of Air*, being the best description available to fit the sightings at that time.

1930s Antarctic Nazi Expeditions

In 1938, and other occasions in the 1930s, Nazi Germany sent a secret expedition to Antarctica. A sea-plane equipped ship, the MS Schwabenland, led by German Navy Captain Alfred Ritscher, ostensibly looking for a site for a whaling station. The Nazis stated aim was also to stake a claim to a chunk of Antarctica they called New Swabia, an area the Norwegians now call Queen Maud Land in their claim of the area.

> Conspiracy theorists claim that as Nazis realised they were going to lose the war, so they set up large bases down there. This may have a direct bearing on the events surrounding **Operation Highjump** discussed below. Transferring the development of UFO type craft down there, possibly assisted by aliens! There is a whole separate storyline behind this involving a supposed crashed saucer near Freiberg in 1933, also Vril and Thule secret societies being involved.

The "Battle" of Los Angeles

On the 24th February 1942, late at night on that date, a large object/s were illuminated by multiple searchlights over Los Angeles, initially suspecting a Japanese attack, this object/s was then subject to a massive anti-aircraft barrage amounting to thousands of rounds of ammunition, despite this continuing until the early hours of the next morning, nothing was brought down.

No bombs were dropped, no retaliation of any kind occurred, so this was the most one-sided "battle" ever known to me. Photographs of this object caught in the searchlights are published and searchable online, no credible explanation has ever been forthcoming for this event.

Foo Fighters

Foo Fighters, as well as a later day pop group, was the name given by US and UK airman to glowing balls of light that were seen close to bombers during raids over Germany in late WW2. When these lights came close to aircraft, engines would cut out. An unknown number of aircraft were affected by this phenomenon, returning aircrew were put under strict orders to keep quiet about this. A German secret weapon was suspected.

Operation Paperclip

The above was the name the US gave to their transferring of over 3000 German personnel, scientists and their assistants, at the end of WW2, to work for the US, no questions asked, histories whitewashed. The most famous of these was Werner von Braun, the developer of the V2 rocket, like many others, any war crimes buried, as long as they helped US science projects. Why were the Germans so way ahead of everyone else, and what other exotic sciences (such as "De Glock" – The Bell, to be mentioned in connection with the Kecksburg incident later) were furthered secretly in the US whilst rocket development made the headlines…

By the later stages of the war, the Krigsmarine had developed large cargo capable submarines from submarine tankers, so a significant transfer of personnel and material was possible by then, and many U-boats were unaccounted for, presumed sunk. Several were reported to have docked in South American ports, then heading south. While there in no evidence for this, what followed in late 1946/7 after the war, adds an interesting twist to the above…

Operation Highjump

This military expedition of mainly US ships, but with UK and Russian participants, was sent down to Antarctica at the end of 1946 supposedly to test equipment under extreme conditions and test the feasibility of establishing a base there.

Organised by Admiral Richard E Byrd (search), and led by Admiral Richard H Cruzen, there were three groups of ships sent down to Antarctica, seemingly organised in great haste after the end of WW2, as if there was unfinished business to be dealt with down there. I will not repeat all of the known and speculated events that try to fill in the veil of secrecy that surrounds this expedition here, but the key known facts are that this operation was called off much earlier than was expected, there was some loss of life, and rumours of a battle taking place. As usual no official confirmation is to be found, but in interesting interview held after the expedition with the *International News Service*, held aboard the command ship of the operation – the USS Mount Olympus – and appearing in the Chilean newspaper *EL Mercurio* on March 5th 1947, states as follows –

"Admiral Byrd warned today that the United States should adopt measures of protection against the possibility of invasion of the country by hostile planes coming from the Polar Regions."

After being welcomed home officially, he was then whisked off to a security debriefing. Just *who* was a threat in 1947 from the Polar Regions, clearly *not* referring to strategic Russian bombers of the following decades. Given the known German involvement in Antarctica just before the war, is there something the US and others is not keen for us to know about the Polar Regions…

Roswell 1947

As there are countless books on this, even those with no interest in this subject have heard of this event, that was let slip in the newspapers of the day, before being quickly retracted a day later, here I will just point out a few interesting disputed events about this event.

The Roswell area at that time was situated close to Walker Air Force Base, at that time the home of the only nuclear bomb equipped squadron in the world, belonging to the Strategic Air Command of the then US Army Air Force, so maybe of interest to someone not keen on our new nuclear capabilities? This being a common thread in some future events, mentioned later.

Why would supposedly advanced craft crash? One possibility is the fact that radar and possibly other beamed frequencies were a new invention for us at that time, and that the frequencies used interfered in guidance or propulsion systems that had as yet no previous experience of these frequencies being deployed nearby. Or, if not so advanced craft, perhaps from Antarctica and of earthly German origins, this might explain the crashes, brought down by new tech of our (US) own.

Child-sized coffins *were* ordered from an undertaker in Roswell, to be delivered as soon as possible to the nearby air force base, where the bodies of supposed small grey aliens, from one, or possibly two crash sites, were taken initially.

There is testimony from people many years later including an on-site nurse, in old age, who says they were warned on pain of death, not to talk of what they witnessed, as in many future cases, only speaking out decades later.

Lt Col P.J. Corso

Lt Col Corso's book (search), *The Day after Roswell*, details his claims that he was part of the US Foreign Technology Division, normally used to reverse engineer recovered Russian or other potentially hostile tech, this was extended to include material recovered from crashed alien craft, then carefully fed to selected US companies – resulting in the US gaining a broad technological edge over the rest of the world, maintained to this day.

Kenneth Arnold 1947

On June 24th 1947, Kenneth Arnold, a businessman, was flying his private plane near Mount Rainier, a 14400 Ft Volcano in Washington state, when he reported seeing nine shiny objects he estimated to be travelling at a minimum speed of 1200 mph, shaped "like a pie plate", "half-moon shaped, oval in front and convex in the rear", describing their erratic motion as like "a fish flipping in the sun" or "a saucer skipped across water" from this the press coined the term Flying Saucer, used ever after to describe many sightings up until recent times where Black Triangles and V-shaped craft are also reported – more on these later in this timeline synopsis.

Kapustin Yar

The above named site was a secret military base of the Soviet Union located in the remote Oblast Astrakhan region; the base was so secret that a nearby town was evacuated then razed to the ground. In 1947, a UFO seen over the base was attacked by a Soviet interceptor, a beam of light was seen to hit the plane, but the UFO was also brought down, extra-terrestrial bodies were supposedly recovered along with remains of the craft. Kapustin Yar is reported to be the Russian equivalent of Area 51, or Dugway proving grounds (search) with underground facilities for storage and reverse engineering of many subsequent retrieved craft.

Korean War UFOs

In May 1951, a company of US soldiers started to launch artillery strikes against a village near Chorwon, in an area known as the "Iron Triangle" about sixty miles north of Seoul. A pulsating light was seen to move down into the area being attacked, but the artillery had no effect against this "craft", instead, after firing at it, a beam of light that could only be seen when aimed at you, according to Private Francis P. Wall, swept across his entire company. The results were a strong tingling sensation, followed by nausea, and general sickness so bad, that the entire company had to be evacuated by ambulances, after roads had to be built just to reach them, many were too weak to walk. Richard F. Haines, a former NASA scientist turned UFO researcher, said the symptoms matched radiation sickness.

Over 40 other UFO sightings were made by Western Troops during the three-year war.

1952 Washington Flap

From July 12th to July 29th, 1952, a large number of flying discs were seen and photographed over Washington DC, the Air Force unable to prevent these incursions over the US capital, radar logs report these objects flying either so slowly they would crash if conventional aircraft, at other times estimated at speeds in excess of 7000 MPH. (Recall Admiral Byrd's warning…)

> Speculation: The above could have been a demonstration of superiority – to bring about a subsequent "deal" mentioned later.

Project "Blue Book" was set up to investigate the above and other sightings, but was "encouraged" by the CIA to debunk or omit serious sightings, senior military compilers of these sightings, originally told to toe the official Air Force line of weather events or anything other than unknown craft, however detailed the report, especially by experienced pilots, (who soon learnt it was not good for their careers to make such reports), eventually, after leaving the military, these authors changed their tune and wrote books citing the true unknown nature of these craft.

J. Allen Hynek is one of the main authors who changed their views when faced with overwhelming evidence that could not be explained away. Edward J. Ruppelt is another early author, bought in to rubber stamp the official line, but soon coming to the same conclusions as Hynek. Project Blue Book is now the subject of a TV series starting at the end of March 2019 on Sky TV, so unseen by me – but hopefully, the story of Hynek, brought in to whitewash the subject, but changing his mind when faced with overwhelming evidence of the truth – that something unknown (to the general public) is going on, will hopefully be related faithfully in this series.

Many further sightings continued in the 1950s, including by military interceptor pilots.

Operation Mainbrace, 1952

In the North Sea, from Norway and Denmark to the east coast of England, one of the largest NATO operations ever undertaken took place in September 1952. 200 ships, around 1000 aircrafts and over 80,000 personnel took part in this 12-day NATO exercise. On Sept 19th, personnel on board the USS, Franklin D Roosevelt, observed a silvery spherical object which was photographed but never released to the public. Earlier the participating Danish Destroyer Willemoes was north of Bornholm Island on Sept 13th, during the night Lieutenant Commander Schmidt Jenson and several other members of the crew saw a bluish glowing triangular object moving at high speed (estimated over 900mph) heading south west.

On Sept 19th, a British Meteor Jet was returning to its airfield in Yorkshire, England. Just before 11 am on approach to landing, a silvery object was observed from the ground following it "swaying back and forth like a pendulum". Lieutenant John W. Kilburn and other observers on the ground said that when the Meteor began circling, the UFO stopped. It was disk-shaped and rotated on its axis while hovering, then took off at high-speed westward, changed course to the southeast before disappearing. Other British and Danish pilots also reported sightings during this major exercise.

Edwards AFB 1954

On the night and early hours of 20-21st February, 1954, President D Eisenhower is alleged to have been taken in secret to Edwards Air force Base, California, for a first contact meeting with extra-terrestrials, supposedly this first meeting was with "Nordic" looking aliens, who were there to dissuade any further nuclear tests, subsequently meetings with "Greys" or worse – (Antarctic Germans). Meetings are alleged to have taken place at Holloman AFB, resulting in an infamous treaty, that allowed "limited" human abduction, if Greys, in return for advanced technology transfer, or, ramped up spaceship production facilities in the US, if Antarctic Germans…

> 1950s "Contactee" George Adamski's "Space brothers" ship photos, look very like a German design from WW2 – the Haunebu.

Antonio Vilas Boas 1957

Antonio Vilas Boas was a Brazilian farmer who claims to have been abducted aboard an alien craft on October 16, 1957, much disputed, this is the first reported story of such an event, he claims to have been induced to have sex with a humanoid female alien, this alien indicating afterwards she was now pregnant. Sickness and nausea occurred after this "event" other symptoms, consistent with radiation poisoning were also reported, this farmer went on to become a lawyer, and so was not an ignorant subsistence farmer, as the ownership of a tractor at that time signifies, he stuck to his story until his death in 1991.

Betty and Barny Hill, 1961

Though there have been a multitude of alleged alien abductions, this one is significant as it is the first widely publicised encounter in the US, and as such, not subject to "Cultural Tracking" the description given to disputed future abduction claims, that sceptics insist are copies of other people's descriptions of encounters. This to me is a double-edged sword, either these events *are* all very similar, which is likely if all part of the same programme, or they are a mixture of hoaxes and events mistaken for the above.

This event took place in rural New Hampshire in September 1961, taken from a car, subjected to tests, samples taken for reproductive purposes, messages about the alien origins after later hypnotic regression brought back "lost" or repressed memories, in short, most of the ingredients of many future abduction claims. Two authors for me stand out in the research on this aspect of UFO lore, the first is **David M. Jackob's**, the second is the late **Budd Hopkins**, there are many others, but I recommend you search out these two for anyone wanting a good overall view on this angle of the subject.

Kecksburg "Crash", 1965

This is an unusual case; in that it has possible connections with a supposed Nazi project from WW2. On December 9th, 1965, after being reported first over Canada then over six US states as a fireball, an object crashed or landed, about thirty miles southeast of Pittsburgh near the village of Kecksburg Pennsylvania. Locals described the object as acorn or bell-shaped, about the size of a small car, with hieroglyphic type markings in a band around its base. The area was soon cordoned off by the military, the locals were sent away from the site but managed to see an object covered by tarpaulin strapped onto to the back of a flatbed truck, as it was taken away under heavy escort.

Stories of a German "Wonder Weapon" developed late in WW2, described by Polish journalist, Igor Witkowski, located at a site in the Polish side of the Czech border. Die Glock (The Bell) was of a similar size and shape to the Kecksburg "acorn", had counter rotating elements, and used a liquid metal related to mercury, reports of anti-gravity properties as well as possible time-travel capabilities are linked with this device, five of seven scientists are supposed to have died working on it, radiation being the possible cause of their demise. Researchers of Die Glock and the Kecksburg event speculate on their similarities of description, along with the time-travel reports, to wonder if both are one and the same. The location of the object taken away from Kecksburg is unknown.

Vietnam War UFOs

In 1968, two US inshore patrol boats in Vietnam were stalked by two UFOs, one patrol boat destroyed, strangely, by their *own* ammunition being returned back to them after being fired at the craft, soon after, an Australian warship took a hit from a missile fired at a UFO, by Phantom F4s, *the day before*, fragments from the missile hit, matching those fired from the jet.

It is claimed General George S Brown, deputy of Air Operations, stated, after the war, "We were plagued by UFOs" during the conflict. It is also claimed that protocols for military aircraft encountering UFOs were changed during that war, after suffering losses as a result of attacking these craft in the Korean, as well as Vietnam war, as well as over the US, going back to the 1948 Mantell incident when Captain T Mantel's P51 mustang crashed after attacking a UFO.

A policy of avoidance seems to be in place to this day, as when the Kurd, Pesh Murga called in a US jet strike against Iraqi forces in that war, but left the area when UFOs were also seen …

Clifford Stone

Former US Army Sgt Clifford Stone was stationed in Vietnam in the 1960s, it was there he claimed to have witnessed his first alien crash retrieval, after which he was recruited into a secret global crash retrieval programme, where he became a "specialist" in interfacing with alien entities. Sworn to secrecy, it was only after his son died in 1995 that he decided to "go public" with his secret work. If even a fraction of Clifford Stone's revelations are true, then life here is far more complex. If not true, then he has a first-class and extensive imagination. There are several interviews of his to be seen on YouTube.

1967 Minuteman Nuke Shutdown

In March 1967, 18 Minuteman ICBM's were shut down at Malmstrom AFB in Montana, USA, one by one. That same day, security guards and maintenance personnel on the base reported a UFO hovering above the missile silos, one guard was so affected by what he saw that he never again worked on security at the site. The missiles were eventually brought back on line. UFOs seem to be seen often near nuclear sites; this event prompted speculation that someone was demonstrating a capability to shut down these weapons at will.

Shag Harbour USO

The small village of Shag Harbour, Nova Scotia, Canada, became a focus of interest on October 4th, 1967, when several people reported seeing an object enter the harbour from the air, after hovering over the water, thought at first to be a crashed aircraft, boats sent out divers, who reported an object on the seabed, a second object then arrived, seeming to come to the aid of the first, both moved off, followed for days by the Canadian Navy, heading north east along the Nova Scotia Coast drawing interest from the US navy and a Russian submarine, before both breaking the surface and disappearing at high speed.

Stanton Friedman

A retired Nuclear Physicist who has worked on classified defence projects in the 1950s and 1960s, the late Stanton Friedman had been a tireless investigator of UFO-related incidents, his books reveal much about the alleged creation of the MJ 12 committee, the organisation set up to control and suppress knowledge of a possible alien presence on and near earth.

Travis Walton, 1975

One of the most famous alien abduction events is claimed to have taken place in the mountains of Arizona, Travis was leaving work in a truck with five other loggers when they saw a bright light nearby in the forest, alone among the loggers. Travis left the truck to investigate, the other loggers saw Travis hit by a beam of light from a craft hovering above him, in a panic, the other loggers drove off, when they returned soon after, he was gone. The five loggers returned without Travis, after a few days with no sign of him, they became under suspicion of murder, but five days after disappearing, he was found, dehydrated and weak, on a road fifteen miles away from where he disappeared.

Since then he has undergone and passed numerous lie detector tests, two books *The Walton Experience*, 1978, and *Fire in the Sky*, 1997, also made into a film, tell this story.

Our Mysterious Spaceship Moon

Published in August 1976 by Don Wilson, this small but influential book, *Our Mysterious Spaceship Moon*, is a thought-provoking book based on Russian scientists test results of seismic tests on objects deliberately crashed into our moon, that reveal that it is much lighter than it should be, as though it is almost hollow. A recent 2017 book, *Secrets of Our Spaceship Moon*, by the same author explores NASA's alleged cover up of what it knows about our moon.

New Zealand 1978 UFO

For some weeks, UFOs had been sighted over the Cook Strait between the North and South Islands of New Zealand. On the 30th December 1978, an Argosy freight plane left Wellington Airport, with a film crew aboard to try to capture some footage of anything strange in the air after repeated reports. Whenever attempts like this are tried, they are usually doomed to failure, however, this was to be *the* exception that proves the rule.

Late that evening, the pilot and a TV reporter both saw a series of five pulsating lights which came closer, at that stage, a cameraman wearing headphones was told by Wellington Air traffic Control that they were being followed. The plane then turned 360 degrees, the occupants then saw "a spinning sphere with lateral lines around it", this object was picked up on Wellington ATC radar, when the Argosy's navigation lights were turned off – the resulting footage was sent all around the world and actually broadcast on the *BBC News*, they had no choice, as the footage was everywhere. On the following night more UFO footage was obtained from the same aircraft.

Alan Godfrey

This case has interesting parallels with a US serving policeman's account near Socorro, New Mexico in 1964, where Lonnie Zamora observed a strange landed craft, with occupants outside of the craft, leaving when they saw him, but leaving burnt vegetation and other traces of the craft's landing. Other witness emerged stating they saw the craft approach its landing sight.

In Alan Godfrey's case, he was also a serving police officer, out on a night shift patrol in his police car in Todmorden, West Yorkshire on the 28th November 1980 when he saw a strange object hovering around five feet off the road ahead of him. He tried to radio his station, but both his car and personnel radio would not work, afraid to leave his car, he made a drawing in his notebook of the craft in front of him – diamond faceted, the top half dark, the lower half rotating fast.

He then inexplicably, found himself driving, about twenty yards past where he saw this craft. He stopped, reversed back to the site. The craft was gone, but where it had hovered, there was a circular dry patch in the ground, it had been raining and the surrounding road was wet. The area surrounding the dry patch piled with leaves that had swirled around the craft while it was rotating. He was then able to contact a fellow officer, who arrived and was able to verify the dry patch and swirled leaves at the location. Other police witnesses also saw strange lights in the sky nearby that night.

It was only after returning to the station that he realised he could not account for a period of time around the event. As earlier in this book, I will admit to a tenuous link to this case, in that at the time I was part of a small group MUFORA, led by Jenny Randles a noted author on this subject, who also investigated the following major Rendlesham Forest incident.

When she learnt of the above event from a local paper, she was able to contact PC Godfrey, who at one point travelled across to central Manchester at Jenny's invitation to where our instigative group met. He gave his account of the event in person to us, responding to questions in an open way. Unknown to the rest of us, he had also agreed to undergo hypnotic regression, though not at that meeting, through a contact of Jenny's. Despite severe headaches after these sessions, to the point of being sick, which he kept to himself at the time, he is recorded as saying that he was in a room with "horrible" small creatures with heads shaped like light bulbs, along with a strange human called Joseph, who was talking to him "in his head". Some sort of clamp was attached to one of his feet. (There was an unexplained tear in his boot from the time of the event) electrodes were also attached, he said under hypnosis. There are other aspects to this case. Now in retirement, in 2017, Alan Godfrey tells his story in a book, co-authored with Jenny Randles. The book is called *Who or what were they?*

With the publicity, came the gradual distancing of his local police force from him, he was first moved to a village nearby, before eventually "invited" to leave the police with an honourable discharge. Zamora, the US Patrolman, faced similarities in his treatment, as do many people when they report events such as these.

Rendlesham Forest

This is the most compelling UFO incident known to have happened on British soil. In late December 1980, a small triangular UFO was reported to have landed near RAF Bentwaters, at that time used by the US Air Force. Tactical nuclear weapons were reported located on this site at that time, at the height of the cold war. The list of events are that base personnel were called out to investigate strange lights in Rendlesham Forest just outside the base. Deputy base commander Lt Col Charles Holt led a team out to where the lights were reported moving through the trees.

As the Col Holt approached, he had switched on his tape recorder, this recording has been much repeated on TV documentaries of this event. Other witnesses alleged to have been present are Sgt Jim Penniston, John Burroughs, and possibly Larry Warren, differing accounts including Jim Penniston's claim of touching this landed black craft, that had hieroglyphic type markings on it is not supported by other witnesses, though he recorded his observations in a now published notebook. Another airman, Larry Warren, claims a different set of events took place that includes the Base Commander Gordon Williams communicating with small aliens near the craft. Many other witnesses, including civilians living nearby, report lights in the sky at the time. Farm animals were making loud disturbed noises, this was also reported by Lt Col Holt's Party. A UFO was seen hovering over the nuclear bunkers sending a beam of light down to them on the base.

Though there are conflicting reports on these incidents that took place over a few days. Investigations by both local UFO groups and Jenny Randles, whom I had some association with for a time, resulted in a book written by her on the events there, in collaboration with local investigators. Search "*Sky Crash*".

Of others, I recommend the late investigative reporter Georgina Bruni's 2001 book about this event, concentrating more on the subsequent cover up, this included an interview with the Prime Minister of the time, Margaret Thatcher, Georgina's book is called *You Can't Tell the People* – a supposed quote from the above-mentioned interview.

Above *Top* Secret, 1988

Timothy Good is a British author who has written several painstakingly researched books on the subject of an alien presence on earth, in particular *The Greys*, as they are known and their possible reason for being here. He has also looked into the extensive cover up and possible collusion of the US and other governments about this presence. *Above Top Secret* is the first of his books.

Bob Lazar, 1989

There is much debate, claim and counter claim about Bob Lazar's work and education background, he says he worked at Los Alamos Laboratories, and MIT, where he claims his Physics degree was earned, claiming records of these have been erased when he started talking about his work at S4, a remote section of Area 51, which was little known until Bob Lazar made his claims about working on alien craft there in the 1970s, reverse engineering these craft for the US military. At the time of writing this, there is renewed debate and a new 2018 documentary about these events, in particular regarding Element 115, which he describes decades before it was added to the Periodic Table – updated info is revealed here, search YouTube, Amazon Prime, or Sky TV.

Laguna Cartagena

A large portion of Porto Rico, called Laguna Cartagena, has been designated a "Wildlife Refuge" in the 1980s. A respected local ufologist called Jorge Martin says this has been done to keep residents away from the area, as frequent and persistent reports of sighting of UFOs and aliens are reported in the area. There is reputed to be an alien base under the area, possibly linked with a US Naval Base. For a synopsis on events there, search Marcus Lowth's, April 14th, 2018, "*The Laguna Cartagena and the UFO significance of Porto Rico*", this article will give you an overview.

JAL-747 Alaska UFO

Japan Airlines cargo flight 1628 was on route from Paris to Tokyo over Eastern Alaska on November 17th, 1986, when the pilot saw two objects approach his aircraft. First he thought them to be military, but the craft manoeuvred in ways no known aircraft could, moving so close at one-point heat could be felt in the cockpit from them. The captain requested permission from Anchorage air traffic control to alter course, before these craft then left their proximity, only to be replaced by a much larger disk-shaped craft the captain described as "twice the size of an Aircraft Carrier". This huge craft followed their turn away from it but was eventually lost from sight. The 747 landed at Anchorage safely.

After reporting the UFO, the captain was grounded for a year before being allowed to resume flying. A FAA meeting was called to present radar and taped air to ground conversations to government "officials" including a Vice Admiral, CIA and FBI personnel, among others. At the end of the meeting, all radar and voice tapes were taken by the CIA. FAA personnel and others present were told by the CIA – 'This meeting never happened, we were never here.'

Surprise, surprise, a few months later, the FAA told the press, that the radar data was a split image – a classic case of witness suppression?

Belgian Flap

On March 30th, 1989, after several reports of a large silent black triangular-shaped craft, including by police, Belgian air force F16s were scrambled to investigate. The F16s were able to pick this craft up on radar, but were unable to get close to the craft before it disappeared at very high speed. The radar logs have been released to the public. Many other sightings at that time over several days were also reported in Belgium.

A similar craft was reported in March 1993, moving slowly on a north-easterly course first seen over Cornwall. Correlation of the sightings by Nick

Pope indicate the same craft was seen as far north as Shropshire over a period of six hours – by multiple witnesses including police.

Height 611 UFO

Reports of UFO events were until recent years harder to come by, and harder still to follow up in such places as the old USSR, but they do happen, one example is the Height 611 incident, where in 1986, on January 29th, on a hill known locally as height 611, around 8 pm near the town of Dalnegorsk. Around twenty witnesses saw a wingless metallic object suddenly lose control and crash on Limestone Mountain, as Height 611 is also known locally. A team from the Russian Academy of Sciences arrived on the 3rd February to investigate the site that was reported to have burnt for hours after the crash. Lead and other metallic elements were collected from the blackened site, including a mesh, with high gold content, along with beads that were mostly composed of lead, silicon and iron, photos of the site appeared blank when developed. The mesh fragments survived tests involving prolonged exposure to strong acids, without dissolving.

Samples of the soil, rock and burnt wood from the site contained a chemical composition similar to samples obtained from the Tunguska Event (search) in 1908.

In November of the following year, 1987, numerous witnesses saw another UFO hovering over the crash site, sending a beam of light down over the area. In 1989, yet more witnesses reported a UFO landing at the exact same sight. It was not until 1995 that these incidents become known of in the West.

Phobos 2 1988

Many space probes sent to Mars fail for one reason or another, both American and Russian. But one of the most interesting is what happened to one of two probes launched in 1988 from Russia to investigate Phobos, one of two Martian moons, that has an irregular orbit around the red planet. The first probe was lost on its journey to Mars, but Phobos 2 made it – almost. Close to Phobos, it took pictures of a cylindrical-shaped shadow on the surface of the moon, but soon afterwards, the probe was destroyed, however, it had sent one more picture back before destruction, this last picture was declared too sensitive to be released to the public. The night that final photo was received, Orthodox Russian Priests were summoned to the Phobos 2 control Centre in Moscow to discuss this picture. This event alone would indicate the Russians are as aware as major Western governments of a presence, they deem not for general release to the public. A disputed photo of a massive 279ft square "Monolith" on the surface of Phobos has since been released from the Mars Reconnaissance Orbiter…

Paul Hellyer

In 1995, ex-Canadian Minister of Defence, Paul Hellyer, started to speak out about what he claims is alien visitations by at least four species, and that top government "officials" from major countries are in constant communication with some species. He also claims some of these aliens have tried to steer us away from current destructive policies, but the US, instead, views them as a threat, and are spending billions of dollars on "Black budget" defence projects, hidden from Senate oversight, aided by one species.

Gary Mckinnon

Mentioned earlier in my narrative, Gary McKinnon was caught hacking into NASA and the Pentagon in 2001/2002, looking for suppressed info on free Zero Point Energy, and Anti-Gravity technology. He found spreadsheets referring to "Non-terrestrial Officers" and ship to ship transfers within the "Solar Warden" fleet, also finding secret NASA photos of UFOs kept in a NASA dept where photographs are "edited" to airbrush out alien-related objects we, the public, are not to know about.

Interestingly, our very own then Home Secretary, ~~Teresa~~ THERESA May, refused repeated American requests for extradition of Gary, citing his Asperger's Syndrome condition as making his mental state too fragile to be safe for his transfer. But what did our Prime Minister learn about this case while in charge of it, and was Gary's health the only reason for his blocked extradition. This long running high-profile case received several reports on mainstream news channels, unusual for this subject matter.

Varginha Incident, 1996

A strange and unusual event took place on January 20th, 1996 in the town of Varginha, southern Brazil. These are the bare bones of the story – three teenage girls came across a green, sulphur smelling, small humanoid being with red eyes, after reporting this, a hunt took place, and at least one more was found, injured, both were captured and taken to a local hospital, medical staff became ill when examining these creatures, which were first taken away by Brazilian Military, before allegedly being handed over to the US, (I smell MJ12 handy work here). For a detailed account of an investigation of this event, I recommend a book by the late Dr Roger Leir – *UFO Crash in Brazil.*

This same Dr Leir, is also known for his surgical removal of claimed alien implants, documented film of which shows close up pictures of small objects that have attached themselves to the nervous system of individuals, possibly to gain a power source, and try to move to avoid removal, these objects are usually found just below the skin, but there is no entry scar tissue above. Examined after removal, they become inert, having an unknown origin. Books about this aspect of the UFO phenomenon are available. Search Dr Roger Leir.

Phoenix Lights

Witnessed by thousands of people, and filmed and photographed from multiple angles, this event, or events, in the skies of Arizona and Nevada and the Mexican state of Sonora, on March 13th 1997, took place over an area along a line 300 miles long between 7.30 and 10.30, local time. Two distinct events took place, a large triangular set of lights (some claim a dark, giant V shape behind the lights) was filmed over Phoenix, passing slowly and silently over the city. A second set of stationary lights were seen in the Phoenix area, the US air force claiming these were their own aircraft's flares.

A second sighting over the area was seen and filmed by the local *Fox News* TV station on February 6th, 2007. A hoax, with helium-filled balloons attached to flares occurred in 2008. The half-mile wide V-shaped earlier sightings have never been explained to witnesses' satisfaction.

Black Triangles

Huge black triangular objects seem to be more prominent in recent years, craft such as over Wolverhampton, UK, from 2008 – 2010, was described as five times larger than a passenger aircraft. Man-made craft, as discovered in Gary Mackinnon's famous "hack" of the Pentagon, describe Triangular "TR3Bs", as well as larger cigar-shaped craft in a "Solar Warden Fleet". Recent claims of Rigid hulled, neutral buoyancy, helium-filled triangular man-made craft may be true, but would not explain the capabilities of craft such as those chased in the 90s "Belgian Flap" by F16's, which were totally outmanoeuvred and left standing by these craft.

So it would seem we may be adding these craft to a broad spectrum, there are likely many sources, some alien, others closer to home. Without official disclosure, there is no definitive proof. I am no confirmed "believer". Only in the extreme likelihood something is going on, given the over 100,000 reports of strange aerial, landed, and underwater objects, regardless of claimed "closer encounters" since the early 1900s.

Bonnybridge, Scotland

In terms of the number of UFO reports from one area, Bonnybridge, near Falkirk, Scotland, with an average in the 1990s of over 300 a year, would make it the world's no 1 hotspot, with diamond-shaped craft, sometimes accompanied by helicopters, a speciality of the area, though US sightings of this type of craft have also been reported – also with a multi-helicopter escort, suggesting human involvement at the very least. Search "The Cash/landrum incident", which actually went to court – over alleged severe health problems caused by exposure to this craft.

Disclosure Project

An ongoing project, headed by **Steven M. Greer, M.D**. This has witness testimony of over 500 people, going back 25 years, some of high-level military and political standing, claiming a cover up of an alien presence here, reverse engineering of alien craft, and Special Access Projects costing billions of dollars, all related to the UFO cover up and development of Zero Point Energy, Gravity Amplification Propulsion, and other technology that would transform our lives if released to the public. "Contact Protocols" are also discussed, along with a possible near future, staged – fake – alien invasion, in order to allow a world government to form. I am somewhat wary of this scenario, as it would be very hard to sustain for long, this theory makes me a little wary of Dr Greer, though he seems to have had access to some very senior figures who have disclosed a lot of possibly valid info, so not quite sure, but one to watch.

A DVD and accompanying Book, *Unacknowledged* by Dr Greer, tells all about the above known to date (2017).

Thank you, those of you who have ploughed through all the incidents mentioned here, all checkable online, or in more detail as I have over the last forty-five years or so, by reading the books painstakingly researched by the authors named in my narrative, plus many others, to which I give again, all credit for what is only highlighted and repeated here.

I must emphasise that these events are only the tip of a very deep iceberg, I have only collated these events at the end of my story, as I do not have enough new knowledge for a book of my own on this subject, but feel these, a representative few, worth reiterating here.

One might well ask why so much of this is American related. Try entering any country online, followed by "UFO reports", very few will have none, France is a rich source of sightings and its government has recently released a lot of info on these. But I along with many others would have to conclude it has to be America's first use of atomic weapons that has concentrated older sightings there, especially in the southwest, where the first tests were conducted. Many encounters, two of which mentioned above seen to indicate alien alarm at this. There are other theories as to this concern, such as environmental pollution, and the elephant in the room that is never mentioned by the media, even though it is the main cause of all planetary harm – unsustainable population growth, which has doubled since I was at school. Last I looked – Earth has not doubled in size. Adjustment may be very severe, if not planned for very soon.

Many long-term investigators point to the fact that some UFOs seem able to not just fly off at incredible speed but just disappear, or fade away on the spot, which suggests some are able to "tune out" of our visible spectrum, in the same way as radio stations are all there, but you are only tuned into one. Could it be that apart from the fact that while some may be true aliens from other star systems, others could well be from our own planet, well hidden, it would explain their extreme concern for our nuclear weapons, if they are also resident in our biosphere.

So for me, it is the countless thousands of sightings, of varying descriptions, some being radar confirmed, plus more detailed claimed encounters and extensive cover up operations, that most convince me all it not quite as it seems. The grave concerns of retaining any authority, depending on the nature and scope of any official disclosure, especially if complicity with "others" is involved, and, or the withholding of technological advancements that could make the use of fossil fuel redundant, means such knowledge could be held back until such time as key decision makers with "oil interests" are no longer in charge of policy, and a way found of a "No mass panic" managed disclosure, agreed by involved worldwide governments – a tall order indeed...

If this subject was not already complicated enough, there is a possible Antarctic twist to weave into this subject. In 1980, a researcher called W.A. Harbinson wrote a story in the form of a novel called *Genesis*. Although a novel, this story relies on known facts regarding German involvement in Antarctica – which started before WW2. Below in table form is a summary, the left column sets out known facts. The middle and right columns deal with supporting information and also draws on at present – unverifiable claims that are extrapolated from this information – much of the right column drawn from Dr Michael Salla's book *Antarctica's Hidden History*. Interesting, if disturbing reading. If any of this turns out to be provable, we live in a more dangerous world than even much of the previous written info suggests...

Antarctic Germans Scenario – included – parts of Dr Michael Salla's Hypothesis

Known Facts (search online)	**Possible Supporting Info to –**	**Claimed events**
German Antarctic claim, 1938 Survey ship with aircraft sent down. German flags scattered from seaplane. Known fact.	U-boats seen heading south from Argentina after WW2. Possible under-ice volcanos found in West Antarctica – 2017 Edinburgh University survey.	Under-ice caverns created by heat from under-ice volcanos. German occupied. Claimed alien help with bases. Submarine accessibility also claimed.
Operation Paperclip 1945. Known fact.	Thousands of German scientists taken to US at end WW2 – to work on advanced projects	Paperclip scientists promoted to head many US secret aerospace projects in 1954 "Deal".
Operation Highjump 1946	American task force sent to Antarctica – returns early with	Claims task force ships attacked by

Known fact.	rumoured losses – admiral in charge claims Polar craft danger.	craft emerging from sea.
Washington "Flap" 1952 Search online. Project Blue book after this event. Known fact.	1952: Many craft seen and photographed over Washington, chased by fighters – totally outmanoeuvred.	1952 event – claimed show of strength by Antarctic Germans, leading to 1954 deal with US.
Eisenhower went "missing" for a claimed dentist appointment 1954. (Search online)	Claimed treaty with aliens 1954/55, but possible deal with Antarctic Germans instead?	A treaty with surviving Nazi Germans with advanced tech, less palatable even than aliens?
Aug 2017, Edinburgh University researchers discover sub ice volcanoes in West Antarctica.	Whistle blower claims under ice caverns accessed by U-boats.	Claims heat from dormant volcanoes created caverns. Now 2017 volcanoes discovered?
New volcanoes discovery could explain excess iceberg carving in west Antarctica (search).	1950s Adamski UFO photo, looks very like Haunebu 11 German WW2 design (search).	Speculation Adamski's "space brothers" were German Thule society – not aliens.
Recent "high-profile" visitors to Antarctica, such as US Senator John Kerry in November 2016.	Dr. Michael E Salla's – "Antarctica's Hidden History" based claims – Columns 2 and 3.	Possible Russian – Lake Vostok, Antarctic "Ruins" discovery. NASA: magnetic anomaly there.
Charles Hapgood, proposed "Sudden Pole Shift theory" searchable online – many books	Hapgood's theory puts Antarctica much further north before Pole shift only thousands of years ago	Matches claims – advanced civilisation was "Flash frozen" after pole shift south.

The above facts in the **left-hand** column I do not dispute.

Recent discoveries of under ice volcanoes, if they are confirmed, make plausible case for ice caverns.

After the German defeats of El Alamein and Stalingrad at the end of 1942, and Kursk in 1943, it would seem logical that if some senior German Military, especially SS, I.E (General Hans Kammler) known to be involved in advanced weapons development, had a remote bolthole/s they might prepare, they would start transfers in earnest by then, knowing they faced a very bleak future in Germany.

Larger, more advanced tanker and cargo-sized German submarines were produced in the later stages of WW2, enabling possible larger scale evacuation, (some forced), also giving good reason for the Baltic German enclave hold out until the surrender, and especially Denmark and Norway, allowing submarine escape into the North Sea or English Channel. Germany, until 1915, had a South West Africa Colony – so a possible German populated covert way station en route maybe, as well as recorded South American U boat sightings heading south at the end of WW2…

The one and only thing that would make aliens look a good scapegoat for all UFOs would be the very unpleasant discovery that America had secretly done a deal with Nazis in Antarctica, sounds mad, but if they were prepared to whitewash the history of German Nazis such as Werner Von Braun, as they did in Operation Paperclip, who went on to head NASA, (rockets no more than a public distraction) with hundreds of other German scientists taken at the end of WW2, whose work is much less accessible but maybe much more advanced, then is it possible, fantastic as it sounds, that after a drubbing in the South Atlantic in 1946 (Operation High-jump) and the 1952 "Washington Flap", (possible Antarctic German superiority demonstration), America made a deal with them that could never be made public.

The later Antarctic Treaty of 1961, making the continent off limits for commercial and mineral exploitation, is a suspiciously (Laudable if innocent) very far-sighted example of co-operation at a time of increasing world tension. Also though, it would be a very convenient way of keeping unwanted scrutiny to a very (manageable) small scale.

I do not know what to believe, but I am aware that the known facts **(above left only-columns)** – lend themselves well to some very contentious claims, some more dire in their content. A multiple alien species visitor scenario would be preferable to some of the extrapolations and claims proposed about the above scenario, regarding transferred slave workers used at these bases.

Interestingly, at the end of 2016, US Senator John Kerry and several other high-profile people visited Antarctica all around the same time, as though there was something new to see, anything to do with Lake Vostok perhaps…

Just a month or so earlier, the largest Marine Protected Area was created – essentially the Ross Sea, preventing shipping from entering. This also is the exact area where the US Navy is rumoured to be at war with undersea-based aliens – all good stuff, let's just say I am aware but not yet convinced.

I am also aware of a possible "False Flag", fake alien invasion in the near future, staged by The US and others – in order to facilitate a world government. Several authors warn of this, again, I hope not to be convinced. While they (US) may well have the hardware hidden away to stage a convincing start, I doubt they could sustain it for long without discovery, especially with many on the lookout for this.

Victor Shauberger: (search) born in 1885 in Austria, an inventor among other things – relevant to this subject in that his water implosion technology led to the development of a Repulsine Saucer which was of interest to Hitler, whom he met in 1943. While it is not known if these were built in Germany, Shauberger was taken to America in Operation Paperclip (scientist grab) at the end of WW2, where his inventions were all patented by the US government, he was then sent back to Austria. He was dead within five days of returning there...

Interestingly, many UFO witness reports include the intake of water from lakes & rivers from some witnessed craft.

Landrillo, North Wales, January 23rd 1974 - (search) Two strange event was recorded close to Landrillo in the nearby mountains, reported as an earthquake of magnitude 3.5, whilst also reported as a crash of something that gave of a bright glow for some time afterwards, witnessed by local people. The whole area was cordoned off by the military for several days. Shepherds were prevented from tending stock nearby for this period. Reports of something being loaded onto a truck & taken away by military personnel were given to investigators. Where this was taken is unknown. (RAF) Rudloe Manor (search) near the town of Corsham is one possible destination. This facility has vast underground caverns, originally a vast marble quarry, used to build much of Bath, is was turned into an aircraft factory in WW2 - the Manor above later housing the Provost & Security Services of the RAF, which also included dealing with UFO reports from the public. I have been told by a former RAF aircraft technician that any radar tapes of an anomalous nature were sent to this facility. Corsham Computer Centre, a Navy facility, with an entrance two miles away is believed to be linked to Rudloe Manor underground. Whilst surface activity has ceased at Rudloe Manor, anyone lingering near its old entrance is under surveillance - & libel to be moved on by police very soon, so underground activity of some sort is happening. Could even be our version of Area 51 – S4, as there are rumours of a recovered crashed UFO dating back to WW2.

Colares island, northern Brazil 1977 - (search). It is rare for multiple sightings in one area over a period of six months, even rarer for many witnesses to claim, and have verified by a local doctor, harm done by UFOs, this case is the exception. Many witnesses (at least forty) on this island claim beams of light struck them – sometimes through walls?, resulting in serious burns, photographed by the local doctor, who said the whole island was in a state of fear for many months, so much so that the Brazilian military was called in. Operation Plate, was a series of observation posts set up to monitor events. As usual the results were never made public. However, the U S NASA contractor (search) **Robert Bigalow**, known to have much information on the UFO subject, which he does not deny, bought the entire files on this event from the Brazilian government. Fisherman in the area report lights over the water to this day.

In case many of you are thinking there have been no recent developments, think on this – As of this year (2019) the U S navy is now in the process of relaxing restrictions on its pilots reporting of unidentified aerial craft after a marked increase of such reports since 2014 off the California coast. This may also be due to a major series of sightings as far back as 2004 by the USS Nimitz lead Carrier Strike Group Eleven (search) "2004 Tic Tac", when two pilots & several radar operators reported the white tic tac shaped craft moving & turning at speeds no known terrestrial aircraft are capable of. Very soon afterwards a helicopter arrived on the accompanying Cruiser Princeton and the radar recordings removed & all related data ordered deleted. Business as usual then. In 2015 many U S Navy pilots are reported to have seen & recorded UFOs tracking their Theodore Roosevelt Carrier strike group all the way from the US Atlantic coast to middle east operation locations.

Helen Sharman – Britain's first astronaut, spending some time on the Mir Space Station, has made a public statement in January 2020 "That aliens definitely exist and could be living among us on earth". What has led her to risk public credibility in making such a statement- repeated very briefly on the BBC's news text service, before being removed. Has she seen or been told something, or just followed the evidence.

POSSIBLE CONCLUSIONS – YOU DECIDE

1) Despite ALL witnessed events collated above, which are a small fraction of the total, every event mentioned or not, can be explained based on the world order as currently presented to the general public.
2) Various very gifted human scientists from Tesla to Shauberger, including many Germans taken to the US, UK, Russia - & Antarctica? after WW2 have had their key inventions kept secret & developed to a point where they alone are responsible for all the thousands of sightings of non-conventional aerial (and submerged) craft. No aliens involved.
3) Aliens are here, and are responsible for virtually all non-conventional craft sightings. Given the variety of sightings, more than one species are present, some may have bases here. There could even be an inter-dimensional element, as some craft display an ability to suddenly appear & disappear, unless this is just a "cloaking device". Our current understanding of physics (String Theory) predicts the possibility of other dimensions. Our major governments are aware – but are afraid to reveal any of the above due to fear of panic & loss of control – or are even colluding to some extent.

4) Both aliens & humans have anti-gravity craft here, aliens being more advanced, ours being a result of back engineering alien craft, & or hand me downs, plus some gifted human work kept secret. Different groups may be operating with different agenda – as with human nations. Human/alien alliances may be included in this scenario, Antarctica & other areas being used as a base for both.

If any of conclusions 2, 3, or 4 are valid, then loss of control by the involved government sub surface factions might not be the only reason for suppressing disclosure. If it became certain public knowledge that there was much more advanced tech beyond our current level, then it is likely that scientific endeavour for advancement would tail off in expectation of advances being handed to us on a plate, resulting in stagnation of scientific advance by our own effort – this could not be risked and could be a valid reason against full disclosure – and continuation of surreptitious trickle feeding of tech pointing us in the right direction, this scenario depending on which of the above conclusions is right.

Let's hope all the above is wrong, or only man made, not as if we need any outside help to ruin our planet.

Others might help us save it - if we were being farmed for our DNA. Bahahaa...

Hamlet – possibly referring to the (Benson & hedges) Hamlet cigar, - shaped UFO, said (more or less) "There are more things in heaven and earth than are dreamt of in your philosophy". Something to shake a spear at then....

Acknowledgements

First SARAH for her memories, filling out my bare bones recall. Me to Sarah – a hundred times whilst writing this – "Do you remember when…"

Whoever created my spellchecker, without which I could not have contemplated this task.

All authors and witnesses I mention, who I encourage you again to search out online.

My smartphone and all the myriad websites accessible from this for checking my facts – especially Wikipedia.

Austin Macauley Publishers Ltd.